RESEARCH IN LABOR ECONOMICS

RESEARCH IN LABOR ECONOMICS

Series Editor: Solomon W. Polachek

IZA Co-Editor: Konstantinos Tatsiramos

Volume 23: Accounting for Worker Well-Being
Edited by Solomon W. Polachek

Volume 24: The Economics of Immigration and Social Diversity
Edited by Solomon W. Polachek, Carmel Chiswick and Hillel Rapoport

Volume 25: Micro-Simulation in Action
Edited by Olivier Bargain

Volume 26: Aspects of Worker Well-Being
Edited by Solomon W. Polachek and Olivier Bargain

Volume 27: Immigration: Trends, Consequences and Prospects for The United States
Edited by Barry R. Chiswick

Volume 28: Work Earnings and Other Aspects of the Employment Relation
Edited by Solomon W. Polachek and Konstantinos Tatsiramos

Volume 29: Ethnicity and Labor Market Outcomes
Edited by Amelie F. Constant, Konstantinos Tatsiramos and Klaus F. Zimmermann

Volume 30: Jobs, Training, and Worker Well-Being
Edited by Solomon W. Polachek and Konstantinos Tatsiramos

Volume 31: Child Labor and the Transition Between School and Work
Edited by Randall K. Q. Akee, Eric V. Edmonds and Konstantinos Tatsiramos

Volume 32: Who Loses in the Downturn? Economic Crisis, Employment and Income Distribution
Edited by Herwig Immervoll, Andreas Peichl and Konstantinos Tatsiramos

RESEARCH IN LABOR ECONOMICS VOLUME 33

RESEARCH IN LABOR ECONOMICS

EDITED BY

SOLOMON W. POLACHEK
Department of Economics, State University of New York at Binghamton and IZA

KONSTANTINOS TATSIRAMOS
University of Leicester and IZA

United Kingdom – North America – Japan
India – Malaysia – China

Emerald Group Publishing Limited
Howard House, Wagon Lane, Bingley BD16 1WA, UK

First edition 2011

Reprints and permission service
Contact: booksandseries@emeraldinsight.com

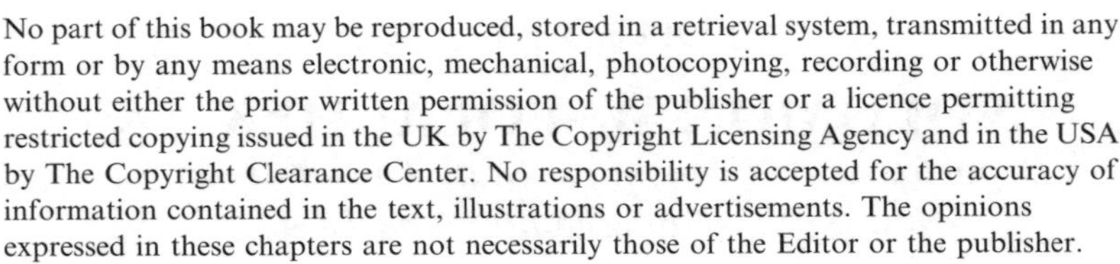

British Library Cataloguing in Publication Data
A catalogue record for this book is available from the British Library

ISBN: 978-1-78052-332-3
ISSN: 0147-9121 (Series)

Emerald Group Publishing Limited, Howard House, Environmental Management System has been certified by ISOQAR to ISO 14001:2004 standards

Awarded in recognition of Emerald's production department's adherence to quality systems and processes when preparing scholarly journals for print

CONTENTS

LIST OF CONTRIBUTORS

Heather Antecol	Robert Day School of Economics and Finance, Claremont McKenna College, Claremont, CA, USA
Olivier Bargain	Department of Economics, University College Dublin, Dublin, Ireland; Institute for the Study of Labor (IZA), Bonn, Germany
Kathleen Beegle	Development Economics Research Group, World Bank, Washington, DC, USA
Rafael E. De Hoyos	Secretariat of Education, Government of Mexico, Mexico
Karina Doorley	CEPS/INSTEAD Research Institute, Esch-sur-Alzette, Luxembourg; Department of Economics, University College Dublin, Dublin, Ireland
Gil S. Epstein	Department of Economics, Bar-Ilan University, Ramat-Gan, Israel
Joop Hartog	Department of Economics, University of Amsterdam, Amsterdam, the Netherlands
Charlene M. Kalenkoski	Department of Economics, Ohio University, Athens, OH, USA; Institute for the Study of Labor (IZA), Bonn, Germany
Michael Lokshin	Development Economics Research Group, World Bank, Washington, DC, USA

Yuval Mazar Research Department, Bank of Israel, Jerusalem, Israel

Alfonso Miranda Department of Quantitative Social Science, Institute of Education, University of London, London, UK

David C. Ribar Department of Economics, University of North Carolina at Greensboro, Greensboro, NC, USA; Institute for the Study of Labor (IZA), Bonn, Germany

Roberta Serafini European Central Bank, Frankfurt am Main, Germany

Leslie S. Stratton Department of Economics, Virginia Commonwealth University, Richmond, VA, USA; Institute for the Study of Labor (IZA), Bonn, Germany

Alessandra Venturini Department of Economics, University of Turin, Turin, Italy

Melanie Ward European Central Bank, Frankfurt am Main, Germany

PREFACE

How individuals allocate their time between work and leisure has important implications regarding worker well-being. For example, more time at work means a greater return to human capital and a greater proclivity to seek more training opportunities. At the same time, hours spent at work decrease leisure and depend on one's home environment (including parental background), health, past migration, and government policies. In short, worker well-being depends on trade-offs and is influenced by public policy. These decisions entail time allocation, effort, human capital investment, health, and migration, among other choices. This volume considers worker well-being from the vantage of each of these alternatives. It contains ten chapters. The first three are on time allocation and work behavior, the next three on aspects of risk in the earnings process, the next two on aspects of migration, the next one on the impact of tax policies on poverty, and finally the last chapter on the role of labor market institutions on sectoral shifts in employment.

Allocation of time starts early. Even children and teenagers make time-allocation decisions that affect their future well-being. But often these decisions are not in isolation; they depend on environmental considerations, especially household characteristics, particularly socioeconomic status. In the first chapter Charlene M. Kalenkoski, David C. Ribar, and Leslie S. Stratton utilize the 2003–2006 American Time Use Survey to examine time allocation among 15 to 18-year-old teenagers. They concentrate on how family and personal characteristics (particularly the effect of living in a single-parent household, having a father in the household who is nonemployed, and having both parents employed) impact on time spent pursuing educational versus noneducational activities. In their analysis they examine whether disadvantaged teenagers adopt adult roles by taking on extra economic and/or household responsibilities, or whether conversely disadvantaged teenagers take on noneducational domestic and other pursuits simply because disadvantaged households provide less supervision. The methodological innovation is to adopt a competing risk hazard model that more closely tracks actual time use throughout the day.

Perhaps discontinuous labor force participation is the most important reason for the gender wage gap. Not only does dropping out reduce lifetime work, but dropping out causes current skills to atrophy with nonuse. Of late, the popular press, including a number of newspapers, report on the "opt-out revolution" in which highly trained women exit the labor force primarily to care for their families. In the second chapter Heather Antecol utilizes data from the US Census in conjunction with the current population survey (1980–2009) to test this "opt-out" proposition, particularly among highly educated women working in fields with long hours and little workplace flexibility. Unlike past research, Antecol zeros in on a particular demographic subgroup and distinguishes between leaving the labor force completely and cutting hours of work. She finds little support that highly educated women exit the labor force to care for their families at higher rates today than in earlier time periods. However, she presents some evidence that white college-educated married women in male-dominated occupations cut hours of work.

Family responsibilities represent one group of considerations affecting female labor force participation, but there are others. In the third chapter Rafael E. De Hoyos looks both at micro and macroeconomic variables that affect female work behavior. He concentrates on Mexico from 1994 to 2000, where female participation rose by 12%, or over 700,000 workers. Based on a structural sector-specific model, he shows that the negative income shocks of the peso crisis at least partially explain the increase in participation observed between 1994 and 1996, and that a relatively higher expected wage in the manufacturing sector and a change in women's willingness to work, both of which were probably brought on by NAFTA, mostly explain the increase in participation during the recovery period 1996–2000. His results underscore the importance of macroeconomic phenomena and ensuing public policies that shape microeconomic labor market activity.

Investing in human capital is not riskless. Earnings vary tremendously even among individuals having similar amounts of school. As a result, one cannot precisely predict one's own future earnings. This incomplete information is exacerbated because one also does not know one's own ability compared to others. For this reason individuals must be rewarded a risk premium to choose occupations with a high wage risk. In the fourth chapter Joop Hartog (along with his associates) concentrate on the wage needed to compensate an individual for not knowing where he or she will lie within the distribution of possible wages. They find consistent evidence that wage compensation depends on the second and third moments. Wages are positively related to variance and negatively to skewness, implying individuals pay a premium for the possibility of high wages, but receive compensation for pure risk. Interestingly, biases in estimating school rates of return are small if one fails to account for these aspects of risk.

The variance and skewness of earnings varies between the public and private sectors. Further, at least in the United States, nearly 20% of employees work in some branch of the government. In addition, governmental pay practices influence pay in other sectors of the economy. As such, understanding how the wage setting mechanism works differently in the for-profit and the not-for-profit sectors is important. Also important is whether differences in pay between these two sectors stimulate mobility between government and private sector jobs. Such public/private differences in the United States were explored in an earlier *Research in Labor Economics* (Volume 12) chapter by Lawrence Katz and Alan Krueger. Whereas a number of subsequent studies explore public and private sector differences for various other countries, few if any analyze these differences in Israel because of difficulties encoding Israeli micro-data for private versus public sector employment. However, utilizing Israeli data widens our understanding of these two sectors worldwide by providing data points for one additional country. In the fifth chapter, Yuval Mazar analyzes differences in wage determination between the Israeli public and private sectors. As is commonly observed in other countries, the public sector has a higher starting wage intercept, but smaller wage-experience and wage-education gradients compared to the private sector. An observed rise in the rate of return in the private compared to the public sector caused 11% of the male skilled workers to switch to the public sector. But there are other differences, as well, and these differences also stimulate mobility between the sectors.

The first, second, and third moments of the earnings distribution represent one form of risk that individuals respond to. Another is the impact of bad health on earnings, to which individuals react by indulging or not indulging in risky behavior such as smoking or drinking. In the sixth chapter, Michael Lokshin and Kathleen Beegle examine the effect of smoking on wages. They use three approaches: a traditional two-stage least squares model, a three-equation system estimated by full information maximum likelihood, and finally a semi-parametric model using a local instrumental variables approach. The latter two control for observed and unobserved characteristics that may be correlated with both smoking and earnings. Unlike most current studies that concentrate on rich Western and North American countries where smoking is on the wane, Lokshin and Beegle examine poorer countries where a larger proportion of the population smokes. In such countries risky behavior can have bigger effects not only because the treatment of heart disease, cancer, and other cigarette-induced health ailments might be inferior, but also because a greater proportion of the population is employed in more menial occupations requiring physical strength. In contrast to US-based studies that find about a 5–10% deleterious effect, Lokshin and Beagle find smoking reduces earnings by 19–23%.

Many economists argue that in-migration increases labor supply, and as a result in-migration decreases wages in a host country. Others argue that in-migration boosts a host country's economic well-being because migrants take jobs too undesirable for natives, as well as stimulate aggregate demand based on their earnings. In the seventh chapter Alessandra Venturini and Gil S. Epstein argue the effects are more complicated than simple supply and demand shifts. They claim one should also consider a country's migration policies which they contend can affect overall worker productivity. As such, they derive an optimal policy based on an effort-enhancing contract. Because of high host country wages compared to wages in the origin country, migrant workers arrive willing to take onerous jobs entailing long hours and hard work. However, the longer they stay the more reluctant they become to continue in these jobs. As such, a policy promoting temporary migration may yield more host country gains. Thus they emphasize policies encouraging a country to import guest workers for short time periods to be replaced by new waves of immigrant workers later on.

Are children from households headed by an immigrant parent less or more likely to graduate from high school? Clearly, the answer to this question is relevant to understand how international migration may affect human capital accumulation in developing countries. In the eighth chapter Alfonso Miranda uses bivariate dynamic random effects probit models (BDPM) to estimate the effects of parental migration on children's high school graduation rates in Mexico. As a backdrop, note how the United States tightened its border to Mexico in the 2000s forcing more migrants to stay in the United States permanently. Miranda's results show that boys from households headed by a migrant are 17% less likely to graduate from high school than boys from households headed by a nonmigrant, and girls 13.5% less likely – this in spite of remittances sent back to the family from the United States. However, a larger number of migrants in the family is associated with a higher probability of graduation from high school. Further, boys from households headed by a migrant are around 30 percentage points more likely to migrate themselves. Thus emigration to the United States may actually be reducing, rather than increasing, the accumulation of human capital in Mexico.

Clearly migration, as well as the other factors examined in this volume, is related to public policy. In the ninth chapter, Olivier Bargain and Karina Doorley examine how to use public policy through the labor market to reduce poverty. They answer this question by analyzing the cushioning and incentive impacts of "make work pay" programs focusing particular attention on Ireland, which since 2008 suffered a deep economic crisis. To do so, Bargain and Doorley utilize the EUROMOD micro-simulation model (see *Research in Labor Economics*, Volume 25) which they link with the 2001 Living in Ireland (LII) Survey to analyze the effects of the Family Income Supplement (FIS) and the British Working Tax Credit (WTC) on work behavior, poverty, and the resulting wage distribution. They find that a full take-up version of the existing FIS scheme would significantly reduce poverty when payments become as generous (in real terms) as in 2008. Adopting the WTC in Ireland would also generate an important though smaller redistributive effect because the incentive for single mothers is more geared toward part-time work, which may not be enough to take them out of poverty. For the most part, these policies have a disincentive effect on married women because they are means-test at the household level. As such, make work pay programs reduce poverty because they create a strong incentive for single parents to work.

Public policy and institutions may not only affect poverty and individual employment decisions; they also affect the sectoral reallocation of the workforce. In this volume's final chapter, Roberta Serafini and Melanie Ward examine why the service sector employment share in Europe is rising less rapidly relative to the United States, and why employment in this sector is distributed differently across subsectors. They concentrate on how institutional impediments hinder the reallocation associated with the shift from manufacturing to services. The analysis is carried out for the aggregate service sector, as well as more narrowly in four subsectors and twelve sector-specific branches over the period 1970–2003. They find that a number of organizational barriers such as union density and the degree of centralized wage bargaining together with the mismatch between workers' skills and job vacancies have affected Europe's ability to reallocate labor from manufacturing into the services.

As with past volumes, we aim to focus on important issues and to maintain the highest levels of scholarship. We encourage readers who have prepared manuscripts that meet these stringent standards to submit them to *Research in Labor Economics* (RLE) via the IZA website (http://www.iza.org/rle) for possible inclusion in future volumes. For insightful editorial advice, we thank Tindara Addabbo, Alpaslan Akay, William T. Alpert, Kate Antonovics, Sowmya Wijayambal Arulampalam, Linda A. Bailey, Olivier Bargain, Michele Belot, Richard Berthoud, Holger Bonin, Andrea Brandolini, Lorenzo Cappellari, Nancy Chau, Lorenzo Corsini,

Francesco D'Amuri, Koen Decancq, Dhaval M. Dave, David L. Dickinson, Michael Elsby, Francesco Figari, Rosa GarcÚa-Fernandez, Hans-Dieter Gerner, Anne Gielen, Donna K. Ginther, Mary Gregory, Peter Haan, Nicolas Herault, Joni Hersch, Michael J. Hilmer, Martin Kahanec, Marco Leonardi, Mark A. Loewenstein, Stéphanie Lluis, Miguel A. Malo, David Marsden, Felice Martinello, Manos Matsaganis, Karine S. Moe, Caitlin Knowles Myers, Shoshana Neuman, Cathal O'Donoghue, Sabrina Wulff Pabilonia, Eugenio Peluso, Victoria Prowse, Helmut Rainer, John Robst, Timothy Smeeding, Bruce Stafford, Yelena Takhtamanova, Jeffrey P. Thompson, Panos Tsakloglou, Arne Uhlendorff, Arthur van Soest, Katharina Wrohlich, and Xing Zhou.

Solomon W. Polachek
Konstantinos Tatsiramos
Editors

CHAPTER 1

HOW DO ADOLESCENTS *SPELL* TIME USE? AN ALTERNATIVE METHODOLOGICAL APPROACH FOR ANALYZING TIME-DIARY DATA

Charlene M. Kalenkoski, David C. Ribar and Leslie S. Stratton

ABSTRACT

We investigate how household disadvantage affects the time use of 15–18 year olds using 2003–2006 data from the American Time Use Survey. Applying competing-risk hazard models, we distinguish between the incidence and duration of activities and incorporate the daily time constraint. We find that teens living in disadvantaged households spend less time in nonclassroom educational activities than other teens. Girls spend some of this time in work activities, suggesting that they are taking on adult roles. However, we find more evidence of substitution into unsupervised activities, suggesting that it may be less-structured environments that reduce educational investment.

Keywords: Time use; adolescence; event-history models

JEL classifications: J22; J13

Research in Labor Economics, Volume 33, 1–44

ISSN: 0147-9121/doi:10.1108/S0147-9121(2011)0000033004

INTRODUCTION

Adolescence is an important stage in a person's development. Neither completely dependent nor wholly independent, adolescents occupy a middle ground in modern societies. Many activities during these years, including time invested in schooling, participation in other enriching activities, experiences with work, and exposure to greater responsibility and autonomy, can yield substantial long-run benefits. However, other activities can either directly lead to detrimental outcomes or crowd out the time available for productive activities. Household circumstances may encourage, shape, or constrain these activities. In particular, disadvantaged youths, such as those living with only one parent, with less-educated parents, or in poorer communities, might not engage in productive activities for as much time as their advantaged peers.

Many studies of the impacts of household circumstances on youths' activities have focused narrowly on only one or a few activities, such as schooling (Crowder & Teachman, 2004; Fischer & Kmec, 2004; South, Baumer, & Lutz, 2003), paid work (Leventhal, Graber, & Brooks-Gunn, 2001; Ruhm, 1995), housework (Call, Mortimer, & Shanahan, 1995; Capizzano, Main, & Nelson, 2004; Demo & Acock, 1993; Gager, Cooney, & Call, 1999; Goldscheider & Waite, 1991; Hilton & Haldeman, 1991; Peters & Haldeman, 1987), or organized activities (Lopoo, 2007). Other studies have investigated the associations between selected activities for youths, most notably work and school activities (see, e.g., Kalenkoski & Pabilonia, 2009a, 2009b). However, with the increasing availability of time-diary data, researchers can now examine the daily time use of teenagers more comprehensively (Marshall, 2007; Porterfield & Winkler, 2007; Raley, 2007; Wight, Price, Bianchi, & Hunt, 2009; Zick, 2010).

A central research question as well as a methodological challenge regarding time use is how time devoted to one activity affects time devoted to other activities. For example, if disadvantaged teens are spending less time in schooling, research should address what they are doing instead. One possibility is that disadvantaged teens are working more in the home, providing more care for siblings, or working more in the labor market (Gennetian et al., 2002; Porterfield & Winkler, 2007). Another is that less-affluent parents provide less supervision, encourage fewer structured activities, and rely more on the "accomplishment of natural growth" (Lareau, 2003). A consideration of these alternatives requires an analysis of the determinants of and relations among several activities.

Such time trade-offs recognize the overall time constraint individuals face, but there are several other methodological challenges to examining time use. One is that time allocations are nonnegative, with many observations for some types of activities grouped at zero. Ordinary least squares (OLS) models fail to account for either the nonnegativity constraint or the mass point at zero, but some techniques that do address these issues, such as the standard Tobit model, can impose other types of unreasonable restrictions. Another challenge is that the distributions of reported time use are not captured well by standard probability functions, such as the normal distribution.

In this study, we use time-diary data collected from 2003 to 2006 by the American Time Use Survey (ATUS) to investigate how household circumstances affect the time that teens spend during the school year in classroom activities, nonclassroom educational activities, work, sleep, and other supervised and unsupervised activities. As with some other comprehensive studies of time use (e.g., Zick, 2010), we define the activities so that they categorize an entire day, allowing us to consider trade-offs among the activities.

We address many other methodological concerns by using the activity data in a spell format and estimating competing-risk hazard (event-history) models of teenagers' continuation in and transitions out of activities. While parallels have been drawn before between time diaries and event-history data (Stafford, 2009), and while a few other studies have applied event-history methods to time-diary data to analyze a limited number of activities (e.g., Bhat, Srinivasan, & Axhausen, 2005; Lee & Timmermans, 2007; Todd, Armeli, & Tennen, 2009), our study is unique in applying multivariate event-history methods to a full diary day of activities. Our event-history approach has several advantages. First, it conforms to the way that the activities themselves are reported – as spells. Previous studies of time use have used aggregate measures of time spent, such as the total daily minutes devoted to a particular activity. Our model works directly with the spell data. Second, our methodology accounts for the times reported in different activities being mutually exclusive and exhaustive. Thus, the technique incorporates the daily time constraint and facilitates the analysis of trade-offs. Third, our approach naturally incorporates distinctions between the incidence and duration of activities. Techniques used by others, such as OLS and Tobit, either ignore or conflate these two processes. Fourth, our methodology allows us to account for other aspects of time-diary data that are difficult to accommodate using other techniques, including the time of day that activities are performed and the tendency of respondents to report durations in round numbers.

Our multivariate event-history models include measures of parents' living and work arrangements, parents' education, the number of other children living in the respondent's household, local labor market conditions, and other personal and household characteristics as explanatory variables. Estimation reveals that teens living in single-parent households and boys living with two working parents spend less time in nonclassroom educational activities than similar teens living in other households. Teens living with less-educated parents also spend less time in nonclassroom educational activities. When we look at teens' other activities, we find that much of the reduction in nonclassroom educational time is accompanied by an increase in unsupervised other activities. There is also evidence of later waking times for some teens. These patterns suggest that a lack of supervision and structure may account for disadvantaged teens' diminished nonclassroom educational activities. For girls, we also find evidence that household disadvantage is associated with more work, suggesting that increased responsibilities may be interfering with studying and other outside-the-classroom educational activities.

LITERATURE REVIEW

Research has consistently found that children who grow up in disadvantaged circumstances tend to obtain less schooling and perform worse on cognitive tests than other children.[1] Such diminished educational attainment can lead to lower earnings and other negative outcomes later in life. The importance of schooling has led researchers to examine whether the day-to-day behaviors of children might differ with socioeconomic status. There is considerable evidence that it does.

The association between household disadvantage and the time that teenagers devote to homework and studying has been examined by several authors. Marshall (2007), Porterfield and Winkler (2007), Wight et al. (2009), and Kalenkoski and Pabilonia (2009b), each found evidence that teenagers in non-intact households and with less-educated parents spend less time doing homework than other teenagers. Zick (2010) reported similar relations between disadvantage and a broader measure of schoolwork that included class time.

There is also evidence that teenagers in disadvantaged circumstances spend less time in other enriching activities. Zick (2010) found that teenagers in single-parent households and with less-educated parents participate in fewer organizationally related activities, such as scouting. Lopoo (2007) also found that family structure and parental education are related to extracurricular activities in cross-sectional models, though his evidence became more equivocal in fixed effects models.

If disadvantaged adolescents are studying less or participating in fewer extracurricular activities, what are they doing instead? One hypothesis is that living in disadvantaged circumstances forces youths to shoulder increased responsibility and take on adult roles earlier than other children. For example, families with single parents or working mothers may lack the time resources of other families, necessitating more housework by adolescents. Numerous researchers, including Peters and Haldeman (1987), Goldscheider and Waite (1991), Hilton and Haldeman (1991), Demo and Acock (1993), Gager et al. (1999), and Capizzano et al. (2004), have found that teenagers, especially girls, living in single-parent households spend more time in housework (including childcare) than those in dual-parent households. Call et al. (1995) reported greater housework among teens with working mothers. However, Goldscheider and Waite (1991) found little evidence that maternal employment affects the extent to which children take responsibility for household tasks.

Greater household needs in the form of a larger household or a greater number of young siblings may also increase the demands on teenagers' time. In their review of the consequences of welfare-to-work programs on adolescents' development, Gennetian et al. (2002) found that adolescent children of welfare recipients who have younger siblings experience larger negative effects on school performance, and are more likely to be suspended or expelled from and to drop out of school, than adolescent children of welfare recipients who are not subject to such policies. Call et al. (1995) reported that household size is an important predictor of the time teenagers spend in housework and caring activities.

Teens may also assume adult roles through paid employment. Such employment may increase skills through experience. At the same time, it may be detrimental to school performance. Marshall (2007) found that teens with demanding paid jobs do significantly less homework than those who are not employed, and Oettinger (1999) found a decline in the grades of minority high-school students who work long hours. Similarly, Tyler (2003) found that employment while in high school has a negative effect on 12th grade math achievement, and Kalenkoski and Pabilonia (2009a, 2009b) found that the employment of high-school students reduces time spent on homework. Not all studies find negative effects of student employment, however (see, e.g., Leventhal et al., 2001; Rothstein, 2007; Ruhm, 1995).

A weakness with the early-adult-roles explanation is that market work and housework account for only small fractions of most teens' days. Wight et al. (2009) estimated that teens spend only about 90 minutes a day in these activities on average and less than an hour a day on school days. Zick (2010) found that recent cohorts of teens have spent substantially less time in paid employment than teens in the 1970s. Her analyses indicated that the time freed from working has not led to more time in school or other enriching activities. Instead, time spent in passive leisure activities has increased.

Research by Zick and others suggests another way that socioeconomic status may translate into poorer schooling outcomes – through reduced parental supervision. Increased autonomy, independence, and disengagement are part of the process of growing up. Nevertheless, some teens may be given too much autonomy and provided with too little supervision too soon. Lareau (2003) has hypothesized that economically advantaged and disadvantaged parents may see their roles differently, with the former utilizing a strategy of "concerted cultivation" to provide lots of structure and organized activities for their children and the latter following a more hands-off approach that allows for the "accomplishment of natural growth."

A lack of structure or supervision might also be a consequence of a shortage of parental time. Burton and Phipps (2007) found evidence in a cross-national study that working parents do experience a "time crunch." However, in a study limited to two-parent families, Bryant and Zick (1996) found that while maternal employment leads to a shift in the type of activities parents share with their children, it does not change the amount of time. Similarly, Bianchi (2000) reported that the time employed and nonemployed mothers spend with their children is remarkably comparable.

Some empirical evidence suggests that how that time is used is different. Raley (2007) found that children in single-parent households spend more time in personal-care activities, including sleep, but less time in "free-time" activities than children living with both parents. Wight et al. (2009) found that teens with more educated parents spend more time studying and less time watching TV, are more likely to eat dinner with a parent, and get less sleep. They also found that teenagers with a single parent go to bed later and are less likely to eat dinner with a parent, and that disadvantaged teens are more likely to work. An increase in work among disadvantaged teens might increase teens' independence and disrupt their parents' ability to supervise their activities. This independence may be seen as a natural stage in development by their parents.

That lack of supervision and underinvestment in youth activities may lead to poorer outcomes is a common perception, but concern has also been expressed that some teens may be over-scheduled and over-involved. Qualitative research by Lareau (2003) described children with little free time. However, quantitative analyses by Mahoney, Harris, and Eccles (2006), Porterfield and Winkler (2007), Raley (2007), Wight et al. (2009), and Zick (2010) indicated that most youths' have ample free time. Further, Mahoney et al. (2006) concluded that most youths are intrinsically motivated to engage in organized activities and experience developmental benefits, even at high levels of participation. Over-scheduling does not appear to be a significant concern.

While these time-use studies have tried to determine how teenagers' daily activities are affected by family circumstances, they fail to take full advantage of the available time-diary data. Our event-history approach incorporates this information more completely and allows us to provide a more detailed and more accurate accounting of teens' time use.

DATA AND METHODOLOGY

We conduct our empirical analyses of teenagers' time allocations using individual-level time-diary data from the 2003–2006 ATUS. The ATUS is a national survey that has been conducted regularly since January 2003 by the U.S. Bureau of the Census for the U.S. Bureau of Labor Statistics. The study first randomly selects households in their last month of participation in the Current Population Survey (CPS). It then selects one person aged 15 or over within each household to participate in a phone interview during which the subject provides a 24-hour time diary and answers other questions. The survey is not restricted to household heads or spouses. Because the ATUS uses the CPS as a sampling frame, it has a stratified design. In addition, the diaries in the ATUS oversample weekends. We use survey-provided sampling weights to make the ATUS representative of the national population and of an average day.

The distinctive feature of the ATUS is that it collects a retrospective, one-day diary, describing how the respondent spent his or her time. Subjects report the activities that they were performing throughout the day in their own words. They also report when these activities began and ended, where the activities occurred, and, for most but not all activities, who else was present.[2] The Census Bureau subsequently codes the responses into standardized activities in an episode format. These episodes are the source material for the activities that we examine.

A critical feature of the ATUS for our purposes is that it supports multivariate analyses of teenagers' behavior. Although teenagers constitute a small proportion of the ATUS study population, there are ample observations to examine because the survey itself is large and because cross-sections can be pooled over time (there were approximately 20,000 respondents in 2003 and 13,000 respondents in each of the subsequent years).

Our analyses focus on 15–18 year olds who live with a single, noncohabiting parent or with a married parent, who do not live with children of their own, who are enrolled in school but have not completed a high-school degree or equivalent, and who provided at least 23 hours of diary information. The restrictions on living arrangements are imposed primarily to focus on dependent adolescents, to allow us to characterize the parents' circumstances, and to abstract from unusual care responsibilities and family situations. The restrictions on enrollment and grade completion are intended to abstract from school dropout and continuation decisions and to concentrate on a similar set of educational activities. The restriction on the amount of usable diary information is made for purposes of data quality. These restrictions are similar to those imposed by Wight et al. (2009) and Zick (2010) in their analyses of adolescent behavior. Taken together, the restrictions produce an analysis sample that is somewhat more advantaged than teenagers generally.

Additionally, and in contrast to the analyses by Wight et al. and Zick, we restrict our analyses to time diaries that describe weekdays and weekends during school weeks.[3] We do this mainly to support analyses of schooling-related activities but also in recognition of the vast differences in activities during and outside the school year. Initial analyses supported this distinction and rejected modeling school-year and nonschool-year activities together.

Activity Spell Data

The ATUS diary data distinguish among several hundred detailed activities. For our analyses, we reclassify these activities into six broad mutually exclusive but exhaustive categories. The first two categories comprise school-related activities. Here we differentiate between classroom time, over which teens have relatively little choice, and homework and other educational activities (not including school sports), over which teens have more discretion.[4] A third category contains market and household work activities, including care for household children and grocery shopping. A fourth category contains sleep- or rest-related activities. The remainder of a teen's time is divided into two "other" categories. These distinguish between activities in which a parent or other adult is present (supervised other activities) and not present (unsupervised other activities). Friends, neighbors, coworkers, and acquaintances age 18 and over are not acknowledged as supervisors.

We then take several steps to simplify our event-history analyses and reduce the number of spells and transitions that we need to consider. First, we treat all consecutive detailed activity spells of the same broad activity type as a single spell of that type. For instance, a spell of doing laundry followed by a spell of vacuuming is treated as a single spell of work. Collapsing the activities this way reduces the number of spells by about half.

Next, we restrict the sample to include only teenagers who were sleeping at or within 10 minutes of 4 a.m. on the initial day of the diary. The diary day starts at 4 a.m. Thus, we only have to consider a single origin type of activity – sleep. This restriction reduces the sample by 62 teenagers. We also concatenate "new" sleep spells that began before 6:30 a.m. and that were preceded by single, short, non-sleep activities with earlier sleep spells, dropping the intervening activities, and treating the initial and subsequent periods of sleep as continuous spells. For example, a teen who woke up, drank a glass of water, and then went back to sleep would have both sleep spells counted as one continuous sleep spell and the time spent drinking water would be ignored. Similarly, we concatenate non-retiring sleep spells that began after 12:30 a.m. with retiring sleep spells. These changes only affect five spells. We then recode all of the remaining (342) noninitial and nonterminal sleep spells (naps) as "unsupervised other" activities. Although we would have liked to examine these sleep spells as such, there were too few to model separately.

Finally, from our concatenated spells, we drop 919 activity spells that were reported to have lasted five minutes or less (a reduction of 4.4% of the available concatenated activities and 0.1% of the total time reported in the diaries).

Explanatory Measures

In addition to the activity data, the ATUS asks each subject to identify who else lives in the household and to list each member's gender, age, and relationship to the subject. We use these rosters to construct household composition measures. Adolescents who report having only one parent present at the time of the time diary and adolescents whose parent indicates being unmarried are coded as living in a single-parent household.[5] Other conditioning variables include indicators for whether the parents in the household worked, the highest level of education attained by the parents, the number of other adults and the number of other adolescents in the household, the number of younger children in different age ranges in the household, indicator variables for the race/ethnicity and age of the teen and the metropolitan status of the household, and the state unemployment rate. In our analysis, we also condition upon whether the diary day fell on a weekend or holiday. We drop 35 observations that are missing information on one or more of the covariates.

Characteristics of the Analysis Sample

Our final analysis sample has information on 9,861 concatenated activity spells for 1,004 teenage girls and 8,963 spells for 1,005 teenage boys.[6] All of the teenagers report at least two activity spells, and the median number of spells is nine. Characteristics of the teenagers in our analysis, including the total minutes and daily incidence of activities, household circumstances, and personal attributes, are shown in Table 1.

The distributions of activities across non-holiday weekdays and across weekends and holidays are shown in Fig. 1 separately for teenage girls and boys. Fig. 1 plainly shows that activities are unevenly distributed across the hours of each day and across different types of days, mostly in ways that we would anticipate. For example, almost all classroom activities occur between 7 a.m. and 3 p.m. on weekdays. Sleep is concentrated early and late in the day, with teenagers rising earlier on weekdays. Work is more likely to occur on weekends or holidays than on weekdays. To the extent that work does take place on weekdays, it tends to occur in the afternoon and early evening. Finally, the graphs show that when teenagers are not attending school, supervised and unsupervised other activities dominate their waking hours. Teenage boys are more likely to be involved in unsupervised other activities than teenage girls, especially outside of regular school hours.

For our event-history analyses, each time diary is divided into 144 10-minute intervals. To conduct the hazard analysis, we identify for each interval whether the activity continued or whether a transition to a different activity occurred. As we would expect given the large number of intervals and the modest number of spells during the day, the vast majority of the

Table 1. Means and Standard Deviations of Analysis Variables.

	Teenage Girls		Teenage Boys	
	Mean	Standard deviation	Mean	Standard deviation
Outcome variables				
Minutes spent in classroom activities	245.65	212.00	243.99	210.70
Any time in classroom activities	0.62	0.49	0.61	0.49
Minutes spent in other educational activities	68.90	96.02	46.45	83.51
Any time in other educational activities	0.54	0.50	0.41	0.49
Minutes spent in household or market work	89.19	134.25	80.58	143.76
Any time in household or market work	0.57	0.50	0.48	0.50
Minutes spent in other supervised activities	173.72	180.56	161.37	184.64
Any time in other supervised activities	0.87	0.34	0.81	0.39
Minutes spent in other unsupervised activities	350.50	200.32	387.77	221.21
Any time in other unsupervised activities	1.00	0.06	0.99	0.09
Minutes spent in sleep	524.04	136.42	530.12	140.54
Explanatory variables				
Two-parent household, only father works[a]	0.19	0.39	0.18	0.38
Two-parent household, both parents work	0.50	0.50	0.50	0.50
Two-parent household, father does not work	0.07	0.26	0.09	0.29
Single-parent household	0.24	0.42	0.23	0.42
Highest education obtained by parents	14.13	3.10	13.96	3.08
Hispanic	0.16	0.37	0.19	0.39
Black	0.13	0.33	0.13	0.34
Number of children aged 0–6 in household	0.15	0.46	0.14	0.41
Number of children aged 7–11 in household	0.30	0.56	0.28	0.54
Number of children aged 12–18 in household	0.74	0.81	0.74	0.76
Number of other adults in household	0.37	0.67	0.42	0.72
Age	16.32	1.00	16.37	1.01
Urban	0.84	0.37	0.82	0.38
State unemployment rate	5.30	1.10	5.39	1.03
Weekend or holiday	0.28	0.45	0.28	0.45
Number of respondents	1004		1005	

Note: Statistics calculated using school-year data for enrolled high-school students from the 2003–2006 ATUS; statistics incorporate sampling weights supplied with ATUS.
[a]Omitted category in multivariate analyses.

interval-to-interval observations are continuations of activities. When we consider the actual changes in activities, we see that most of these involve transitions into or out of the supervised and unsupervised other activities. There are relatively few transitions among the remaining activities.

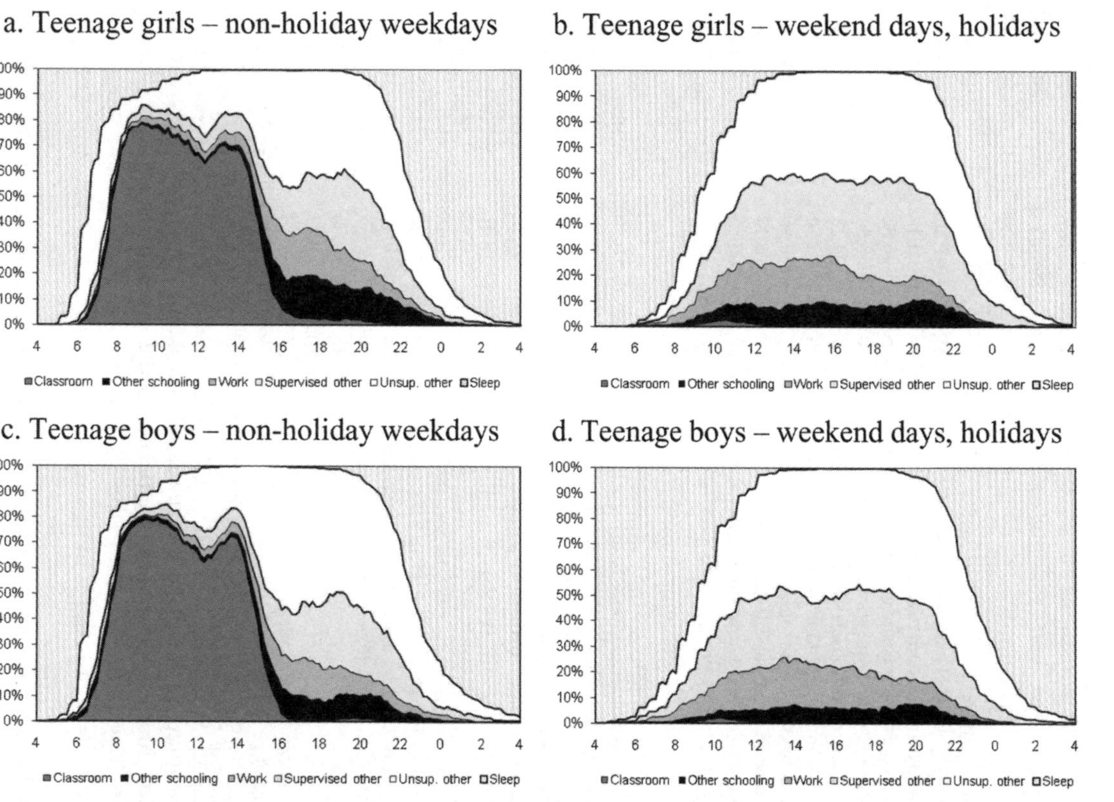

Fig. 1. Distributions of Teenagers' Time Use Across the Day During the School Year. *Note*: Statistics calculated using school-year data for enrolled high-school students from the 2003–2006 ATUS; statistics incorporate sampling weights supplied with ATUS. The horizontal axes in each figure indicate the hour of the day in military (24-hour) time.

ECONOMETRIC MODEL

We model the transitions among the broad groups of activities defined in the previous section using discrete-time, competing-risk hazard methods. Let j and k be index variables that denote different activities (= 0 if morning sleep, 1 if classroom schooling activities, 2 if other educational activities, 3 if work, 4 if "other" supervised activities, 5 if "other" unsupervised activities, and 6 if retiring sleep). Let h_{jk} be the hazard of transitioning from activity j to activity k. As we mentioned, morning sleep ($j=0$) is the origin activity for everyone in the analysis sample. If j equals 0, the teenager's "choice set," M_0, is to continue sleeping or to transition to any of the other activities except retiring sleep ($M_0=\{0, 5\}$). Once the teenager has woken up and transitioned to one of the other activities (1–5), he or she can continue in that activity or transition to any of the other activities, except for morning sleep ($M_j=\{1, 6\}$ for j in $\{1, 5\}$). Retiring sleep is modeled as a terminal activity; once a teenager has transitioned into retiring sleep, he or she is assumed to remain in that activity ($M_6=\{6\}$). This gives rise to 6 types of spells and 36 types of transitions to model.[7] All of the activity spells except morning and retiring sleep can have multiple episodes during the day.

We adopt the discrete-time, competing-risk hazard framework described by Allison (1982) and model each transition as a function of the duration of the spell (d), the time of day (t), family structure and economic circumstances (F), and other observed covariates (X), using a multinomial logit specification

$$h_{j,k}(d,t) = \frac{\exp\left(\alpha_{jk}A_d + \beta_{jk}B_t + \gamma_{jk}F + \delta_{jk}X\right)}{\sum\limits_{m\in M_j}\exp\left(\alpha_{jm}A_d + \beta_{jm}B_t + \gamma_{jm}F + \delta_{jm}X\right)} \tag{1}$$

where A_d is a vector of duration controls for the spell, B_t is a vector of time-of-day and cumulative activity duration controls, and α_{jk}, β_{jk}, γ_{jk}, and δ_{jk} are vectors of coefficients to be estimated.[8] The specification is a type of proportional hazards model in which the term $\alpha_{jk}A_d$ accounts for the baseline duration dependence pattern and the other terms shift this pattern up or down. In estimating the model, the coefficients associated with continuation in a given activity – α_{jj}, β_{jj}, γ_{jj}, and δ_{jj} – are normalized to zero.

As we discussed in the previous section, there are numerous transitions into and out of the supervised and unsupervised other activities but relatively few transitions directly between the remaining activities. The "thin" transitions (e.g., $1\rightarrow2$, $1\rightarrow3$, $1\rightarrow6$, $2\rightarrow1$) do not have enough observations to support estimating all of the coefficients in specification (1). For these transitions, we instead estimate a restricted specification, consisting of an intercept and an indicator for whether the activity took place on a weekend or holiday.

As a sensitivity test, we also estimate models that include a common unobserved variable or factor, η, to control for the possibility of spurious duration dependence within spells and for potential associations in behavior across spells that may arise from unmeasured, person-specific characteristics. These models take the form

$$h_{j,k}(d,t) = \frac{\exp\left(\alpha_{jk}A_d + \beta_{jk}B_t + \gamma_{jk}F + \delta_{jk}X + \lambda_{jk}\eta\right)}{\sum_{m \in M_j} \exp\left(\alpha_{jm}A_d + \beta_{jm}B_t + \gamma_{jm}F + \delta_{jm}X + \lambda_{jm}\eta\right)} \tag{2}$$

where λ_{jk} is an additional coefficient. For the distribution of the unobserved factor, we adopt a semi-parametric, discrete distribution following the approach of Heckman and Singer (1984). These distributions include two points of support, and the locations and probabilities of these points are estimated using the aML software package (Lillard & Panis, 2003).

Although our event-history approach is more complicated than the OLS and Tobit approaches usually employed to examine daily time-use data, we see several crucial advantages to this technique. Most importantly, our approach conforms to the underlying structure of the data and the reporting process for activities in the ATUS. Event-history models are a natural way to model the duration of spells and hence activities, but they also respect other features of the data. In particular, they allow us to model entry into different activities, thus letting us examine and distinguish between characteristics that contribute to the incidence of an activity and the duration of the activity. This is an improvement over single-index OLS and Tobit specifications. The models also fully account for the fact that the uses of time are reported as mutually exclusive events. In previous research, the restrictions associated with mutual exclusivity and the daily time constraint for multiple activities have only been addressed informally, such as through correlated model specifications (e.g., Kalenkoski, Ribar, & Stratton, 2005, 2007; Zick, 2010). Through the spell duration, cumulative duration, schedule, and finite-mixture heterogeneity controls, the models account for the distributions of activity times in a comprehensive and logically consistent way. We avoid the strong distributional restrictions inherent in standard Tobit models and can apply the methods in circumstances where other less-restrictive approaches, such as censored least absolute deviations (CLAD), cannot be applied.[9] Nevertheless, our approach still addresses the same underlying censoring and nonnegativity issues associated with time allocations. Finally, we account for other relevant features of time-use data, such as time-of-day effects and heaped reporting times. Although some multivariate studies have considered the timing of activities over the day (e.g., Hamermesh, 1999, 2005; Hamermesh, Myers, & Pocock, 2008; Stewart, 2010), such studies remain rare and generally only consider the incidence of activities at particular times and not their durations or daily cumulations.

General Specification Issues

Our event-history models incorporate parametric controls for current spell duration and time-of-day effects. While the controls we adopt are relatively flexible, some initial specification decisions are still required. After an examination of the spell distributions and some initial testing, we adopted piecewise linear specifications (linear splines) for the current spell duration dependence patterns, with the segments connecting at two-hour intervals during a spell up to the eighth hour. Unlike a series of dummy-variable (step-function) controls, the piecewise linear specifications avoid discrete jumps at the connecting points of the baseline hazard function. That said, descriptive analyses did reveal that all of the hazards exhibited spikes at regular 30- and 60-minute intervals – these occur because people tend to report activities in half-hour and hour increments. To account for this reporting behavior, all of our models include dummy controls for spell intervals that end in a 30- or 60-minute increment. While the locations of the connecting segments and the dummy controls are fixed, the other shape parameters – the slopes along the piecewise linear functions and the levels of the spikes associated with the dummy controls – are all estimated and therefore determined by the data.

Our model also allows for separate time-of-day effects depending on whether the activity occurred on a weekday or on a weekend or holiday. For each type of day and for most of our activities, we specify piecewise linear functions that are constrained to be flat from 4 a.m. to 7 a.m., to have a two-hour segment running to 9 a.m., and to have three-hour segments thereafter through either 9 p.m. or 12 a.m., depending on the activity. The transition to nighttime sleep is specified differently with a long flat segment running through 6 p.m. and two three-hour spline segments thereafter. In each of the models, the flat segments early and late in the day correspond to times when there were very few transitions. These restrictions are needed to avoid conditioning (near-complete sample separation) problems in the models at thin points in the time-of-day distributions. Again, the slopes of the other segments of the piecewise linear functions are estimated.

In addition to these controls, all of our models, except the hazard function for morning sleep, incorporate measures for the cumulative amounts of time spent in sleep, classroom activities, other educational activities, work, and other supervised time from 4 a.m. till the present time. These cumulative duration effects are identified separately from the within-spell duration effects by times spent in previous spells.

RESULTS

As the description of the econometric specifications indicates, we jointly estimate numerous transitions among daily activities, utilizing a broad array of control variables. We have organized the results tables for our primary specification first by gender and then by the type of transition. Tables 2a and 2b list selected coefficient estimates and estimated standard errors from the models for teenage girls, and Tables 3a and 3b list the results for boys.

The first two columns in Tables 2a and 3a contain coefficients corresponding to the transitions from initial morning sleep into supervised other activities and unsupervised other activities. The coefficients for the remaining three "thin" transitions into classroom schooling, other educational activities, and work activities are omitted from the tables but available upon request (recall that the coefficients for these transitions are limited to an intercept and an indicator for weekends or holidays). The next two columns in Tables 2a and 3a list coefficients corresponding to the transitions from classroom activities into supervised and unsupervised other activities. The next two columns contain coefficients for the transitions from other educational activities into supervised and unsupervised other activities. The final two columns contain coefficients corresponding to the transitions from work into supervised and unsupervised other activities.

In Tables 2b and 3b, the first five columns contain coefficients corresponding to the transitions from supervised other activities into each of the possible remaining activities, while the final five columns list coefficients for the transitions from unsupervised other activities into the remaining activities. All of the estimates come from multinomial discrete-time transition models in which transitions are modeled relative to continuation in the original activities.

The estimated coefficients and standard errors for specific control variables are listed by row in the tables. The variables associated with disadvantage are laid out first, and we focus our discussion on these variables. The first three rows in each table list the coefficients for the parents' living arrangements and work status. The estimates from Table 2a indicate that living in a household in which both parents work or in which the father does not work (as opposed to a "traditional" two-parent household where only the father works) reduces the risk of girls transitioning from classroom activities to supervised other activities. Living with a nonworking father also reduces the risks of girls leaving other educational activities for supervised other activities. As Table 2b indicates, parents' work status is not strongly associated with girls' exits from supervised other activities. The net effect of having two working parents or a nonworking father on the total time spent in supervised other activities is therefore negative.[10] Having two working parents or a nonworking father also increases girls' transition rates from unsupervised other activities to work. All told these results suggest that girls who live with both parents and whose mother works spend more time on educational and work activities and less time in supervised other activities. Looking at the effect that living with a single parent is estimated to have on transitions to and from supervised activities and other educational activities suggests that living with a single parent reduced girls' time in these quality activities.

Table 3a shows that, among boys, having a working mother in a two-parent household increases transitions out of other educational activities into supervised other activities and that living with a single parent reduces transitions from work to supervised other activities, lengthening work spells. Table 3b shows that living with a single parent increases transitions from supervised other time to unsupervised other time and generally reduces transitions out of unsupervised other time, increasing the length of unsupervised other activity spells.

The next key explanatory variable in the tables is parental education. Girls with more educated parents sleep later and have longer other educational activity spells than girls with less-educated parents. Parental education also increases girls' transitions from supervised and unsupervised other activities into other educational activities. Among boys, having more educated parents also reduces the transition rate out of and increases the transition rate into these other educational activity spells and also increases the transition rate into classroom activities. For both girls and boys, the association between parental education and the amount of time spent in other educational activities appears to be unambiguously positive.

Race and ethnicity are significantly associated with time use for all adolescents. There is evidence that black boys and perhaps black girls wake later than nonblack adolescents. Black girls have longer spells of unsupervised activities and of other educational activities than nonblack

Table 2a. Coefficient Estimates for Transitions to Supervised and Unsupervised Other Activities: Girls.

Initial State	Initial Sleep		Classroom		Other Education		Work	
Ending State	Supervised other time	Unsupervised other time	Supervised other time	Unsupervised other time	Supervised other time	Unsupervised other time	Supervised other time	Unsupervised other time
Two-parent household, both parents work	−0.092	0.034	−0.626***	−0.125	−0.308	−0.091	−0.234	−0.080
	(0.281)	(0.103)	(0.219)	(0.106)	(0.202)	(0.143)	(0.183)	(0.145)
Two-parent household, father does not work	−1.025	0.127	−0.782*	0.158	−0.697*	0.031	−0.135	−0.155
	(0.658)	(0.164)	(0.415)	(0.177)	(0.401)	(0.234)	(0.264)	(0.217)
Single-parent household	−0.295	−0.067	−0.305	−0.129	−0.400	0.214	−0.080	−0.025
	(0.340)	(0.122)	(0.257)	(0.128)	(0.300)	(0.182)	(0.212)	(0.163)
Highest education obtained by parents	−0.066*	0.005	−0.045	0.017	−0.052*	−0.027	0.039	0.005
	(0.040)	(0.014)	(0.031)	(0.015)	(0.029)	(0.020)	(0.024)	(0.018)
Hispanic	−1.058***	−0.078	−0.963**	−0.398***	−0.625**	−0.293	0.179	0.152
	(0.403)	(0.116)	(0.304)	(0.136)	(0.299)	(0.180)	(0.174)	(0.136)
Black	−0.714	0.089	−0.382	−0.095	−0.654**	−0.062	−0.140	0.142
	(0.445)	(0.124)	(0.312)	(0.127)	(0.328)	(0.182)	(0.217)	(0.139)
Number of children aged 0–6	−0.041	−0.094	−0.235	−0.119	−0.133	0.004	0.118	0.079
	(0.288)	(0.090)	(0.219)	(0.099)	(0.279)	(0.164)	(0.119)	(0.087)
Number of children aged 7–11	−0.162	0.029	−0.217	0.051	−0.164	−0.058	0.110	0.167**
	(0.231)	(0.073)	(0.175)	(0.074)	(0.181)	(0.112)	(0.109)	(0.081)
Number of children aged 12–18	−0.202	0.024	−0.018	−0.049	0.042	0.042	−0.073	0.077
	(0.155)	(0.049)	(0.108)	(0.049)	(0.107)	(0.070)	(0.084)	(0.062)
Number of other adults	−0.166	0.054	0.106	0.157**	−0.011	0.063	−0.093	−0.044
	(0.199)	(0.057)	(0.150)	(0.068)	(0.149)	(0.092)	(0.092)	(0.062)
Age 16	0.152	−0.025	0.110	0.042	−0.408*	−0.037	−0.030	−0.257*
	(0.279)	(0.104)	(0.237)	(0.107)	(0.229)	(0.146)	(0.170)	(0.137)
Age 17	−0.326	−0.035	0.130	0.108	−0.072	−0.120	−0.446**	−0.221*
	(0.293)	(0.103)	(0.237)	(0.107)	(0.211)	(0.152)	(0.175)	(0.131)

Age 18	−0.908**	−0.269**	0.764**	0.246	−0.351	−0.001	−0.592***	−0.429***
	(0.434)	(0.130)	(0.306)	(0.150)	(0.329)	(0.201)	(0.213)	(0.154)
Urban residence	0.139	−0.033	0.138	0.017	−0.586***	−0.177	−0.010	−0.220
	(0.295)	(0.103)	(0.244)	(0.113)	(0.227)	(0.164)	(0.193)	(0.137)
Unemployment rate	0.026	−0.047	−0.030	−0.055	−0.036	−0.086	0.107*	−0.024
	(0.115)	(0.039)	(0.096)	(0.044)	(0.088)	(0.057)	(0.065)	(0.048)
Cumulative time in classroom			0.024	0.013	0.015	−0.009	0.011	−0.006
			(0.024)	(0.012)	(0.009)	(0.006)	(0.007)	(0.005)
Cumulative time in other education			0.056	0.021	0.002	−0.016*	0.031**	−0.011
			(0.036)	(0.021)	(0.016)	(0.010)	(0.013)	(0.012)
Cumulative time in work			0.051	0.052**	0.005	−0.008	0.007	−0.016**
			(0.041)	(0.024)	(0.013)	(0.008)	(0.009)	(0.007)
Cumulative time in unsupervised other activities			0.068**	0.026	0.001	−0.002	0.015*	−0.007
			(0.027)	(0.018)	(0.012)	(0.007)	(0.008)	(0.007)
Cumulative time in sleep			0.049**	0.002	−0.024*	−0.006	0.001	−0.006
			(0.024)	(0.012)	(0.014)	(0.009)	(0.009)	(0.007)

Note: The estimated coefficients and standard errors come from discrete-time, competing-risk (multinomial logit) hazard specifications that also include year dummies, weekend/weekday-specific time-of-day splines, duration splines, and dummy controls for 30 and 60-minute spells. The models were estimated using school-year data for enrolled high-school students from the 2003–2006 ATUS. Estimated standard errors appear in parentheses.

*Significant at the 0.10 level, **significant at the 0.05 level, and ***significant at the 0.01 level.

Table 2b. Coefficient Estimates for Girls from Supervised and Unsupervised Other Time.

Initial State	Supervised Other Time					Unsupervised Other Time				
Ending State	Class-room	Other education	Work	Unsupervised other time	Retiring sleep	Class-room	Other education	Work	Supervised other time	Retiring sleep
Two-parent household, both parents work	0.076 (0.298)	−0.235 (0.172)	0.116 (0.164)	0.045 (0.086)	−0.112 (0.217)	−0.080 (0.102)	−0.020 (0.134)	0.303** (0.139)	−0.082 (0.082)	−0.199* (0.112)
Two-parent household, father does not work	0.355 (0.424)	−0.128 (0.313)	−0.332 (0.313)	−0.005 (0.147)	0.260 (0.348)	0.003 (0.178)	−0.085 (0.231)	0.389** (0.198)	−0.127 (0.135)	0.018 (0.188)
Single-parent household	0.382 (0.344)	−0.800*** (0.255)	−0.121 (0.202)	−0.109 (0.106)	−0.321 (0.252)	−0.061 (0.121)	−0.158 (0.172)	0.427*** (0.157)	−0.308*** (0.103)	−0.142 (0.133)
Highest education obtained by parents	−0.040 (0.043)	0.065** (0.026)	−0.001 (0.023)	0.021* (0.012)	−0.089*** (0.029)	0.006 (0.015)	0.079*** (0.020)	0.003 (0.017)	0.017 (0.012)	−0.001 (0.016)
Hispanic	−0.623 (0.395)	−0.146 (0.242)	0.139 (0.181)	0.005 (0.101)	−0.510* (0.273)	0.121 (0.123)	−0.285 (0.187)	0.189 (0.133)	0.056 (0.098)	0.178 (0.121)
Black	0.125 (0.397)	−0.146 (0.286)	0.294 (0.214)	0.079 (0.116)	−0.125 (0.275)	−0.078 (0.124)	−0.034 (0.165)	−0.289* (0.153)	−0.252** (0.109)	0.007 (0.133)
Number of children aged										
0–6	−0.337 (0.304)	−0.159 (0.187)	0.252** (0.102)	−0.096 (0.079)	0.073 (0.170)	−0.005 (0.090)	−0.125 (0.136)	0.259*** (0.084)	0.085 (0.069)	−0.089 (0.102)
7–11	0.528*** (0.190)	−0.320** (0.154)	0.072 (0.116)	−0.041 (0.063)	0.026 (0.146)	−0.064 (0.077)	0.097 (0.097)	0.234*** (0.078)	0.053 (0.058)	0.157* (0.082)
12–18	0.118 (0.160)	−0.257** (0.102)	0.229*** (0.080)	−0.023 (0.044)	−0.067 (0.107)	−0.006 (0.049)	0.130** (0.064)	0.081 (0.058)	0.005 (0.042)	0.136** (0.054)
Number of other adults	0.205 (0.204)	0.039 (0.119)	0.216** (0.096)	0.043 (0.053)	−0.140 (0.140)	0.009 (0.062)	0.015 (0.088)	−0.067 (0.069)	0.013 (0.051)	0.090 (0.061)
Age 16	0.153 (0.331)	−0.216 (0.185)	0.249 (0.177)	0.012 (0.088)	0.217 (0.220)	−0.168 (0.104)	0.167 (0.142)	0.064 (0.138)	0.043 (0.083)	−0.235** (0.113)

Age 17	0.287	−0.277	0.168	−0.125	−0.414*	−0.008	0.212	0.374***	−0.216**	−0.234**
	(0.323)	(0.191)	(0.184)	(0.092)	(0.234)	(0.104)	(0.144)	(0.132)	(0.089)	(0.113)
Age 18	0.653*	−0.671**	0.230	−0.153	−0.335	−0.324**	0.068	0.783***	−0.057	−0.180
	(0.382)	(0.298)	(0.226)	(0.117)	(0.316)	(0.141)	(0.194)	(0.147)	(0.113)	(0.146)
Urban residence	0.100	0.138	0.233	0.048	0.297	−0.110	0.079	0.262*	−0.026	0.017
	(0.294)	(0.198)	(0.186)	(0.089)	(0.243)	(0.108)	(0.147)	(0.135)	(0.086)	(0.112)
Unemployment rate	−0.026	−0.059	0.083	−0.008	0.068	−0.075*	0.027	−0.099**	−0.029	−0.085**
	(0.114)	(0.076)	(0.067)	(0.034)	(0.088)	(0.040)	(0.053)	(0.048)	(0.034)	(0.042)
Cumulative time in										
Classroom	0.073***	0.032***	0.008	−0.003	−0.017**	0.124***	0.031***	−0.009*	0.006	0.005
	(0.024)	(0.009)	(0.008)	(0.004)	(0.008)	(0.014)	(0.007)	(0.006)	(0.004)	(0.004)
Other education	0.052	0.032***	−0.011	−0.016*	0.015	0.051*	0.044***	−0.018	−0.013*	0.021***
	(0.048)	(0.012)	(0.015)	(0.006)	(0.011)	(0.028)	(0.009)	(0.012)	(0.008)	(0.005)
Work	0.002	0.014	0.016*	−0.005	−0.021***	0.051**	0.016**	0.021***	0.008	0.000
	(0.043)	(0.010)	(0.009)	(0.004)	(0.008)	(0.022)	(0.008)	(0.006)	(0.005)	(0.004)
Unsupervised other activities	−0.039	−0.003	0.003	−0.014***	−0.012*	0.044**	0.009	−0.007	0.013***	0.012***
	(0.046)	(0.012)	(0.010)	(0.004)	(0.007)	(0.022)	(0.008)	(0.008)	(0.005)	(0.004)
Sleep	−0.009	0.013	0.013	−0.003	−0.032***	0.003	0.007	−0.011*	0.002	−0.011*
	(0.025)	(0.012)	(0.009)	(0.005)	(0.011)	(0.012)	(0.009)	(0.007)	(0.005)	(0.006)

Note: The estimated coefficients and standard errors come from discrete-time, competing-risk (multinomial logit) hazard specifications that also include year dummies, weekend/weekday-specific time-of-day splines, duration splines, and dummy controls for 30 and 60-minute spells. The models were estimated using school-year data for enrolled high-school students from the 2003–2006 ATUS. Estimated standard errors appear in parentheses.

*Significant at the 0.10 level, **significant at the 0.05 level, and ***significant at the 0.01 level.

Table 3a. Coefficient Estimates for Transitions to Supervised and Unsupervised Other Activities: Boys.

Initial State	Initial Sleep		Classroom		Other Education		Work	
Ending State	Supervised other time	Unsupervised other time	Supervised other time	Unsupervised other time	Supervised other time	Unsupervised other time	Supervised other time	Unsupervised other time
Two-parent household, both parents work	0.025	−0.106	−0.016	−0.115	0.793***	0.141	0.316	−0.150
	(0.298)	(0.108)	(0.252)	(0.115)	(0.306)	(0.173)	(0.204)	(0.142)
Two-parent household, father does not work	0.242	0.018	0.138	−0.105	0.923**	0.174	0.214	0.023
	(0.427)	(0.156)	(0.360)	(0.169)	(0.375)	(0.256)	(0.301)	(0.202)
Single-parent household	−0.398	0.004	0.092	−0.110	−0.500	0.145	−0.617**	−0.094
	(0.385)	(0.124)	(0.292)	(0.132)	(0.445)	(0.217)	(0.284)	(0.171)
Highest education obtained by parents	−0.038	−0.018	−0.019	0.008	−0.065*	−0.058***	0.023	−0.004
	(0.039)	(0.014)	(0.031)	(0.015)	(0.037)	(0.022)	(0.028)	(0.020)
Hispanic	0.069	−0.107	−0.052	−0.220*	−0.802**	−0.115	0.442*	0.436**
	(0.311)	(0.113)	(0.227)	(0.116)	(0.355)	(0.179)	(0.250)	(0.173)
Black	−1.126**	−0.211*	−0.088	−0.241*	1.110**	0.465*	0.021	0.125
	(0.487)	(0.120)	(0.303)	(0.136)	(0.437)	(0.271)	(0.260)	(0.159)
Number of children aged 0–6	0.042	0.131	0.264	−0.010	0.343	0.192	0.207	0.138
	(0.288)	(0.096)	(0.202)	(0.111)	(0.343)	(0.197)	(0.148)	(0.119)
Number of children aged 7–11	−0.064	0.085	0.359**	−0.032	−0.712**	0.131	−0.248*	0.050
	(0.234)	(0.074)	(0.152)	(0.080)	(0.283)	(0.129)	(0.131)	(0.090)
Number of children aged 12–18	0.207	−0.015	0.397***	−0.035	−0.207	−0.032	0.016	−0.160**
	(0.150)	(0.053)	(0.110)	(0.055)	(0.136)	(0.081)	(0.097)	(0.074)
Number of other adults	0.211	−0.039	0.070	−0.056	−0.095	−0.083	0.217**	0.159**
	(0.136)	(0.054)	(0.120)	(0.059)	(0.166)	(0.105)	(0.101)	(0.066)
Age 16	−0.493	0.050	−0.427*	0.064	−0.106	−0.019	−0.474**	−0.562***
	(0.316)	(0.106)	(0.231)	(0.109)	(0.267)	(0.178)	(0.220)	(0.166)
Age 17	−0.058	0.103	−0.310	0.095	−0.353	0.225	−0.582***	−0.385**
	(0.283)	(0.103)	(0.222)	(0.106)	(0.270)	(0.170)	(0.206)	(0.155)

Age 18	−0.703**	−0.342***	−0.298	0.212	−0.665	0.013	−0.656***	−0.997***
	(0.351)	(0.131)	(0.321)	(0.150)	(0.500)	(0.272)	(0.250)	(0.184)
Urban residence	0.022	−0.087	−0.567***	−0.021	−0.704**	−0.040	−0.336*	−0.027
	(0.320)	(0.101)	(0.203)	(0.102)	(0.275)	(0.189)	(0.179)	(0.139)
Unemployment rate	−0.109	−0.005	0.210**	−0.001	0.167	−0.039	0.066	0.136**
	(0.120)	(0.042)	(0.089)	(0.044)	(0.118)	(0.074)	(0.083)	(0.057)
Cumulative time in classroom			0.044*	0.024*	0.000	0.006	−0.002	−0.022***
			(0.026)	(0.013)	(0.014)	(0.008)	(0.009)	(0.005)
Cumulative time in other education			0.147***	0.016	−0.008	−0.011	0.008	0.003
			(0.040)	(0.024)	(0.016)	(0.010)	(0.017)	(0.012)
Cumulative time in work			−0.239*	−0.108**	−0.016	0.003	−0.013	−0.016**
			(0.131)	(0.051)	(0.017)	(0.010)	(0.010)	(0.006)
Cumulative time in unsupervised other activities			0.059**	−0.002	0.016	0.014	0.024***	−0.015**
			(0.029)	(0.021)	(0.013)	(0.009)	(0.007)	(0.007)
Cumulative time in sleep			0.070**	0.024*	0.000	0.014	0.009	−0.014**
			(0.030)	(0.014)	(0.018)	(0.011)	(0.011)	(0.007)

Note: The estimated coefficients and standard errors come from discrete-time, competing-risk (multinomial logit) hazard specifications that also include year dummies, weekend/weekday-specific time-of-day splines, duration splines, and dummy controls for 30 and 60-minute spells. The models were estimated using school-year data for enrolled high-school students from the 2003–2006 ATUS. Estimated standard errors appear in parentheses.

*Significant at the 0.10 level, **significant at the 0.05 level, and ***significant at the 0.01 level.

Table 3b. Coefficient Estimates for Boys from Supervised and Unsupervised Other Time.

Initial State	Supervised Other Time					Unsupervised Other Time				
Ending State	Classroom	Other education	Work	Unsupervised other time	Retiring sleep	Classroom	Other education	Work	Supervised other time	Retiring sleep
Two-parent household, both parents work	0.225	0.143	0.031	−0.033	0.071	−0.258**	−0.172	0.026	−0.078	0.016
	(0.273)	(0.220)	(0.216)	(0.091)	(0.260)	(0.120)	(0.169)	(0.142)	(0.085)	(0.111)
Two-parent household, father does not work	0.018	0.135	−0.073	−0.227	0.791**	−0.222	0.138	0.125	−0.231*	−0.056
	(0.401)	(0.324)	(0.308)	(0.142)	(0.353)	(0.173)	(0.233)	(0.197)	(0.133)	(0.166)
Single-parent household	0.066	−0.403	−0.033	0.188*	−0.003	−0.193	−0.357*	−0.221	−0.277***	−0.231*
	(0.377)	(0.316)	(0.287)	(0.111)	(0.310)	(0.134)	(0.212)	(0.170)	(0.104)	(0.130)
Highest education obtained by parents	−0.012	0.065**	0.033	0.011	−0.100***	0.037**	0.093***	−0.017	−0.009	−0.056***
	(0.040)	(0.031)	(0.031)	(0.013)	(0.035)	(0.015)	(0.023)	(0.018)	(0.012)	(0.016)
Hispanic	−0.154	0.457**	−0.343	0.033	−0.216	−0.185	0.120	−0.382**	−0.188**	0.015
	(0.310)	(0.232)	(0.279)	(0.102)	(0.280)	(0.124)	(0.174)	(0.160)	(0.091)	(0.120)
Black	−0.025	−0.221	−1.462***	−0.002	0.068	−0.138	−1.029***	0.074	−0.503***	−0.113
	(0.351)	(0.330)	(0.491)	(0.118)	(0.319)	(0.143)	(0.302)	(0.146)	(0.115)	(0.126)
Number of children aged										
0–6	0.415*	0.247	0.261*	0.007	−0.200	−0.009	−0.041	−0.050	−0.022	−0.020
	(0.233)	(0.195)	(0.152)	(0.083)	(0.293)	(0.111)	(0.174)	(0.118)	(0.080)	(0.106)
7–11	0.137	−0.101	0.033	0.173***	−0.296	0.024	−0.212	0.391***	0.063	−0.049
	(0.190)	(0.159)	(0.152)	(0.059)	(0.191)	(0.084)	(0.134)	(0.081)	(0.059)	(0.076)
12–18	−0.276**	−0.077	0.219**	−0.014	−0.081	0.018	0.103	0.034	0.132***	0.109**
	(0.126)	(0.116)	(0.111)	(0.047)	(0.127)	(0.059)	(0.085)	(0.069)	(0.042)	(0.055)
Number of other adults	−0.326*	0.095	0.351***	−0.065	−0.056	−0.014	−0.211**	0.089	0.079*	0.053
	(0.188)	(0.113)	(0.100)	(0.048)	(0.109)	(0.056)	(0.104)	(0.063)	(0.043)	(0.059)
Age 16	−0.511*	−0.151	−0.148	0.019	−0.682***	0.064	0.163	0.426***	0.134	−0.055
	(0.281)	(0.225)	(0.231)	(0.091)	(0.238)	(0.113)	(0.180)	(0.153)	(0.085)	(0.114)
Age 17	−0.301	0.130	0.092	−0.021	−1.006***	0.048	0.377**	0.600***	−0.150*	−0.304***
	(0.276)	(0.208)	(0.216)	(0.091)	(0.245)	(0.110)	(0.165)	(0.145)	(0.086)	(0.109)

Age 18	−0.461	−0.243	−0.188	−0.166	−1.713***	−0.422***	−0.203	0.532***	−0.060	−0.507***
	(0.350)	(0.308)	(0.275)	(0.116)	(0.321)	(0.160)	(0.256)	(0.175)	(0.105)	(0.137)
Urban residence	−0.165	0.139	0.002	0.008	−0.080	−0.222**	0.363*	0.147	−0.022	−0.038
	(0.256)	(0.221)	(0.210)	(0.087)	(0.230)	(0.104)	(0.187)	(0.136)	(0.083)	(0.107)
Unemployment rate	0.008	−0.011	−0.069	0.060	−0.054	−0.008	0.157**	−0.046	0.041	−0.044
	(0.113)	(0.092)	(0.094)	(0.038)	(0.101)	(0.046)	(0.072)	(0.056)	(0.035)	(0.047)
Cumulative time in										
Classroom	0.019	0.039***	0.007	−0.007*	0.003	0.089***	0.029***	−0.001	0.011***	0.001
	(0.026)	(0.010)	(0.010)	(0.004)	(0.008)	(0.016)	(0.009)	(0.006)	(0.004)	(0.004)
Other education	−0.032	0.049***	0.026*	−0.006	0.015	−0.010	0.033***	−0.018	0.024***	0.012**
	(0.051)	(0.011)	(0.015)	(0.007)	(0.012)	(0.028)	(0.011)	(0.014)	(0.007)	(0.005)
Work	−0.154	0.002	0.027***	−0.002	0.013*	−0.013	0.010	0.020***	0.024***	0.000
	(0.124)	(0.012)	(0.009)	(0.004)	(0.008)	(0.048)	(0.010)	(0.006)	(0.005)	(0.004)
Unsupervised other activities	−0.135*	−0.011	0.003	−0.010***	−0.005	0.018	0.014	−0.010	0.032***	0.009***
	(0.075)	(0.011)	(0.010)	(0.004)	(0.006)	(0.027)	(0.009)	(0.008)	(0.004)	(0.003)
Sleep	−0.076***	0.015	0.002	−0.002	−0.021*	−0.028*	−0.002	−0.021***	0.018***	−0.023***
	(0.026)	(0.014)	(0.011)	(0.005)	(0.011)	(0.015)	(0.011)	(0.007)	(0.005)	(0.006)

Note: The estimated coefficients and standard errors come from discrete-time, competing-risk (multinomial logit) hazard specifications that also include year dummies, weekend/weekday-specific time-of-day splines, duration splines, and dummy controls for 30 and 60-minute spells. The models were estimated using school-year data for enrolled high-school students from the 2003–2006 ATUS. Estimated standard errors appear in parentheses.

*Significant at the 0.10 level, **significant at the 0.05 level, and ***significant at the 0.01 level.

girls. Black boys, however, have longer classroom spells and shorter other educational spells. Black boys also have lower rates of transition from supervised other activities into work and from unsupervised activities into supervised other activities and into other educational activities. In general, black teenagers appear to spend substantially more time in unsupervised other activities than other teenagers. For Hispanic girls, there is also evidence of a time-shifted day with them both rising and going to bed later than non-Hispanic girls. Furthermore, there is evidence that all Hispanic teens devote more time schooling – both in and out of the classroom – than non-Hispanics. For Hispanic boys, some of this comes at the expense of work spells as the coefficient estimates suggest they are less likely to enter work spells and more likely to exit them.

Other characteristics have rather predictable effects. For example, older teens and those living in areas with lower unemployment rates are predicted to have longer work spells. As childcare time is classified here as "work," teens living in households with other children present also have longer work spells.

To control for dependencies across the uses of time, our models include the cumulative amounts of time that teenagers have spent so far during the day in certain activities as explanatory variables. Our results indicate that the cumulative time spent in an activity is a significant determinant of subsequent time use. For example, sleeping later in the morning is associated with a lower probability of continuing a classroom activity for girls and boys.

Simulation Results

The coefficients from the multinomial logit models in Tables 2a–3b are difficult to interpret. Each coefficient represents an estimated conditional association between an explanatory variable and an underlying index. The transition outcomes in the models depend on several indices and do so in a nonlinear way. The transition probabilities, in turn, are hard to interpret because they are expressed conditionally as hazard probabilities and further depend on the person's uses of time up to that possible transition. For example, the hazard at the eighth hour of an activity spell could be very high, but the practical impact could be negligible if few people continue in that activity for that long. Ultimately, we are interested in the associations of observed characteristics with teenagers' total daily time use, which depend cumulatively on the person's complete sequence of transitions.

To better examine the implications of the transition models, we conduct a series of simulations. The simulations apply the coefficient estimates from

Tables 2a–3b to samples in which we replicate each observation from the 2,009-person analysis sample 25 times. For each replicated person, we simulate transitions between activities by calculating hazard probabilities at each point in time throughout a day conditioned on what was simulated for the person previously in the day. Each hazard is then compared to a random draw to simulate a possible transition. Time use patterns throughout the day and time use amounts for the entire day are then calculated based on the simulated transition paths. We use this methodology for two purposes – to demonstrate the predictive ability of our econometric approach and to generate empirical estimates of the marginal impact of observed characteristics on the incidence and amount of time spent in each activity.

With respect to the predictive ability of our econometric approach, we first compare how well our simulations of the incidence and the distributions of the amount of total time spent in each activity match actual time and predicted time distributions from comparable Tobit and OLS specifications. The results for incidence, specifically the fraction of the sample spending time in each activity, are reported in Fig. 2.[11] The upper panel shows results for girls, the lower panel results for boys. As everyone in the sample slept, no incidence comparison for sleep time is provided. Clearly, the fraction ever reporting no time in unsupervised activities is also very low – less than 1%. This fact plus the observation that 13% of the women and 19% of the men report no time in supervised activities provides further support for the conclusion that over-scheduling is not a substantial concern for teenagers. When we consider all of the outcomes together, our event-history modeling approach clearly fits the data best, with predictions that are virtually identical to the actual data for all of the activities except work. In contrast, the Tobit models overpredict the incidence of classroom activities by nearly 10-percentage points, underpredict the incidence of supervised other activities by similar margins, and underpredict the incidence of unsupervised other activities by 3 to-percentage points. Predictions from the OLS models are even worse than those from the Tobit models.

Figs. 3 and 4 illustrate actual and simulated distributions of positive amounts of time for each activity and each specification for girls and boys, respectively. In the case of unsupervised other and sleep time, because incidence is so close to 100%, the Tobit and OLS predictions are essentially identical. Again, overall, our event-history approach provides very close fits to the actual distributions. Only in the case of the spikes for classroom time around seven to eight hours and for sleep time around eight to nine hours does our model fail to track total actual hours fairly closely, and in this case neither OLS nor Tobit predictions are any better. OLS and Tobit

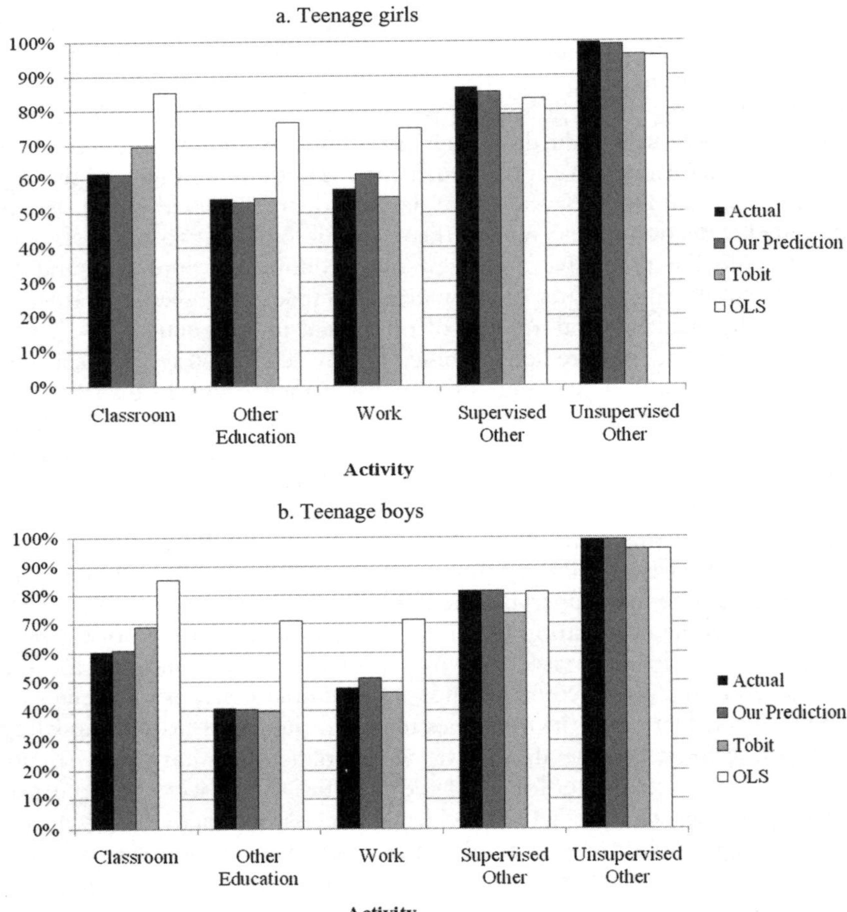

Fig. 2. Comparing Actual and Simulated Incidence of Time Use Percent Reporting Time in Each Activity.

predictions do about as well as our simulations for unsupervised other and sleep time, the activities for which incidence is close to 100%. OLS predictions do particularly poorly at mimicking actual other education time. Neither OLS nor Tobit do as well as the event-history approach at capturing the large fraction of time spent in small amounts of work and unsupervised other time. The event-history approach also provides the best fit for other

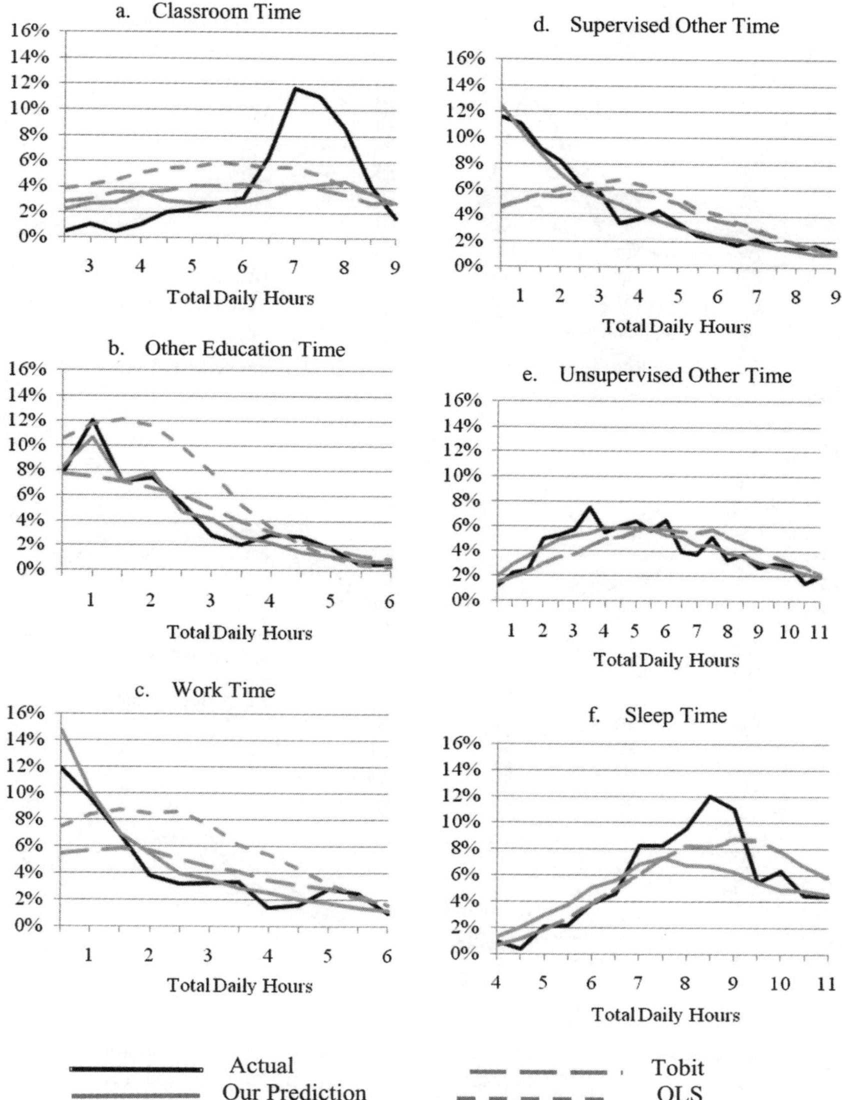

Fig. 3. Distributions of Teenage Girls' Actual and Simulated Total Hours in Activities.

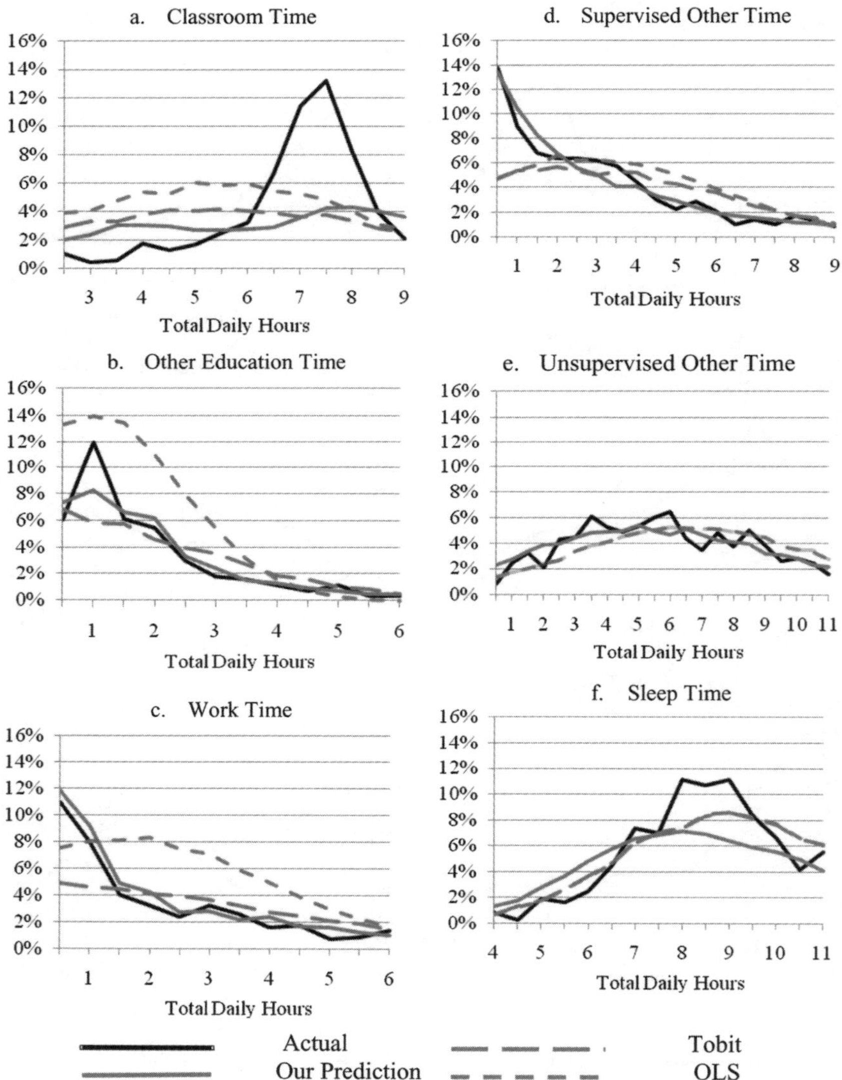

Fig. 4. Distributions of Teenage Boys' Actual and Simulated Total Hours in Activities.

education time. That the event-history approach does so well comparatively at simulating total time spent in each activity is remarkable as total time is not itself the dependent variable in event-history modeling, while it is for OLS and Tobit.

Finally, Fig. 5 illustrates the simulated distribution of time use across the day for girls and boys using the event-history approach. Such a simulation is not possible using a Tobit or OLS specification. As the event-history model is fit to transitional probabilities and not specifically to the distribution of time use over the day, there is no guarantee that this model will mimic the observed pattern of time, though our time-of-day and duration controls help in this regard. Nevertheless, a comparison of Figs. 1 and 5 reveals that the simulations also do a good job of capturing the distribution of teenagers' time use by time of day. The most noticeable feature that they appear to miss is a return to classroom activities on weekdays following lunch.

Simulated estimates of the marginal impact observed characteristics have on the incidence and amount of time spent in each activity are reported in Tables 4a and 4b. The first rows of Tables 4a and 4b provide baseline estimates of the fraction of individuals observed and the average amount of time spent in each of our six activities. The "marginal associations" of changes in the observed characteristics with the incidence and amount of time use are calculated by systematically changing characteristics from the analysis sample while holding the other observed characteristics fixed and then simulating the changes in the outcomes. Results from these simulations are reported in the second and subsequent rows of Table 4a for girls and Table 4b for boys. In addition to reporting the mean time and incidence for each change, we also report the percentage change in each from the relevant base case in parentheses below. In some cases we see that the change in incidence moves in the opposite direction from the change in amount. Single-index models are not able to capture such different effects.

The first four of these change simulations assign different family structures and parental work patterns to the teenagers. In particular, simulations are conducted assuming that all of the teenagers live in households with (1) two parents where the father works but the mother does not (the relevant base case for family structure/work pattern parameters), (2) two working parents, (3) two parents but a nonworking father, and (4) a single parent. Relative to girls living with a working father and a nonworking mother, the models indicate that girls living in other arrangements spend more time in work, less time in supervised other activities, and more time in unsupervised activities. Girls living with single parents also spend substantially less time in other educational activities.

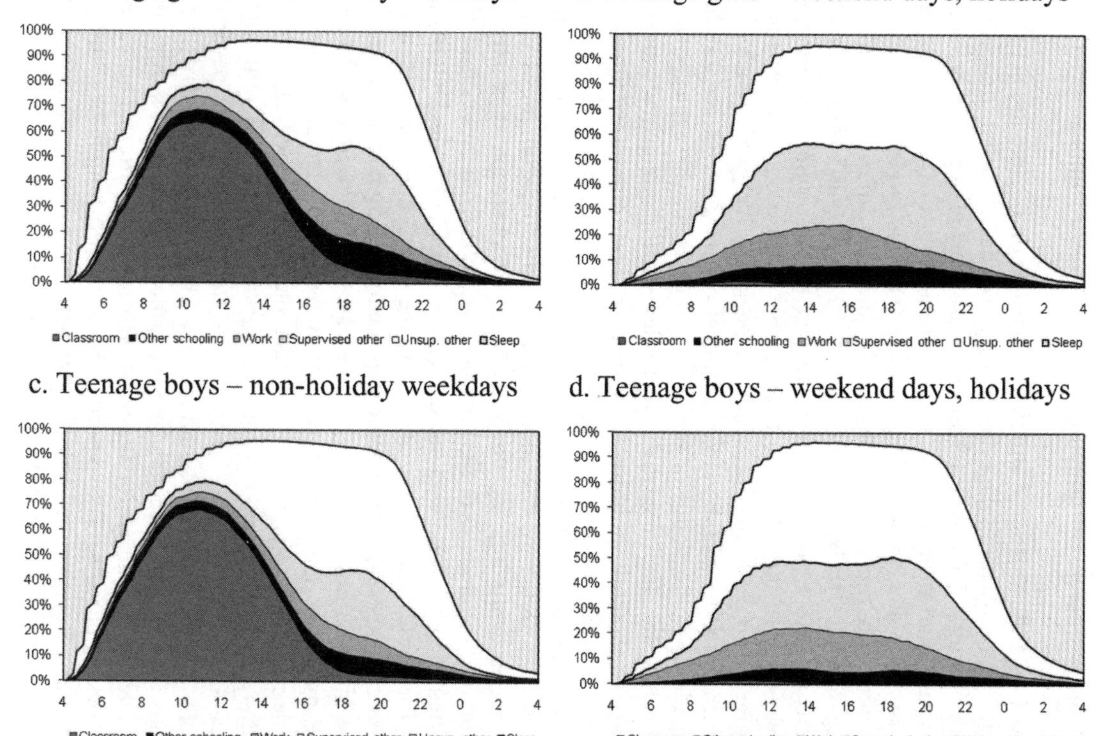

Fig. 5. Simulated Distributions of Teenagers' Time use Across the Day During the School Year.

Notes: Simulated distributions calculated using school-year data for enrolled high-school students from the 2003–2006 ATUS and coefficient estimates from Tables 2a–3b. Statistics incorporate sampling weights supplied with the ATUS. The horizontal axes in each figure indicate the hour of the day in military (24-hour) time.

Table 4a. Simulation Results for Girls.

	Classroom		Other Schooling		Work		Supervised Other Activities		Unsupervised Other Activities	Sleep
	Minutes (% change)	Incidence (% change)	Minutes (% change)	Incidence (% change)	Minutes (% change)	Incidence (% change)	Minutes (% change)	Incidence (% change)	Minutes (% change)	Minutes (% change)
Baseline	228.9	61.4%	65.4	53.1%	85.4	61.3%	168.9	85.3%	348.7	542.8
Two-parent HH, only father works[a]	225.8	61.8%	69.0	55.9%	70.5	57.3%	185.2	88.7%	337.5	552.0
Two-parent HH, both parents work[a]	230.7 (2.1%)	61.5% (−0.5%)	69.7 (1.0%)	54.4% (−2.7%)	90.1 (23.0%)	62.7% (8.7%)	163.5 (−12.8%)	85.6% (−3.7%)	348.9 (3.2%)	537.2 (−2.7%)
Two-parent HH, father does not work[a]	234.6 (3.9%)	63.2% (2.3%)	67.5 (−2.4%)	53.3% (−4.7%)	88.4 (21.0%)	60.7% (5.5%)	152.4 (−19.4%)	82.3% (−7.6%)	344.7 (2.0%)	552.4 (0.1%)
Single parent HH[a]	225.5 (−0.1%)	60.6% (−1.9%)	52.3 (−25.6%)	46.9% (−16.9%)	87.9 (20.4%)	63.1% (9.5%)	175.2 (−5.9%)	83.6% (−6.0%)	359.3 (6.2%)	539.9 (−2.2%)
Highest education obtained by parents	228.7 (−0.1%)	61.3% (−0.2%)	69.8 (6.7%)	54.6% (2.9%)	84.6 (−0.9%)	61.2% (−0.1%)	167.3 (−1.0%)	85.1% (−0.2%)	347.1 (−0.4%)	542.5 (−0.1%)
White[b]	226.3	61.9%	65.0	53.8%	87.6	61.6%	176.2	86.9%	344.4	540.6
Hispanic[b]	237.4 (4.9%)	59.6% (−3.8%)	64.4 (−0.9%)	48.2% (−10.6%)	85.8 (−2.0%)	64.2% (4.3%)	171.4 (−2.9%)	84.3% (−3.0%)	329.4 (−4.3%)	551.6 (2.0%)
Black[b]	236.9 (4.6%)	62.4% (0.8%)	69.8 (7.3%)	53.7% (−0.1%)	76.6 (−12.8%)	58.1% (−5.7%)	130.6 (−27.0%)	79.7% (−8.3%)	391.9 (13.6%)	534.2 (−1.2%)

Table 4a. *(Continued)*

	Classroom		Other Schooling		Work		Supervised Other Activities		Unsupervised Other Activities	Sleep
	Minutes (% change)	Incidence (% change)	Minutes (% change)	Incidence (% change)	Minutes (% change)	Incidence (% change)	Minutes (% change)	Incidence (% change)	Minutes (% change)	Minutes (% change)
Number of children aged										
0–6	220.8	59.1%	60.1	49.4%	95.2	67.9%	184.7	86.8%	334.0	545.1
	(−3.5%)	(−3.8%)	(−8.1%)	(−7.0%)	(11.5%)	(10.8%)	(9.4%)	(1.7%)	(−4.2%)	(0.4%)
7–11	231.6	62.5%	65.4	51.6%	88.9	66.1%	171.4	85.2%	333.5	549.3
	(1.2%)	(1.8%)	(−0.0%)	(−2.8%)	(4.1%)	(7.8%)	(1.5%)	(−0.1%)	(−4.4%)	(1.2%)
12–18	232.9	61.7%	65.3	53.3%	91.0	64.3%	165.2	84.8%	338.1	547.6
	(1.7%)	(0.4%)	(−0.2%)	(0.4%)	(6.5%)	(5.0%)	(−2.2%)	(−0.6%)	(−3.0%)	(0.9%)
Number of other adults	229.0	62.5%	66.2	53.8%	90.1	62.1%	157.7	84.9%	354.8	542.2
	(0.1%)	(1.8%)	(1.1%)	(1.4%)	(5.5%)	(1.3%)	(−6.6%)	(−0.4%)	(1.8%)	(−0.1%)
Unemployment rate	222.4	60.1%	66.7	52.2%	82.0	60.6%	169.8	85.8%	356.9	542.2
	(−2.8%)	(−2.2%)	(1.9%)	(−1.6%)	(−4.0%)	(−1.1%)	(0.5%)	(0.6%)	(2.4%)	(−0.1%)

The baseline results are derived from a simulation conducted using the characteristics actually observed in the data.
[a]Changes in household type are identified relative to two-parent households in which only the father works.
[b]Changes in race/ethnicity are identified relative to white persons.

Table 4b. Simulation Results for Boys.

	Classroom		Other Schooling		Work		Supervised Other Activities		Unsupervised Other Activities	Sleep
	Minutes (% change)	Incidence (% change)	Minutes (% change)	Incidence (% change)	Minutes (% change)	Incidence (% change)	Minutes (% change)	Incidence (% change)	Minutes (% change)	Minutes (% change)
Baseline	238.4	60.9%	46.1	40.5%	78.9	51.0%	155.8	81.0%	379.3	541.5
Two-parent HH, only father works[a]	247.7	62.3%	54.4	43.5%	78.4	51.8%	163.2	82.1%	356.2	540.2
Two-parent HH, both parents work[a]	233.1 (−6.1%)	60.1% (−3.8%)	44.6 (−21.2%)	41.3% (−5.6%)	77.4 (−1.3%)	51.9% (0.2%)	167.9 (3.0%)	83.3% (1.5%)	368.8 (3.3%)	548.3 (1.5%)
Two-parent HH, father does not work[a]	242.2 (−2.3%)	61.6% (−1.3%)	51.2 (−6.8%)	45.2% (4.2%)	77.0 (−1.8%)	53.3% (2.9%)	167.3 (2.7%)	81.0% (−1.3%)	356.1 (−0.0%)	546.1 (1.1%)
Single parent HH[a]	243.9 (−1.6%)	61.5% (−1.4%)	41.7 (−27.4%)	36.2% (−18.1%)	80.3 (2.4%)	47.6% (−8.1%)	119.6 (−28.0%)	75.4% (−8.3%)	429.1 (19.2%)	525.4 (−2.7%)
Highest education obtained by parents	238.1 (−0.1%)	60.7% (−0.3%)	50.8 (10.1%)	42.7% (5.3%)	78.1 (−1.0%)	50.5% (−1.1%)	154.3 (−1.0%)	80.7% (−0.3%)	380.5 (0.3%)	538.3 (−0.6%)
White[b]	242.7	61.9%	48.0	41.7%	87.8	53.1%	160.5	83.0%	362.1	538.8
Hispanic[b]	232.2 (−4.4%)	59.4% (−4.1%)	60.6 (27.3%)	45.7% (10.0%)	49.1 (−49.1%)	44.0% (−17.7%)	150.4 (−6.5%)	80.3% (−3.4%)	437.2 (19.8%)	548.0 (1.7%)
Black[b]	227.1 (−6.5%)	57.8% (−6.9%)	22.4 (−55.6%)	28.2% (−33.3%)	72.0 (−20.0%)	48.8% (−8.3%)	133.5 (−17.4%)	72.6% (−12.8%)	399.8 (9.9%)	547.8 (1.7%)

Table 4b. *(Continued)*

	Classroom		Other Schooling		Work		Supervised Other Activities		Unsupervised Other Activities	Sleep
	Minutes (% change)	Incidence (% change)	Minutes (% change)	Incidence (% change)	Minutes (% change)	Incidence (% change)	Minutes (% change)	Incidence (% change)	Minutes (% change)	Minutes (% change)
Number of children aged										
0–6	252.4	63.4%	46.8	43.4%	74.1	52.7%	150.2	81.8%	390.1	526.4
	(5.9%)	(4.2%)	(1.6%)	(7.1%)	(−6.1%)	(3.2%)	(−3.6%)	(1.0%)	(2.8%)	(−2.8%)
7–11	245.1	62.4%	43.0	38.6%	105.0	59.6%	142.4	81.1%	376.7	527.9
	(2.8%)	(2.5%)	(−6.7%)	(−4.9%)	(33.1%)	(16.9%)	(−8.7%)	(0.2%)	(−0.7%)	(−2.5%)
12–18	232.0	60.5%	49.7	41.8%	90.4	53.6%	174.1	84.5%	348.4	545.5
	(−2.7%)	(−0.6%)	(7.7%)	(3.2%)	(14.6%)	(5.1%)	(11.7%)	(4.3%)	(−8.2%)	(0.8%)
Number of other adults	232.4	59.9%	45.1	38.8%	80.3	55.5%	171.4	83.3%	366.4	544.4
	(−2.5%)	(−1.6%)	(−2.3%)	(−4.2%)	(1.8%)	(8.7%)	(10.0%)	(2.8%)	(−3.4%)	(0.6%)
Unemployment rate	235.9	60.8%	49.8%	42.9%	71.2	49.8%	159.3	82.6%	383.2	540.6
	(−1.1%)	(−0.1%)	(8.1%)	(6.0%)	(−9.8%)	(−2.4%)	(2.2%)	(2.1%)	(1.0%)	(−0.2%)

The baseline results are derived from a simulation conducted using the characteristics actually observed in the data.

[a]Changes in household type are identified relative to two-parent households in which only the father works.

[b]Changes in race/ethnicity are identified relative to white persons.

Boys living with two working parents spend less time in classroom and other schooling activities than boys living with a working father and a nonworking mother. Boys living with a single parent spend less time in other educational activities, less time in supervised other activities, and substantially more time (over an hour more) in unsupervised activities. Boys living with both parents but whose father is not working appear to report a higher incidence of other educational activities, but average less time in those activities.

Increased years of parental education are associated with both girls and boys spending additional time in other educational activities. The marginal associations imply that children of parents with a bachelor's degree spend a quarter to a third of an hour more than children of parents with only a high-school diploma on such activities. Parental education has little other association with teenagers' time use.

An additional child of any age increases teenage girls' average work time, with the largest effect occurring for an additional child aged 0–6. An additional child aged 0–6 also increases the time girls spend in supervised activities but decreases the time they spend in unsupervised activities and classroom and other educational activities, suggesting that teenage girls may be required to help more around the house when young children are present. For boys, an additional child aged 0–6 increases the time spent in classroom activities and in unsupervised activities. An additional child aged 7–11 is estimated to increase boys' time in work activities by 26 minutes. While this does not change the probability of having supervised time, it does decrease the time spent in supervised activities by on average 13 minutes. Finally, an additional child aged 12–18 increases boys' time spent in work and supervised other activities while decreasing their time spent in unsupervised activities. Similarly, the presence of other adults contributes to a reallocation among boys from unsupervised to supervised other activities.

The simulations indicate that black girls and boys spend substantially more time in unsupervised other activities and less time in work and supervised other activities than nonblack teenagers. Black boys also appear to spend significantly less time in classroom and other educational activities. Hispanic boys spend more time in unsupervised other activities and other educational activities and less time in work and supervised other activities than non-Hispanics. Interestingly, Hispanic girls are a bit less likely to spend time either in the classroom or in other educational activities, but when they do they spend substantially more time – over 30 more minutes in the class and almost 15 more minutes in other educational activities. These results indicate that Hispanic and especially black teens are generally engaging in less schooling, less work, and less-supervised activities, but more unsupervised activities than other teens.

Finally, the simulations reveal that higher unemployment rates are associated with less time in work and more time in unsupervised other activities. The association with work is stronger for boys, while the association with unsupervised other activities is stronger for girls.

Sensitivity Analyses

The transition models presented in Tables 2a–3b incorporate numerous specialized controls, including controls for spell durations, cumulative time use, heaped reporting, and weekday and weekend/holiday time-of-day effects. Specification tests revealed that each set of controls was jointly significant and improved the fit of the models. To examine their substantive impact, we reestimated the models without selected controls and then simulated the total daily time allocation distributions, as we had done with our preferred model. The alternative specifications did not reproduce the distributions as well as our preferred specification. Time-of-day controls were especially critical. Models without these controls substantially over-predicted sleep and underpredicted other activities.[12]

We also estimated transition models that included controls for unobserved heterogeneity, as described in Eq. (2). The unobserved components were specified as discrete distributions with two points of support. We estimated an "unrestricted" specification for girls and a partially restricted specification for boys.[13] These led to small changes in the estimated duration effects but no appreciable changes in the estimated effects of the observed variables and other controls. The inclusion of these controls also did not alter the simulation results. Detailed results are available upon request.

CONCLUSION

We use time diaries from the 2003–2006 ATUS and an innovative application of competing-risk hazard models to examine how teenagers' daily time allocations are affected by family and personal characteristics. Our methodology has substantial advantages over other techniques. Analyzing activity spells within a hazard framework conforms to the way that activities in the ATUS and other time diaries are reported, as a series of spells. In addition, our approach recognizes the mutually exclusive nature of activities and the daily time constraint in a logically consistent way. It also allows us to distinguish between the incidence and the duration of an activity, and to incorporate time-of-day effects, heaped reporting, and some dependencies within and across activity spells. As a result, our competing-risk hazard approach more closely reproduces time-of-day patterns, the distributions of total daily activity times, and differences in the implied effects of observed characteristics on the incidence and total time allocation of activities than the approaches that have been applied in previous studies. Although our method of analyzing time-diary data addresses many features of the data, we estimate our principal models using standard multinomial logit software. Thus, this approach can be easily implemented by most researchers.

We are especially interested in how characteristics associated with household disadvantage, such as living in a single-parent family or with an out-of-work father, living with less-educated parents, or living in a high-unemployment area, affect teenagers' time investments in classroom activities and in other educational activities. This distinction is critical as time devoted to other educational activities appears to be sensitive to several aspects of disadvantage while time devoted to classroom activities is much less so. Our results indicate that teenagers of both sexes who lived in single-parent families or with less-educated parents spent substantially less time in other educational activities than other, comparable teenagers. Additionally, boys who lived with two working parents devoted less time to other educational activities than boys who lived with a working father but a nonworking mother, and black boys were estimated to spend less than half as much time as white boys in these activities. While the ATUS data are limited to a single day's time allocations and thus lack long-run outcome measures such as standardized test scores and future labor market outcomes, these results suggest that one potential mechanism through which disadvantage negatively affects future outcomes is through reduced homework time and reduced participation in extracurricular activities.

We are also keenly interested in how household disadvantage alters teenagers' other uses of time. Given the daily time constraint, these reductions in schooling investments must be counterbalanced by increases in other uses of time. Prior research has only addressed offsetting time use in a limited way if at all. A key advantage of our approach is that it naturally incorporates all uses of time. In particular, we group teenagers' noneducational activities into four categories: work, sleep, other activities where an adult is present and available to supervise, and other activities without an adult. This decomposition, in turn, facilitates an investigation of two hypotheses regarding why disadvantage might affect schooling. The first hypothesis is that teenagers in disadvantaged households might have to adopt adult roles and take on extra economic or household responsibilities. This could result in their work hours increasing. The second hypothesis is that disadvantaged households may provide less supervision or provide less-structured environments, leading teenagers to spend more time in unsupervised other activities.

We find some evidence supporting the early-adult-role hypothesis for girls. Girls who live in single-parent households, but also those who live in two-parent households with a working mother or a nonworking father, devote 12–15 more minutes to work than girls in traditional households. Girls with very young siblings also work more than other girls.

We find much more evidence for the supervision/structure hypothesis, especially for boys. Boys living in single-parent households are estimated to spend nearly an hour and 15 minutes more per day in unsupervised other activities than boys living with a working father and a nonworking mother. For girls, this same difference in living arrangements is associated with a third of an hour increase in unsupervised activities.

Evidence regarding supervision and structure also can be seen in other ways such as the timing of teenagers' days and employment trade-offs. Girls with less-educated parents tend to sleep later than other girls. Black boys and Hispanic girls follow a similar pattern. Higher local unemployment rates and minority status reduce work time generally. To a substantial degree, the reduction in work time is offset by an increase in unsupervised time.

The less-structured environment of disadvantaged youths may therefore be a key mechanism explaining their reduced investment in education. Policy initiatives designed to provide more structure and supervision may help ameliorate this differential. These would include mentoring programs, such as Big Brothers and Big Sisters, for teens in single-parent households. They might also include after-school programs, such as homework clubs and intensive tutoring, for teens with working and/or less-educated parents. These could provide both educational assistance and structure to enhance schooling achievement. Counseling and workshop programs for disadvantaged parents may also help them to supervise more effectively. In addition, our findings regarding girls' work suggest that their schooling might benefit from expanded day care facilities for their younger siblings.

NOTES

1. Reviews of the extensive literature on adolescent attainments are available in Haveman and Wolfe (1994), Duncan and Brooks-Gunn (1997), and Bowles, Gintis, and Groves (2005).

2. Respondents were not asked who else was present when they reported sleeping, grooming, working, or taking a class. They also were not asked when they refused to classify or could not remember the type of activity.

3. We excluded the weeks between the Memorial Day and Labor Day holidays and the nine days from Christmas Eve to New Years day. Wight et al. (2009) and Zick (2010) pooled data from the entire year and included dummy variables to account for summer observations.

4. These other schooling-related activities include extracurricular club activities, music and performance activities, student government, research, and homework. We exclude sports from other education activities because the ATUS does not identify which activities are and are not school related. We also considered examining sports/exercise as a separate activity within our framework but were not able to because of the very small amount of time spent in such activities.

5. We code married couples who are living apart as single-parent households because the household time constraints more nearly resemble those of single-parent households. We drop teenagers with cohabiting parents because very few of them were in this situation.

6. There were 2,509 15–18 year-olds in the ATUS who had not completed high school and provided diary information during the school year. Our exclusions for school enrollment, living arrangements, missing information, and activity patterns reduce the sample by 20%.

7. There is a 37th transition (from one period of retiring sleep to another) that does not need to be modeled.

8. To reduce the amount of notation, we omit subscripts identifying the teenager and the spell.

9. CLAD can only be applied if the incidence of an activity is more than 50%.

10. Factors that increase the probability of entering an activity or decrease the probability of exiting that activity act to increase time in that activity. Conversely, factors that decrease the probability of entering an activity or increase the probability of exiting that activity act to reduce time in that activity.

11. It is straightforward to predict the incidence of an activity from the event-history models (the person transitions into the activity at least once) and from the Tobit models (the latent index for the activity is positive). However, the incidence has to be inferred for OLS models. We assume that predictions of positive amounts of time from the OLS models indicate that the activity was undertaken.

12. The biggest issue was that these models predicted a constant rate of entry into retiring sleep, which is a terminal event. Once observations were simulated to enter this activity, they were not available to enter into other activities.

13. Identification for these models requires at least one factor loading (λ_{jk} coefficient from specification 2) to be fixed. The model for girls incorporated this minimal restriction; however, we were unable to obtain estimates of the model for boys unless a second factor was fixed.

ACKNOWLEDGMENTS

The authors thank Deborah Cobb-Clark, Nancy Folbre, Daniel Hamermesh, Robert Pollak, Jay Stewart, two anonymous reviewers, and participants at numerous workshops and conferences for their helpful comments.

REFERENCES

Allison, P. D. (1982). Discrete-time methods for the analysis of event histories. *Sociological Methodology*, *13*, 61–98.

Bhat, C. R., Srinivasan, S., & Axhausen, K. W. (2005). An analysis of multiple interepisode durations using a unifying multivariate hazard model. *Transportation Research*, *39*(Part B), 797–823.

Bianchi, S. M. (2000). Maternal employment and time with children: Dramatic change or surprising continuity. *Demography*, *37*(4), 401–414.

Bowles, S., Gintis, H., & Groves, M. O. (Eds.). (2005). *Unequal chances: Family background and economic success*. New York, NY: Russell Sage Foundation.

Bryant, W. K., & Zick, C. D. (1996). An examination of parent-child shared time. *Journal of Marriage and the Family*, *58*(1), 227–237.

Burton, P., & Phipps, S. (2007). Families, time and money in Canada, Germany, Sweden, the United Kingdom and the United States. *Review of Income and Wealth*, *53*(3), 460–483.

Call, K. T., Mortimer, J. T., & Shanahan, M. J. (1995). Helpfulness and the development of competence in adolescence. *Child Development*, *66*(1), 129–138.

Capizzano, J., Main, R., & Nelson, S. (2004). *Adolescents assuming adult roles: Factors associated with teens providing child care for younger siblings*. Unpublished data. The Urban Institute, Washington, DC.

Crowder, K., & Teachman, J. (2004). Do residential conditions explain the relationship between living arrangements and adolescent behavior?. *Journal of Marriage and the Family*, *66*(3), 721–738.

Demo, D. H., & Acock, A. C. (1993). Family diversity and the division of domestic labor: How much have things really changed? *Family Relations*, *42*(3), 323–331.

Duncan, G. J., & Brooks-Gunn, J. (Eds.). (1997). *Consequences of growing up poor*. New York, NY: Russell Sage Foundation.

Fischer, M. J., & Kmec, J. A. (2004). Neighborhood socioeconomic conditions as moderators of family resource transmission: High school completion among at-risk youth. *Sociological Perspectives*, *47*(4), 507–527.

Gager, C. T., Cooney, T. M., & Call, K. T. (1999). The effects of family characteristics and time use on teenagers' household labor. *Journal of Marriage and the Family*, *61*(4), 982–994.

Gennetian, L. A., Duncan, G. J., Knox, V. W., Vargas, W. G., Clark-Kauffman, E., & London, A. S. (2002). *How welfare and work policies for parents affect adolescents: A synthesis of research*. MDRC report, MDRC, New York.

Goldscheider, F. K., & Waite, L. J. (1991). *New families, no families? The transformation of the American home*. Berkeley, CA: University of California Press.

Hamermesh, D. S. (1999). The timing of work over time. *Economic Journal*, *109*(542), 37–66.

Hamermesh, D. S. (2005). Routine. *European Economic Review*, *49*(1), 29–53.

Hamermesh, D. S., Myers, C. K., & Pocock, M. L. (2008). Cues for timing and coordination: Latitude, letterman, and longitude. *Journal of Labor Economics*, *26*(2), 223–246.

Haveman, R., & Wolfe, B. (1994). *Succeeding generations: On the effects of investments in children*. New York, NY: Russell Sage Foundation.

Heckman, J. J., & Singer, B. (1984). A method for minimizing the impact of distributional assumptions in econometric models of duration data. *Econometrica*, *52*(2), 271–320.

Hilton, J. M., & Haldeman, V. A. (1991). Gender differences in the performance of household tasks by adults and children in single-parent and two-parent, two-earner families. *Journal of Family Issues*, *12*(1), 114–130.

Kalenkoski, C. M., & Pabilonia, S. W. (2009a). Does working while in high school reduce study time in the U.S.? *Social Indicators Research*, *93*(1), 117–121.

Kalenkoski, C. M., & Pabilonia, S. W. (2009b). *Time to work or time to play: The effect of student employment on homework, sleep, and screen time*. IZA Discussion paper no. 4666. Institute for the Study of Labor (IZA), Bonn, Germany.

Kalenkoski, C. M., Ribar, D. C., & Stratton, L. S. (2005). Parental child care in single parent, cohabiting, and married couple families: Time diary evidence from the United Kingdom. *American Economic Review Papers and Proceedings*, *95*(2), 194–198.

Kalenkoski, C. M., Ribar, D. C., & Stratton, L. S. (2007). The effect of family structure on parents' child care time in the United States and the United Kingdom. *Review of Economics of the Household*, *5*(4), 353–384.

Lareau, A. (2003). *Unequal childhoods: Class, race, and family life*. Berkeley, CA: University of California Press.

Lee, B., & Timmermans, H. J. P. (2007). A latent class accelerated hazard model of activity episode durations. *Transportation Research*, *41*(Part B), 426–447.

Leventhal, T., Graber, J. A., & Brooks-Gunn, J. (2001). Adolescent transitions to young adulthood: Antecedents, correlates, and consequences of adolescent employment. *Journal of Research on Adolescence*, *11*(3), 297–323.

Lillard, L., & Panis, C. (2003). *aML multilevel multiprocess statistical software, Version 2.0*. Los Angeles, CA: EconWare, Inc.

Lopoo, L. M. (2007). While the cat's away do the mice play? Maternal employment and the after-school activities of adolescents. *Social Science Quarterly*, *88*(5), 1357–1373.

Mahoney, J. L., Harris, A. L., & Eccles, J. S. (2006). Organized activity participation, positive youth development and the over-scheduling hypothesis. *Social Policy Report*, *20*(4), 1, 3–31.

Marshall, K. (2007). The busy lives of teenagers. *Perspectives*, 5–15.

Oettinger, G. S. (1999). Does high school employment affect high school academic performance? *Industrial and Labor Relations Review*, *53*(1), 136–151.

Peters, J. M., & Haldeman, V. A. (1987). Time used for household work. *Journal of Family Issues*, *8*(2), 212–225.

Porterfield, S. L., & Winkler, A. E. (2007). Teen time use and parental education: Evidence from the CPS, MTF, and ATUS. *Monthly Labor Review*, *130*(5), 37–56.

Raley, S. (2007). Children's time use: Too busy or not busy enough. In: S. M. Bianchi, J. P. Robinson & M. A. Milkie (Eds.), *Changing rhythms of American family life*. New York, NY: Russell Sage Foundation.

Rothstein, D. S. (2007). High school employment and youths' academic achievement. *Journal of Human Resources*, *42*(1), 194–213.

Ruhm, C. J. (1995). The extent and consequences of high school employment. *Journal of Labor Research*, *16*(3), 293–304.

South, S. J., Baumer, E. P., & Lutz, A. (2003). Interpreting community effects on youth educational attainment. *Youth & Society*, *35*(1), 3–36.

Stafford, F. (2009). Timeline data collection and analysis: Time diary and event history calendar methods. In: R. F. Belli, F. P. Stafford & D. F. Alwin (Eds.), *Calendar and time diary methods in life course research* (pp. 13–30). New York, NY: Russell Sage Foundation.

Stewart, J. (2010). The timing of maternal work and time with children. *Industrial and Labor Relations Review*, *64*(1)article 9.

Todd, M., Armeli, S., & Tennen, H. (2009). Interpersonal problems and negative mood as predictors of within-day time to drinking. *Psychology of Addictive Behaviors*, *23*(2), 205–215.

Tyler, J. H. (2003). Using State child labor laws to identify the effect of school-year work on high school achievement. *Journal of Labor Economics*, *21*(2), 353–380.

Wight, V. R., Price, J., Bianchi, S. M., & Hunt, B. R. (2009). The time use of teenagers. *Social Science Research*, *38*(4), 792–809.

Zick, C. D. (2010). The shifting balance of adolescent time use. *Youth & Society*, *41*(4), 569–596.

CHAPTER 2

THE OPT-OUT REVOLUTION: RECENT TRENDS IN FEMALE LABOR SUPPLY

Heather Antecol

ABSTRACT

Using data from the U.S. Census in conjunction with data from the Current Population Survey (1980–2009), I find little support for the opt-out revolution – highly educated women, relative to their less-educated counterparts, are exiting the labor force to care for their families at higher rates today than in earlier time periods – if one focuses solely on the decision to work a positive number of hours irrespective of marital status or race. If one, however, focuses on both the decision to work a positive number of hours and the decision to adjust annual hours of work (conditional on working), I find some evidence of the opt-out revolution, particularly among white college educated married women in male-dominated occupations.

Keywords: Opting out; female labor supply; extensive/intensive margin; race/ethnicity

JEL classifications: J13; J15; J16; J22

Research in Labor Economics, Volume 33, 45–83

ISSN: 0147-9121/doi:10.1108/S0147-9121(2011)0000033005

INTRODUCTION

> Workplace flexibility isn't just a women's issue. It's an issue that affects the well-being of our families and the success of our businesses. It affects the strength of our economy – whether we'll create the workplaces and jobs of the future that we need to compete in today's global economy. (President Obama, March 31, 2010, Workplace Flexibility Forum)

Recent national media accounts have drawn attention to the growing concern that highly educated women, relative to their less-educated counterparts, are exiting the labor force to care for their families at higher rates today than in earlier time periods. This stylized fact, known as the "opt-out revolution," was first sensationalized by Lisa Belkin in a 2003 *New York Times* article.[1] Given women are more likely to graduate college than men (Hewlett, 2007), this could have extremely large consequences for women, the firms for which they work, and society as a whole. While women's role in society has changed dramatically over the last 50 years (i.e., increased labor force participation and declining fertility rates, particularly among married women), casual empiricism suggests that the societal organization of the workplace has yet to catch up. While the media accounts suggest it is family pulls (e.g., the birth of a child) that cause women to exit, workplace pushes (e.g., lack of workplace flexibility and extreme work hours) may in fact be at play as well. The goal of this study, however, is not to shed light on the underlying causes of opting out but to shed light on whether or not women, particularly highly educated women who work in fields that do not tend to afford them workplace flexibility and are prone to extreme work hours (e.g., 60+ hours/week), are indeed "opting out" of the labor market.[2]

A number of recent studies have attempted to find evidence of the opt-out revolution. The preponderance of these studies focus on the employment side of opting out (i.e., conditional on having children women exit the labor market)[3] and generally conclude that there is no evidence to support the popular press' notion of an opt-out revolution, that is, the effect of children is not found to be higher for highly educated women compared to less-educated women in recent years (see, e.g., Boushey, 2005, 2008; Cohany & Sok, 2007; Fortin, 2008; Goldin, 2006; Percheski, 2008; Vere, 2007).[4]

What can account for the discrepancy in the press' accounts of the opt-out revolution and the studies of the employment side of the opt-out revolution (henceforth referred to as the opt-out literature)? One possibility is the opt-out literature tends to focus on the effect of children unadjusted for demographic characteristics, such as marital status and race/ethnicity (henceforth referred to as race).[5] The labor supply decisions of prime-aged women (henceforth referred to as women) with children who are not married are likely to be very different than those of their married women counterparts, particularly at the top of the education distribution, as these women are likely married to men who are also highly educated and have high-earning power, affording them the ability to exit the labor market when they have children (see, e.g., Williams, Manvell, & Bornstein, 2006).[6] Indeed, highly educated married women tend to be the focus of the media accounts (Williams et al., 2006). In addition, in 2000 marriage rates among women are higher at the top of the education distribution than at the bottom of the education distribution; this is in stark contrast to 1980 where highly educated women are generally less likely to get married than their less-educated counterparts.[7] Marriage rates have fallen over time as well (see Table 1). Thus, by combining married and non-married women, one may be underestimating the effect of children, particularly in recent years.

Similarly, the labor supply decisions of non-Hispanic white (henceforth referred to as white) women with children are likely to be very different than those of their nonwhite counterparts. The media attention is generally more focused on white affluent women in white-collar jobs (Williams et al., 2006). Furthermore, white women are generally more attached to the labor market, more likely to have a college education, more likely to be married, and less likely to have children, and if they do have kids, they have fewer of them, relative to their nonwhite counterparts (see Table 1). Moreover, racial differences in educational attainment have become more pronounced over time. All of these racial differences suggest that the effect of children may differ substantially by race, and these differences may shed light on the discrepancies between the results presented in the media and the opt-out literature.

Another possibility is the opt-out literature generally focuses on one aspect of female labor supply, the decision to work a positive number of hours (i.e., the extensive margin), as opposed to conditional on participating in the labor market, the decision to adjust annual hours of work (i.e., the intensive margin).[8] I argue focusing on both margins may be important because women, particularly highly educated women, may not be choosing to exit the labor market entirely, but may be opting for reduced hours of work. There is support for this in the qualitative literature on opting out (see, e.g., Hewlett, 2007; Hewlett et al., 2005; Stone, 2008), that is, highly educated women are seeking alternative occupations that are less demanding, afford them more flexibility, and require a reduced time commitment. Moreover, Belkin (2003) recognized this possibility in her *New York Times*

Table 1. Summary Statistics by Race/Ethnicity and Year (Women Aged 25–44).

Variables	Total			Non-Hispanic White			Non-Hispanic Black			Hispanic			Asian		
	1980	1990	2000	1980	1990	2000	1980	1990	2000	1980	1990	2000	1980	1990	2000
	(1)	(2)	(3)	(4)	(5)	(6)	(7)	(8)	(9)	(10)	(11)	(12)	(13)	(14)	(15)
Race/Ethnicity[a]															
WHITE	0.81	0.77	0.71												
BLACK	0.10	0.11	0.11												
HISPANIC	0.06	0.08	0.11												
ASIAN	0.02	0.03	0.05												
Labor supply															
AHRS	1032.74	1296.97	1393.57	1031.52	1327.86	1438.58	1131.59	1286.48	1444.46	866.78	1062.63	1125.51	1097.25	1244.07	1271.62
WKSWRK	28.10	33.91	35.76	28.24	34.93	37.11	29.96	32.82	36.30	23.16	27.49	28.92	28.47	31.23	31.63
UHRS	24.21	28.79	30.04	24.17	29.29	30.70	26.03	28.81	31.54	21.21	24.78	25.48	25.54	27.56	27.77
CAHRS[b]	1519.44	1679.63	1770.24	1507.02	1676.94	1775.69	1609.80	1718.35	1795.67	1495.89	1626.96	1689.56	1620.49	1760.41	1804.16
LFA	0.68	0.77	0.79	0.68	0.79	0.81	0.70	0.75	0.80	0.58	0.65	0.67	0.68	0.71	0.70
Education															
LTHIGH	0.18	0.11	0.09	0.15	0.07	0.05	0.29	0.15	0.10	0.46	0.35	0.32	0.18	0.13	0.08
HIGH	0.44	0.33	0.28	0.46	0.34	0.27	0.41	0.37	0.33	0.33	0.30	0.29	0.26	0.22	0.17
SOMECOL	0.19	0.32	0.34	0.20	0.33	0.35	0.19	0.33	0.38	0.13	0.24	0.25	0.19	0.25	0.23
COLLEGE	0.19	0.24	0.30	0.20	0.26	0.33	0.11	0.15	0.19	0.07	0.10	0.14	0.38	0.40	0.52
Family relationship															
MARRIED	0.73	0.66	0.63	0.77	0.70	0.68	0.47	0.37	0.35	0.69	0.62	0.63	0.78	0.73	0.71
NCHILD	1.68	1.40	1.39	1.62	1.34	1.33	1.94	1.54	1.47	2.10	1.77	1.73	1.50	1.34	1.19
NCHLT5	0.35	0.35	0.34	0.34	0.34	0.33	0.34	0.32	0.29	0.48	0.44	0.42	0.44	0.38	0.36
NOKID	0.25	0.32	0.33	0.26	0.33	0.34	0.23	0.28	0.31	0.20	0.26	0.27	0.30	0.35	0.39
KIDLT5	0.28	0.27	0.27	0.27	0.27	0.26	0.27	0.25	0.23	0.37	0.34	0.33	0.35	0.30	0.29
Age															
AGE	33.40	34.11	34.95	33.45	34.23	35.21	33.18	33.79	34.70	33.17	33.37	33.90	33.30	34.21	34.33
N	1,296,068	1,635,258	1,589,181	1,052,561	1,283,288	1,152,947	131,166	158,876	164,045	76,955	126,889	165,967	26,514	51,220	65,403

Source: U.S. Census (IPUMS). All observations with flagged values on any of the variables of interest are dropped from the analysis. Sampling weights used. See Table A1 for variable definitions.

[a]Does not sum to one as Native Americans and other races not included.

[b]Number of observation is lower because they refer only to those working positive hours.

Magazine article. This then suggests that defining opting out simply on a woman's decision to exit the labor market may be masking some of the employment aspect of the opt-out revolution.

A third possibility is defining highly educated women simply as college educated may obscure the opt-out phenomenon. It may be that it is college-educated women in specific managerial/professional occupations, particularly male-dominated occupations (e.g., architects, engineers, lawyers, and physicians), that are more likely to opt out of the labor market in terms of both the extensive and intensive margin.[9] On the one hand, women in these occupations may be more inclined to exit the labor market entirely because these occupations offer the least amount of job flexibility (see Stone, 2008). On the other hand, women in these types of occupations likely worked extreme hours (e.g., 60+ hours/week) prior to having their child/children, and may be able to adjust their hours down to accommodate their new family roles. In addition, it is this group of women that the media tends to focus on (see Williams et al., 2006).

Using data from the U.S. Census in conjunction with data from the Current Population Survey (1980–2009), I find little support for the opt-out revolution – highly educated women, relative to their less-educated counterparts, are exiting the labor force to care for their families at higher rates today than in earlier time periods – if one focuses solely on the decision to work a positive number of hours irrespective of marital status or race. If one, however, focuses on both the decision to work a positive number of hours and the decision to adjust annual hours of work (conditional on working), I find some evidence of the opt-out revolution, particularly among white college educated married women in male-dominated occupations.

The remainder of the chapter is as follows. The data is discussed in the second section. Third section examines labor force attachment (LFA) by presence of young children, year, education, marital status, and race. Fourth section presents the results for the "child effect" decomposition. Fifth section presents an in-depth analysis for white college educated married women. The conclusions are presented in the sixth section.

DATA

For the main analysis I use data from the *Integrated Public Use Microdata Series* (IPUMS) 5% sample of the 1980, 1990, and 2000 U.S. Census (Ruggles et al., 2010). This data is ideal for my purposes because it has detailed information on family characteristics (marital status and presence of children), labor market characteristics (usual hours worked per week, weeks worked in the past calendar year, and occupation), and demographic characteristics (age and education), as well as having large samples of women within educational, racial/ethnic, and occupational categories.

I also supplement the U.S. Census data with data from the *Integrated Public Use Microdata Series* (IPUMS) March Current Population Survey (CPS) samples (King et al., 2010) to get information on the years between the censuses (i.e., 1981–1989 and 1991–1999), as well as information beyond 2000 (i.e., 2001–2009). Unfortunately, due to small sample sizes I am unable to examine all educational, racial/ethnic, and occupational categories using the CPS. Despite this shortcoming, I am able to use the CPS data to investigate the opt-out phenomenon for non-Hispanic white college educated married women. This analysis is presented in detail in the fifth section.

I restrict the sample to women between the ages of 25 and 44 who are employed in the civilian labor force and do not have allocated values on any of the variables of interest.[10] I focus on 25–44 year olds to ensure that women have completed their formal education, as well as allowing them sufficient time to begin forming their families. I only focus on the civilian labor force as the armed forces labor force is very different and likely attracts women with different preferences for work and family.

I consider four racial groups: non-Hispanic white, non-Hispanic black, Hispanic, and Asian, henceforth referred to as white, black, Hispanic, and Asian. These are constructed as indicator variables equal to 1 if the respondent is of that particular race, and 0 otherwise.[11] Table 1 presents summary statistics by race and year. The proportion of the female population that is white (nonwhite) decreased (increased) over the time period, with the biggest increase realized by Hispanics. Whites (Hispanics) accounted for 80.7% (6.1%), 76.5% (8.1%), and 70.7% (10.9%) of the female population in 1980, 1990, and 2000, respectively.

I consider three measures of labor supply. The first measure of labor supply considered is unconditional annual hours of work. This is defined as usual hours per week times weeks worked in the past calendar year. It therefore includes women who are not working, as by construction it includes 0 values. I also consider conditional annual hours of work measured as annual hours of work conditional on working positive annual hours of work. Finally, I consider LFA that is defined to equal 1 if a respondent worked positive annual hours, and 0 otherwise.[12] By focusing on these three measures, I am able to examine both the intensive and extensive margins (discussed in detail below).

Women were more attached to the labor market in 2000 relative to 1980 irrespective of the labor supply measure considered, although the biggest increase in labor supply occurred between 1980 and 1990. For example, LFA rates in 1980, 1990, and 2000 are 68.3%, 77.2%, and 78.7%, respectively. The same general pattern holds for all races, although it is more pronounced for white women. Focusing again on LFA, white women's LFA rates increased 12.3 percentage points between 1980 and 2000 while black, Hispanic, and Asian women's LFA rates increased by 9.8, 8.1, and 2.3 percentage points, respectively, in this time period.

To determine the "child effect," information on presence of children in the household is needed. I use the family relationship variables constructed in the IPUMS data to ascertain the presence of children. The first indicator variable is constructed based on the number of own children (biological, adopted, or step children) in the household (NCHILD). Specifically, I create an indicator variable equal to 1 if there are no own children in the household, and 0 otherwise. A second indicator variable is constructed based on the number of own children under age five in the household (NCHLT5). Specifically, I create an indicator variable equal to 1 if there are any own children less than five in the household, and 0 otherwise. For prime-aged women, own children in the household is a relatively good approximation for fertility (see Rindfuss, 1976). The number of own children decreased from 1.668 in 1980, to 1.399 in 1990, and 1.386 in 2000 while the proportion of women who had no children increased from 25.6% to 31.6% in 1990, and 33.0% in 2000. The proportion of women having children less than five is relatively stable between 1980 and 2000; 27.6%, 27.2%, and 26.5% in 1980, 1990, and 2000, respectively. While the levels are different across racial groups (e.g., nonwhites have more children than their white counterparts), the overall patterns tend to hold for all racial groups.

I also create a marital status indicator variable equal to 1 for married, spouse present, and 0 otherwise. Marriage rates have fallen over time from 72.9% in 1980, to 65.6% in 1990, and to 63.4% in 2000. Blacks experienced the largest decline in marriage rates between 1980 and 2000 (11.8 percentage points) followed by whites (8.6 percentage points), Asians (6.8 percentage points), and Hispanics (6.8 percentage points).

In addition, I consider four educational categories: less than high school (grade 11 or less), high school (grade 12), some college (1–3 years of college), and college (4+ years of college).[13] These are constructed as indicator variables equal to 1 if the respondent has attained that particular level of education, and 0 otherwise. Women have acquired more education between 1980 and 2000; 18.0% (18.5%), 10.9% (23.7%), and 8.8% (29.6%) of women had a less than high-school (college) degree in 1980, 1990, and 2000, respectively. The increase in college attendance between 1980 and 2000 is highest for Asians (37.2%–51.5%), followed by whites (19.9%–32.7%), blacks (11.1%–19.1%), and Hispanics (7.4%–13.7%).

Finally, I examine detailed occupations that fall into three occupational categories within the managerial/professional occupations: male-dominated (roughly 70% male or higher in 1980, 1990, and 2000), female-dominated (roughly 30% male or lower in 1980, 1990, and 2000), and mixed occupations (roughly between 40% and 60% male in 1980, 1990, and 2000). These categories are constructed based on the "occupation, 1990 basis" (OCC1990) variable in the IPUMS data for individuals between the ages of 18 and 64. An ideal feature of the IPUMS occupation question is that it applies to individuals who had worked within the previous five years, which allows one to examine both the extensive margin and intensive margin. Moreover, the five-year time frame coincides with the presence of young children, that is, children less than five years of age. See Table A2 for a detailed list of occupations by year that fall under each occupation category, as well as the percent male within each detailed occupation category.

Unfortunately due to small sample sizes (particularly in male-dominated occupations), I am only able to consider a subset of detailed occupations within each occupation type (see Table A2 for the sample size of white college educated married women by occupation, year, and presence of children).[14] The detailed male-dominated occupations considered are architects, electrical engineers, physicians, lawyers, and clergy/religious workers. The detailed female-dominated occupations considered are registered nurses, dieticians/nutritionists, occupational therapists, primary school teachers, and librarians. The mixed occupations considered are human resources and labor relations manager (henceforth referred to as human resources), accountants and auditors, secondary school teachers, economists and market researchers (henceforth referred to as economists), and editors/reporters.

LABOR FORCE ATTACHMENT BY PRESENCE OF YOUNG CHILDREN, YEAR, EDUCATION, MARITAL STATUS, AND RACE

Following the opt-out literature, I first focus on the extensive margin (i.e., the decision to work a positive number of hours). Fig. 1 presents the

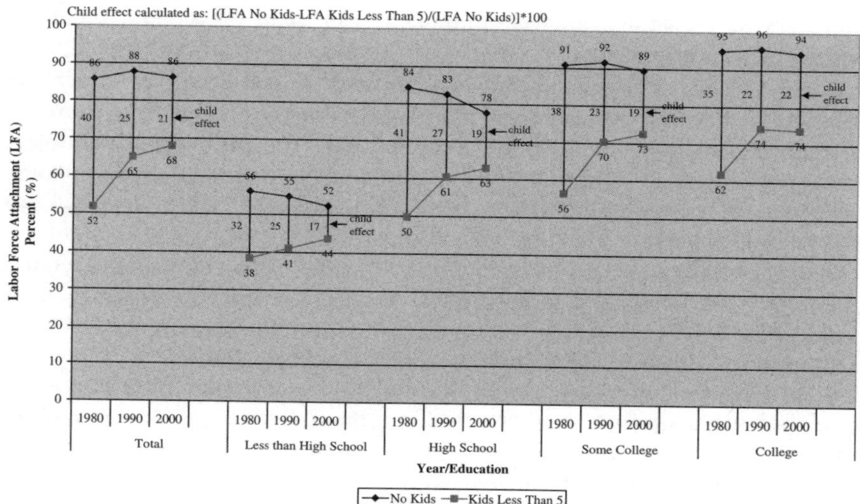

Fig. 1. Labor Force Attachment (LFA) by Presence of Young Children, Education, and Year (Women Aged 25–44).

LFA rates for all women aged 25–44 by presence of young children, year, and education. Fig. 1 also presents the "child effect" measured as:

$$\frac{\overline{LFA}_{NK} - \overline{LFA}_{KLT5}}{\overline{LFA}_{NK}} \quad (1)$$

where $\overline{LFA}$ is mean labor force attachment and NK and KLT5 denote women without children and women with young children, respectively.[15]

There are several noteworthy patterns. First, LFA of women with young children has increased over time irrespective of education category, although the increase is more pronounced between 1980 and 1990 than between 1990 and 2000. For example, the LFA rate for women with young children increased from 52.0% in 1980 to 65.0% in 1990 and 68.0% in 2000. Perhaps surprisingly, the same is not true for women without children. For less educated (high school or below) the LFA of childless women decreased over time (e.g., 56.5%, 54.8%, and 52.4% in 1980, 1990, and 2000 for women with less than high school) while for more educated (some college and above) the LFA of childless women remained relatively flat between 1980 and 2000 (e.g., 94.9%, 95.6%, and 94.4% in 1980, 1990, and 2000 for women with college).

Second, LFA is higher among women with higher levels of education relative to their less-educated counterparts irrespective of year or presence of children. Focusing on 2000, it can be seen that the LFA rate for childless women with less than high school is 52.4% while their high school, some college, and college counterparts have LFA rates of 77.7%, 89.5%, and 94.4%, respectively.

Third, childless women have higher LFA rates than women with young children. This is again true regardless of the education category or year considered. For example, in 1990 the LFA rate for childless women is 77.6% while the LFA rate for women with young children is 64.5%.

Fourth, there is no clear pattern by education in the child effect in a given year. In 1980 and 1990, the child effect rises (falls) as one acquires more education at the bottom (top) of the education distribution while in 2000 the child effect generally rises with education. For example, in 1980 (2000) the child effect for women with less than high school, high school, some college, and college is 31.7% (16.6%), 40.7% (18.9%), 37.5% (18.9%), and 34.2% (21.8%), respectively. There is, however, a clear pattern in the child effect over time in a given education category. Specifically, the child effect fell between 1980 and 1990 for all education groups while between 1990 and 2000 it fell (although a much smaller decline than in the previous time period) for all education groups except college-educated women where the effect remained relatively constant. For instance, the child effect for high-school educated women went from 40.6% in 1980, to 26.6% in 1990, to 18.9% in 2000 while for college-educated women the child effect went from 34.2% in 1980, to 22.2% in 1990, to 21.8% in 2000. Taken together, these results provide little support for the media accounts of the opt-out revolution.[16]

Fig. 1 combines all women irrespective of marital status. As previously discussed, the media tends to focus on highly educated married women who may have the luxury to opt out of the labor market because they tend to be married to highly educated men with high-earning potential (see, e.g., Williams et al., 2006). Moreover, marriage rates for college-educated women in 2000 are higher than those of their less-educated counterparts; this was not true in 1980. Marriage rates have fallen over time as well (see Table 1), although less so for college-educated women. By combining married women with non-married women, one may be underestimating the child effect, particularly in recent years. Thus, for the remainder of the analysis I focus on married women. Fig. 2 presents the LFA rates and the child effect for married women by presence of young children, education, and year. While

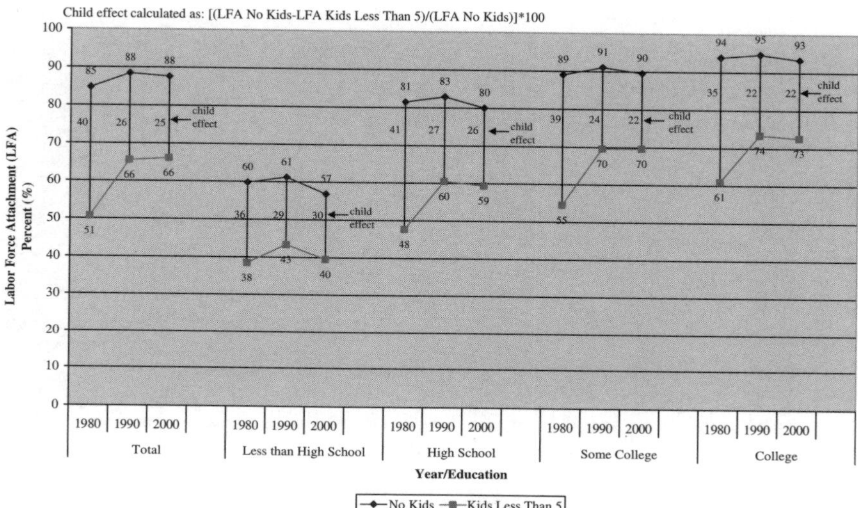

Fig. 2. Labor Force Attachment (LFA) by Presence of Children, Education, and Year (Married Women Aged 25–44).

there is evidence that the child effect is underestimated in recent years (particularly at the bottom of the education distribution), it remains the case that the child effect did not rise between 1990 and 2000 for college-educated women.

Allowing for differential effects by race may help shed light on the discrepancy between the media accounts of the opt-out revolution and the results presented to this point. Specifically, it is unlikely that the child effect will be the same by race given there are substantial racial differences in LFA, educational attainment, marital status, and presence of children (see Table 1). Figs. 3–6 present the LFA rates and the child effect for married women by presence of young children, education, and year for whites, blacks, Hispanics, and Asians, respectively.

Not surprisingly, the results for married white women (Fig. 3) mirror those presented for all married women (Fig. 2) given white women make up such a large share of the total population. The patterns for nonwhite married women differ somewhat from their white counterparts. In particular, the child effect generally falls as nonwhites acquire more education irrespective of year.[17] The child effect is generally smaller in

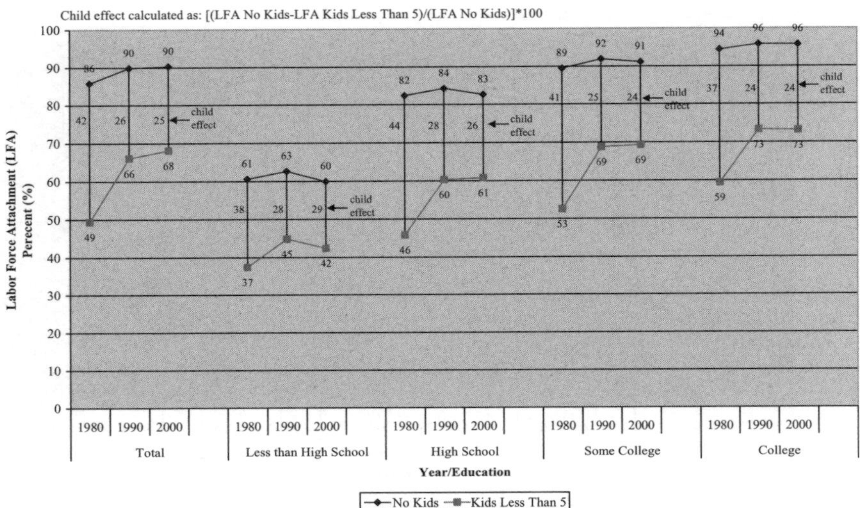

Fig. 3. Labor Force Attachment (LFA) by Presence of Young Children (Married Non-Hispanic White Women Aged 25–44).

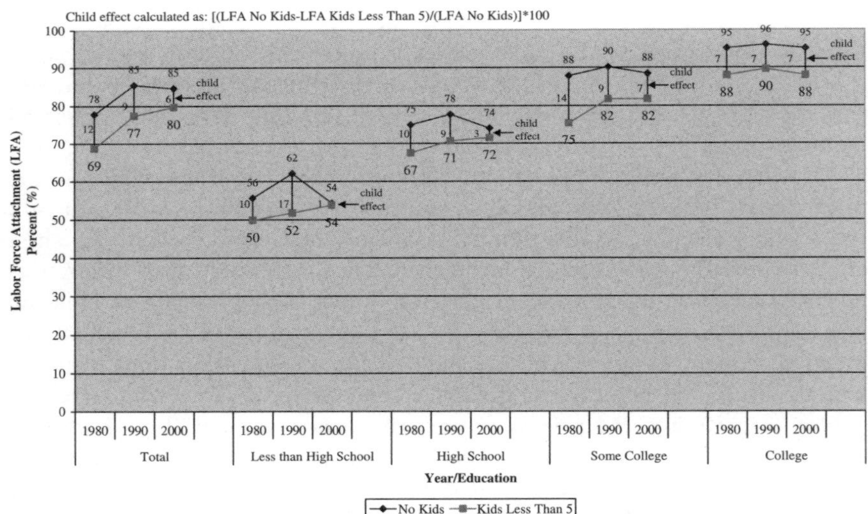

Fig. 4. Labor Force Attachment (LFA) by Presence of Young Children (Married Non-Hispanic Black Women Aged 25–44).

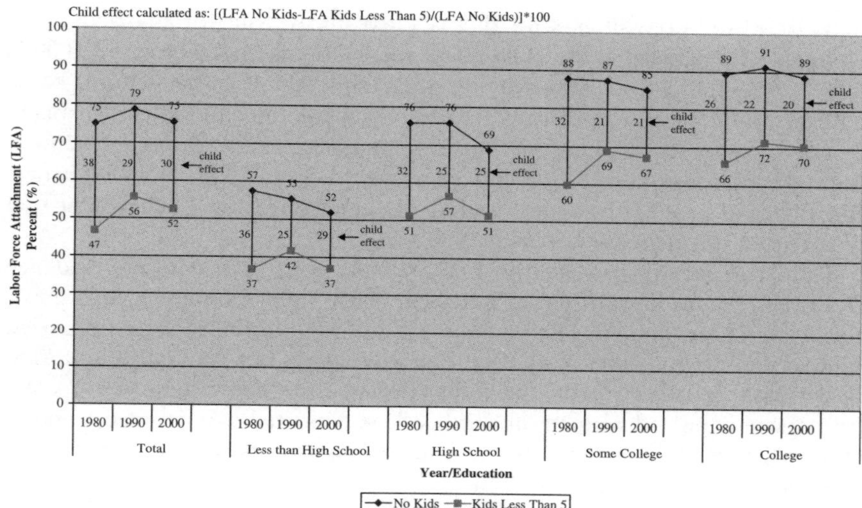

Fig. 5. Labor Force Attachment (LFA) by Presence of Children (Married Hispanic Women Aged 25–44).

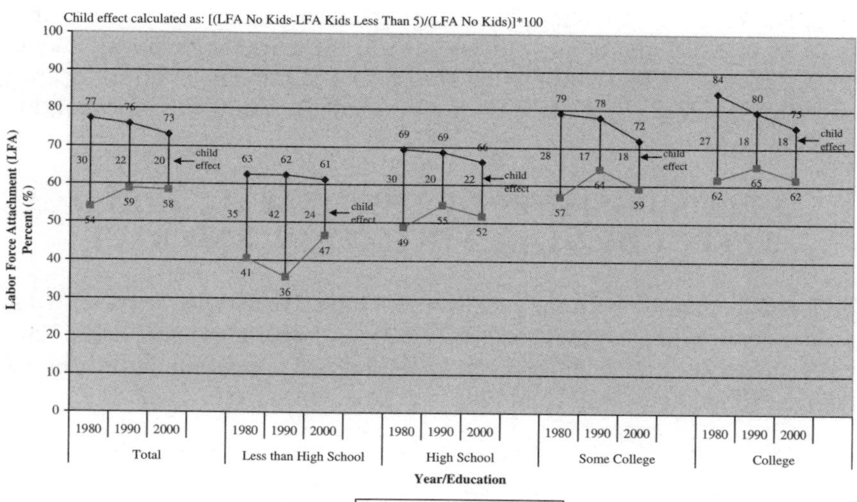

Fig. 6. Labor Force Attachment (LFA) by Presence of Young Children (Married Asian Women Aged 25–44).

magnitude for nonwhites, and this is particularly true for married black women.[18] For example, the child effect for white married women in 2000 is 29%, 26%, 24%, and 24% for less than high school, high school, some college, and college, respectively (see Fig. 3) while the child effect for black married women in 2000 is 1%, 3%, 7%, and 7% for less than high school, high school, some college, and college, respectively (see Fig. 4). What is true for all racial groups, however, is that the child effect for college-educated women did not increase between 1990 and 2000.

The LFA patterns revealed in Figs. 1–6 are consistent with the evidence from the opt-out literature (see Boushey, 2005, 2008; Cohany & Sok, 2007; Percheski, 2008) and suggest that the opt-out revolution, as sensationalized by Lisa Belkin in a 2003 *New York Times* article, is not generally supported in the data. In other words, the child effect did not increase in recent years for college-educated women, nor did college-educated women face a higher child effect relative to their less-educated counterparts within a given year, irrespective of race or marital status.[19]

This conclusion, however, is based on the extensive margin (i.e., the decision to work a positive number of hours) and does not consider the intensive margin (i.e., conditional on participating in the labor market, the decision to adjust annual hours of work). I argue this is important because women, particularly highly educated women, may not be choosing to exit the labor market entirely, but may be opting for reduced hours of work. This then suggests that defining opting out as simply labor market attachment may be masking some of the "opt-out revolution." The remainder of the chapter examines the child effect based on both the extensive and intensive margin.

DECOMPOSITION OF THE OVERALL CHILD EFFECT BY YEAR, EDUCATION, AND RACE

To formally analyze both the extensive and intensive margin, I first note that mean unconditional annual hours is equal to conditional annual hours times LFA. Given this, the child effect in unconditional annual hours (henceforth referred to as the overall child effect) can be written as

$$\frac{\overline{UAH}_{NK}^{M} - \overline{UAH}_{KLT5}^{M}}{\overline{UAH}_{NK}^{M}} = \frac{\overline{CAH}_{NK}^{M} \times \overline{LFA}_{NK}^{M} - \overline{CAH}_{KLT5}^{M} \times \overline{LFA}_{KLT5}^{M}}{\overline{UAH}_{NK}^{M}} \quad (2)$$

where $\overline{UAH}$ is mean unconditional annual hours, $\overline{CAH}$ is mean conditional annual hours, $\overline{LFA}$ is mean labor force attachment, and M, NK, and KLT5 denote married, women without children, and women with young children, respectively. I now add and subtract from the numerator of the right-hand side (RHS) of Eq. (2) the counterfactual mean unconditional annual hours for married women without children if they had the mean LFA of married women with young children ($\overline{CAH}^M_{NK} \times \overline{LFA}^M_{KLT5}$):

$$\frac{\overline{UAH}^M_{NK} - \overline{UAH}^M_{KLT5}}{\overline{UAH}^M_{NK}} = \frac{\overline{CAH}^M_{NK} \times \overline{LA}^M_{NK} - \overline{CAH}^M_{NK} \times \overline{LA}^M_{KLT5} + \overline{CAH}^M_{NK} \times \overline{LA}^M_{KLT5} - \overline{CAH}^M_{KLT5} \times \overline{LA}^M_{KLT5}}{\overline{UAH}^M_{NK}} \quad (3)$$

Collecting terms:

$$\frac{\overline{UAH}^M_{NK} - \overline{UAH}^M_{KLT5}}{\overline{UAH}^M_{NK}} = \frac{(\overline{LA}^M_{NK} - \overline{LA}^M_{KLT5}) \times \overline{CAH}^M_{NK}}{\overline{UAH}^M_{NK}} + \frac{(\overline{CAH}^M_{NK} - \overline{CAH}^M_{KLT5}) \times \overline{LA}^M_{KLT5}}{\overline{UAH}^M_{NK}} \quad (4)$$

The first term on the RHS of Eq. (4) represents the portion of the overall child effect due to the extensive margin and the second term represents the portion of the overall child effect due to the intensive margin.[20] Dividing each term on the RHS of Eq. (4) by the overall child effect (and multiplying by 100) gives the percent explained by the extensive and intensive margin, respectively.[21]

Before focusing on the decomposition results, it is worthwhile to discuss the patterns in female labor supply based on unconditional annual hours, as well as the patterns in the overall child effect. Unconditional annual hours have generally increased for married women irrespective of presence of children or level of education (see Fig. 7).[22] For example, college educated childless women worked 1,624 unconditional annual hours in 1980 compared to 1,835 and 1,887 unconditional annual hours in 1990 and 2000, respectively. While this rise in unconditional annual hours holds for white married women (see Fig. 8), it does not for their nonwhite counterparts (see Figs. 9–11). For example, black married childless women with lower levels of education (high school or less) experience a fall in unconditional annual hours between 1990 and 2000 (see Fig. 9). In addition, the overall child effect is higher than the child effect in LFA irrespective of race, education level, and year, suggesting the importance of accounting for both the extensive and intensive margin. For example, for college educated

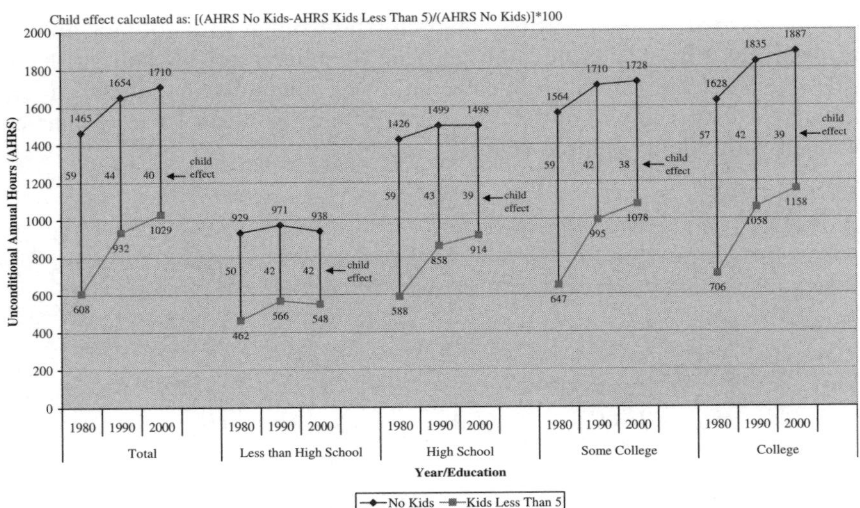

Fig. 7. Unconditional Annual Hours (AHRS) by Presence of Children, Education, and Year (Married Women Aged 25–44).

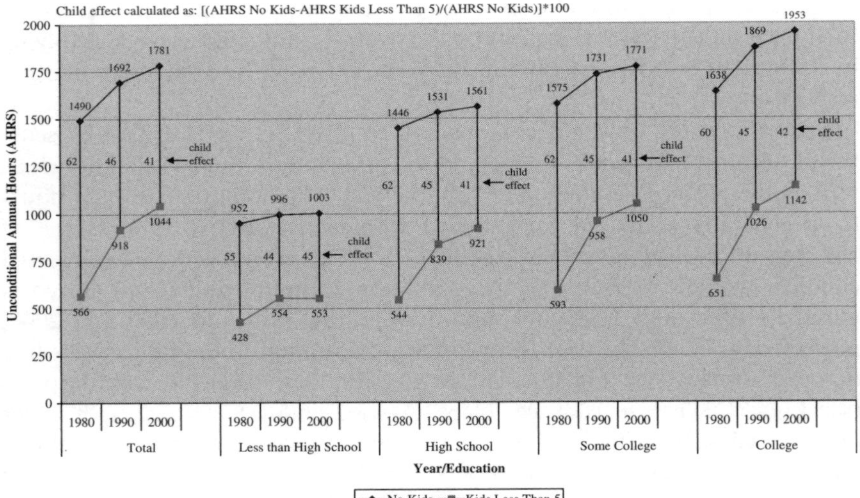

Fig. 8. Unconditional Annual Hours (AHRS) by Presence of Young Children, Education, and Year (Married Non-Hispanic White Women Aged 25–44).

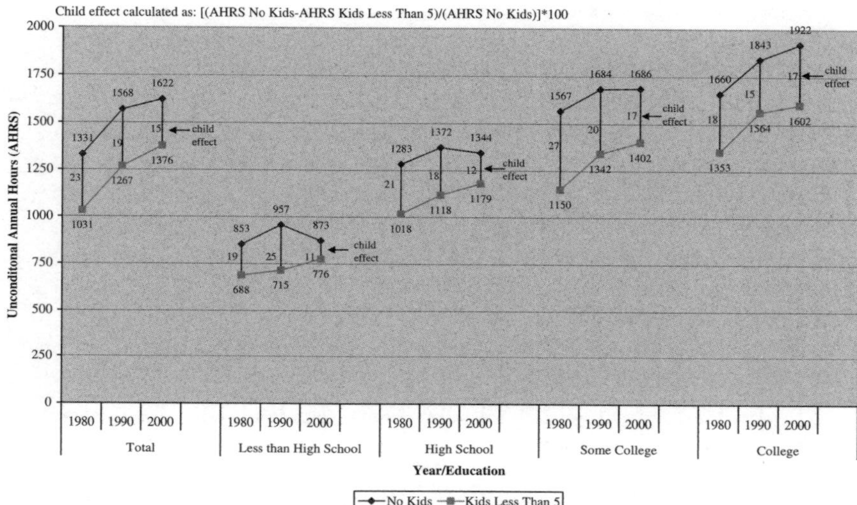

Fig. 9. Unconditional Annual Hours (AHRS) by Presence of Young Children, Education, and Year (Married Non-Hispanic Black Women Aged 25–44).

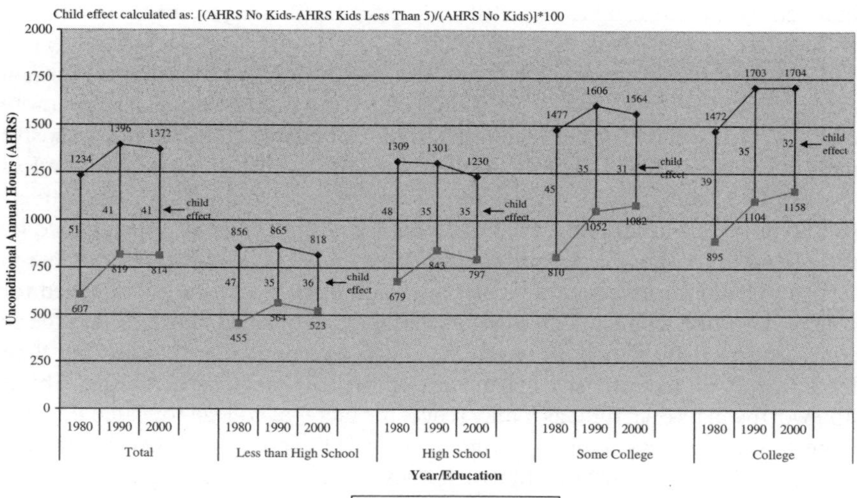

Fig. 10. Unconditional Annual Hours (AHRS) by Presence of Children, Education, and Year (Married Hispanic Women Aged 25–44).

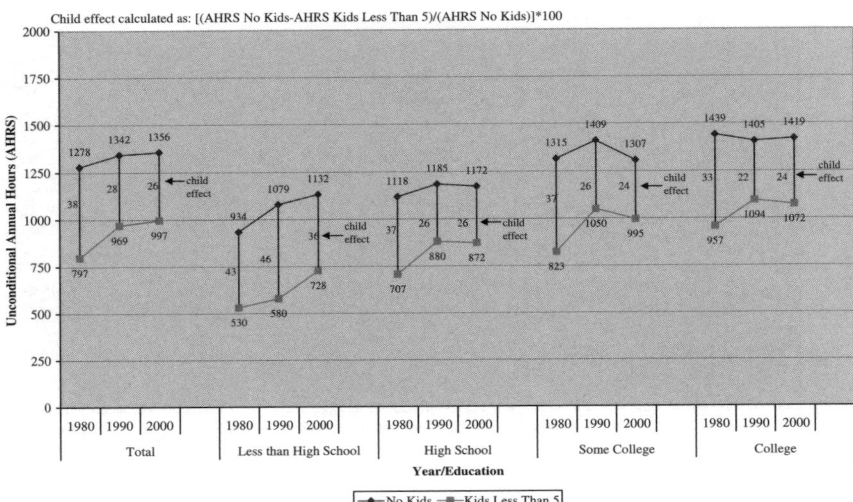

Fig. 11. Unconditional Annual Hours (AHRS) by Presence of Young Children, Education, and Year (Married Asian Women Aged 25–44).

married women in 2000 the overall child effect is 38.6% (see Fig. 7) while the child effect in LFA is 21.8% (see Fig. 1).

Turning to the decomposition results (see Table 2), I find the intensive margin explains a larger share of the overall child effect as married women acquire more education irrespective of the year considered. For example, in 2000 the intensive margin explains 26.6%, 33.9%, 40.9%, and 42.8% of the overall child effect for less than high school, high school, some college, and college, respectively (see column 3). Interestingly, the portion of the overall child effect explained by the extensive margin decreased between 1980 and 1990 and increased between 1990 and 2000 for all education categories, although it is more pronounced for college-educated women. This suggests that married women, particularly college educated married women, in recent years are reverting back to adjusting their labor supply on the extensive margin as opposed to the intensive margin. This is noteworthy in its own right as it may reflect the fact that college educated married women may have less of an opportunity to adjust their hours of work any further due to workplace hour constraints. If they require more flexibility than their workplace can provide, then they may feel they are left with no choice but to exit the labor market. This phenomenon has been documented in the qualitative literature (see, e.g., Stone, 2008).

Table 2. Decomposition of the Child Effect in Unconditional Annual Hours by Race/Ethnicity, Year, and Education (Married Women Aged 25–44).

	Total			Non-Hispanic White			Non-Hispanic Black			Hispanic			Asian		
	1980 (1)	1990 (2)	2000 (3)	1980 (4)	1990 (5)	2000 (6)	1980 (7)	1990 (8)	2000 (9)	1980 (10)	1990 (11)	2000 (12)	1980 (13)	1990 (14)	2000 (15)
Total															
Child effect	58.53	43.64	39.84	62.01	45.71	41.42	22.54	19.20	15.17	50.77	41.34	40.69	37.64	27.77	26.47
Extensive margin	40.20	25.89	24.55	42.41	26.40	24.53	11.71	9.40	5.80	37.73	29.26	30.41	30.01	22.46	20.02
% Explained	(68.68)	(59.32)	(61.62)	(68.40)	(57.74)	(59.22)	(51.93)	(48.94)	(38.21)	(74.31)	(70.79)	(74.74)	(79.73)	(80.87)	(75.65)
Intensive margin	18.34	17.76	15.29	19.60	19.32	16.89	10.84	9.80	9.37	13.04	12.07	10.28	7.63	5.31	6.44
% Explained	(31.32)	(40.68)	(38.38)	(31.60)	(42.26)	(40.78)	(48.07)	(51.06)	(61.79)	(25.69)	(29.21)	(25.26)	(20.27)	(19.13)	(24.35)
Less than high school															
Child effect	50.29	41.69	41.54	55.01	44.36	44.89	19.39	25.26	11.14	46.90	34.73	36.06	43.19	46.30	35.72
Extensive margin	35.65	29.22	30.48	38.30	28.37	29.28	10.30	16.61	0.89	36.07	24.78	28.69	35.07	42.90	23.91
% Explained	(70.89)	(70.08)	(73.39)	(69.63)	(63.96)	(65.23)	(53.13)	(65.77)	(7.97)	(76.91)	(71.35)	(79.57)	(81.21)	(92.66)	(66.93)
Intensive margin	14.64	12.47	11.05	16.71	15.99	15.61	9.09	8.65	10.26	10.83	9.95	7.37	8.12	3.40	11.81
% Explained	(29.11)	(29.92)	(26.61)	(30.37)	(36.04)	(34.77)	(46.87)	(34.23)	(92.03)	(23.09)	(28.65)	(20.43)	(18.79)	(7.34)	(33.07)
High school															
Child effect	58.76	42.74	39.00	62.39	45.24	40.97	20.70	18.48	12.24	48.16	35.18	35.22	36.76	25.70	25.58
Extensive margin	41.43	27.05	25.79	44.38	28.38	26.41	10.10	9.15	3.45	32.42	25.49	25.38	29.58	20.43	21.63
% Explained	(70.51)	(63.29)	(66.13)	(71.13)	(62.74)	(64.46)	(48.80)	(49.50)	(28.15)	(67.33)	(72.45)	(72.06)	(80.47)	(79.52)	(84.58)
Intensive margin	17.33	15.69	13.21	18.01	16.86	14.56	10.60	9.33	8.80	15.73	9.69	9.84	7.18	5.26	3.94
% Explained	(29.49)	(36.71)	(33.87)	(28.87)	(37.26)	(35.54)	(51.20)	(50.50)	(71.85)	(32.67)	(27.55)	(27.94)	(19.53)	(20.48)	(15.42)
Some college															
Child effect	58.65	41.84	37.61	62.36	44.65	40.71	26.58	20.28	16.83	45.15	34.50	30.80	37.44	25.53	23.85
Extensive margin	38.75	23.58	22.22	41.29	25.13	23.97	14.14	9.28	7.48	31.84	21.06	20.88	27.93	17.42	17.73
% Explained	(66.08)	(56.36)	(59.09)	(66.21)	(56.29)	(58.88)	(53.18)	(45.77)	(44.41)	(70.52)	(61.04)	(67.78)	(74.61)	(68.24)	(74.35)

Table 2. (*Continued*)

	Total			Non-Hispanic White			Non-Hispanic Black			Hispanic			Asian		
	1980 (1)	1990 (2)	2000 (3)	1980 (4)	1990 (5)	2000 (6)	1980 (7)	1990 (8)	2000 (9)	1980 (10)	1990 (11)	2000 (12)	1980 (13)	1990 (14)	2000 (15)
Intensive margin	19.90	18.26	15.39	21.07	19.52	16.74	12.45	11.00	9.36	13.31	13.44	9.92	9.51	8.11	6.12
% Explained	(33.92)	(43.64)	(40.91)	(33.79)	(43.71)	(41.12)	(46.82)	(54.23)	(55.59)	(29.48)	(38.96)	(32.22)	(25.39)	(31.76)	(25.65)
College															
Child effect	56.61	42.31	38.62	60.25	45.11	41.55	18.49	15.13	16.63	39.20	35.16	32.04	33.47	22.11	24.42
Extensive margin	35.05	22.40	22.11	37.06	23.53	23.60	7.45	6.65	7.39	26.18	21.65	20.44	26.85	17.94	18.11
% Explained	(61.92)	(52.94)	(57.24)	(61.52)	(52.16)	(56.78)	(40.29)	(43.96)	(44.42)	(66.79)	(61.59)	(63.80)	(80.22)	(81.16)	(74.15)
Intensive margin	21.56	19.91	16.51	23.19	21.58	17.96	11.04	8.48	9.24	13.02	13.50	11.60	6.62	4.17	6.31
% Explained	(38.08)	(47.06)	(42.76)	(38.48)	(47.84)	(43.22)	(59.71)	(56.04)	(55.58)	(33.21)	(38.41)	(36.20)	(19.78)	(18.84)	(25.85)

Source: U.S. Census (IPUMS). All observations with flagged values on any of the variables of interest are dropped from the analysis. Sampling weights used.

Numbers do not always add up due to rounding.

The overall patterns hide some important racial differences. While similar results are found for white and Hispanic married women, the same is not true for black and Asian married women. For black married women, the intensive margin plays the biggest role for college-educated women relative to their less-educated counterparts in 1980 and 1990 (see columns 7 and 8) while in 2000 it is least important for college-educated women relative to their less-educated counterparts (see column 9). This is largely explained by the fact that the LFA rates of black married women with less than high school in 2000 were virtually identical, not because black married women with young children substantially increased their LFA between 1990 and 2000 in this education category but because childless black married women with less than high school substantially reduced their LFA during this time period (see Fig. 4). There are no clear patterns in the importance of the intensive margin by level of education for Asian married women.[23] For black (Asian) married college-educated women, on the other hand, the relative role of the extensive margin remained roughly the same (decreased) between 1990 and 2000.

Despite the fact that the aforementioned patterns illustrate the importance of accounting for both the extensive and intensive margins, as with the child effect in LFA, the overall child effect does not increase in recent years for married college-educated women (see Fig. 7). This, however, masks important racial differences. Specifically, the child effect for black (Asian) college educated married women increases by 1.5 (2.3) percentage points between 1990 and 2000 (see Fig. 9 (11)). For white and Hispanic college educated married women, the child effect falls by 3.6 and 3.1 percentage points, respectively, between 1990 and 2000 (see Figs. 8 and 10, respectively). These patterns continue to suggest limited evidence in support of the opt-out revolution, particularly for white college educated married women who tend to be the focus of the media. This may be driven by the fact that college education is too coarse of a definition for this group. Thus, the remainder of the chapter presents an in-depth examination of white college educated married women.

A FURTHER INVESTIGATION OF NON-HISPANIC WHITE COLLEGE EDUCATED MARRIED WOMEN

The opt-out phenomenon among non-Hispanic white (henceforth referred to as white) college educated married women may be obscured for a number of reasons. First, it may be that limiting the analysis to 2000 is too early a time period in which one could detect the opt-out phenomenon, which was not brought to the public's attention until Belkin's 2003 *New York Times* article. Second, it may be that the propensity to opt-out of the labor market varies by age for college-educated women as there may be large differences in the work behavior of young women relative to older women due to, for example, a change in preferences toward work and family (i.e., culture). Finally, it may also be that college-educated women across occupation categories have different propensities to opt out of the labor market as the opportunities for workplace flexibility vary by occupation. Each of these possibilities is examined in turn.

Table 3 presents the decomposition of the overall child effect for white college educated married women by year – 1980, 1981–1983, 1984–1986, 1987–1989, 1990, 1991–1993, 1994–1996, 1997–1999, 2000, 2001–2003, 2004–2006, and 2007–2009. The data for 1980, 1990, and 2000 continue to be based on the U.S. Census data, while the data for the intervening years are from *Integrated Public Use Microdata Series* (IPUMS) March Current Population Survey (CPS) samples. The CPS data is ideal because IPUMS constructs the variables to align with those in the census data; however, the CPS sample sizes are small.[24] Given the small sample sizes, I pool over three-year periods in the CPS. Interestingly, it can be seen that, if anything, evidence of the opt-out phenomenon actually occurs between the latter half of the 1990s and the early 2000s, as opposed to the mid- to the late-2000s.[25] Specifically, the overall child effect falls continuously from 60.3% in 1980 to 40.2% in 1997–1999, increases to 41.6% in 2000 and 42.2% in 2001–2003,[26] then falls thereafter (39.9% in 2004–2006 and 38.3% in 2007–2009). However, labor force participation (annual hours and LFA) fell for all white married college-educated women in this period, not just those with children. Moreover, a similar effect is found for less educated white married women, suggesting that the decline in participation is not distinct to white married college educated women.[27] These patterns are consistent with the results found by Boushey (2005, 2008) who argues the decline in women's labor force participation over this time period is due to a downturn in the economy rather than the presence of children.

Table 4 presents the decomposition of the overall child effect for white college educated married women by year and four age groups: 25–29, 30–34, 35–39, and 40–44 (see Table A3 for a cohort analysis).[28] Not surprisingly, the overall child effect is smaller for the youngest women (25–29) and steadily increases until the oldest age group (40–44) where it begins to decline irrespective of year. For example, in 2000 the overall child effect is

Table 3. Decomposition of the Child Effect in Unconditional Annual Hours by Year (Non-Hispanic White College Educated Married Women).

	1980	1981–1983	1984–1986	1987–1989	1990	1991–1993	1994–1996	1997–1999	2000	2001–2003	2004–2006	2007–2009
	(1)	(2)	(3)	(4)	(5)	(6)	(7)	(8)	(9)	(10)	(11)	(12)
Child effect	60.25	55.09	48.23	46.66	45.11	41.44	40.03	40.17	41.55	42.22	39.90	38.31
Extensive margin	37.06	30.07	25.95	24.56	23.53	20.66	19.98	20.13	23.60	23.46	22.56	21.09
% Explained	(61.52)	(54.59)	(53.81)	(52.65)	(52.16)	(49.84)	(49.90)	(50.12)	(56.78)	(55.57)	(56.54)	(55.04)
Intensive margin	23.19	25.02	22.27	22.09	21.58	20.78	20.05	20.04	17.96	18.75	17.34	17.22
% Explained	(38.48)	(45.41)	(46.19)	(47.35)	(47.84)	(50.16)	(50.10)	(49.88)	(43.22)	(44.43)	(43.46)	(44.96)

Source: U.S. Census (IPUMS) in gray and the March Current Population Survey (IPUMS). All observations with flagged values on any of the variables of interest.

Table 4. Decomposition of the Child Effect in Unconditional Annual Hours by Year and Age (Non-Hispanic White College Educated Married Women).

	Total			25–29			30–34			35–39			40–44		
	1980	1990	2000	1980	1990	2000	1980	1990	2000	1980	1990	2000	1980	1990	2000
	(1)	(2)	(3)	(4)	(5)	(6)	(7)	(8)	(9)	(10)	(11)	(12)	(13)	(14)	(15)
Total															
Child effect	60.25	45.11	41.55	54.46	38.85	34.12	62.47	46.14	42.77	64.20	48.33	45.47	59.95	44.29	41.89
Extensive margin	37.06	23.53	23.60	29.50	16.97	16.01	39.23	23.73	23.25	43.46	26.50	26.96	41.00	25.85	24.90
% Explained	(61.52)	(52.16)	(56.78)	(54.16)	(43.68)	(46.91)	(62.81)	(51.43)	(54.35)	(67.70)	(54.84)	(59.29)	(68.39)	(58.37)	(59.44)
Intensive margin	23.19	21.58	17.96	24.96	21.88	18.12	23.23	22.41	19.53	20.74	21.83	18.51	18.95	18.44	16.99
% Explained	(38.48)	(47.84)	(43.22)	(45.84)	(56.32)	(53.09)	(37.19)	(48.57)	(45.65)	(32.30)	(45.16)	(40.71)	(31.61)	(41.63)	(40.56)

Source: U.S. Census (IPUMS). All observations with flagged values on any of the variables of interest are dropped from the analysis. Sampling weights used. Numbers do not always add up due to rounding.

34.12%, 42.77%, 45.47%, and 41.89% for white college educated married women aged 25–29, 30–44, 35–39, and 40–44, respectively. Moreover, the intensive margin is of greater importance for young women relative to their older counterparts for all years. This lends support to the hypothesis that work behavior differs by age. Despite these age differences, there continues to be little support for the opt-out revolution for white college educated married women. In particular, the overall child effect falls substantially between 1980 and 1990, and continues to fall between 1990 and 2000 although to a lesser extent, irrespective of the age group considered.[29]

Table 5 presents the decomposition of the overall child effect by year and occupation. I focus on managerial/professional occupations for a number of reasons. First, managerial/professional occupations tend to be the focus of the media (see Williams et al., 2006). Second, lack of workplace flexibility in these occupations (see Stone, 2008) may result in women choosing to exit the labor market entirely on the one hand while on the other hand extreme hours in these types of occupations may afford women the ability to reduce their hours in light of new family responsibilities. This further highlights the importance of accounting for both the extensive and intensive when examining managerial/professional occupations.

Table 5 reveals that white college educated married women in managerial/professional occupations are more likely to adjust their hours (conditional on working) than exit the labor market, suggesting ignoring the intensive margin (as Belkin, 2003 suggests) misses a large portion of the story. Despite this, it is still the case that white college educated married women in managerial/professional occupations experience a fall in the overall child effect between 1990 and 2000 (36.29%–32.05%).

Looking at all managerial/professional occupations, however, combines all occupations irrespective of their gender mix. Given workplace flexibility and extreme hours likely vary a great deal by an occupation's gender mix, I look at detailed occupations in three occupation categories: male-dominated occupations (architects, electrical engineers, physicians, lawyers, and clergy/religious workers), female-dominated occupations (registered nurses, dieticians/nutritionists, occupational therapists, primary school teachers, and librarians), and mixed occupations (human resources, accountants and auditors, secondary school teachers, economists, and editors/reporters). See the data section for a detailed discussion of occupation definitions.

The results are striking. For male-dominated occupations, the child effect in unconditional annual hours generally falls between 1980 and 1990 and generally increases between 1990 and 2000.[30] For example, the child effect in unconditional annual hours increased from 35.2% to 39.5% for architects

Table 5. Decomposition of the Child Effect in Unconditional Annual Hours by Year and Occupation (Non-Hispanic White College Educated Married Women).

	Managerial/Professional		
	1980	1990	2000
Child effect	49.19	36.29	32.05
Extensive margin	21.89	13.02	12.39
% Explained	(44.50)	(35.89)	(38.67)
Intensive margin	27.30	23.27	19.65
% Explained	(55.50)	(64.11)	(61.33)

Traditionally male-dominated occupations

	Architects			Electrical engineers			Physicians			Lawyers			Clergy/Religious workers		
	1980	1990	2000	1980	1990	2000	1980	1990	2000	1980	1990	2000	1980	1990	2000
Child effect	51.44	35.16	39.51	27.25	25.66	27.20	28.46	19.88	23.81	24.02	24.53	26.97	46.99	47.77	43.24
Extensive margin	10.60	9.35	15.12	25.12	9.05	14.11	6.27	3.24	2.22	8.10	8.89	7.97	18.94	14.33	9.66
% Explained	(20.61)	(26.58)	(38.26)	(92.20)	(35.25)	(51.85)	(22.03)	(16.28)	(9.32)	(33.73)	(36.23)	(29.57)	(40.30)	(29.99)	(22.34)
Intensive margin	40.84	25.82	24.39	2.13	16.62	13.10	22.19	16.64	21.59	15.92	15.64	18.99	28.05	33.45	33.58
% Explained	(79.39)	(73.42)	(61.74)	(7.80)	(64.75)	(48.15)	(77.97)	(83.72)	(90.68)	(66.27)	(63.77)	(70.43)	(59.70)	(70.01)	(77.66)

Traditionally female-dominated occupations

	Registered nurses			Dieticians/Nutritionists			Occupational therapists			Primary school teachers			Librarians		
	1980	1990	2000	1980	1990	2000	1980	1990	2000	1980	1990	2000	1980	1990	2000
Child effect	49.97	38.05	32.99	48.69	38.44	40.63	49.75	38.38	33.53	48.33	32.26	28.94	49.48	36.48	34.67
Extensive margin	16.40	9.30	9.56	19.92	9.56	13.43	20.40	6.68	8.04	25.65	14.08	14.16	25.93	16.59	14.78

% Explained	(32.81)	(24.43)	(28.97)	(40.90)	(24.86)	(33.06)	(41.01)	(17.40)	(23.99)	(53.08)	(43.64)	(48.92)	(52.40)	(45.46)	(42.63)
Intensive margin	33.57	28.76	23.44	28.78	28.89	27.20	29.35	31.70	25.48	22.68	18.18	14.78	23.55	19.89	19.89
% Explained	(67.19)	(75.57)	(71.03)	(59.10)	(75.14)	(66.94)	(58.99)	(82.60)	(76.01)	(46.92)	(56.36)	(51.08)	(47.60)	(54.54)	(57.37)

Mixed occupations

	Human resources			Accountants/Auditors			Secondary school teachers			Economists			Editors/Reporters		
	1980	1990	2000	1980	1990	2000	1980	1990	2000	1980	1990	2000	1980	1990	2000
Child effect	38.57	30.46	26.37	43.03	35.09	33.31	45.49	31.72	29.61	41.18	38.93	28.85	56.35	42.27	40.89
Extensive margin	29.02	17.29	14.35	23.05	15.04	13.00	21.67	13.82	11.80	23.30	21.31	10.81	23.28	13.70	12.69
% Explained	(75.22)	(56.77)	(54.42)	(53.55)	(42.86)	(39.02)	(47.65)	(43.56)	(39.83)	(56.58)	(54.75)	(37.45)	(41.31)	(32.42)	(31.04)
Intensive margin	9.56	13.17	12.02	19.99	20.05	20.31	23.81	17.90	17.82	17.88	17.62	18.05	33.07	28.57	28.20
% Explained	(24.78)	(43.23)	(45.58)	(46.45)	(57.14)	(60.98)	(52.35)	(56.44)	(60.17)	(43.42)	(45.25)	(62.55)	(58.69)	(67.58)	(68.96)

Source: U.S. Census (IPUMS). All observations with flagged values on any of the variables of interest are dropped from the analysis. Sampling weights used.

Numbers do not always add up due to rounding.

See Table A2 for percent male in the occupation and sample sizes.

between 1990 and 2000. This rise between 1990 and 2000 is in sharp contrast to the patterns found for female-dominated occupations (with the exception of dieticians/nutritionists) and mixed occupations.[31] Perhaps not surprisingly, women are generally more likely to adjust their hours of work (conditional on working) in male-dominated occupations. In female-dominated occupations, the importance of the intensive margin varies depending on specialty. In the medical specialty (i.e., registered nurses, dieticians/nutritionists, and occupational therapists) the intensive margin is of more importance than in the education specialty (i.e., primary school teachers, and librarians). For mixed occupations, the relative role of the extensive and intensive margin is closer together, particularly in earlier years. These patterns illustrate that accounting for differences in workplace flexibility and the incidence of extreme hours across occupations is important. Moreover, these patterns provide support for the popular press' notion of the opt-out revolution, particularly among white college educated married women in male-dominated occupations.

CONCLUSION

The "opt-out revolution" was first sensationalized in a 2003 *New York Times* article by Lisa Belkin and suggests that highly educated women (relative to their less-educated counterparts) are exiting the labor market to care for their children more in recent years, that is, highly educated women face a higher child effect than their less-educated counterparts. This spurred a flurry of media attention to the issue, as well as increased interest among academics across the social sciences. The majority of the studies examine the employment side of the opt-out revolution (i.e., conditional on having children women exit the labor market).[32] With the exception of Vere (2007), they find little support for the media's account of highly educated women's recent exodus from the labor market to care for their children (see, e.g., Boushey, 2005, 2008; Cohany & Sok, 2007; Fortin, 2008; Goldin, 2006; Percheski 2008).

The purpose of this study is to further document the evidence on the employment side of the opt-out revolution by allowing for differential effects of children on female labor supply by race, marital status, and occupation, as well as examining both the extensive margin (i.e., the decision to work a positive number of hours) and the intensive margin (i.e., conditional on participating in the labor market, the decision to adjust annual hours of work) of female labor supply.

Using data from the U.S. Census in conjunction with data from the Current Population Survey (1980–2009), I find little support for the opt-out revolution – highly educated women, relative to their less-educated counterparts, are exiting the labor force to care for their families at higher rates today than in earlier time periods – if one focuses solely on the decision to work a positive number of hours irrespective of marital status or race. If one, however, focuses on both the decision to work a positive number of hours and the decision to adjust annual hours of work (conditional on working), I find some evidence of the opt-out revolution, particularly among white college educated married women in male-dominated occupations.

Given male-dominated occupations tend to be those that have higher earnings, this could lead to a widening in gender inequality, as well as have severe labor market consequences for firms and society as a whole since women now comprise a larger fraction of college graduates than do men. Understanding what causes women in these types of professions to "opt out" of the labor market is an extremely important public policy issue, one that is recognized by the current administration. Thus, future work is needed to provide explanations for the patterns documented in this chapter. Why do the opt-out patterns vary by race? Is it an artifact of cultural factors (i.e., different preferences for work and family)? Why do women opt out? Is it family pulls (e.g., birth of a child), or is it workplace pushes (e.g., lack of flexibility on the job)? Or is it a combination of the two?[33] Does the importance of pulls versus pushes vary by race? Conditional on exiting the labor market, how long do women remain out of the labor market? What types of occupations do they transition back into? How long do the transitions back into the labor market typically take?[34] Does race play a role in reentry? Why do the opt-out patterns vary by occupation? Is it an artifact of differences in workplace flexibility and the incidence of extreme hours?

NOTES

1. Many other media reports followed (see, e.g., Story, 2005; Trunk, 2005; Wallis, 2004).

2. The notion of "opting out" of the labor market is not new to labor economists; in fact it is a reincarnation of "intermittent/discontinuous" labor force participation first proposed by Mincer and Polachek (1974, 1978) almost 40 years ago.

3. Several studies examine the fertility side of opting out. The results are mixed; Vere (2007) and Shang and Weinberg (2009) find increased fertility among college-educated women while Percheski (2008) finds no change in fertility among

professional women. Others have examined the impact of opting out on labor market outcomes among alumni from top-ranked colleges. Goldin and Katz (2008) find no evidence of the opt-out revolution among Harvard University alumnae but do find that opting out impacts earnings, although differentially by occupation. Herr and Wolfram (2009) find that alumnae from Harvard University are less likely to stay attached to the labor market if their workplace lacks family friendly policies. Bertrand, Goldin, and Katz (2010) find that the gender wage gap among MBA graduates from the University of Chicago's Booth School of Business can largely be explained by career interruptions from childbirth. Several studies also seek to understand why highly educated women are exiting the labor market and what the associated costs of exiting may be (see, e.g., Hewlett, 2007; Hewlett et al., 2005; Stone, 2008; Stone & Lovejoy, 2004; Williams et al., 2006); these studies tend to be more qualitative in nature.

4. The one exception is Vere (2007) who does find evidence that highly educated women with children are exiting the labor market at higher rates than their less educated counterparts. However, he only focuses on women 27 years of age which is very young for childbearing, particularly in later cohorts for highly educated women.

5. Boushey (2005) does allow for intercept effects of race/ethnicity and marital status when estimating the effect of children on women's labor force attachment but does not allow for slope effects (i.e., she does not interact marital status or race/ethnicity with children). While Boushey (2008) does estimate the effect of young children (under the age of 6) on women's employment separately by marital status, race, education, and age, she does run a fully interacted model where the effect of children is interacted concurrently with marital status, race, education, and age (e.g., she does not estimate the child effect for black married college educated women). Cohany and Sok (2007) do report labor force participation by race, however, they only do so for married women with infants. While Fortin (2008) estimates the effect of children on women's labor force participation separately by marital status and education, she only stratifies by two education categories: less than college and college graduates. Fortin (2008) also analyzes the effect of children on black women's labor force participation, however, she does not allow for differential effects of children by education or marital status for this group of women. Another demographic characteristic is immigrant status. Results that focus solely on nonimmigrants are generally similar and available upon request.

6. Cha (2010) finds that professional women with children, married to professional men, were substantially more likely to exit the labor market if their partner worked extreme hours (>60 hours) relative to their childless counterparts whose partners did not work extreme hours.

7. The marriage rates for women aged 25–44 in 1980 are 69% (less than high school), 76% (high school), 72% (some college), and 69% (college). The marriage rates for women aged 25–44 in 1990 are 58% (less than high school), 68% (high school), 66% (some college), and 66% (college). The marriage rates for women aged 25–44 in 2000 are 57% (less than high school), 63% (high school), 63% (some college), and 66% (college).

8. Percheski (2008) does consider alternative measures of labor supply (full-time year round employment and works 50 + hours/week) but does not try to disentangle the relative roles of extensive and intensive margin.

9. While Percheski (2008) does examine women in managerial/professional occupations, as well as the subset of traditionally male- and female-dominated occupations within this occupational category, she does not examine detailed occupations in managerial/professional occupations, traditionally male occupations, or traditionally female occupations. Focusing on aggregate categories may mask the opt-out phenomenon as there are different degrees of flexibility and the incidence of extreme hours in the detailed occupations within each occupation category.

10. Specifically, I drop an individual if they have an allocated value for age, sex, race, Hispanic, education, usual hours of work, weeks worked per year, employment status, marital status, and relationship to household head.

11. In order to construct these variables I rely on two IPUMS variables: race (RACED) and Hispanic origin (HISPAND).

12. Alternatively I could have used labor force participation (LFP) that equals one if a respondent was employed or actively seeking employment in the reference week, and zero otherwise. While this is the measure generally considered in the opt-out literature, for my purposes labor force attachment (LFA) is needed to determine the relative roles of the intensive and extensive margins of labor supply. Results based on LFP are very similar to results based on LFA and are available upon request.

13. These categories are constructed based on the educational attainment recode variable (EDUREC) in the IPUMS data which combines two separate IPUMS variables HIGRADE and EDUC99. The former is available from 1940 to 1980 and the latter is available from 1990–2000. The recoded variable was constructed to allow for analysis across the years. The main differences are high school based on EDUC99 is 12th grade no diploma and high school diploma or GED while high school based on HIGRADE (EDUREC) is grade 12, some college based on EDUC99 is some college no degree, occupational associate degree, and academic associate degree while some college based on HIGRADE (EDUREC) is 1–3 years of college, and college based on EDUC99 is a bachelor's degree, master's degree, professional degree and doctorate degree while college based on HIGRADE (EDUREC) is 4+years of college.

14. An occupation is considered if there are at least 25 women without kids/with kids less than 5 in each year.

15. Percheski (2008) measures the effect of children analogously, although she labels it the "child penalty."

16. The same patterns are found if one examines the child effect by education, age, and year, as well as by education, age, and birth cohort (results available upon request). This is discussed in greater detail for a subset of the sample in fifth section.

17. The main exception is for black married college educated women in 2000 who face a higher child effect than their less-educated counterparts.

18. The main exception is for Asian married women with less than high school in 1990 who face a child effect of 42% (see Fig. 6) while their white married counterparts face a child effect of 28% (see Fig. 3).

19. The main exception is for black college educated married women in 2000 who face a child effect of 7%, while black married women with less than high school, high school, and some college face a child effect of 1%, 3%, and 7%, respectively (see Fig. 4).

20. Instead, I could have added and subtracted from Eq. (3) the counterfactual mean unconditional annual hours for married women without children if they had the mean conditional annual hours of married women with young children ($\overline{\text{CAH}}^{\text{M}}_{\text{KLT5}} \times \overline{\text{LA}}^{\text{M}}_{\text{NK}}$). This adjusts the intensive margin, as opposed to the extensive margin (as is done in Eq. (3)). While this yields a slightly larger role for the intensive margin, the overall patterns are the same (results available upon request).

21. Antecol and Steinberger (2011) use a similar technique to examine differences in labor supply between married women and partnered lesbian women.

22. The main exception is for married women with young children who have less than high school between 1990 and 2000 where unconditional annual hours marginally fell.

23. According to Table 2 (columns 13–15), the relative importance of the intensive margin in 1980 is higher for Asian married women with some college, followed by less than high school, college, and high school while in 1990 (2000) the relative importance of the intensive margin is higher for Asian married women with some college (less than high school) followed by high school (college), college (some college), and less than high school (high school).

24. Ideally, one would use this data throughout the analysis, however, due to small sample sizes this is not possible for all educational, racial/ethnic, and occupational categories.

25. Interestingly, a similar pattern is found if one solely examines the extensive margin. In particular, the child effect in labor force attachment continuously falls from 37.1 in 1980 to 20.1 in 1997–1999, increases to 23.6 in 2000, and then falls thereafter (23.5 in 2001–2003, 22.6 in 2004–2006, and 21.1 in 2007–2009).

26. If one pools the CPS over 1999–2001 in an attempt to get an approximation of the 2000 Census number (41.6), the child effect is 42.0, which is very much in line with the Census data.

27. This is generally true for all levels of education, although it is noisier in the 1990s for white married women with less than high school due to small cell sizes. Moreover, this holds true for white married college educated women across the age distribution.

28. Table A3 reveals that the results are very similar if I instead employ a cohort analysis, that is, I do not find evidence of the opt-out phenomenon among white college educated married women. Specifically, support of the opt-out phenomenon requires that the overall child effect rises for more recent birth cohorts relative to earlier birth cohorts. I find, however, that the overall child effect becomes smaller as one moves from earlier birth cohorts to more recent birth cohorts for all age groups for white married college educated women.

29. The patterns by age groups mirror those for the overall college-educated sample for blacks, Hispanics, and Asians presented in Table 2. Results are available upon request.

30. The main exception is clergy/religious workers. This occupation category, as defined by the Census (http://www.census.gov/hhes/www/ioindex/ioindex02/txtnew02.html#21-2099) includes clergy ("Conduct religious worship and perform other spiritual functions associated with beliefs and practices of religious faith or denomination. Provide spiritual and moral guidance and assistance to members"), directors, religious activities and education ("Direct and coordinate activities of a denominational group to meet religious needs of students. Plan, direct, or coordinate

church school programs designed to promote religious education among church membership. May provide counseling and guidance relative to marital, health, financial, and religious problems"), and all other religious workers ("All religious workers not listed separately."). The latter two categories are likely dominated by women, make up the bulk of the women in the overall clergy/religious workers occupation, and more closely resemble occupations in female-dominated occupations (e.g., teachers). The overall results for clergy/religious workers, therefore, more closely align with female dominated, rather than male-dominated occupations.

31. Analysis on alternative female-dominated occupations and mixed occupations yield similar results and are available upon request.

32. There are several other aspects of the opt-out literature. Vere (2007), Percheski (2008), and Shang and Weinberg (2009) examine the fertility side of opting out. Goldin and Katz (2008), Herr and Wolfram (2009), and Bertrand et al. (2010) examine the impact of opting out on labor market outcomes among alumni at Harvard University and the University of Chicago's Booth School of Business, respectively. Stone and Lovejoy (2004), Hewlett et al. (2005), Williams et al. (2006), Hewlett (2007), and Stone (2008) seek to understand why highly educated women are exiting the labor market and what the associated costs of exiting may be.

33. There is a growing literature that is investigating this, although it is generally focused on highly educated professional women (see Herr & Wolfram, 2009; Hewlett et al., 2005; Hewlett 2007; Stone, 2008; Stone & Lovejoy, 2004).

34. Hewlett et al. (2005) and Hewlett (2007) provide evidence on reentry for highly qualified professionals.

REFERENCES

Antecol, H., & Steinberger, M. (2011). Labor supply differences between married heterosexual women and partnered lesbians: A semi-parametric decomposition approach. *Economic Inquiry*.

Belkin, L. (2003). The opt-out revolution. *New York Times Magazine*, October 26, pp. 42–47, 58, 85–86.

Bertrand, M., Goldin, C., & Katz, L. F. (2010). Dynamics of the gender gap for young professionals in the financial and corporate sectors. *American Economic Journal: Applied Economics*, *2*(3), 228–255.

Boushey, H. (2005, November). *Are women opting out? Debunking the myth*. Center for Economic Policy Research, Briefing paper.

Boushey, H. (2008). "Opting out?" The effect of children on women's employment in the United States. *Feminist Economics*, *14*(1), 1–36.

Cha, Y. (2010). Reinforcing the "separate spheres" arrangement: The effect of spousal overwork on the employment of men and women in dual-earner households. *American Sociological Review*, *75*(2), 303–329.

Cohany, S. R., & Sok, E. (2007). Trends in labor force participation of married mothers of infants. *Monthly Labor Review* (Feb), 9–16.

Fortin, N. (2008). *Gender role attitudes and women's labor market participation: Opting-out and the persistent appeal of housewifery*. Working Paper. Department of Economics, University of British Columbia, Vancouver, BC.

Goldin, C. (2006). The quiet revolution that transformed women's employment, education, and family. *American Economic Review Papers and Proceedings*, *96*(2), 1–21.

Goldin, C., & Katz, L. (2008). Transitions: Career and family life cycles of the educational elite. *American Economic Review Papers and Proceedings*, *98*(2), 363–369.

Herr, J. L., & Wolfram, C. (2009). *Opt-out rates at motherhood across high-education career paths: Selection versus work environment*. NBER Working Paper no. 14717. Cambridge, MA.

Hewlett, S. A., Luce, C. B., Shiller, P., & Southwell, S. (2005, March). *The hidden brain drain: Off-ramps and on-ramps in women's careers*. Research Report no. 9491. Harvard Business Review, Boston, MA.

Hewlett, S. A. (2007). *Off-ramps and On-ramps: Keeping talented women on the road to success*. Boston, MA: Harvard Business School Press.

King, M., Ruggles, S., Alexander, J. T., Flood, S., Genadek, K., Schroeder, M. B., Trampe, B., & Vick, R. (2010). *Integrated Public Use Microdata Series, Current Population Survey: Version 3.0* [Machine-readable database]. Minneapolis, MN: University of Minnesota.

Mincer, J., & Polachek, S. (1974). Family investments in human capital: Earnings of women. *The Journal of Political Economy*, *82*(2), S76–S108. (Part 2).

Mincer, J., & Polachek, S. (1978). An exchange: The theory of human capital and the earnings of women: Women's earnings reexamined. *The Journal of Human Resources*, *13*(1), 118–134.

Percheski, C. (2008). Opting out? Cohort differences in professional women's employment rates from 1960 to 2005. *American Sociological Review*, *73*(June), 497–517.

Rindfuss, R. (1976). Annual fertility rates from census data on own children: Comparisons with vital statistics data for the United States. *Demography*, *13*(2), 235–249.

Ruggles, S., Alexander, J. T., Genadek, K., Goeken, R., Schroeder, M. B., & Sobek, M. (2010). *Integrated Public Use Microdata Series: Version 5.0* [Machine-readable database]. Minneapolis, MN: University of Minnesota.

Shang, Q., & Weinberg, B. (2009). *Opting for families: Recent trends in the fertility of highly educated women*. NBER Working Paper 15074. Cambridge, MA.

Stone, P. (2008). *Opting out? Why women really quit careers and head home*. Berkeley, CA: University of California Press.

Stone, P., & Lovejoy, M. (2004). Fast-track women and the "choice" to stay home. *The Annals of the American Academy*, *596*(November), 62–83.

Story, L. (2005). Many women at elite colleges set career path to motherhood. *New York Times*, September 20, p. A1.

Trunk, P. (2005). New generation puts the focus on family. *The Boston Globe*, April 17, p. G1.

Vere, J. P. (2007). "Having it all" no longer: Fertility, female labor supply, and the new life choices of generation X. *Demography*, *44*(4), 821–828.

Wallis, C. (2004). The case for staying home. *Time Magazine*, March 22, p. 50.

Williams, J., Manvell, J., & Bornstein, S. (2006). *"Opt-Out" or Pushed Out? How the press covers work/family conflict. The untold story of why women leave the workforce*. Working Paper. Work Life Law, UC Hastings College of Law, San Francisco, CA.

TABLES A1–A3

Table A1. Variable Definitions.

Variable	Definition
Labor supply	
UAHRS	= unconditional annual hours = (WKSWRK*UHRS)
WKSWRK	= weeks worked last year
UHRS	= usual hours worked per week
CAHRS	= conditional annual hours = UAHRS if UAHRS > 0
LFA	= labor force attachment = 1 if UAHRS > 0, 0 otherwise
LFP	= labor force participation = 1 if EMP or UNEMP, 0 otherwise
EMP	= 1 if employed, 0 otherwise
UNEMP	= 1 if unemployed, 0 otherwise
Education	
LTHIGH	= 1 if less than high school, 0 otherwise
HIGH	= 1 if high school (with or without degree), 0 otherwise
SOMECOL	= 1 if some college, 0 otherwise
COLLEGE	= 1 if ba or higher, 0 otherwise
Race/Ethnicity	
WHITE	= 1 if non-Hispanic white, 0 otherwise
BLACK	= 1 if non-Hispanic black, 0 otherwise
HISPANIC	= 1 if Hispanic, 0 otherwise
ASIAN	= 1 if Asian, 0 otherwise
NATIVE	= 1 if Native American, 0 otherwise
OTHE RACE	= 1 if other race, 0 otherwise
Family relationship	
MARRIED	= 1 if married spouse present, 0 otherwise
NCHILD	= number of own children in the household
NCHLT5	= number of own children less than 5 in the household
NOKID	= 1 if no own children present in the household, 0 otherwise
KIDLT5	= 1 if any own children less than 5 present in the household, 0 otherwise
Age	
AGE	= age

Table A2. Descriptive Statistics for Detailed Occupations by Occupation Type and Year.

	1980			1990			2000		
	%Male	*N* (No kids)	*N* (Kids < 5)	%Male	*N* (No kids)	*N* (Kids < 5)	%Male	*N* (No kids)	*N* (Kids < 5)
Male-dominated occupations									
Chief executives and public administrators	0.747	14	8	0.703	4	5	0.800	381	487
Funeral directors	0.912	3	2	0.864	6	4	0.819	7	10
Purchasing agents and buyers, of farm products	0.904	0	2	0.799	2	2	0.754	4	2
Construction inspectors	0.948	1	0	0.929	3	7	0.890	3	5
Architects	0.905	64	25	0.835	155	169	0.778	178	183
Aerospace engineer	0.966	10	0	0.913	76	52	0.904	34	64
Metallurgical and materials engineers, variously phrased	0.947	8	1	0.865	9	14	0.886	16	10
Petroleum, mining, and geological engineers	0.954	2	1	0.934	11	11	0.928	7	11
Chemical engineers	0.946	12	6	0.882	50	32	0.845	52	64
Civil engineers	0.966	26	12	0.926	90	96	0.888	132	137
Electrical engineer	0.947	52	25	0.899	238	179	0.892	115	114
Industrial engineers	0.898	44	13	0.853	84	77	0.825	122	135
Mechanical engineers	0.976	14	4	0.945	48	51	0.932	75	91
Not-elsewhere-classified engineers	0.957	34	25	0.896	221	174	0.880	178	179
Physicists and astronomers	0.940	7	4	0.852	18	13	0.860	10	10
Atmospheric and space scientists	0.858	1	3	0.877	7	1	0.878	10	5
Geologists	0.871	35	10	0.834	79	53	0.742	133	111
Agricultural and food scientists	0.752	17	10	0.707	35	42	0.726	33	34

Foresters and conservation scientists	0.877	16	8	0.852	36	20	0.841	36	33
Physicians	0.849	257	207	0.778	562	853	0.715	629	1142
Dentists	0.918	30	23	0.857	108	170	0.802	95	159
Optometrists	0.902	9	3	0.821	33	44	0.693	52	77
Podiatrists	0.909	0	2	0.891	5	5	0.821	10	17
Clergy and religious workers	0.851	78	138	0.766	153	63	0.702	214	361
Lawyers	0.844	542	262	0.734	1310	1333	0.682	1350	1728
Announcers	0.790	16	7	0.780	24	29	0.764	16	14
Female-dominated occupations									
Registered nurses	0.039	2027	2853	0.054	3099	6284	0.074	2835	5784
Dieticians and nutritionists	0.096	183	180	0.099	225	417	0.094	211	350
Occupational therapists	0.073	106	94	0.113	206	329	0.096	313	495
Physical therapists	0.257	186	185	0.236	342	507	0.269	520	830
Speech therapists	0.099	329	386	0.072	382	710	0.069	512	722
Therapists, n.e.c.	0.299	106	86	0.259	214	239	0.238	264	270
Kindergarten and earlier school teacher	0.031	410	1058	0.019	254	1037	0.019	508	1257
Primary school teachers	0.219	8251	12576	0.204	6989	11640	0.200	6993	11536
Special education teachers	0.300	89	85	0.163	164	314	0.128	522	688
Librarians	0.167	533	401	0.196	382	403	0.176	256	242
Dancers	0.218	10	4	0.212	16	17	0.130	8	11
Mixed occupations									
Legislators	0.614	5	11	0.573	14	10	0.555	12	8
Human resources and labor relations manager	0.615	184	94	0.493	365	267	0.432	540	607
Managers in education and related field	0.596	422	308	0.466	726	813	0.384	675	844
Postmasters and mail superintendents	0.572	1	2	0.540	4	11	0.445	6	7
Managers of properties and real estate	0.550	43	56	0.507	197	209	0.454	181	235

Table A2. (*Continued*)

	1980			1990			2000		
	%Male	*N* (No kids)	*N* (Kids < 5)	%Male	*N* (No kids)	*N* (Kids < 5)	%Male	*N* (No kids)	*N* (Kids < 5)
Accountants and auditors	0.588	894	537	0.453	2768	2752	0.405	2688	3967
Other financial specialists	0.516	313	210	0.461	739	742	0.489	734	899
Personnel, HR, training, and labor relations specialists	0.504	491	275	0.416	757	662	0.325	1419	1450
Buyers, wholesale, and retail trade	0.517	158	71	0.439	207	197	0.434	185	224
Medical scientists	0.579	32	28	0.558	75	68	0.524	119	103
Subject instructors (HS/college)	0.590	878	1156	0.559	1023	1237	0.510	1460	1684
Secondary school teachers	0.405	2586	3380	0.414	1386	1907	0.396	1462	1975
Archivists and curators	0.504	41	12	0.440	69	44	0.411	69	62
Economists, market researchers and survey researchers	0.691	151	75	0.549	376	289	0.513	203	238
Social scientists, n.e.c.	0.576	26	16	0.518	44	41	0.485	72	51
Writers and authors	0.507	79	77	0.480	200	281	0.439	247	405
Designers	0.453	380	296	0.408	817	831	0.416	968	1078
Art makers: painters, sculptors, craft-artists, and print-markers	0.484	223	159	0.446	308	77	0.505	258	220
Editors and reporters	0.477	429	306	0.467	576	554	0.489	506	487

Note: %Male is the percent of the occupation that is male for all individuals between the ages of 18 and 64. *N* (No Kids) and *N* (Kids < 5) are the sample sizes for college educated Non-Hispanic white married women between the ages of 25 and 44 without and with kids less than 5, respectively.

Source: U.S. Census (IPUMS). All observations with flagged values on any of the variables of interest are dropped from the analysis. Sampling weights used.

Table A3. Decomposition of the Child Effect in Unconditional Annual Hours by Birth Cohort and Age (Non-Hispanic White College Educated Married Women).

	Age			
	25–29	30–34	35–39	40–44
Overall child effect				
Birth cohort				
1936–1945			64.203	59.954
1946–1955	54.463	62.466	48.330	44.291
1956–1965	38.851	46.142	45.475	41.887
1966–1975	34.123	42.772		
Extensive margin				
Birth cohort				
1936–1945			43.463	41.002
1946–1955	29.499	39.233	26.502	25.853
1956–1965	16.972	23.730	26.960	24.897
1966–1975	16.005	23.246		
Intensive margin				
Birth cohort				
1936–1945			20.741	18.952
1946–1955	24.964	23.233	21.828	18.437
1956–1965	21.879	22.412	18.514	16.990
1966–1975	18.118	19.526		

Source: U.S. Census (IPUMS). All observations with flagged values on any of the variables of interest are dropped from the analysis. Sampling weights used.
Numbers do not always add up due to rounding.

CHAPTER 3

FEMALE LABOR PARTICIPATION AND OCCUPATION DECISIONS IN POST-NAFTA MEXICO

Rafael E. De Hoyos[1]

ABSTRACT

The objective of this chapter is to estimate the parameters defining female labor participation and occupation decisions in mexico. Based on a theoretical framework, we use micro data to estimate the wage-participation elasticity in urban Mexico. Consistency between the selectivity-adjusted wages and the multinomial participation equations is achieved via a two-step estimation procedure following Lee (1983). We use the results of our model to test and quantify three hypotheses explaining recent increases in female labor participation in urban mexico. Our results show that the observed 12 percent increase in female labor participation in mexico between 1994 and 2000 is explained by the combination of a negative income shock caused by the 1994–1995 participation; wage differentiaeso crisis, the increase in expected wages taking place in the manufacturing sector during the post-North American Free Trade Agreement (NAFTA) period, and a reduction in female reservation wage.

Keywords: Participation; wage differentials; microsimulation; Mexico

JEL classifications: C34; J23; J24; J31

Research in Labor Economics, Volume 33, 85–127

ISSN: 0147-9121/doi:10.1108/S0147-9121(2011)0000033006

INTRODUCTION

Increasing female labor participation is an important aspect that is contributing to the development process in many emerging economies. Identifying the determinants of female labor participation and occupation decisions improves our understanding of the dynamics of labor supply and its interaction with economic development. The objective of the present study is to estimate the determinants of female labor participation and occupation decisions within a structural, utility-maximizing framework, and to use them to explain the recent increase in female participation in the Mexican labor market.

Based on the relationships described by the structural model, the chapter develops a microeconometric model to obtain the determinants of labor participation and occupation decisions. The starting point is a utility-maximizing setting where individuals' choice depends on a set of comparisons between *expected* market wages and a subjective *reservation* wage. Although the agent's choice depends, ultimately, on personal and household characteristics and a subjective valuation of leisure, we estimate the way in which participation reacts to changes in expected wages (participation-wage elasticity). Given that participation/occupation decisions are the outcome of a nonrandom utility-maximizing process, we model *expected* wages taking selectivity into account; therefore, selectivity-adjusted wages and labor participation/occupation functions are estimated using a two-step procedure.

The structural models of labor occupation developed in Heckman and Sedlacek (1985) and Heckman and Honore (1990) are based on Roy's (1951) concept of comparative advantage. These papers show that agents' occupation decisions are not entirely determined by differences in market wages; personal preferences also play a significant role in the *selection* process. These findings, together with the fact that the econometrician only observes market wages and not personal preferences, have led almost all labor supply studies to use reduced-form estimations where wages are substituted by their determinants (i.e., observed personal characteristics within a human capital framework). An exception to this is van Soest (1995) and Gong and van Soest (2002) who develop a model that explicitly links expected wages with labor participation and occupation decisions. Using data for Mexico, Gong and van Soest (2002) find that higher wages have a positive effect on women's participation and their occupational choices.

The present study contributes to our understanding of the determinants of female labor participation in urban Mexico. With respect to previous studies on Mexican labor markets, our approach is novel in two respects: (1) using micro data for several years we uncover the dynamics of intrahousehold female labor participation dependence and (2) the participation and occupation effects of exogenous shocks (currency crisis and liberalizing reforms) are evaluated using microsimulation techniques.

The model is estimated using biannual Mexican household data for the years 1994–2000. This interval allows us to test changes in female labor participation/occupation wage elasticities during a period of liberalizing reforms. Female labor participation in urban Mexico increased by 12 percent between 1994 and 2000, representing a total of more than 700,000 new entrants during the first six years of NAFTA. Given the simultaneity of these two events, it is tempting to infer a causal relationship, explaining the increase in female participation as a result of NAFTA. Our model allows us to create a *hypothetical* economy where the participation/occupation structure is free of "trade-induced" changes in labor market parameters. Hence, using microsimulation techniques, we can quantify how much of the increase in female participation was brought about by changes in expected wages (market conditions affected by trade liberalization) versus changes explained by shifts in structural parameters determining female *reservation wage* function.

The chapter is organized in the following way. In the next section, we develop the model, stressing the necessary assumptions to identify the parameters in our empirical strategy. Third section shows the results of the model using Mexican household data for the period 1994–2000. In fourth section, we carry out a microsimulation analysis to test the impact of exogenous changes in parameters on the employment and the occupation structure. Finally, a summary and conclusions are shown in the last section.

THE MODEL

Theoretical Framework

Following Heckman (1974), we assume that an agent's participation decision is determined by the difference between market wages and a reservation wage function (what Heckman calls shadow prices of female time). Heckman develops a model for the binomial choice problem; however, it can easily be extended to a multinomial one. Define a reservation wage, w_{ij}^{*}, as the minimum wage required to observe individual

i working in occupation j. Such a reservation wage will be determined by the agent's personal and household characteristics and preferences:

$$w_{ij}^* = w_j^*(\boldsymbol{X}_i, \boldsymbol{Z}_i) \quad \forall\ j = 1 \ldots J \tag{1}$$

where $\boldsymbol{X}_i$ and $\boldsymbol{Z}_i$ are vectors of personal and household characteristics of individual i, respectively. Instead of having a single reservation wage function for each individual (as in Heckman's model), we have J of them, that is, as many as the number of remunerated choices (occupations). The J reservation wages derived from the assumption that occupations have different characteristics, apart from monetary ones, that have a value for the individuals making them a function of personal preferences. Allowing for different reservation wages across choices is justified on the basis of differences in observable characteristics (e.g., working conditions) and unobservable ones (e.g., an individual preference for a particular occupation) across occupations. Therefore, individuals attach a different personal valuation to each occupation. A well-documented example of this is the institutional rigidities present in the labor market, where the lack of working hours flexibility can be substituted by occupational choices (see Deaton & Muellbauer, 1980, p. 86). The utility valuation given to the different occupational characteristics is captured – indirectly – by vectors $\boldsymbol{X}_i$ and $\boldsymbol{Z}_i$. On the other hand, expected market wages, following conventional human capital theory, are defined by the well-known function $\hat{w}_{ij} = \boldsymbol{X}_i\hat{\boldsymbol{\beta}}_j$, where w_{ij} is the log of hourly wages.

Once a reservation (w^*) and an expected market wage ($\hat{w}$) are defined for each occupation and each individual, agents' choices will be based on a series of pair comparisons between $\hat{w}_j$ and w_j^*. The utility-maximizing choice will depend not merely on the level of these two components but also on the difference between them, (i.e., $\hat{w}_{ij} - w_{ij}^*$). In this framework, the conventional reservation wage (i.e., whether an individual decides to work or not) is defined implicitly by the same set of pair comparisons. An individual participates in the labor market as long as one of the differences $\hat{w}_{ij} - w_{ij}^*$ is positive, but the final occupational choice will be the one which maximizes the gap between them. There is an implicit *utility* function embedded in this maximizing process that can be defined as follows:

$$V_{ij} = V(\hat{w}_{ij} - w_{ij}^*), \quad \forall j \tag{2}$$

Notice that while V_{ij} is defined by elements $\hat{w}$ and w^*, reservation wages will depend, in turn, on individual preferences; *utility* is thus ultimately defined by monetary income, a personal valuation of it and individual preferences.[2]

A reduced form of (2) takes into account the fact the we do not observe w^*_{ij} and hence we can only include the observable components that determine reservation wages, that is, $\boldsymbol{X}_i$ and $\boldsymbol{Z}_i$. Assuming that *utility*, $V(\cdot)$, is a linear function of its arguments and adding a random component, it can be defined as follows:

$$V_{ij} = \lambda \hat{w}_{ij} - (\boldsymbol{X}_i \gamma'_j + \boldsymbol{Z}_i \gamma_j) + \eta_{ij} \tag{3}$$

where η_{ij} is a stochastic component. We are implicitly assuming that, controlling for differences in $\boldsymbol{X}_i$ and $\boldsymbol{Z}_i$, the marginal utility of monetary income, λ, is constant across individuals and occupations; therefore, λ is a scalar parameter.[3] Since $\hat{w}_i$ is fully determined by $\boldsymbol{X}_i$, a major problem with Eq. (3) is that we cannot identify both sets of parameters, λ and γ'_j, at the same time. Changes in $\boldsymbol{X}_i$ will have a double and simultaneous effect, on the one hand on expected market wages and, on the other, on reservation wages. To tackle this problem, as an alternative to (3), we define a less flexible but more parsimonious version of the *utility* function. Substitute the reduced-form version of the expected (log) wage function $(\boldsymbol{X}_i \hat{\boldsymbol{\beta}}_j)$ into (3):

$$V_{ij} = \lambda(\boldsymbol{X}_i \hat{\boldsymbol{\beta}}_j) - (\boldsymbol{X}_i \gamma'_j + \boldsymbol{Z}_i \gamma_j) + \eta_{ij} \tag{4}$$

Simplify:

$$V_{ij} = (\lambda - \gamma'_j / \hat{\boldsymbol{\beta}}_j) \boldsymbol{X}_i \hat{\boldsymbol{\beta}}_j - \boldsymbol{Z}_i \gamma_j + \eta_{ij} \tag{5}$$

Define $\delta_j = (\lambda - \gamma'_j / \hat{\boldsymbol{\beta}}_j)$:

$$V_{ij} = \delta_j \hat{w}_{ij} - \boldsymbol{Z}_i \gamma_j + \eta_{ij} \tag{6}$$

Notice that the wage-participation parameter, δ_j, will be positive if and only if $\lambda^* \hat{\boldsymbol{\beta}}_j > \gamma'_j$. Therefore, $(\lambda^* \hat{\boldsymbol{\beta}}_j)$ and (γ'_j) can be interpreted as the substitution and income effects of changes in personal endowments $\boldsymbol{X}_i$, respectively. Participation will increase as a result of higher expected wages as long as the substitution effect is larger than the income effect, or, in other words, as far as the marginal utility of monetary income is larger than the increase in reservation wages. Eq. (6) allows the marginal utility of fitted wages, $\hat{w}_{ij}$, to differ across choices, capturing the unobservable effects deriving from the reservation wage function (γ'_j) and the remunerations of personal characteristics across occupations $(\hat{\boldsymbol{\beta}}_j)$. Moreover, the first element of $\boldsymbol{Z}_i$ is a column of ones (i.e., there is a different intercept for each occupation), accounting for the utility effects of occupation-specific attributes such as working conditions or working hours flexibility. Based on specification (6), individual i will choose occupation j if and only if:

$$V_{ij} > \max_{m \neq j}\{V_{im}\} \ \forall j \tag{7}$$

Framework (1)–(7) combines Heckman's (1974) reservation wage concept and McFadden's (1974) multinomial utility maximization criteria. Unifying both approaches helps us understand the dynamic processes that might lie behind the data we observe. Our focus solely on participation and occupation decisions rather than endogenizing hours of work is based on the institutional rigidities present in many developing countries, where working hours are not freely chosen.[4]

Empirical Strategy

This section elaborates on the aspects that we have to take into account in order to obtain a set of equations that are suitable for estimation. The advantage of having a structural model behind the estimations is that we can interpret the parameters in a way that is consistent with the theoretical framework.

From (3) we know that a change in one of the elements of $\boldsymbol{X}_i$ will have a double – and possibly opposing – effect on the probability of participating in the labor market. On the one hand, an increase in $\boldsymbol{X}_i$ will tend to increase the agent's expected wage and this might have a positive effect on participation. On the other hand, the same increase in $\boldsymbol{X}_i$ can rise the agent's reservation wage and hence reduce his or her participation probability. Although we do not observe this second effect, we could estimate a specification like (3) and try to identify both effects. However, as we have already pointed out, we cannot identify the parameters on $\hat{w}_{ij}$ and $\boldsymbol{X}_i$ simultaneously. Furthermore, even using a parsimonious specification like (6) and a simple empirical strategy like the one developed in McFadden's (1974), the interpretation of δ_j is not straightforward. Given the normalization assumption that is necessary to estimate the probability of participation and occupation based on the criteria described in (7), allowing the parameters on expected wages to vary across outcomes will be misleading in terms of our theoretical model. Say that we normalize by making the parameters of outcome "not active" equal to 0. For every possible occupation, we will have an expected wage, but the interpretation of the parameters for all of them would be in terms of the base category (not active). In terms of our structural model, an increase in the expected wage in occupation j does not have an effect on the probability of participating in occupation j' *relative to being not active*; therefore, there is no basis for including all J expected wages as if they were characteristics of the individuals. Instead of allowing expected wages to enter (6) as if they were characteristics of the individuals, we restrict δ_j to be the same for all occupations (δ). Thus, we interpret expected wages as an outcome's *attribute* rather than a characteristic of the individuals.[5]

Before estimating the model, we need one further assumption. The random components of (6), η_{ij}, can follow many distributions, for example, normal, poisson, extreme value or a combination of various distributions (logit kernel or mixed logit). For simplicity, we assume that η_{ij} are i.i.d. with extreme value distribution. With all our assumptions at hand, the probability that agent i will choose occupation s is defined as follows:

$$\Pr(i = s) = \frac{\exp[\delta \hat{w}_{is} + Z_i \gamma_s]}{\sum_{j=1}^{J} \exp[\delta \hat{w}_{ij} + \boldsymbol{Z}_i \gamma_j]} \tag{8}$$

Eq. (8) combines *attributes* of the occupations, $\hat{w}_{ij}$, with *characteristics* of the individual $\boldsymbol{Z}_i$, in other words it is a generalized multinomial model combining McFaddens conditional logit and the multinomial logit (MNL).[6] According to Maddala (1983) "…the main difference between the McFadden logit model and the MNL model [considered here] is that the McFadden model considers the effects of choice characteristics on the determinants of choice probabilities as well, whereas the MNL model [considered here] makes the choice probabilities dependent on individual characteristics only" (p. 42). Specification (8) is a combination of a conditional and an MNL with $\hat{w}_{ij}$ varying across individuals and occupations and $\boldsymbol{Z}_i$ varying only across individuals.[7]

Selectivity and Expected Wages

Let us define the log of hourly wages net of taxes, w_i, as a linear function of formal years of schooling, years of schooling interacting with a dummy variable for higher education, experience, experience squared, and a regional dummy variable.[8] These variables plus a constant are the elements of $\boldsymbol{X}_i$. We allow for different parameters across occupations, estimating a separate wage equation for each of them assuming that their residuals are only related via the selection criteria (7). Our working age population is defined as women between 12 and

65 years old without a physical impediment to work and not being full-time students. Women within this classification face the following set of choices: (i) to participate in the labor market as self-employed or informal worker,[9] (ii) work in the manufacturing sector, (iii) work in other formal sectors, or (iv) not to participate in the labor market at all (not active).[10]

As we have already specified, the workers observed in each sector are not the outcome of a random process, indeed they follow criteria (7). Therefore, to estimate parameters that are valid for the whole population, the wage equations in each of the three remunerated sectors have to account for selectivity. Following (8), we can obtain the conditional probabilities of labor participation for each sector and, given a parameterization rule, include them in the wage equation to control for selectivity.[11] The problem is that, as we can see from (8), the conditional probabilities obtained from the MNL, $\Pr(\cdot)$, are themselves a function of expected wages; therefore, we have the following simultaneous equation model:

$$\hat{w}_{ij} = w[\boldsymbol{X}_i, \Pr(\hat{w}_{ij}, \boldsymbol{Z}_i)] \tag{9}$$

To solve the simultaneity, we estimate (9) following a two-step procedure.[12] In the first step, we estimate $\Pr(\cdot)$ using a reduced form of it with expected wages being substituted by its determinants $\boldsymbol{X}_i$: $\Pr(\boldsymbol{X}_i, \boldsymbol{Z}_i)$, where $\boldsymbol{X}_i$ captures, in an indirect fashion, the wage effects on $\Pr(\cdot)$. In the second step, the conditional probabilities $\Pr(\boldsymbol{X}_i, \boldsymbol{Z}_i)$ are included in the wage equations based on the results by Lee (1983). Define z_i as a vector containing $\boldsymbol{X}_i$ and $\boldsymbol{Z}_i$; selectivity-adjusted wage equations are estimated in the following way (we exclude the individual subindex for clarity):

$$w_s = \boldsymbol{X}\beta_s + \sigma_s\rho_s\left(\frac{\phi(H_s(z\gamma_s))}{F_s(z\gamma_s)}\right) + \varepsilon_s \tag{10}$$

where $\sigma_s\rho_s$ are parameters capturing the covariance between the wage and selection equations; $H_s(z\gamma_s)$ is a transformation of the MNL index, $z\gamma_s$, into a standard normal distribution; ϕ is the standard normal density function and $F_s(z\gamma_s)$ is the marginal distribution of the MNL residuals. Since the wage equations and the conditional probabilities from the selection equation share vector $\boldsymbol{X}$, the identifying variables or exclusion restrictions in Eq. (10) are contained in $\boldsymbol{Z}$ (instruments). We define $\boldsymbol{Z}$ bearing in mind that its components must affect reservation wages but not market wages. In the case of female laborers, $\boldsymbol{Z}$ includes the number of children in the household (less than 7-year-old); a dummy variable equal to 1 if the woman is not head of the household and the head is active; the income of all other household members and its quadratic form. As has been argued in Attanasio, Low, and Sánchez-Marcos (2004), female labor participation is closely linked to household income variability and economy-wide shocks. To take this into account, the last element of $\boldsymbol{Z}$ is a measure of the variation in all other household members' income.[13] All these variables are expected to have a significant effect on female reservation wages without affecting their expected market remuneration.

Estimation of informal sector "wages" using specification (10) implicitly assumes that this sector is *complete*, and therefore it remunerates the marginal productivity of labor as the outcome of personal characteristics. Marcouiller, Ruiz, and Woodruff (1997) find that returns to personal characteristics in the Mexican informal sector behave quite like those in the formal sector. The same study and those by Maloney (1999) and Gong, van Soest, and Villagomez (2000) suggest that, controlling for personal characteristics, the informal sector in Mexico is a desirable destination rather than an inferior forced option. As it was mentioned in the theoretical section, the different occupations can have certain attributes valued by agents. A special feature that is present in the informal sector that might have an advantage over its formal counterpart is the flexibility in working hours. To account for this occupational *attribute*, we include the standard deviation of working hours ($\tilde{h}$) in each sector as a determinant of participation and occupation. A note of caution is necessary at this point. Notice that $\tilde{h}$ will only vary across occupations but not between individuals. The same can be said about the intercept in (6) – the first element of $\boldsymbol{Z}$. Therefore, including $\tilde{h}$ and allowing for a different intercept for each occupation will result in perfect multicollinearity. To avoid this problem, our estimations assume that the intercept for the informal sector equation is equal to 0. In other words, all particular attributes attached to the informal sector (apart from $\hat{w}$) will be captured by $\tilde{h}$.

Finally, the structural participation and occupation function is estimated using a *generalized* MNL[14] including the exponential of the fitted values of the wage Eq. (10), $\hat{W}$, $\tilde{h}$, and $\boldsymbol{Z}_i$ as regressors:[15]

$$\text{Prob}(i = s) = \frac{\exp[\delta \hat{W}_{is} + \varphi \tilde{h}_s + \text{Z}_i \gamma_s]}{\sum_{j=1}^{J} \exp[\delta \hat{W}_{ij} + \varphi \tilde{h}_j + \boldsymbol{Z}_i \gamma_j]} \tag{11}$$

Although rather standard, the empirical strategy described in this section is well-suited for answering the question in hand: what explains the increase in female labor participation observed in post-NAFTA Mexico? Other more sophisticated models such as van Soest (1995), exploiting variations in hours worked, would add little – if any – to our understanding of the factors behind the increase in female labor participation in Mexico. Additionally, as it will become clear from fifth section, estimating Eq. (11) will allow us to quantify the relative importance of three possible explanations behind the increase in female labor participation: (a) the negative income effect brought about by the 1995 economic crisis; (b) a positive substitution effect (increase in relative wages) after 1996, explained by the increase in female labor demand in the manufacturing sector; and (c) changes in female reservation wage functions favoring participation.

DATA

The model described in second section is estimated using Mexican household survey data (ENIGH) for households located in urban areas (communities with 15,000 inhabitants or more) for the years 1994, 1996, 1998, and 2000, respectively. Between 1994 and 1996, Mexico experienced great macroeconomic turbulence as a result of the Peso crisis that erupted in December 1994. In 1994, the country embarked on a free trade agreement with Canada and the United States. The years between 1996 and 2000 were a time of economic recovery, with high rates of growth mainly boosted by manufacturing exports. All these changes could have had a significant impact on female labor participation and occupation decisions.

To summarize the most important changes taking place in the Mexican female labor market, in Fig. 1 we show the percentage change in labor participation and the time trend in real wages.[16] Female labor participation increased during the period of analysis with the proportion of active women rising from 41.6 percent in 1994 to 46.6 percent in 2000, representing a 12 percent increase in a period of only six years. An increase of 5 percentage points might seem to be a small change, but when we consider the number of total women entering the labor market during those years, the increase is far from being trivial. An increase in female participation of 5 percentage points of the 1994 female working age population represents a total of 707,993 female laborers entering the market over and above the effects due to demographic trends.[17] Of the total amount, around 338,794 of the new entrants took place in the manufacturing sector, 244,684 new laborers went into other formal sectors, and 124,514 ended up in the informal sector. During these period, the manufacturing sector absorbed most of the new female entrants into the labor marker despite its relatively small size in

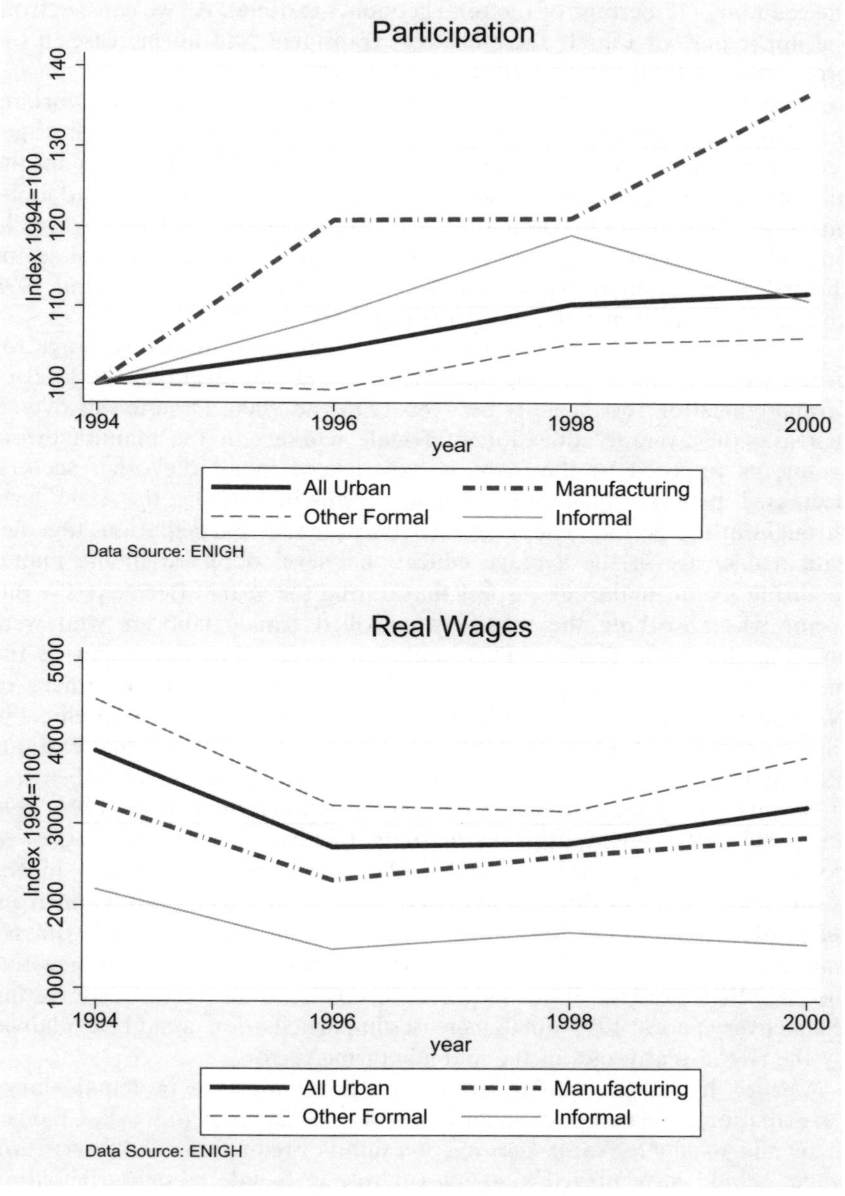

Fig. 1. Female Participation and Real Wages.

the economy (17 percent of the total economy in 1994). As we can see from the upper part of Fig. 1, these changes translated into an increase in the proportion of total female laborers in the manufacturing sector.

After the Peso crisis (1994–1995), real average wages for women working in urban areas decreased 30 percent. Although urban areas average wages remained practically unchanged between 1996 and 1998, wages in the manufacturing sector rose 13 percent during the same period. Manufacturing wages kept rising between 1998 and 2000, time during which wages in other formal sectors began to recover. Real wages in the informal sector showed no constant trend, with a positive change between 1996 and 1998 and an unexpected negative shift between 1998 and 2000.

In Fig. 2, we show the average years of schooling and average age for urban women within working age. We find that, on average, the level of formal education rose steadily between 1994 and 2000. Despite this overall increase, the average education of female workers in the manufacturing sector, as opposed to the increase experienced in all the other sectors, decreased between 1994 and 1996 and remained below the 1994 level throughout the period. The large increase in female participation, together with a decrease in the average educational level observed in the manufacturing sector, makes us suspect that during the years after NAFTA this sector was absorbing the relatively unskilled female laborers who were entering the labor market. This could be a sign that the boom in the manufacturing sector after the Peso devaluation and the enactment of NAFTA made many unskilled Mexican women more likely to participate in the labor market. Finally, the lower right part of Fig. 2 shows that entrants into the informal sector were younger, on average, than the incumbents.

Despite the opposite trends in real wages between the periods 1994–1996 and 1996–2000, participation in the manufacturing sector always showed positive shifts. The explanation for the increasing participation in the manufacturing sector during the period 1994–1996 might be different from the explanation behind the increase during 1996–2000. Perhaps women's participation between 1994 and 1996 was a response to the large negative income effect brought about by the Peso crisis; on the other hand, during the recovery period 1996–2000, increases in participation could be explained by the rise in real wages in the manufacturing sector.

A third hypothesis explaining the observed increase in female labor participation is related to changes in women's *willingness* to work. Changes in female *shadow price of leisure*, for example, reductions in "reservation wage," could have played a significant role in female labor participation decisions. For example, in a relatively traditionalist society like the Mexican

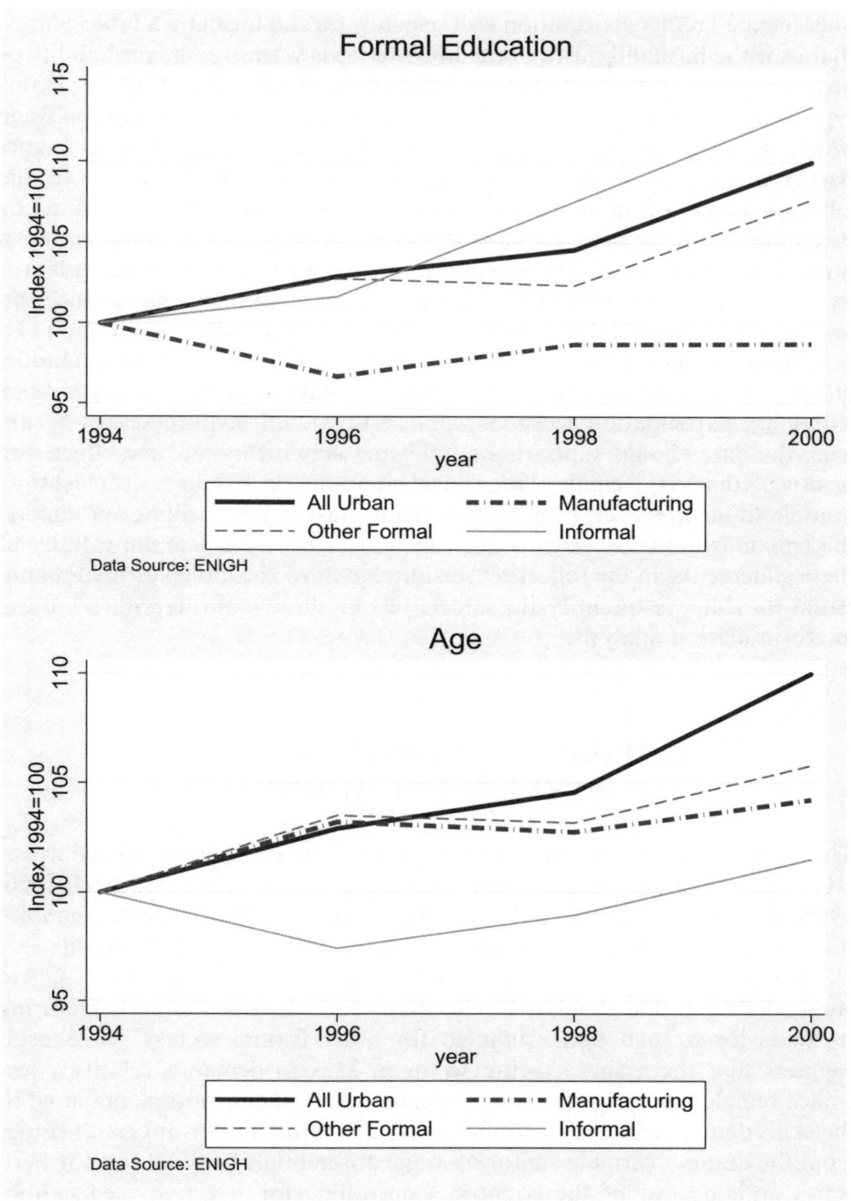

Fig. 2. Years of Schooling and Age.

one, female labor participation still depends on the husband's labor status; that is, if the husband (head of the household) is working, the probability of observing an active spouse is lower than if the head was not active. If this type of *dependency*, or any other factor affecting the female reservation wage function, is changing throughout the period in a way that favors participation, then we could conclude that the observed increase in female labor participation in Mexico between 1994 and 2000 can be explained by three effects: (a) the negative income effect brought about by the crisis; (b) a positive substitution effect (increase in relative wages) after 1996, explained by the increase in female labor demand in the manufacturing sector; and (c) changes in female reservation wage functions favoring participation. To be able to test these hypotheses and quantify their effects, a structural model linking exogenous income effects, market wages, and female *dependency* with labor participation decisions will be estimated. If hypotheses (a)–(c) are true, the data should support the following statements: income effects are positive, that is, female labor participation probability decreases as household income rises; wage-participation elasticity is positive; and finally, the female reservation wage is decreasing over time. To test the validity of these statements, in the following sections we show the model estimates and, based on this, we quantify the effects of our three main hypotheses using microsimulation analysis.

EMPIRICAL ESTIMATES OF THE STRUCTURAL MODEL

This section presents the estimation results for the selectivity-adjusted wages (10) and the participation and occupation Eq. (11) for the years 1994, 1996, 1998, and 2000, respectively.[18] Given the large amount of results, the tables with the wage equation's estimates for each sector are placed in Appendix C.[19]

An important result to notice from the wage equations (Tables C.1–C.3 in Appendix C) is that the average return to schooling in the manufacturing sector is lower than that estimated for other formal sectors. This result suggests that the manufacturing sector in Mexico demands relatively less skilled female laborers (measured in years of formal education) compared to the skills demanded in other formal sectors. Another important result comes from the dummy variable capturing wage differentials between the northern states and the rest of the country. Controlling for selectivity, education, and experience, during the recovery years 1996–2000, female laborers in manufacturing industries located in the north of Mexico earned, on average, 20 percent more than their northern counterparts working in other formal sectors and 25 percent more than manufacturing laborers in other regions. This result supports the hypothesis of an increase in female labor demand in the manufacturing industry explained, in turn, by the rapid growth in exports in this sector during those years.[20]

Table 1 shows the estimation results of the participation and occupation Eq. (11) taking "not active" as the base category; therefore, all the parameters (except for the wage-participation elasticity) are interpreted as changes in the probability of choosing a particular occupation relative to not being active.[21] The first two rows contain the estimates of two occupation attributes, that is, expected wages ($\hat{W}$) and the standard deviation of working hours ($\tilde{h}$). Regarding the latter, the results show that female workers (or possible ones) perceive working hours stability as a positive attribute; therefore, a ceteris paribus increase in the variance of working hours in a particular occupation reduces its probability of being chosen. As we would have expected a priori, an increase in expected wages in a particular sector increases the likelihood of observing workers in that sector. Following our theoretical model, a value of δ of, say, 1 implies a value of λ (the marginal utility valuation of money income) greater than 1. The probability of observing a worker participating increases as a result of an exogenous increase in $\hat{W}$ (i.e., $\delta > 0$).

Based on the estimates of δ, we compute the wage-participation elasticity. The estimated wage-participation elasticity is quite stable over time, ranging from 0.33 in 1998 to 0.39 in 2000 (see dashed line in Fig. 3).[22] This result supports hypothesis (b) postulated in third section, that is, participation can be partly explained by positive changes in real wages occurring in the export-oriented manufacturing sector. The continuous line in Fig. 3 shows the average fitted values of the log of hourly wages ($\hat{w}$) notice the large positive reaction of fitted values of wages between 1996 and 1998 – although still below the pre-crisis level. In the next section, we will quantify the labor participation effects of these changes in expected wages.

From the third row of Table 1 onward, we show the participation and occupation effects of household characteristics $\boldsymbol{Z}$. Remember that all variables included in $\boldsymbol{Z}$ (instruments) affect reservation wages without changing market wages. Hence $\boldsymbol{Z}$'s estimated parameters should be seen as the determinants of females' reservation wage function and orthogonal to $\hat{W}_{ij}$.

Despite an expected a priori negative sign on the parameter relating participation to the number of children in the household, we find that, for many years, this relationship is not significantly different from zero. A

Table 1. Structural Model Results.

	1994	1996	1998	2000
$\hat{W}$	1.3 (0.077)***	1.45 (0.08)***	1.11 (0.087)***	1.5 (0.101)***
$\tilde{h}$	−0.15 (0.008)***	−0.11 (0.007)***	−0.11 (0.007)***	−0.1 (0.008)***
Manufacturing earner (Tradable)				
Intercept	−1.88 (0.161)***	−2.58 (0.165)***	−2.54 (0.201)***	−3.4 (0.216)***
Children	−0.37 (0.085)***	−0.18 (0.078)**	−0.14 (0.066)	−0.02 (0.094)
H_s^a	−1.13 (0.191)***	−1.14 (0.133)***	−1.01 (0.148)***	−0.77 (0.222)***
H_d^a	0.61 (0.181)***	0.78 (0.165)***	1.05 (0.164)***	1.46 (0.232)***
Y_m^0	−5.62 (1.24)***	−9.68 (1.559)***	−10.95 (1.53)***	−10.48 (1.713)***
$(Y_m^0)^2$	1.02 (0.22)	1.31 (0.672)	6.81 (1.377)*	5.88 (1.232)
$Var(Y_m^0)$	0.002 (0.001)	0.002 (0.004)	0.001 (0.001)	−0.033 (0.023)
Other earner (nontradable)				
Intercept	−0.8 (0.122)***	−1.15 (0.118)***	−0.44 (0.152)***	−2.23 (0.249)***
Children	−0.16 (0.055)**	−0.23 (0.036)***	−0.13 (0.042)*	−0.21 (0.085)**
H_s^a	−1.14 (0.096)***	−1.14 (0.085)***	−0.95 (0.088)***	−0.97 (0.115)***
H_d^a	0.62 (0.119)***	0.17 (0.107)	0.64 (0.108)***	0.71 (0.193)***
Y_m^0	−3.91 (0.602)***	−5.02 (0.764)***	−7.62 (1.085)***	−5.33 (1.113)***
$(Y_m^0)^2$	0.7 (0.122)	0.56 (0.639)	6.0 (1.404)*	2.21 (1.035)
$Var(Y_m^0)$	0.002 (0.001)*	0.002 (0.004)	0.001 (0.001)**	0.001 (0.002)
Informal sector				
Children	−0.12 (0.066)	−0.11 (0.05)	−0.12 (0.059)	−0.04 (0.066)
H_s^a	−0.68 (0.162)***	−0.67 (0.121)***	−0.6 (0.135)***	−0.52 (0.182)***
H_d^a	−0.97 (0.221)***	−0.71 (0.207)***	−0.58 (0.251)**	−0.2 (2.62)
Y_m^0	−9.93 (1.422)***	−13.19 (1.694)***	−11.67 (1.624)***	−11.4 (2.301)***
$(Y_m^0)^2$	1.8 (0.226)	1.93 (0.668)	6.89 (1.372)**	3.96 (4.442)
$Var(Y_m^0)$	0.002 (0.001)	0.002 (0.004)	0.002 (0.001)**	0.002 (0.003)
GF	63.12	61.63	59.06	59.42
R^2	0.325	0.293	0.261	0.275
N	32,284	36,292	27,492	24,240

Notes: *, **, *** significant at the 10 percent, 5 percent, and 1 percent level, respectively (with bootstrapped SE).
Standard errors in parenthesis.
GF refers to the goodness of fit of the model, measured as the percentage of cases predicted correctly, respectively.

plausible explanation for this can lie in the strong family ties observed in Mexico, where the presence of grandparents in the household reduces (or eliminates) child care costs. A very interesting pattern arose in the parameters estimating labor participation dependence of female household

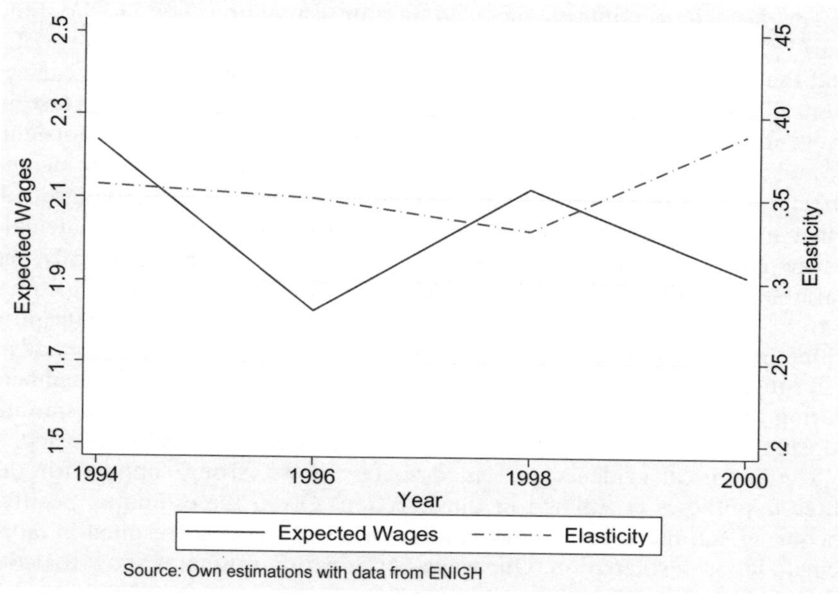

Fig. 3. Wage-Participation Elasticity.

members with respect to the labor status of the head of household. We allow for spouses and daughters to have a different response to the head of the household's participation decision. H_s^a and H_d^a are dummy variables taking a value of one when the woman is a nonhead of household (spouse or daughter, respectively) and the head of the household is actively participating in the labor market. In the case of female spouses, the probability of participation decreases when their husband is working ($H_s^a < 0$). However, notice that this effect is decreasing over time, suggesting that women's participation decisions are becoming less dependent on their husband's labor status. In the case of daughters, the story is completely different, with the probability of being employed in formal sectors increasing when the male head of the household is active, $H_d^a > 0$, and increasing over time. These results suggest that the Mexican labor market is changing in a way such that women's labor participation is less subject to their husband's labor status. Another way of interpreting this result is as a reduction in females' reservation wage or, equivalently, an increase in their *willingness* to work. Therefore, hypothesis (c) suggested in third section also finds support in the data.

The last three controls included in our estimation, Y^0_m, $(Y^0_m)^2$, and $\mathrm{Var}(Y^0_m)$, are capturing, respectively, the income effect, a quadratic form of it and the variance of all other household members' incomes.[23] As we can see from Table 1, the income effect is always *positive*, that is, an increase in exogenous income reduces female labor participation, and with a notsignificant second-order contribution. Only in year 1998 the second-order income effect ($(Y^0_m)^2$) is positive and significant, implying that a positive change in all other household members' income will decrease the probability of female participation and this will be stronger at lower levels of income. Finally, the variable capturing the variance of all other household members' income, $\mathrm{Var}(Y^0_m)$, shows the expected positive sign, although it is only significantly different from zero in 1998. A rise in the variance of household income had as a result an increase in labor participation of female household members during 1998. This could be seen as a rational reaction to try to smooth consumption in a country with strong borrowing constraints like Mexico.

The empirical evidence presented so far shows strong support for the three hypotheses postulated in third section. Given the estimated positive income effect, the negative shock caused by the Peso crisis resulted in more female labor participation. Our wage-participation estimates show that the observed increases in real wages in the manufacturing sector after 1996 also accounts for part of the increase in female participation. Finally, reductions in the dependency between women's labor decisions and the head of household's labor status also played a significant role in explaining the observed increase in female labor participation.

Although this rather simple female labor participation model is able to explain less than a third of the total variation in participation and occupation status of urban women in Mexico, it is enough to predict correctly 60 percent of the cases (see bottom part of Table 1). Appendix D shows that the model has around the same goodness of fit regardless of the age, years of schooling of women, or the size of the household. However, it shows a considerable better fit for women with incomes above \$5,000 pesos per month and those that are not heads of households. Finally, we test the robustness of our results using two other methods of selection-adjustment proposed in Dubin and McFadden (1984) and Bourguignon, Fournier, and Gurgand (2004). Although the value of the parameters changes under these alternative selectivity-correction methods, all the qualitative results hold, making us confident about the robustness of importance played by the three effects described in this section.

The remaining of this chapter quantifies the *relative* importance of the three hypotheses in explaining the increase in labor participation. As we would explain in details in the following section, the microsimulation analysis quantifies the ceteris paribus labor participation effect of changes in the estimated parameters and independent variables. Given the lack of robustness in the *value* (point estimator) of the estimated parameters, the results of the microsimulation analysis should be seen as a first approximation of the quantitative impact on female labor participation of the three competing hypothesis used in the present study: (i) negative income effect brought about by the economic crisis, (ii) increase in real wages in the manufacturing as a result of trade liberalization, and (iii) emancipation of female labor participation decisions.

MICROSIMULATION ANALYSIS

How much of the total increase in female labor participation between 1994 and 2000 can we attribute to the negative income effect caused by the Peso crisis of 1994–1995? What proportion of the increase in participation is explained by changes in female expected wages? How many of the net entrants in the different occupations reported in third section are the outcome of changes in females' reservation wage function? Using a microsimulation exercise helps us understand what are the factors behind the increase in female labor participation in post-NAFTA Mexico.[24]

Define Ω_t as a vector containing all the estimated parameters from the participation function at time t:

$$\boldsymbol{\Omega}_t = (\hat{\delta}_t, \hat{\phi}_t, \hat{\gamma}_t)$$

Similarly, define $\boldsymbol{\chi}_t$ as a vector containing all variables explaining female labor participation and occupation at time t:

$$\boldsymbol{\chi}_t = (\hat{w}_t, \tilde{h}_t, \boldsymbol{Z}_t)$$

Finally introduce a time subindex in the random component of the *utility* function, η. Female labor participation and occupation decisions at time t are hence a function of the three components just defined:

$$\Pr(\cdot)_t = \Pr(\boldsymbol{\Omega}_t, \boldsymbol{\chi}_t, \eta_t) \qquad (12)$$

Therefore, any change in the probability of female participation between t and t' can be decomposed into changes in parameters (Ω), exogenous variables ($\boldsymbol{\chi}$), and residuals (η).

As we discussed in third and fourth sections, there are three tested hypotheses explaining the increase in female labor participation: (a) a negative income shock caused by the Peso crisis, (b) a trade-induced positive shift in female labor demand, particularly in the manufacturing sector, and (c) a long-run negative trend in women's reservation wage function. Simulating changes in the components of (12) help us quantify the ceteris paribus labor participation and occupation effects of our three hypotheses.

Measuring the Effects of Changes in $\hat{\boldsymbol{\beta}}$

An exogenous macro shock, for example, currency crisis and trade liberalization, will manifest itself as a change in the relative prices of the economy (both for men and women). In the labor market, the most important "price" is the wage that, in turn, is defined by a set of "prices" or returns to personal characteristics, $\hat{\boldsymbol{\beta}}$. Between 1994 and 1996, we would expect to observe a negative impact on "prices" of personal characteristics of men and women in all occupations as a consequence of the Peso crisis. If this is the case, then *expected* wages, $\hat{w}$, would decrease and, given a positive participation-wage elasticity, participation should be lower as a consequence of the crisis. On the other hand, according to the results of our labor participation model, the same negative shock on the "price" of personal characteristics would reduce household incomes and this, in turn, increases the probability of female participation. To quantify these effects, in our labor participation function, exogenous changes in "prices" will affect elements $\hat{w}$ and $\boldsymbol{Z}$ of component $\boldsymbol{\chi}$. Therefore, the *value* of some of the independent variables defining female participation, $\boldsymbol{\chi}$ (husband's labor participation and all other household member's income), will be a function of the returns to personal characteristics, $c = \chi(\hat{\boldsymbol{\beta}}, \ldots)$.[25] To account for the overall $\hat{\boldsymbol{\beta}}$-induced changes in household incomes and husband's labor participation, it is necessary to parameterize wages and participation decisions for men. This allows us to find out the ceteris paribus effect of changes in "prices" on variables: H_s^a, H_d^a, Y_m^0, and $(Y_m^0)^2$. Remember that H_s^a and H_d^a are dummy variables indicating the labor status of the head of the household (usually the husband) and Y_m^0 measures all other household members' income (strongly dependent on husband's income). Thus, variables H_s^a, H_d^a, Y_m^0, and $(Y_m^0)^2$ will be affected by changes in returns to personal characteristics both in the men's and women's labor market.[26] We, therefore, estimate men's wage equations and participation functions following the same empirical strategy as we did for women; the details of the estimation of husband's wage and participation function can be found in De Hoyos (2005b).[27]

A hypothetical or simulated set of expected wages and household characteristics, $\hat{w}^i$ and $\boldsymbol{Z}^i$, are created by substituting the estimated returns to personal characteristics for year t', $(\hat{\boldsymbol{\beta}}_{t'})$, into the database for year t. The new vector of returns to personal characteristics will have a direct household income effect via the change in labor income. Furthermore, while simulating household incomes, we allow the men in our sample to re-optimize their labor participation and occupation decisions given the new set of expected wages. The procedures we undertake are the following: (1) Estimate the model for men and women using the cross-sectional data for year t and t'. (2) "Import" the wage parameters of year t' into the parameterized model for t. (3) Compute the new set of hypothetical expected wages and household incomes. (4) Allow male household members to change their occupational status given the new value of expected wages and household income. (5) Simulate household incomes using the hypothetical set of wages and men's occupational status. (6) Finally, we simulate the ceteris paribus female participation effects of changes in $\hat{\boldsymbol{\beta}}$ via the expected wages channel $(\hat{w})$ and the exogenous household income channel $(\boldsymbol{Z})$. This allows us to measure the impact – through its different channels – that an exogenous change in the market returns to personal characteristics $(\hat{\boldsymbol{\beta}})$ between t and t' has on female labor participation:

$$\Pr(\cdot)_t^i = \Pr[\boldsymbol{\Omega}_t, \boldsymbol{\chi}_t^i, \eta_t] \tag{13}$$

where $c_t^i = \chi_t^i[\hat{w}^i(\hat{b}_{t'}), Z^i(\hat{b}_{t'})...]$; $\Pr(\cdot)_t^i$ is a *simulated* probability (since it is not observed) at the *micro* level (since we compute one for each individual in the sample). Using the estimation results of our model plus the estimated parameters for men, the three components of (13), Ω_t, $\boldsymbol{\chi}_t^i$, and η_t, are observed. To summarize our procedure, we are "importing" the estimated wage equation parameters $(\hat{\boldsymbol{\beta}})$ for year t' into the data set for year t. Once the parameters are in the database for year t, we simulate a hypothetical expected wage and household income ($\hat{w}^i$ and $\boldsymbol{Z}^i$) that we then use to construct $\boldsymbol{\chi}_t^i$. Finally we multiply $\boldsymbol{\chi}_t^i$ by Ω_t and add the residual terms η_t. This will create a new *utility*-maximizing decision, and therefore a new set of participation/occupation probabilities for each woman within working age (actual and potential worker). We undertake three separate simulations, taking 1994 as the base year and "importing" the estimated wage parameters for the years 1996, 1998, and 2000, respectively. The simulation results are summarized in Fig. 4.

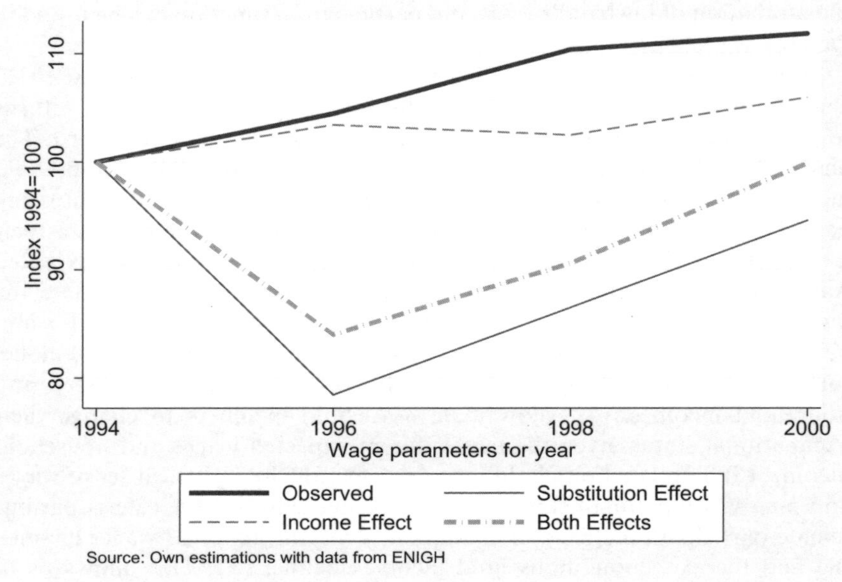

Fig. 4. Simulated Participation Effect of $\Delta\hat{\boldsymbol{\beta}}$.

In Fig. 4, we graph the time trend of the observed and simulated change in participation (with respect to 1994) due to a change in the wage equation parameters. To decompose the effect of $\Delta\hat{\boldsymbol{\beta}}$ even further, we perform three different simulations for each "imported" $\hat{\boldsymbol{\beta}}$ we compute: (1) a simulation where only expected wages, $\hat{w}$, are allowed to change (continuous thin line); (2) a second one where only the household income elements of $\boldsymbol{Z}$ change (dashed thin line), and (3) a third one where both $\hat{w}$ and $\boldsymbol{Z}$ are changing as a consequence of $\Delta\hat{\boldsymbol{\beta}}$ (dashed thick line).[28] We perform these separate simulations because we can interpret the first and second simulations as the *substitution* and *income effects*, respectively, of changes in returns or prices of personal characteristics.

For the moment, let us concentrate on the changes taking place between 1994 and 1996. The observed change in participation (the continuous thick line in Fig. 4) is positive. According to our model, if expected wages were the only element changing during those years of deep economic crisis, female participation would have been reduced by 22 percent (continuous thin line).

Given the positive wage-participation elasticity found in fourth section, this result is explained by the reduction in average expected wages ($\hat{w}$) between 1994 and 1996 (see Fig. 3), which is, in turn, caused by a reduction in returns to personal characteristics ($\hat{\boldsymbol{\beta}}$). Concerning the income effects of the crisis, the estimated reduction in payments to personal characteristics had a negative effect on household's income (Y^0) and also on men's participation decisions.[29] The ceteris paribus simulated participation effect of $\boldsymbol{Z}^i$ is shown in Fig. 4 (dashed thin line). We can see that had the change in household incomes and head of the household participation decisions – as a consequence of a negative shock in $\hat{\boldsymbol{\beta}}$ – been the only change taking place between 1994 and 1996, then female labor participation would have increased as much as the observed increase during those years. This is explained by the crisis' negative income effect that "pushed" more women into the labor market. The final simulation presented in Fig. 4 includes both changes, $\hat{w}^i$ and $\boldsymbol{Z}^i$, together in the same simulation. The simulated net participation effect is negative, in other words, had remunerations to personal characteristics decreased in the way they did between 1994 and 1996, female participation would have decreased 13 percent, ceteris paribus.

Let us now analyze the changes that occurred during the recovery period 1996–2000. As $\hat{\boldsymbol{\beta}}$ experienced a positive change, household incomes increased and, given the positive income effect estimated, the participation rate attributable to the income effect decreased, although it remained above the 1994 value (thin dashed line). Regarding wage effects, the increase in returns to personal characteristics taking place between 1996 and 1998 (see Fig. 3) explains the simulated increase in female labor participation between 1996 and 1998 (continuous thin line), although still below the 1994 participation rate. These results show that, controlling for all other changes taking place in the economy between 1994 and 2000, shifts in the returns to personal characteristics would have *decreased* the participation rate by 0.2 percent out of a total *increase* of 12 percent observed during that period.[30]

So far, we have simulated the participation rate that we would have observed if returns to personal characteristics were the only elements changing in the economy, but what about the simulated occupation effects? In Appendix F we present the simulated percentage change in the female participation rate in the manufacturing, other formal and informal sectors. As we can see, the simulated change in participation attributable to shifts in $\hat{w}$ in the manufacturing sector between 1994 and 1996 is positive. Quite the opposite can be said for other formal sectors. These results suggest that, in the absence of labor rationing, the isolated participation effects of changes in $\hat{\boldsymbol{\beta}}$ would have triggered female labor participation in the manufacturing sector and reduced participation in other formal sectors during the crisis years 1994–1996. The effect is explained by the increase in $\hat{\boldsymbol{\beta}}$ taking place in the manufacturing sector even during a time of general contraction of the economy (1994–1996).[31] The positive simulated participation trend in the manufacturing sector remains between the years 1996 and 1998 and then slows down in the period 1998–2000. The figures in Appendix F illustrate the simulated wedge in labor participation that opened between the manufacturing and other formal sectors during the crisis. The negative participation effect brought about by the Peso crisis was cushioned by a trade agreement such as NAFTA, triggering manufacturing exports, increasing relative expected wages, and labor participation. Regarding the occupational changes brought about by the 1994–1996 negative income shock, notice how it has a much larger effect on participation in the informal sector (a 20 percent increase). This result suggests that in the presence of borrowing constraints, the informal sector absorbed part of the female laborers, particularly young ones, that were "pushed" into the labor market by the negative income shock.

To summarize, we have shown that the positive post-1994 trend in overall urban labor participation described in Fig. 1 is explained partly by increases in manufacturing sector participation and, to a lesser extent, by an increase in participation in the informal sector. The explanations behind these shifts are completely different. On the one hand, the positive trends in manufacturing participation are explained by positive shifts in $\hat{\boldsymbol{\beta}}$ for manufacturing female laborers. On the other hand, the increase in the informal sector participation is explained by a negative income shock. Therefore, the data supports the hypothesis of a trade-induced increase in female labor demand taking place in the manufacturing sector between 1994 and 2000 and an increase in participation as a consequence of the 1994–1995 Peso crisis, primarily in the informal sector.

Measuring the Effects of Changes in Ω

The previous simulations uncovered the participation and occupation effects of exogenous changes in wage functions parameters that in turn affected the vector of explanatory variables, $\boldsymbol{\chi}$. All the counterfactuals constructed so far had evaluated the labor participation effects of changes in "prices" of personal characteristics. Assuming that in the short run labor supply is close to being constant, these changes are basically capturing trade and devaluation-induced shifts in labor demand. In this section, we simulate the participation and occupation effects that are attributable to changes in the parameters defining the "reservation wage function," $\boldsymbol{\gamma}$ in Eq. (11).

We are interested in quantifying the participation and occupation effects of changes in reservation wage function parameters *free* of labor market effects. To do so, let us separate the variables in $\boldsymbol{Z}$ into two different matrices: $Z = (Z_{w^*}, Z_y)$. Z_{w^*} contains variables that are strictly affecting female's reservation wage function without being affected by the prevailing market conditions, hence $Z_{w^*} = (H_s^a, H_s^a, \text{Children})$. $\boldsymbol{Z}_y$, on the other hand, contains all the income variables: Y_m^0, $(Y_m^0)^2$ and $\text{Var}(Y_m^0)$, which are, as a matter of fact, capturing the Peso devaluation shock. The only parameters that are allowed to vary in the simulations are those in Z_{w^*}. The parameters in the income variables (Y_m^0, $(Y_m^0)^2$, and $\text{Var}(Y_m^0)$) are kept constant since they are highly unstable across cross-sections, capturing part of the instability brought about by the Peso crisis. Furthermore, we also keep constant the parameters on δ and φ. Changes in the price-wage elasticity (δ) and the parameter for the standard deviation of hours worked (φ) are not allowed to vary since, as we saw in second section, these parameters are determined by the interaction between expected wages and a female's reservation wage function (see Eqs. (5 and 6)). The varying parameters in the simulation (i.e., those of variables H_s^a, H_s^a, and Children), on the other hand, are parameters that affect female's reservation wage function without affecting market wages; moreover, the parameters of these variables are much more stable in time and are not affected by market conditions. Changes in parameters γ_{w^*} would capture the ceteris paribus participation effects of changes in female reservation wage function parameters. A hypothetical value of Ω will be defined as follows:

$$\boldsymbol{\Omega}_t^i = (\hat{\delta}_t, \hat{\varphi}_t, \hat{\gamma}_t^i)$$

where $\hat{\gamma}_t^i$ is a hypothetical vector containing the estimated parameters $\hat{\gamma}_{y,t}$ and the "imported" ones $\hat{\gamma}_{w^*,t'}$. Following last section's counterfactual analysis, to capture the dynamics of changes in $\hat{\gamma}_{w^*}$, we take the year 1994 as the base and "import," in separate simulations, the "reservation wage function" parameters for the years 1996, 1998, and 2000, respectively. The way we interpret these results is similar to the interpretation given in section "Measuring the Effects of Changes in $\hat{\boldsymbol{\beta}}$"; that is, the simulated participation and occupation decisions yield the ceteris paribus effect of changes in $\hat{\gamma}_{w^*}$ observed between t and t'. Based on our structural model, we can think of changes in $\hat{\gamma}_{w^*}$ as changes in women's reservation wage function parameters, or their subjective *willingness* to work. As we mentioned before, parameters $\hat{\gamma}_{w*}$ of the participation function (Eq. (11)) should not be affected by changes in market conditions; therefore, the simulations can be interpreted as capturing *exogenous* changes in women's willingness to work. The results of the simulations are shown in Fig. 5.

From Fig. 5 we can see that if the only changes observed between 1994 and 1996 had been the changes in participation function parameters $\hat{\gamma}_{w*}$, then we would have seen a decrease in participation of almost 3 percent. Given that the net participation effect of changes in $\boldsymbol{\chi}$ during the crisis years 1994–1996 was negative (see Fig. 4), we can infer that the observed increase in female participation after the Peso crisis was, at least partly, the result of a negative income shock affecting household incomes over and above the reduction in returns to personal characteristics. The rather small participation effects of changes in $\hat{\gamma}_{w*}$ are not surprising given the small pace at which preferences tend to change. In the case of Mexico, we can see that there is a relatively large change in preferences favoring female participation between 1996 and 1998. Although the parametric changes captured by our

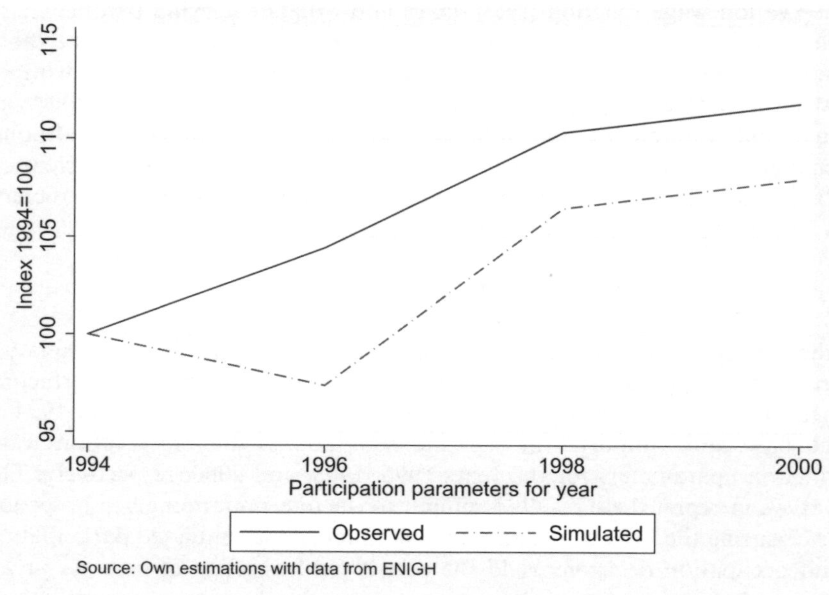

Fig. 5. Simulated Participation Effect of $\hat{\gamma}_{w*}$.

simulations are *free* of market shocks, they might still be capturing, in an indirect fashion, the effects of macroeconomic turmoil. It is difficult to measure the extent to which this result is actually triggered – although indirectly – by the macro shocks of 1995 (NAFTA/devaluation), but certainly these changes help explain the increase in participation in the recovery years 1996–2000.[32] Shifts in $\hat{\gamma}_{w*}$ are enough to explain almost 8 percent of a total increase of 12 percent occurring between 1994 and 2000.

In Appendix G, we present the simulated changes in occupation given the new set of parameters $\hat{\gamma}_{w*}$. The results are revealing. The change in participation function parameters between 1994 and 1996 made participation in the manufacturing sector more likely and quite the opposite for the nonmanufacturing sectors. This could be seen as a sign of a general increase, during the crisis years of 1995–1996, in female preferences for manufacturing sectors as opposed to the nonmanufacturing ones. Nevertheless changes in $\hat{\gamma}_{w*}$ can only explain 6 percent of the total 20 percent increase in female participation in the manufacturing sector. Hence, the observed increase in this sector after NAFTA and the Peso devaluation is explained mainly by the relative increase in returns to personal characteristics in the manufacturing sector $\hat{\boldsymbol{\beta}}_{\text{manu}}$, and to a lesser extent by changes in $\hat{\gamma}_{w*}$.

The simulated changes in $\hat{\gamma}_{w*}$ in the nonmanufacturing formal sectors follows quite closely the observed overall participation performance in those sectors. This is not the case for the informal sector, where the simulated participation is actually moving opposite the trend shown by the observed informal sector participation. This last result suggests that, although participation in the informal sector was increasing during the crisis years, this sector was seen as an unwanted option. Therefore, during the years of economic crisis, the informal sector represented a labor option that was chosen more as a mean for increasing household incomes than as a real preferred alternative.

We showed that although some of the parameters defining female reservation wage function moved in a way that favored labor participation, once we quantify their simultaneous changes, they cannot explain the observed increase in female labor participation between 1994 and 1996. During the recovery period 1996–2000, the positive change in participation is explained by an increase in expected wages (see section "Measuring the Effects of Changes in $\hat{\boldsymbol{\beta}}$"), on the one hand, and changes in women's *willingness to work* on the other. As we discussed in section "Measuring the Effects of Changes in $\hat{\boldsymbol{\beta}}$," the occupational effect of changes occurring during the crisis shows that the trade-driven buoyant manufacturing sector was absorbing most of the new entrants throughout this period.

Our microsimulation exercises undertaken in sections "Measuring the Effects of Changes in $\hat{\beta}$" and "Measuring the Effects of Changes in Ω" showed the usefulness of this type of analysis in terms of quantifying several changes occurring at the same time. Nevertheless, they also exhibit the weakness of the microsimulation analysis in a framework with few time periods and large parameter volatility.

SUMMARY AND CONCLUSIONS

We developed a structural model describing female labor participation and occupation decisions. In our model, women's participation and occupation decisions are taken in a simultaneous way, with participation decisions being embedded in the occupational one. The structural model is used to define and interpret a microeconometric model suitable for estimation. We correct for selectivity in the wage equations by parameterizing the conditional probabilities of labor participation as suggested by Lee (1983). Our model creates an explicit and causal relationship between expected selectivity-adjusted wages and participation/occupation decisions. Other factors such as the labor status of the head of the household, the number of children, and all other household members' incomes are used as controls within a generalized MNL framework.

We apply the model to Mexican urban household data for the years 1994, 1996, 1998, and 2000, respectively. The estimated wage-participation elasticity shows stability fluctuating from a lower value of 0.33 to an upper one of 0.39. Between 1994 and 2000, female participation in Mexico rose by 12 percent. Three hypotheses for the documented increase in female labor participation have been suggested and tested in this chapter: (a) a negative income shock caused by the Peso crisis of 1994–1995, (b) a trade-induced increase in female labor demand in the manufacturing sector, and (c) a change in the female reservation wage function favoring participation. The results from our micro model support all three hypotheses suggesting that the observed increase was the outcome of simultaneous and, sometimes, opposing effects being at work between 1994 and 2000.

Using microsimulation techniques, we were able to quantify the female participation/occupation effects attributable to changes in the parameters defining the participation and wage functions between 1994 and 2000. The results show that the increase in participation observed between 1994 and 1996 is partly explained by the negative income shocks of the Peso crisis. During the recovery period 1996–2000, increasing female participation is the outcome of relatively higher expected wages in the manufacturing sector and changes in women's *willingness* to work, the reservation function parameters.

There is still plenty of scope for future increases in female labor participation in Mexico. We found a significant expansion in female labor market opportunities, primarily in the export-oriented manufacturing sector. Nonmarket-related changes in women's *willingness* to work also help to explain the recent positive trend. As we have shown, women's reaction to market incentives are increasing over time, with higher wage-participation elasticities, and less labor dependency with respect to the (male) head of the household. Most of the positive shifts in female participation are explained by relative increases in real wages in trade-driven manufacturing sector. Therefore, trade policy in manufacturing-intensive less developed countries can be seen as a tool to increase female labor participation (see Bussolo & De Hoyos, 2009). The Mexican government should, therefore, promote export-oriented firms and investment, while creating training programs so that more women presently employed in informal sectors can find a place in the manufacturing industry.

NOTES

1. Elizabeth Monroy and Ricardo Charles provided useful data assistance. The usual caveat applies.
2. In the empirical section, the term utility defined here should be taken with caution since probably it embeds demand-side restrictions in the labor market, hence the observed *choice* might not be entirely the outcome of a personal utility-maximizing process.
3. To clarify the notation, λ is a scalar, γ'_j and γ_j are vectors of size K_1 and K_2 reflecting the effects of personal and household characteristics, respectively, on reservation wages measured in utility units.
4. As stated by Heckman: "Participation (or employment) decisions generally manifest greater responsiveness to wage and income variation than do hours-of-work equations for workers" (Heckman, 1993, p. 117).
5. A sufficient assumption to have a single parameter for expected wages across all outcomes is that $\gamma'_j/mib\hat{\boldsymbol{\beta}}_j = c \; \forall \; j$ where c is a constant (see Eq. (5)). This is equivalent to imposing a constant ratio of marginal market *price* of characteristics $\boldsymbol{X}_i$ relative to its subjective valuation (in terms of reservation wage) across occupations. In other words, every time personal characteristics increase their market remuneration in a particular occupation, individuals will increase, in the same proportion, their subjective valuation of them. This implies, obviously, a constant wage-participation elasticity across all individuals and occupations; this is certainly a restrictive assumption.

6. Notice that Eq. (8) imputes an estimated wage for each of the J possible occupations for each women, regardless of their working status. In the case of "nonactive," the impute wage is zero.

7. This model, as opposed to others such as the multinomial probit or the random effects model, has the drawback that it imposes the independence of irrelevant alternatives (IIA) assumption. Therefore, all our results should be analyzed bearing this restriction in mind.

8. Experience is measured as age minus years of schooling minus 6; the regional dummy variable takes the value of 1 when the state is in the north of Mexico. The mean and standard deviation of all the variables included in our model are shown in Appendix A.

9. We classify workers as being in the informal sector when they are nonprofessional self-employed workers. We exclude family workers who get no monetary remuneration (see Maloney, 1999).

10. Not active agents include women who were actively looking for a job (unemployed), not active housewives, and "other not active" (e.g., women such as pensioners and landladies). Housewives and "other not active" women account for 95 percent and 3 percent of the total inactive female population, respectively. Less than 2 percent of the female inactive population in 2000 was actively looking for a job; hence, the use of a theoretical framework where one of the utility-maximizing choices is to be inactive is, at least, a plausible first approximation of the participation decision process.

11. As it is shown in Heckman's (1979) influential paper, sample selection bias can be thought as a specification error. Including a transformation of the conditional probability of participation is enough to control for selection bias. For a more recent discussion of the advantages and disadvantages of the different ways to control for sample selection bias using a MNL, see Bourguignon et al. (2004).

12. Given the two-step nature of the procedure, all the standard errors presented in fourth section are corrected via bootstrapping methods.

13. To construct this variable, we segmented the population into different labor cohorts (education, experience, and working position); we used this information to compute the variance of all other household members' income (see Appendix B for details.)

14. In our case, a combination of a conditional and a MNL. Maddala (1983) shows that these two models are mathematically the same; hence, I will simply refer to it as a MNL.

15. Notice that expected wages in (11) are in levels so the expected wage of outcome "not active" is equal to zero.

16. Since ENIGH is not a probabilistic survey, we account for sampling design taking expansion factors, stratification, and clustering into account. All the statistical analysis carried out throughout the paper accounts for survey design (see De Hoyos (2005a) for details).

17. The actual increase in female labor participation observed between 1994 and 2000 is 1,779,105 new entrants. The difference between the net entrants (707,993) and the actual one (1,779,105) is explained by an increase in the base population, that is, by demographic and population changes as well as rural–urban migration during those years.

18. Equation (10) is estimated using our own Stata command, *svyselmlog*. *svyselmlog* is the survey version of the original *selmlog*. The command estimates the parameters of the main equation (in this case wages) correcting for selectivity using a MNL and accounting for survey design effects; several forms of selectivity correction are available. *svyselmlog* is available from the SSC (Boston College) archives (De Hoyos, 2005c).

19. Because of space limitations, we do not present the results from the first-stage estimations, Pr($\boldsymbol{X}$, $\boldsymbol{Z}$); however, they are available from the author upon request.

20. Most of the "maquiladoras" (export processing zones) created after 1994 were located in the north of Mexico (Nicita, 2009; De Hoyos & Lustig, 2009).

21. In fact, the parameters in Table 1 are the effects on the latent function determining the participation probabilities – the utility function (6); the marginal effect of $\hat{W}$ on the probability of being active is shown in Fig. 3.

22. The wage-participation elasticity figures in 1998 and 2000 are not statistically different from each other.

23. For presentational purposes, all income variables were rescaled to 1:100,000.

24. For a detailed explanation on the microsimulation technique used in this section, see Bourguignon and Ferreira (2005).

25. The income variables used in the participation functions (Y_m^0) include the sum of income of *all other* household members; hence, although they are being parameterized here, they can be seen as being strictly exogenous for each particular individual.

26. If our database was longitudinal, we wouldn't have to compute these hypothetical $\boldsymbol{Z}$ values, we could have used the *observed* change in income for each household. However, we cannot identify the same family in two different points in time; therefore, we have to simulate the *exogenous* change in household income based on the observed changes in "prices" of personal characteristics.

27. The variables determining men's wages are the same as the ones used for women ($\boldsymbol{X}$). The identification variables $\boldsymbol{Z}$ for men include the size of the household and all other household members' income and its squared form. All the estimation results for men are available from De Hoyos (2005b).

28. Although the sum of the substitution and income effects are very close to the simulation where both effects are allowed, the decomposition methodology that we use does not show additive properties. Therefore, the sum of the effects brought about by the different elements in Eq. (12) is not necessarily equal to the total effect.

29. See Appendix E with the simulated mean household income brought about by $\Delta\hat{\boldsymbol{\beta}}$.

30. This result depends very much on the nonrationed labor markets assumption; that is, labor participation and occupation decisions are purely the outcome of a utility-maximizing process and do not face labor demand restrictions.

31. At this point, is it worthwhile to remind the reader that, since we are controlling for selectivity, $\hat{\boldsymbol{\beta}}_j$ can be interpreted as a sector *j*-specific *treatment* effect; that is, a relative increase in $\hat{\boldsymbol{\beta}}$ in the manufacturing sector, compared to other sectors, is indicating a manufacturing-specific wage premium.

32. In fact, the microsimulation exercise undertaken here uncovers a weakness of this type of analysis. As we mentioned before, the microsimulation analysis relies on certain degree of parameter stability. When parameters are not stable (or not significant), it is cumbersome to make any inference based on a ceteris paribus

change in parameters between two points in time. A solution for this could be to smooth the estimated parameters with a time trend polynomial term; however, fitting a polynomial term with only four points in time tends to be a rather meaningless exercise.

ACKNOWLEDGMENTS

For their comments I am grateful to Ajit Singh, Jaime Ruiz-Tagle, Hamish Low, seminar participants at EDGE, Universita' Bocconi, Milan and two anonymous referees.

REFERENCES

Attanasio, O., Low, H., & Sánchez-Marcos, V. (2004). Female labour supply as insurance against idiosyncratic risk. *Journal of the European Economic Association, Papers and Proceedings, 3*, 755–764.

Bourguignon, F., & Ferreira, F. (2005). Decomposing changes in the distribution of household incomes: Methodological aspects. In: F. Bourguignon, F. Ferreira & N. Lustig (Eds.), *The microeconomics of income distribution dynamics in East Asia and Latin America*. New York: Oxford University Press.

Bourguignon, F., Fournier, M., & Gurgand, M. (2004). Selection bias correction based on the multinomial logit model: Monte-Carlo comparisons. *Mimeo* DELTA, Paris.

Bussolo, M., & De Hoyos, R. E. (Eds.). (2009). *Gender aspects of the trade and poverty nexus: A macro-micro approach*. London: Palgrave Macmillan.

Deaton, A., & Muellbauer, J. (1980). *Economics and consumer behavior*. New York, NY: Cambridge University Press.

De Hoyos, R., & Lustig, N. (2009). Apertura comercial, desigualdad y pobreza. Reseña de los enfoques metodológicos, el estado del conocimiento y la asignatura pendiente. *El Trimestre Económico*, *LXXVI*(302), 283–328 (abril-jun).

De Hoyos, R. E. (2005a). Constructing inequality and poverty indexes using Mexican ENIGH. Retrieved from http://www.econ.cam.ac.uk/phd/red29/

De Hoyos, R. E. (2005b). *The microeconomics of inequality, poverty and market liberalizing reforms. UNU-WIDER* Resaerch Paper 2005/63, Helsinki.

De Hoyos, R. E. (2005c). *SVYSELMLOG: Stata module to compute selectivity adjustment based on the multinomial logit for survey design. Statistical Software Components*, no. S454901, Boston: Boston College.

Dubin, J. A., & McFadden, D. (1984). An econometric analysis of residential electric appliance holdings and consumption. *Econometrica*, *52*, 2.

Gong, X., & van Soest, A. (2002). Wage differentials and mobility in the urban labor market: A panel data analysis for Mexico. *Labor Economics*, *9*, 513–529.

Gong, X., van Soest, A., & Villagomez, E. (2000). *Mobility in the urban labor market: A panel data analysis for Mexico*. CentER discussion paper. Tilburg University, Tilburg, The Netherlands.

Heckman, J. (1974). Shadow prices, market wages and labor supply. *Econometrica, 42*, 4.

Heckman, J. (1979). Sample selection bias as a specification error. *Econometrica, 47*, 1.

Heckman, J. (1993). What has been learned about labor supply in the past twenty years? *The American Economic Review, 83*, 2.

Heckman, J., & Honore, B. E. (1990). The empirical content of the Roy model. *Econometrica, 58*, 5.

Heckman, J., & Sedlacek, G. (1985). Heterogeneity, aggregation, and market wage functions: An empirical model of self-selelction in the labor market. *Econometrica, 93*, 6.

Lee, L. F. (1983). Generalized econometric models with selectivity. *Econometrica, 51*, 507–512.

Maddala, G. (1983). *Limited dependent and quantitative variables in econometrics*. Cambridge: Cambridge University Press.

Maloney, W. (1999). Does informality imply segmentation in urban labor markets? Evidence from sectoral transitions in Mexico. *The World Bank Economic Review, 13*, 2.

Marcouiller, D., Ruiz, V., & Woodruff, C. (1997). Formal measures of the informal sector wage gap in Mexico, El Salvador, and Peru. *Economic Development and Cultural Change, 45*, 2.

McFadden, D. (1974). The measurement of urban travel demand. *Journal of Public Economics, 3*.

Nicita, A. (2009). The price effect of tariff liberalization: Measuring the impact on household welfare. *Journal of Development Economics, 89*(1), 19–27.

Roy, A. D. (1951). Some thoughts on the distribution of earnings. *Oxford Economic Papers, 3*.

van Soest, A. (1995). Structural models of family labor supply. *The Journal of Human Resources, XXX*(1), 63–88.

APPENDIX A: DESCRIPTIVE STATISTICS OF THE VARIABLES USED IN THE MODEL

	1994	1996	1998	2000
Notactive				
Hourly wages (W)	0	0	0	0
Hours worked	0	0	0	0
Children	0.823	0.852	0.770	0.718
	(0.983)	(0.985)	(0.949)	(0.913)
H_s^a	0.642	0.637	0.655	0.664
	(0.479)	(0.481)	(0.475)	(0.472)
H_d^a	0.157	0.168	0.149	0.133
	(0.364)	(0.374)	(0.356)	(0.340)
Y_m^0	0.119	0.083	0.083	0.098
	(0.158)	(0.14)	(0.094)	(0.121)
$(Y_m^0)^2$	0.039	0.027	0.016	0.024
	(0.457)	(0.595)	(0.079)	(0.120)
$Var(Y_m^0)$	11.271	6.717	9.867	6.629
	(79.472)	(129.104)	(59.598)	(60.599)
Schooling	6.790	7.059	7.160	7.549
	(3.824)	(3.759)	(3.756)	(3.878)
Schooling * $I(Y_s > 11)$	1.842	1.675	1.656	2.257
	(4.624)	(4.561)	(4.556)	(5.187)
Experience	22.753	22.387	23.194	23.533
	(15.171)	(14.978)	(14.93)	(14.826)
Experience	747.855	725.535	760.869	773.648
	(827.305)	(807.355)	(814.037)	(805.865)
North	0.336	0.352	0.368	0.368
	(0.472)	(0.478)	(0.482)	(0.482)
Manufacturing earner (tradable)				
Hourly wages (W)	2.807	2.468	2.536	2.752
	0.845	0.891	0.874	0.839
Hours worked	47.422	47.473	47.414	47.181
	10.736	10.520	9.486	9.526
Children	0.489	0.631	0.590	0.629
	(0.780)	(0.985)	(0.856)	(0.884)
H_s^a	0.341	0.314	0.343	0.331
	(0.474)	(0.481)	(0.475)	(0.471)

	1994	1996	1998	2000
H_d^a	0.319	0.359	0.337	0.391
	(0.466)	(0.374)	(0.473)	(0.488)
Y_m^0	0.091	0.059	0.062	0.065
	(0.102)	(0.14)	(0.077)	(0.052)
$(Y_m^0)^2$	0.019	0.006	0.010	0.007
	(0.082)	(0.595)	(0.051)	(0.013)
$Var(Y_m^0)$	14.770	7.275	17.130	1.931
	(74.576)	(129.104)	(157.016)	(7.756)
Schooling	8.539	8.252	8.428	8.435
	(3.279)	(3.759)	(3.268)	(3.307)
Schooling * $\mathrm{I}(Y_s > 11)$	2.663	1.961	2.158	2.051
	(5.463)	(4.561)	(5.136)	(5.015)
Experience	12.963	14.134	13.830	14.231
	(10.555)	(14.978)	(10.740)	(11.205)
Experience	279.455	328.551	306.611	328.067
	(432.293)	(807.355)	(437.686)	(483.550)
North	0.495	0.434	0.508	0.597
	(0.500)	(0.478)	(0.500)	(0.490)
Other earner (nontradable)				
Hourly wages (*W*)	2.985	2.623	2.633	2.819
	0.964	0.930	0.984	0.905
Hours worked	45.219	45.551	45.273	45.292
	14.753	14.929	15.042	14.230
Children	0.590	0.574	0.569	0.467
	(0.873)	(0.845)	(0.876)	(0.767)
H_s^a	0.371	0.407	0.404	0.416
	(0.483)	(0.491)	(0.491)	(0.493)
H_d^a	0.296	0.224	0.268	0.245
	(0.456)	(0.417)	(0.443)	(0.430)
Y_m^0	0.110	0.074	0.078	0.089
	(0.124)	(0.093)	(0.110)	(0.097)
$(Y_m^0)^2$	0.028	0.014	0.018	0.017
	(0.101)	(0.126)	(0.241)	(0.070)
$Var(Y_m^0)$	25.756	74.821	37.540	11.889
	(140.278)	(2496.283)	(336.419)	(55.853)
Schooling	9.643	9.911	9.870	10.386
	(4.516)	(4.427)	(4.549)	(4.426)

	1994	1996	1998	2000
Schooling * $I(Y_s > 11)$	5.593	5.430	5.327	5.959
	(7.081)	(7.181)	(7.254)	(7.449)
Experience	16.141	16.989	16.923	17.237
	(11.76)	(11.877)	(12.393)	(12.266)
Experience^2	398.827	429.702	439.974	447.570
	(520.172)	(537.881)	(559.289)	(541.501)
North	0.351	0.332	0.335	0.325
	(0.477)	(0.471)	(0.472)	(0.468)
Informal sector				
Hourly wages (W)	2.491	2.068	2.113	1.985
	1.072	1.533	1.833	1.197
Hours worked	42.293	40.973	40.815	41.461
	21.766	21.321	21.387	19.898
Children	0.666	0.674	0.615	0.580
	(0.842)	(0.885)	(0.893)	(0.824)
H_s^a	0.529	0.529	0.549	0.560
	(0.499)	(0.499)	(0.498)	(0.496)
H_d^a	0.073	0.077	0.088	0.069
	(0.261)	(0.267)	(0.284)	(0.254)
Y_m^0	0.068	0.047	0.054	0.056
	(0.075)	(0.045)	(0.058)	(0.048)
$(Y_m^0)^2$	0.010	0.004	0.006	0.005
	(0.035)	(0.011)	(0.025)	(0.011)
$Var(Y_m^0)$	17.697	4.605	27.901	7.383
	(104.926)	(21.75)	(251.354)	(41.474)
Schooling	5.761	5.856	6.195	6.535
	(3.811)	(3.947)	(3.929)	(4.017)
Schooling * $I(Y_s > 11)$	1.319	1.180	1.322	1.561
	(3.919)	(3.945)	(4.161)	(4.404)
Experience	28.577	27.446	27.725	28.412
	(13.885)	(13.671)	(13.611)	(13.332)
Experience	1009.462	940.149	953.938	985.005
	(860.215)	(796.212)	(792.715)	(807.199)
North	0.357	0.325	0.308	0.302
	(0.479)	(0.468)	(0.461)	(0.459)

Note: Standard errors in parenthesis.

APPENDIX B: MEASURING HOUSEHOLD INCOME VARIANCE

To estimate the way in which household income variations affects female labor participation, we have to construct a variable able to capture variations in household incomes as *perceived* by *each* household member. Let us start by defining a measure of household income variance. In a cross-sectional framework, we cannot estimate the time variation in household incomes; therefore, we have to use the observed variation within socioeconomic and demographic groups. These groups were defined according to the following observable characteristics: gender, formal education, experience, and position in their working place. The combination of these characteristics formed a total of 263 groups each of them containing different average income (μ) and variance [Var(Y)]. Household income variance is computed using the within population cohorts variance. The way in which the population cohort and the household variances are linked must be consistent with a measure of household variance showing some desired properties. Following Attanasio, Low, and Sánchez-Marcos (2004), we define Axiom 1:

> **Axiom 1.** In the presence of borrowing constraints, where rational agents' optimal choice is to smooth consumption, women's participation probability increases as a response to a rise in the *expected* variance of household incomes. Therefore, the *observed* income variance of a household whose female member is active should be smaller than the one that we would have observed had participation not occurred.

Our preferred measure of household income should comply with Axiom 1. It turned out that the measure of household income variance that we propose here satisfies Axiom 1.

While forming income variance expectations, agents are aware of all other household members' characteristics; for example, a household wife knows the characteristics of her husband and children. Assume that the mean income and variance attached to each of the 262 population cohorts is constant over time and that this information is known by each of the

Table B.1. Average Income and Variance.

	Men	Women
μ	4,704	3,358
$Var(Y)$	5.24e+07	1.14e+07

household members. In the process of deciding whether to participate in the labor market or not, agents form their personal *perception* of what the variance of household income will be. This personal *perception* is the expected value of the variance of all other household members' income. For agents who are not participating in the labor market:

$$\mathrm{Var}(Y_h^i) = \sum_j^m \frac{\mu_j}{\sum_j^m \mu_j} \mathrm{Var}(Y_j) \quad \forall\ j = 1...m : \text{Active Members} \tag{14}$$

Each nonactive household member's expectation will be a weighted average of income variance of all active members. The weight assigned to each active member *j* is formed by the average income within *j*'s population cohort divided by the sum of average incomes of all population cohorts where active household members belong to. In the case of active members, the expected variance will be formed by the variance that they would observe if they decided to abandon the labor market. This is equivalent to create a household income variance with the following counterfactual: what would the variance look like had the agent decided not to participate. This definition of variance for the active members is comparable to the one computed for nonactive members, since it is computing the household variance as if the active member became not active:

$$\mathrm{Var}(Y_h^{i'}) = \sum_j^{m-1} \frac{\mu_j}{\sum_j^{m-1} \mu_j} \mathrm{Var}(Y_j) \quad \forall\ j = 1...m : \text{Active Members} \tag{15}$$

Given our definition of household income variance, a sufficient condition for it to satisfy Axiom 1 is:

Axiom 2. The population cohort variance [Var(*Y*)] of the marginal women entering the labor market is smaller than the observed weighted average values for all other household members.

If Axiom 2 is true, then the counterfactual variance – that is, the variance in the absence of their participation – for participating women will be larger than the observed one. Equivalently, the total household income variance should decrease as an outcome of their participation. If Axiom 1 is true and this information is known by female household members, then participating in the labor market is a consumption-smoothing decision. This is exactly the property stated by Axiom 1. For the Mexican labor market, Axiom 2 turns out to be an empirical regularity; that is, the observed income variance within female population subgroups is less than the observed statistic for male subgroups.

APPENDIX C: SELECTIVITY-ADJUSTED WAGES

Table C.1. Wage Functions for the Manufacturing Sector.

	1994	1996	1998	2000
Schooling	0.138***	0.105***	0.149***	0.111***
Schooling * $I(Y_s > 11)$	−0.004	0.022*	0.003	0
Experience	0.068***	0.042***	0.071***	0.031**
Experience^2	−0.001***	−0.001**	−0.001***	0
North	0.074	0.141**	0.269***	0.333***
Pr(manufacture)†	0.275	0.142	−0.076	0.105
Intercept	0.355	0.579*	0.295	0.801**
R^2	0.267	0.246	0.28	0.236
N	491	609	511	428

Notes:
*, **, *** significant at the 10 percent, 5 percent, and 1 percent level, respectively.
Bootstrapped standard errors with 200 replications.
Data source: ENIGH 1994, 1996, 1998, and 2000.
Pr(·)† are computed accordingly to Eq. (10).

Table C.2. Wage Functions for Other Earning Sectors.

	1994	1996	1998	2000
Schooling	0.148***	0.136***	0.143***	0.131***
*Schooling** $I(Y_s > 11)$	0.020***	0.014***	0.021***	0.011*
Experience	0.077***	0.069***	0.060***	0.057***
Experience^2	−0.001***	−0.001***	−0.001***	−0.001***
North	−0.046	0.004	0.083*	0.105**
Pr(other earner)†	0.290***	0.245***	0.243*	0.065
Intercept	0.337**	0.21	0.059	0.637***
R^2	0.468	0.374	0.409	0.402
N	2,213	2,393	1,950	1,850

Notes:
*, **, *** significant at the 10 percent, 5 percent, and 1 percent level, respectively.
Bootstrapped standard errors with 200 replications.
Data source: ENIGH 1994, 1996, 1998, and 2000.
Pr(·)† are computed accordingly to Eq. (10).

Table C.3. Wage Functions for the Informal Sector.

	1994	1996	1998	2000
Schooling	0.081***	0.064***	0.052**	0.037
Schooling $I(Y_s > 11)$	0.013	0.004	0.034*	0.026
Experience	0.023	0.046***	0.033*	0.063**
Experience^2	0.0	−0.001**	0.0	−0.001*
North	−0.124	0.034	−0.076	−0.096
Pr(informal)†	0.062	0.364	0.143	0.701*
Intercept	1.368**	0.272	0.902	−0.23
R^2	0.053	0.062	0.052	0.084
N	620	857	663	581

Notes:
*, **, *** significant at the 10 percent, 5 percent, and 1 percent level, respectively.
Bootstrapped standard errors with 200 replications.
Data source: ENIGH 1994, 1996, 1998, and 2000.
$\Pr(\cdot)^\dagger$ are computed accordingly to Eq. (10).

APPENDIX D: GOODNESS OF FIT OF THE MODEL

Table D.1. Proportion of Correct Predictions by Sociodemographic Group (%).

		1994	1996	1998	2000
Age	1	65.3	63.0	60.1	60.7
	0	60.2	59.7	57.5	57.3
Years of schooling	1	59.8	59.8	58.7	61.7
	0	64.0	62.5	59.4	59.9
Income	1	85.9	89.0	86.6	86.1
	0	24.0	26.6	27.9	27.5
Household size	1	63.5	61.1	58.9	61.5
	0	62.8	62.1	59.2	57.0
Head	1	48.3	47.2	45.2	45.4
	0	64.8	63.5	61.0	61.4

Notes:
All sociodemographic characteristics are captured by dummy variables.
"Age"' gets the value of 1 if woman is 30 years or older.
"Years of schooling"' get the value of 1 if woman has 11 or more years of formal schooling.
"Income"' gets the value of 1 if personal monthly income is higher than $5,000.
"Household size" gets the value of 1 if the household is composed of 4 or more members.

APPENDIX E: SIMULATED HOUSEHOLD INCOME EFFECTS OF $\Delta\hat{\beta}$

In order to capture within-household participation effects of $\Delta\hat{\beta}$ we parameterize household incomes, including female and male members. We assume that men's participation decisions are independent from all other household member's labor status. Female household members, on the other hand, decide whether to enter the labor market or not taking into account all other household member's income (Y_m^0) and the head of the household labor status (H^a). H^a and Y_m^0 are endogenous once full household incomes have been parameterized. Hence, an economy-wide shock on $\hat{\beta}$ will have an effect on these two variables. In the next table, we show the simulated values of H^a and Y_m^0 for the different estimated values of β. The change in remunerations to personal characteristics resulted in an increase in male participation – the result is totally explained by increases in manufacturing expected wages. Therefore, had the change in β been the only change occurring between 1994 and 1996, the proportion of active men would have increased from 88.8 percent to 92.1 percent. The simulated values correspond with the observed increase in the male participation rate between 1994 and 1998. Regarding simulated Y_m^0, the trend is following very closely the observed path, with a huge negative shock between 1994 and 1996 and a gradual recovery thereafter. The advantage of the microsimulation over a simple distributional-neutral change in average incomes is that we can capture the changes in each and every household in our dataset. Hence, we do not need to assume that overall economy shocks have an homogeneous effect on every household.

	1994	1996	1998	2000
H^a				
Observed	0.888	0.889	0.902	0.920
Simulated	–	0.921	0.929	0.843
Y_m^0				
Observed	10,955	7,539	7,825	8,912
Simulated	–	7,091	7,950	8,807

Income figures are in real Pesos of August 2002.

APPENDIX F: SIMULATED OCCUPATION EFFECT OF $\Delta\hat{\beta}$

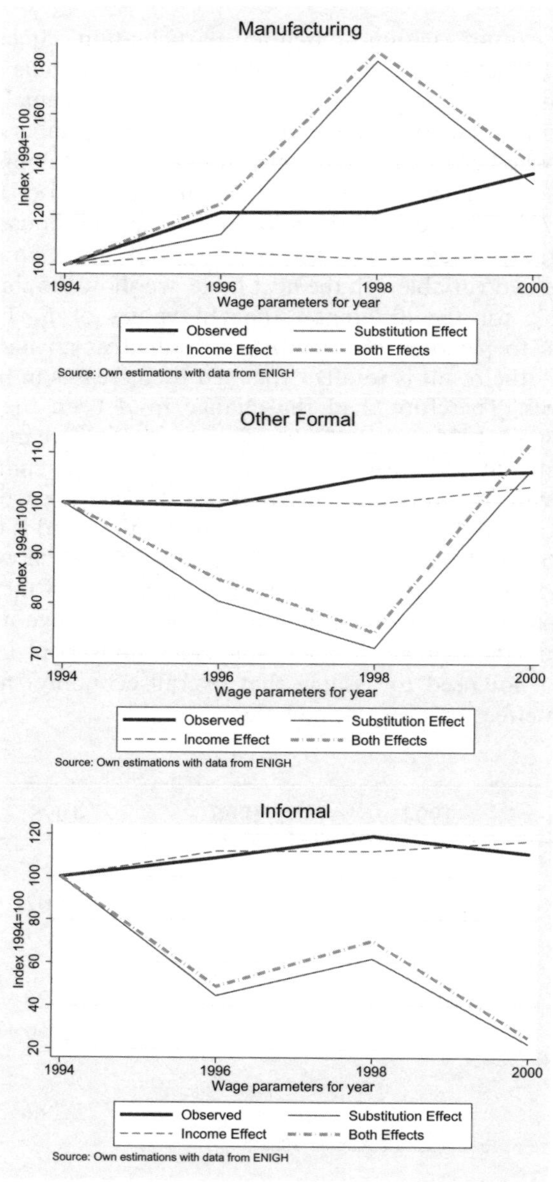

APPENDIX G: SIMULATED OCCUPATION EFFECT OF $\Delta\Omega$

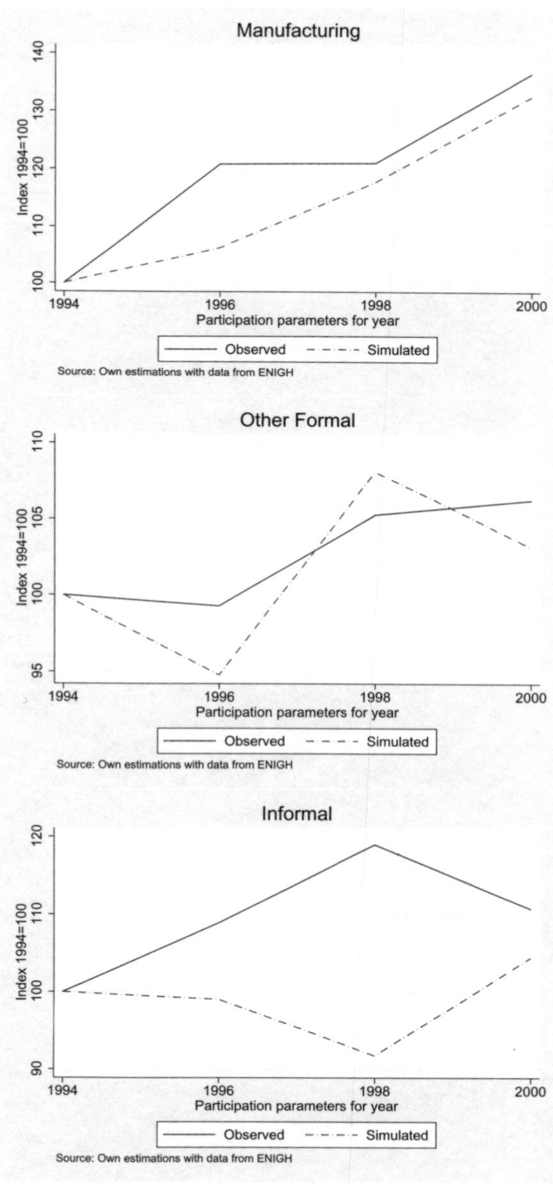

CHAPTER 4

A RISK AUGMENTED MINCER EARNINGS EQUATION? TAKING STOCK

Joop Hartog[☆]

ABSTRACT

We survey the literature on the Risk Augmented Mincer equation that seeks to estimate the compensation for uncertainty in the future wage to be earned after completing an education. There is wide empirical support for the predicted positive effect of wage variance and the negative effect of wage skew. We discuss robustness of the findings across specifications, potential bias from unobserved heterogeneity and selectivity and consider the core issue of students' information on benefits from education.

Keywords: Wages; human capital; risk; compensating differentials

JEL classifications: J31; D8

☆This paper is based on a research project in cooperation with Simona Bajdechi Raita, Peter Berkhout, Jose Cabral Vieira, Luis Diaz Serrano, Bas Jacobs, Helena Skyt Nielsen, Hans van Ophem, Erik Plug, Juerg Schweri, Wim Vijverberg, Dinand Webbink, Stefan Wolter

Research in Labor Economics, Volume 33, 129–173

ISSN: 0147-9121/doi:10.1108/S0147-9121(2011)0000033007

BASIC HYPOTHESIS

Suppose, individuals can either go to work or first go to school for five years. The post-school log wage is 0.325 higher than the wage from going straight to work. Then, in the basic Mincer framework[1] the rate of return to schooling would be 6.5%. Now suppose, the direct, unschooled wage is fixed, but the post-school wage is uncertain, at a realistically modest standard deviation of 0.25. Then, if an individual would make it to one standard deviation above the mean in the post-school distribution, the rate of return would be 11.3%, but if he would not reach above one standard deviation below the mean, his return would not surpass 1.3%. Instead of a single return of 6.5% for everyone, two-thirds of all individuals would have a return somewhere in the wide interval between 1.3% and 11. 3%.

Of course, the essential question would be which part of this variation is risk and which part is known to the student but hidden as unobserved heterogeneity to the outsider. Yet, there can be no doubt that the decision to engage in an education is a decision under uncertainty. There are at least three dimensions in which information is incomplete. The potential student will generally not fully grasp the requirements of the school curriculum and of the occupations available after graduation, she will usually not even be fully sure of her own abilities and preferences and she will not know what the exact returns to the investment will be. With uncertainties so prominent, one is inevitably led to expect that the returns to education will be shaped not only by compensation for postponing earnings but also by compensation for risk. In fact, however, the basic Mincer earnings equation is derived under conditions of certainty on future earnings in the alternatives and the estimations similarly ignore the impact of uncertainty. Research on returns to education has focussed for decades on getting an unbiased estimate of the causal effect of schooling on earnings. Main emphasis is on the proper econometric modelling to deal with omitted ability bias, measurement errors in education and the endogeneity of the schooling decision. Admittedly, these are serious and stubborn problems, as illustrated by the fact that the dust has not settled down and that there is as yet no consensus on true, causal, rates of return to education and their variation in response to individual and institutional conditions. Perhaps all we can be confident about is an interval of the return for an additional year of education between a few percent to an upper limit of some 20%.

With uncertainty so prominent, one might have thought that there is a large literature to deal with it. In fact, analyses investigating the consequences of uncertain completion of an education, incomplete information on abilities and even preferences and on the poor predictability of the career development that comes with an education are very scarce.[2] This chapter can only make a small contribution, by treating just one aspect of the pervasively present uncertainty. We focus on the notion that an individual contemplating an education does not anticipate a given post-school wage rate but rather an entire wage *distribution*, without knowing exactly where in that distribution she will end up. As the individual perceives that the returns to his investment are not certain, he will demand compensation. This chapter is about the existence and magnitude of a risk premium in the returns to education. It turns out that a basic idea on an econometric approach to this problem has been around for a long time.[3] The literature has started with King (1974), who used aggregate data by occupation to estimate the effect of variance and skew of wages within an occupation on the mean occupational wage. The variance of earnings is taken as a measure of risk that individuals want compensation for. Positive skewness of the earnings distribution points to the opportunity of attaining real high earnings and this is something people want to pay for with reduced expected earnings. With microdata one may proceed in two steps. First, estimate a standard Mincer earnings equation, group the residuals by education–occupation classification and take the within-group distribution of residuals as indicating the uncertainty associated with choosing the particular education–occupation combination. In the second stage, add the variance of these education–occupation residuals to the earnings function and estimate risk compensation as the regression coefficient of earnings on the variances. The two-stage approach was first applied by McGoldrick (1995). Following King (1974), she also included the skew of residuals by occupation in the regression equation.

Compensation for earnings risk has now been estimated in close to 20 studies. Generally, the studies report an earnings premium for risk and a rebate for skew, as theory predicts. In this chapter, we review these studies and assess the evidence so far. In the second section, we present a formal model underlying the estimations, in third section the empirical specifications. In fourth section, we present estimation results. Fifth section addresses the problems of bias from heterogeneity and presents estimates that control for these problems. Sixth section considers self-selection and the information set that potential students have. Seventh section presents supporting evidence, and eighth section discusses alternative explanations for our results. Ninth section wraps up, with conclusions and a research agenda.

A SIMPLE FORMAL MODEL

To derive the compensation for earnings postponement and for accepting earnings uncertainty, we will first consider schooling choice under utility maximisation rather than earnings maximisation (which is unavoidable if we analyse uncertainty in a utility framework). In the next stage, we will examine earnings uncertainty proper.

Utility Maximisation in the Absence of Uncertainty

Individuals face two alternatives: go straight to work and earn an annual non-stochastic income Y_0 for the rest of their working life, or go to school for s years, and then after school earn a non-stochastic income Y_s for the rest of their working life. We assume individuals have an uninhibited choice between alternatives. In equilibrium, lifetime utility should be equal. We seek to derive the premium M_s that accomplishes equilibrium, hence

$$Y_0 = (1 - M_s)Y_s \tag{1}$$

that is, M_s is the mark-off on Y_s to equate lifetime utility. Discounting at a rate δ and setting utility of zero income at zero, we get

$$\int_0^\infty U(Y_0)e^{-\delta t}\,\mathrm{d}t = \int_s^\infty U(Y_s)e^{-\delta t}\,\mathrm{d}t \tag{2}$$

where $U(Y)$ is a standard utility function. With time-independent income (and utility) this solves into

$$U(Y_0) = e^{-\delta s}U(Y_s) \tag{3}$$

A simple first-order expansion of $U(Y_0)$ around Y_s generates

$$\begin{aligned} U(Y_0) &= U(Y_s) + (Y_0 - Y_s)U'(Y_s) \\ &= U(Y_s) - M_s Y_s U'(Y_s) \end{aligned} \tag{4}$$

Combining (3) and (4) yields the solution for M_s:

$$M_s = \left(1 - e^{-\delta s}\right)\frac{U(Y_s)}{U'(Y_s)}\frac{1}{Y_s} \tag{5}$$

Clearly, this is a generalisation of Mincer's earnings function. The last two terms jointly are the inverse of the income elasticity of utility. Under earnings maximisation, $U(Y) = Y$, and (5) reduces to the term in parentheses, implying $\ln Y_s = \ln Y_0 + \delta s$, the standard Mincer equation.

Assuming a constant income elasticity of utility simplifies Eq. (5). Specifically, with constant relative risk aversion (CRRA).

$$U(Y) = \frac{1}{1-\rho} Y^{1-\rho} \tag{6}$$

we get

$$M_s = \frac{1 - e^{-\delta s}}{1-\rho} \tag{7}$$

In an expected utility framework, monetary returns will be depreciated by the declining marginal utility of income.

Uncertainty: Risk Aversion and Skewness Affection

Consider an individual who must choose between two options, one with a fixed income Y^* and the other with random income Y at an expected income of $E[Y] = \mu$. Define Θ as the generalised absolute risk premium: $\Theta = E[Y] - Y^* = \mu - Y^*$: an individual in the risky situation receives an expected income that exceeds the income of the risk-free activity by an amount of Θ.

We seek to establish the equilibrium risk premium Θ, that is, the gap between expected income in both positions at which a utility maximising individual is indifferent between the two positions. Utility is defined again as a continuous differentiable function of income $U(Y)$, with $\partial U/\partial Y > 0$. We also assume risk aversion $\partial^2 U/\partial Y^2 < 0$. Indifference requires

$$U(\mu - \Theta) = E[U(Y)] \text{ with } E[Y] = \mu \tag{8}$$

To solve for Θ, we follow Pratt (1964, his Eqs. (4)–(7)). For the left-hand side of (8), we write

$$U(\mu - \Theta) = U(\mu) - \Theta U'(\mu) \tag{9}$$

where $U'(\mu)$ is $\partial U/\partial Y$ evaluated at $Y = \mu$. For the right-hand side, we retain one more term than Pratt did in his Taylor series expansion:

$$U(Y) = U(\mu) + (Y-\mu)U'(\mu) + \frac{1}{2}(Y-\mu)^2 U''(\mu) + \frac{1}{6}(Y-\mu)^3 U'''(\mu) \tag{10}$$

where $U''(\mu) = \partial^2 U/\partial Y^2$ evaluated at $Y = \mu$, and $U'''(\mu) = \partial^3 U/\partial Y^3$ at $Y = \mu$.

Hence

$$E[U(Y)] = U(\mu) + \frac{1}{2}m_2U''(\mu) + \frac{1}{6}m_3U'''(\mu) \tag{11}$$

since $E[Y] = \mu$, and with m_2 and m_3 defining the second and third moments of Y (the variance and the skewness) around μ. Equating (9) and (11), we are now able to solve for Θ:

$$\Theta = \frac{1}{2}V_a m_2 + \frac{1}{6}V_a \frac{U'''(\mu)}{U''(\mu)} m_3 \tag{12}$$

where $V_a = -U''(\mu)/U'(\mu)$ is the degree of absolute risk aversion. If, by analogy to risk aversion, we define absolute skewness affection as $F_a = -U'''(\mu)/U''(\mu)$, we may write

$$\Theta = \frac{1}{2}V_a m_2 - \frac{1}{6}V_a F_a m_3 \tag{13}$$

Eq. (13) is the standard equation for a risk premium as derived by Pratt (1964) and Arrow (1965), but now expanded with skewness affection. In this chapter, we refer to the second moment as risk.

The sensitivity of absolute risk aversion to income (or wealth) Y can be derived as follows:

$$\frac{\mathrm{d}}{\mathrm{d}Y}\left[-\frac{U''}{U'}\right] = \frac{-U'U''' + (U'')^2}{(U')^2} \tag{14}$$

As Arrow (1965) argues, increasing absolute risk aversion is an absurd assumption, as it would imply investing less in risky alternatives if income (wealth) increases. Assuming the same holds for choice in the labour market, we require *decreasing* absolute risk aversion: the expression in Eq. (14) ought to be negative. For this to hold, a necessary but not sufficient condition is $U''' > 0$, as was first pointed out by Tsiang (1972, p. 359): 'Thus, if we regard the phenomenon of increasing absolute risk aversion as absurd, we must acknowledge that a normal risk-averse individual would have a preference for skewness in addition to an aversion to dispersion (variance) of the probability distribution of returns'. Since, for a risk averter, V_a is positive and since F_a is positive if we assume decreasing absolute risk aversion, we conclude from (13) that the absolute risk premium Θ is positive in risk (variance) and negative in skewness. This motivates our terminology of skewness affection; for evidence on skewness affection from choices made in gambling and betting, see Garrett and Sobel (1999) and Golec and Tamarkin (1998). In the literature on lifetime wealth accumulation, skewness affection is called prudence (Gollier, 2001, p. 238).

The empirical model derives more naturally when the compensation for uncertainty is expressed through a relative, rather than absolute, risk premium. It is straightforward to rewrite (13) as an equation for the generalised relative risk premium $\Pi = \Theta/\mu$ (and hence, $Y^* = (1 - \Pi)\mu$). Dividing (13) by μ and slightly rewriting yields

$$\Pi = \frac{\Theta}{\mu} = \frac{1}{2} V_r \frac{m_2}{\mu^2} - \frac{1}{6} V_r F_r \frac{m_3}{\mu^3} \tag{15}$$

where relative risk aversion is given by

$$V_r = V_a \mu = -\frac{U''(\mu)}{U'(\mu)} \mu > 0$$

and relative skewness affection by

$$F_r = F_a \mu = -\frac{U'''(\mu)}{U''(\mu)} \mu > 0$$

Note that without further assumptions, V_r and F_r depend on μ. But under CRRA as in Eq. (6), we would have $V_r = \rho$ and $F_r = \rho + 1$; thus the relative risk premium would be constant.

Combining Earnings Postponement and Uncertainty

Now, let us apply the risk compensation argument in the context of the Mincer framework. We know that there are two compensation arguments: earnings postponement and uncertainty compensation. In a non-stochastic world, as lifetime post-school income Y_s^f would be equivalent with a lifetime income of Y_0. However, after s years of schooling the individual in our case faces a stochastic income Y_s, with expectation $E[Y_s] = \mu_s$ and second and third moments around the mean m_{2s} and m_{3s}. We now seek the risk premium on this fixed post-school income that would compensate for the earnings uncertainty. We express this as a mark-off on the expected income in the risky situation, that is, we replace Y_s^f by $(1 - \Pi_s)\mu_s$ where, as before, Π_s is the risk premium. Lifetime equal utility requires

$$\int_s^\infty U\big((1 - \Pi_s)\mu_s\big) e^{-\delta t}\, \mathrm{d}t = E\left[\int_s^\infty U(Y_s) e^{-\delta t}\, \mathrm{d}t\right] \tag{16}$$

Clearly, the discounting factors drop out as income is as yet time independent. Expanding the left-hand side around μ_s in first order, and the right-hand side around μ_s up to the third order, the earlier result simply re-appears, and we can write

$$\Pi_s = \frac{1}{2}\frac{m_{2s}}{\mu_s^2} V_r - \frac{1}{6}\frac{m_{3s}}{\mu_s^3} V_r F_r \tag{17}$$

We now combine compensation for schooling and for risk by writing the non-stochastic earnings option as a Mincer mark-up on the riskless no-schooling alternative. Thus, we write

$$E[Y_s] = \mu_s = (1 - \Pi_s)^{-1}(1 - M_s)^{-1} Y_0 \tag{18}$$

Suppose, we apply the CRRA simplification, such that

$$M_s = \frac{1 - e^{-\delta s}}{1 - \rho} \tag{19}$$

$$\Pi_s = \frac{1}{2}\frac{m_{2s}}{\mu_s^2}\rho - \frac{1}{6}\rho(\rho + 1)\frac{m_{3s}}{\mu_s^3} \tag{20}$$

and we take Taylor expansions

$$-\ln(1 - M_s) = -\ln\left(1 - \frac{1 - e^{-\delta s}}{1 - \rho}\right) \approx -\ln\left(1 - \frac{\delta s}{1 - \rho}\right) \approx \frac{\delta s}{1 - \rho} \tag{21}$$

$$-\ln(1 - \Pi_s) \approx \Pi_s \tag{22}$$

Furthermore, rewrite the second- and third-order terms in Eq. (17):

$$\frac{m_{2s}}{\mu_s^2} = \frac{E\left[(Y_s - \mu_s)^2\right]}{\mu_s^2} = E\left[\left(\frac{Y_s - \mu_s}{\mu_s}\right)^2\right] \tag{23}$$

$$\frac{m_{3s}}{\mu_s^3} = \frac{E\left[(Y_s - \mu_s)^3\right]}{\mu_s^3} = E\left[\left(\frac{Y_s - \mu_s}{\mu_s}\right)^3\right] \tag{24}$$

Then, the earnings function would read

$$E(\ln Y_s) = \ln Y_o + \frac{\delta}{1-\rho}s + \frac{1}{2}\rho\frac{m_{2s}}{\mu_s^2} - \frac{1}{6}\rho(\rho+1)\frac{m_{3s}}{\mu_s^3} \tag{25}$$

which is a simple equation in schooling years, variance term (23) and skewness term (24). Hence with observations on relative variance and relative skewness, we could estimate a Mincer earnings equation augmented with risk compensation, the *Risk Augmented Mincer* equation (RAM). Wages respond positively to risk and negatively to skewness when individuals decide on an education based on their knowledge of the second and third moment of the wage distribution associated with an education. If we don't assume CRRA, the parameters of (25) will not be constant but depend on income levels. However, as a linearisation, it would still be a good starting point for empirical work.[4]

By necessity, the model is a simplification. It is an extension, with stochastic rather than deterministic post-school earnings, of the framework specified by Jacob Mincer, still the basis for all routine estimates of returns to education. Mincer (1974, pp. 9–11) did not even bother to spell out the strong underlying assumptions on market structure, individual abilities and information, except for a brief reference in the introduction. More elaborate estimates of the causal effect of schooling on earnings are often based on Card (1999). Card's model endogenises schooling, allows for unobserved heterogeneity in individuals' cost and benefits but does not allow for any imperfect information by individuals: they know all their cost and their prospective returns with certainty. Card's problem is an ignorant researcher looking at an omniscient individual. His model serves his purpose, but it is not the single best model to serve all purposes. Clearly, in our model we make very strong assumptions. But so did Mincer and so did Card. In fact, our model is quite similar to Levhari and Weiss (1974), the seminal paper on human capital investment under uncertainty. They also use a two-period model with uncertain second period returns to investment made in the first period. As shown in Appendix A, our basic equation can also be derived from their model.

A key assumption of our approach is that individuals cannot insure the risk of their investment. To us, this is obvious. We simply do not observe individuals commencing a college education and at the same time buying insurance or an optimal investment portfolio that completely eliminates the risk of their venture. Davis and Willen (2000) assume they would do so and compute optimal portfolios for some occupations. They find completely unrealistic values. For example, a 40-year old truck driver (in 1982) should hold a portfolio of \$550,000, including a short position in one portfolio of \$141,000. Our view is shared by, for example, Blanchard and Fisher (1989, p. 283) and by Shaw (1996, p. 626) who states: 'The methods of reducing riskiness that are available in financial markets, namely, diversification, exchange, and insurance, are not options for reducing the riskiness of returns to human capital investments'. Palacios-Huerta (2003) studies the relationship between human capital risk and financial investment in a life cycle consumption framework and reports supporting evidence. He finds that at the aggregate level, the mean–variance frontier does not improve if returns from financial assets are added to returns from human capital: adding an optimal financial investment portfolio does not improve the payoff to risk taking. In the converse case (adding human capital to financial assets), the frontier does improve. For separate demographic groups, the results vary by level of education. Shaw (1996) reports a similar result, based on her own analysis and reference to earlier work: the covariance between human and financial wealth is zero, leaving no scope to reduce human capital risk by adequate financial investment.

Note that in the simple formulation of the model given above, the only uncertainty is the post-school wage rate. It's hard to see how this risk can be insured. Of course, there is also substantial uncertainty about the further development of earnings during the individual's career. One might argue that an individual does not have to accept uncertain earnings over the life cycle as an inescapable event, as it is always possible to apply consumption smoothing. However, this is of course not without cost. Consider uncertainty about income in a simple two-period model: all an individual knows is the probability distribution of income in the next period. A risk-neutral agent (a bank?) would be willing to replace the individual's uncertain future income by its expectation $E\{Y\}$, which would then be the individual's sure consumption. But why would this agent leave all the utility gain to the individual? A bank certainly would charge a fee. The fee would probably be declining in $E\{Y\}$, as banks are more interested in attracting larger sums (they also pay higher interest on larger deposits). But the fee will no doubt be increasing in the variance of Y, as banks will not accept higher risk without compensation. They even dislike volatility, as is shown by the premium they pay on long-term deposits, or the penalty they charge for withdrawals. Homemade consumption smoothing is neither costless. Suppose an individual has random income Y in every period and seeks a stable consumption level C, by saving $Y–C$ if positive and borrowing $C–Y$ in the opposite case. Assume the bank will accommodate all the individual's actions, but it will do so at different interest rates for saving and borrowing. In a symmetric probability distribution, ignoring carryover between periods (accumulating savings, or debts), the expected amount saved will be equal to the expected amount borrowed. But expected interest on savings will be less than expected interest on loans, and this will reduce C below $E\{Y\}$. The gap $E\{Y\}-C$ is a good measure of the cost of risk. Expected savings and expected loans will increase with the variance of the distribution of Y. Hence, the cost of risk will also increase in the variance. Intuitively, one expects it to decrease in skewness, as savings are favoured over loans. But these are of course just the predictions needed for the basic hypothesis. One may sense that this intuitive argument survives in a multiple period model where savings (and debts) can be accumulated, but with the outcome conditioned by the serial correlation of the income draws.[5] Of course, the literature on stochastic dynamic programming has been developed precisely because an individual cannot smooth consumption by replacing uncertain future income by its expected value (see, e.g., Carroll, 2001; Low, 2005). There can be little doubt that lifetime welfare is declining in wage volatility.

EMPIRICAL SPECIFICATIONS

Much debate in the empirical work centres on how to measure risk. Before giving a survey of empirical studies we start, in Box 1, with just an overview of the definitions that have been applied. Later on, we clarify and motivate the specifications and discuss quality and relevance of these measures.

The first analysis, by King (1974), used variance and skew of earnings in occupational cells and estimated Eq. (25) at the aggregate level. Feinberg (1981) used a short panel to estimate each individual's coefficient of variation over six years. McGoldrick (1995) introduced the two-step procedure. With cross-section data, she first estimated an earnings function

$$\ln Y_{ij} = X_i\beta + \sum_j \alpha_j \mathrm{d}_j + \varepsilon_{ij} \qquad (26)$$

where the subscripts i and j denote individuals and the education cell the individual belongs to respectively. The d_j are dummy variables for education cells (fixed effects). The variables included in X are years of education, age and age squared and, depending on specification, dummies for gender and ethnicity. Generally, no other explanatory variables in X are included, as the common variables that may be available (such as industry, firm and job

Box 1. Measuring Risk and Skew

Standard deviation and third moment of wages by occupation or education
King (1974); Johnson (1977); Hartog and Vijverberg (2007)
Standard deviation of residual earnings
McGoldrick(1995); McGoldrick and Robst (1996)
Standard deviation, third moment of exp (ε_{ij}), where ε_{ij} is residual from log earnings equation, for individual i in job j
Berkhout and Hartog (2006); Berkhout et al. (2006); Diaz Serrano (2000); Diaz Serrano, Hartog, and Skyt Nielsen (2004); Diaz Serrano and Hartog (2006); Ma (2005)
Coefficient of variation in individual earnings over time
Feinberg (1981); Moore (1995); Diaz Serrano et al. (2004)
Relative variance and skew (Eqs. (23) and (24)); interquartile range
Hartog and Vijverberg (2007)
Difference in schooling returns between highest and lowest quantile
Pereira and Martins (2002)
Probability mass in segments of wage distribution
Schweri, Hartog, and Wolter (2008)

characteristics) are all unknown to the individual when deciding on education.[6] The education fixed effects α_j are included to pick up effects of omitted variables that may bias the measures of risk and skew within an education cell. Estimated residuals are used to compute measures of R and K

$$R_j = \frac{1}{N_j}\sum_i \left(e_{ij} - \bar{e}_j\right)^2 \quad K_j = \frac{1}{N_j}\sum_i \left(e_{ij} - \bar{e}_j\right)^3 \tag{27}$$

where e_{ij} is the exponential of the estimated residuals ε_{ij} in Eq (26) and N_j is the number of observations in cell j. In (27), R and K are simply estimated as the second and third moment of the distribution of exp(ε_j). In the second step, the estimated values for R and K are included in the wage equation

$$\ln Y_{ij} = X_i\beta + \gamma_R R_j + \gamma_K K_j + \varepsilon_{ij} \tag{28}$$

Dummies for education cells cannot be included in (28) since R and K are already fixed in a given education cell.

Hartog and Vijverberg (2002) introduced a specification that is closer to the model in the second section. First, estimate

$$LnW_{ji} = X_i\beta + \varepsilon_{ji} \tag{29}$$

where i indicates the individual and j indicates the occupation-schooling group that the individual belongs to. Years educated is one of the variables in the matrix X. Define σ_j^2 as the variance of the disturbance ε_{ji} in occupation/education cell j. Use the estimated parameter vector $\hat{\beta}$ and the estimated variance $\hat{\sigma}_j^2$ to predict the wage rate for each individual through:

$$\hat{W}_{ji} = \exp\left(X_i\hat{\beta} + \hat{\sigma}_j^2/2\right) \tag{30}$$

Finally, calculate wage deviations $W_{ji} - \hat{W}_{ji}$ and from these the relative variance R_j and relative skewness K_j, defined as

$$R_j = \frac{1}{I_j}\sum_{i=1}^{I_j}\left(\frac{W_{ji} - \hat{W}_{ji}}{\hat{W}_{ji}}\right)^2 \tag{31}$$

$$K_j = \frac{1}{I_j}\sum_{i=1}^{I_j}\left(\frac{W_{ji} - \hat{W}_{ji}}{\hat{W}_{ji}}\right)^3 \tag{32}$$

In (30), the variance term is added to the mean to reflect that the disturbances of the earnings distributions are approximately lognormal, as is commonly assumed. Were the distribution indeed lognormal, Eq (30) would hold exactly.[7] R and K are the sample estimates of relative variance and relative skew, as defined in Eqs. (23) and (24). In practice, (27) and (31)–(32) are equivalent: in Danish panel data (Diaz Serrano et al., 2004) the measures in (31) and (32) correlate better than 0.99 in each of 17 years with those in (27).

ESTIMATES OF THE RISK AUGMENTED MINCER EQUATION

In Table 1, we present estimates of the RAM. Grosso modo one could say these are first-generation estimates, where risk and skewness are measured within occupations. Whenever relevant, the regressions include a parabolic age (experience) profile. Sometimes there are additional controls, in particular in the second stage (the first stage should not control for effects

Table 1. The Risk Augmented Mincer Equation: Occupations.

Author	Country	Data/Year	N	R, K	Elasticity R	Elasticity K	Controls
King (1974) Table 2, row 3							
	USA	1960 Census	37 occupations (professions, 4 years college)	Standard deviation. Third moment	1.22[a] (8.71)	−4.44 E-3[a] (4.77)	Ability (Project Talent)
Johnson (1977)							
	USA	1970 Census	55–107 occupations	Standard deviation	0.11[b]	–	Within age-education groups
Feinberg (1981) Table 1, column (1)							
	USA	1971–1976 PSID panel	1419 individuals	Individual coefficient of variation over 6 years	0.01 (2.53)	–	IQ, education, occupation; higher compensations for the more risk averse
McGoldrick and Robst (1996), p. 230							
	USA	PSID 1979–1984	528 women, 937 men	Standard deviation residual earnings (time, time square)	M: 0.17 (11.57) F: 0.50 (6.87)		Mobility, 7 occupations
Ma (2005)							
Table 8.6	China	1991 Urban Household Survey	41 education–occupation	$\exp(e_j)$	M: 0.05 (1.90) F: −0.23 (8.14)	0.05 (7.92) −0.006 (0.96)	
Table 8.5		2000	51 education–occupation	$\exp(e_j)$	M: 0.18 (3.70) F: 0.65 (10.75)	0.02 (0.80) −0.09 (3.26)	

Hartog et al. (2003) Tables 1 and 2							
	Netherlands	OSA 1999	40 occupations	exp(e_j)	M: 0.18 (10.02)	−0.05 (8.18)	6 industry dummies
					F: 0.15 (3.96)	−0.06 (3.32)	
	West Germany	SOEP 1992	41 occupations	exp(e_j)	M: 0.11 (4.02)	−0.02 (3.07)	6 industry dummies
					F: 0.25 (6.06)	−0.05 (4.42)	
	East Germany	SOEP 1992	28 occupations	exp(e_j)	M: 0.12 (5.03)	−0.01 (0.91)	6 industry dummies
					F: 0.08 (2.64)	−0.02 (1.57)	
	Portugal	Quadros Pesoal 1992	70 occupations	exp(e_j)	M: 0.37 (33.35)	−0.17 (24.08)	6 occupation dummies, 7 industry dummies, tenure, firm size, ownership and age
					F: 0.76 (30.65)	−0.03 (2.32)	
Hartog et al. (2003) Tables 1 and 2							
	Spain	Estructurra Salarial 1995	83 occupations	exp(e_j)	M: 0.29 (58.11)	−0.02 (8.45)	Bargaining regime, public/private, 6 industry dummies, 6 occupation dummies, city size
					F: 0.10 (11.65)	−0.02 (35.83)	

Table 1. *(Continued)*

Author	Country	Data/Year	N	R, K	Elasticity R	Elasticity K	Controls
Hartog and Vijverberg (2004) Tables 3 and 4							
	USA	NBER-CPS 1995–1999	129 education–occupation	Relative variance, skew	M: 0.16 (15)	−0.06 (26)	Elasticities, t-values averaged
					F: 0.05 (4)	−0.17 (14)	
			104 education–occupation	Interquantile ranges	M: 0.44 (20)	−0.26 (12)	
					F: 0.08 (3)	−0.45 (15)	
Diaz Serrano (2000) Table 7.3							
	Spain	EPF 1990	83 occupations	$\exp(e_j)$	M: 0.02 (7.4)	−0.02 (2.8)	Family status, region, industry, skill level
					F: 0.04 (4.2)	−0.10 (4.8)	
Moore (1995) Table 4							
	USA	PSID 1978–1987	856 individuals	Individual's coefficient of variation	Union −0.08 (0.39) Non-union 0.09 (?)		Risk interacted with union dummy

t-values refer to estimated coefficient, not to elasticity.
[a]Regression coefficients: units and means not reported.
[b]Relative effect of one standard deviation on mean earnings, averaged over 18 age-education categories. All coefficients significant at conventional levels.

that the individual cannot anticipate when choosing an education, such as, e.g., firm size). The estimates strongly support the basic hypothesis of risk compensation. The coefficient for risk is positive in all but one case and significant, usually at high levels in all studies except the study with union interaction. The elasticity is mostly in the interval 0.1–0.2. The coefficient of skewness is negative, except in 4 out of the 19 cases, usually but not always at high levels of statistical significance. The elasticity is small, mostly below 0.10. The study with union interaction, by Moore (1995), focuses on benefits that unions bring their members. Compensation for wage risk is insignificant in both unionised and non-unionised jobs. Interestingly, in jobs covered by union contract workers have less wage variability and more hours variability, suggesting that unions manage to reduce wage risk, but pay for it with higher hours risk. They also bring higher compensation for wage risk than in the non-union sector, but the difference is statistically not significant.

The early studies and the replications suffer from flaws that have to be addressed before any firm conclusions can be drawn. First, earnings risk is measured at the level of occupations, and thus will be sensitive to selective mobility. Individuals who are not successful in an occupation may try their luck elsewhere.[8] With overrepresentation of workers with good draws, observed earnings overestimate the earnings of all those who tried this occupation. With truncation of the earnings distribution at the low end, observed variance of earnings is an underestimate of risk, while skewness is overestimated. Thus, the risk coefficient will be overestimated. The effect on the coefficient of skewness cannot be predicted as both expected earnings and skewness are overestimated. Better estimates can be obtained with observations grouped by education, as one cannot escape bad draws after the education has been completed. If risk induced mobility between occupations is important, one must predict that education-based estimates give lower estimated risk compensation than occupation-based estimates, while the effect on estimated skewness affection cannot be predicted.

The studies in Table 1 also fail to recognise a complication in the estimated standard errors. As noted by Moulton (1986), with R and K measured at group level, errors may be correlated within these groups and estimated standard errors should be corrected for this clustering within cells.[9]

Table 2 presents second-generation estimates, with risk and skewness measured by education and with standard errors corrected for clustering, or with mean earnings regressed on mean risk and skewness. The basic conclusion is unaffected: a positive effect of risk and a negative effect of

Table 2. The Risk Augmented Mincer Equation: Education.

Author	Country	Data/Year	N	R, K	Elasticity R	Elasticity K	Controls
Diaz Serrano et al. (2004) Table 2							
	Denmark	1984–2000	75 educations	$\exp(e_j)$	0.03[a]	−0.005[a]	Men, aged 30–40 clustered
Berkhout, Hartog, and Webbink (2006) Table 1, all							
	Netherlands	LSO 1997	66 educations	$\exp(e_j)$	0.2 (3.69)	−0.1 (2.57	Clustered
–	–	Elsevier/SEO 1996–2001	100 educations	$\exp(e_j)$	0.08 (4.53	−0.04 (3.25)	Starting salaries, tertiary education clustered
Diaz Serrano and Hartog (2006) Table 3							
Model 1	Spain	1995	53 educations	$\exp(e_j)$	0.222 (16.50)	−0.034 (2.42)	Clustered
Model 2				Relative error	0.202 (16.96)	−0.008 (10.00)	
Model 3				Interquartile ranges	0.035 (11.67)	−0.016 (2.50)	
Berkhout and Hartog (2006)							
	Netherlands	Elsevier/SEO 1996–2006	111 educations	$\exp(e_j)$	M: 0.05 (2.19)	−0.13 (5.50)	Regression on mean earnings by education, personal characteristics clustered; starting salaries
					F: 0.04 (2.43)	−0.10 (6.43)	
Hartog and Vijverberg (2007) Table 2							
	USA	NBER-CPS 1995–1999	34 DOT–GED cells	Standard deviation of wages	M: 1.07 (9.34)		Region, ethnicity, working conditions
					F: 0.86 (5.41)		

t-values refer to estimated coefficient, not to elasticity.

[a]Elasticity averaged over 17 annual estimates (all significant); mean R and K from IZA discussion paper no. 963.

skewness, both statistically significant. We cannot compare the magnitudes of the coefficients (elasticities) between Tables 1 and 2, as they are based on different datasets and different controls, so we cannot test the prediction that education-based measures lead to lower elasticities than occupation-based measures. As we noted above, there is no difference between measuring risk and skewness with the exponential specification or as relative measures (Eqs. (27) vs. (31)–(32)). In Diaz Serrano and Hartog (2006), we have also tested another specification, with R and K based on interquartile ranges. As R and K will be sensitive to outliers, we have calculated the percentile distribution of the residuals in the first stage, and defined R as the difference between the 75th and the 25th percentile and K as $(P_{75} - P_{50})/(P_{50} - P_{25})$. As can be seen both in Tables 1 and 2, we still obtain significant effects with the proper signs.

On top of the Moulton problem, we have to realise that R and K are measured from a first-stage regression and will be subject to sampling errors. Murphy and Topel (1985) have presented a method for consistent estimation of the variances of the second-stage parameter estimates. In Diaz Serrano and Hartog (2006), the corrections for clustering and generated regressors are combined, by replacing the conventional OLS covariance matrix estimator in Moulton's adjustment by the covariance estimator proposed by Murphy and Topel. The Moulton correction for clustering is important, but the additional correction for generated regressors has negligible effect on estimated standard errors.

With R and K fixed for a given occupation or education, second-stage regressions cannot include a fixed effect. Thus, it may be that R and K do not measure any dimension of risk but simply some fixed effect of occupation of risk that is not picked up by the controls. In Diaz Serrano et al. (2004), we have regressed education fixed effects from the first-stage earnings functions on R and K (both permanent and transitory, see below). The effect of R and K on these fixed effects was not statistically significant, thus indicating that R and K are not just representing education fixed effects through the backdoor. In Diaz Serrano and Hartog (2006), we applied the same test to our estimates for Spain, with the same result. We can be pretty confident that R and K are not just unidentified education effects.

It's worth pointing out that our results appear not due to omitted job quality. In Hartog and Vijverberg (2002), we report that the estimates are insensitive to the inclusion of a long list of measures of job disamenities such as physical burdens and exposure to toxic conditions.

BIAS FROM UNOBSERVED HETEROGENEITIES?

An immediate objection to using the observed distribution of earnings residuals is the possible confounding of risk and heterogeneity. The (residual) distribution of earnings will be affected by many variables that for an individual may not pose any risk at all. Probably the most prominent of these variables is individual ability. But individuals may also differ in risk attitudes and they may even face individually different risk. To address these issues, Jacobs, Hartog, and Vijverberg (2008) set up a simple model with a safe fixed wage job (with wage W_s) and a risky job with stochastic wage, at expectation $E(W_r)$. We did not refer specifically to educations as the problem is identical in a situation where individuals can choose a job or an occupation without first spending time in school (the required Mincer compensation for postponing earnings can simply be added to earnings). We consider only risk and ignore skewness.

If individuals are identical in all aspects (risk aversion ρ, risk σ^2 and 'ability' expressed as expected productivity in the risky job – in the safe job they have equal productivity anyway), in equilibrium the expected risky wage will just compensate for risk and allocation will be arbitrary. Risk is properly estimated as observed wage variance in the risky job; the coefficient of risk compensation is estimated as the observed wage gap divided by wage variance, without bias, from the equilibrium condition $E(W_r) = W_s + \rho\sigma^2/2$. This is a stripped down version of the model in the second section. Note that ρ is estimated from the wage gap divided by half the variance.

To assess the effects of heterogeneity, we distinguish three cases. First, we assume that individuals only differ in risk attitudes, and have identical abilities and risk. This poses no special problem. The wage gap between risky and safe jobs is now determined by the risk attitude of the marginal individual, and this is just what is estimated in the OLS regression. Second, if individuals only differ in the magnitude of risk and are otherwise identical, residual earnings variance underestimates true risk of the marginal worker, as only low-risk individuals enter the risky job. As a consequence, risk compensation is overestimated. If individuals differ in both risk and risk attitude, the case is rather unusual. The threshold for entering the risky job is now defined as a critical value of the product of risk and risk attitude: the threshold for entry is a contour of combinations of the two variables that separate entry from non-entry in the risky job. There is no single critical value of any of these variables and by consequence they cannot be estimated. The coefficient that is estimated in the RAM can now be interpreted as the maximum value of risk aversion for the individual who has the mean value of risk among those individuals who actually chose the risky job. The third case is where individuals only differ in ability, reflected in their expected earnings in the risky job; assuming individuals know their ability and the researcher does not, we have a garden variety of selectivity. The observed wage gap between the two jobs is now an overestimate of the wage premium, as the mean value of the risky wage also includes the effect of ability for those who chose the risky job (only more able individuals enter the risky job, as the ability premium should serve as a premium for accepting higher risk). Observed wage variance in the risky job is an overestimate of risk, as it also includes the variance of ability between individuals. With risk aversion estimated as the ratio between wage gap and observed variance, we cannot predict the sign of the bias, as both numerator and denominator are biased upward. To assess this case, we revert to simulation. We find that the ambiguity in the sign of the bias cannot be resolved by restriction to reasonable or plausible parameter values: depending on parameter values it may just as well be positive as negative. Considering the plausibility of parameter values we tend to conclude that underestimation of risk aversion is probably more likely than overestimation. But the key implication is that one cannot dismiss the risk compensation estimates as unreliable because they always produce an overestimated coefficient.

Below, we discuss extensively whether ability is known to the individual and may generate an unobserved heterogeneity for the researcher, or whether individuals are also poorly informed. Here, we just note that observations on ability are available in several datasets, and that we are in a position to assess the effect of omitted ability bias in our estimates. Interestingly, the very first tests of the risk compensation hypothesis already allowed for ability differences. King (1974) controlled for ability as measured in the Project Talent. Significant effects of risk and skewness were found while controlling for five ability measures: mathematics, English, reading comprehension, abstract reasoning and arithmetic reasoning. The basic conclusion was also upheld after splitting the sample in two classes of competing groups: technical and non-technical (a distinction confirmed by discriminant analysis on the basis of the five abilities). Estimation separately within the two groups, with their own measures of risk and skewness, confirmed the basic results. Feinberg (1981), testing on a panel with individual intertemporal variance as his measure of risk, found support in regressions that include IQ (a sentence completion test, on which no further information is given).

In Berkhout et al. (2006), we analyse starting salaries for graduates from tertiary education in the Netherlands. Instead of using R and K for all individuals with the same education, we calculate these measures for ability quartiles as measured by the individuals' average grades for their secondary school final exam. This is a relevant stratification, as it is based on information for which we are sure that the individuals themselves also have it at their disposal. The model underlying the risk compensation hypothesis assumes that students perceive their risk and then decide on education. If desired, they could use the same information as we do, by stratifying on secondary school grades. As the results in Table 3 indicate, after controlling for ability in this way the basic results are upheld. In fact, if we compare the results in detail (differentiating by gender and two types of tertiary education, that is, higher vocational and university), we find regression coefficients for R and K that barely differ. There is no bias from omitting ability that can be picked up by secondary school grade quartile.

Panel data are interesting for at least two reasons. By considering individual wage variation over time, unobserved heterogeneity is eliminated. Some of the first-generation studies used panel data, and measured risk as the individual variance over time. Feinberg (1981) and McGoldrick and Robst (1996) each used six waves of the PSID and found statistically significant effects of individually measured risk, although the magnitude of the effect in the former study was very small. Moore (1995) measures risk individually

Table 3. Regressing Log Wage on Risk R and Skewness K; R and K Measured Within the Individual's Secondary School Grade Quartile (*SEO/Tertiary Starters*).

	R	T	K	t	N
All tertiary					
All	2.67	3.95	−3.19	3.33	45020
Men	1.96	4.07	−2.66	3.98	19659
Women	2.44	3.01	−2.14	1.98	25361
Vocational					
All	2.99	4.80	−3.66	4.01	21431
Men	1.86	3.43	−2.55	3.61	8600
Women	2.97	4.59	−2.68	2.72	12831
University					
All	2.80	4.89	−3.83	4.40	23,589
Men	1.65	3.30	−1.92	2.19	11,059
Women	2.57	1.77	−3.07	1.74	12,530

Source: Berkhout et al. (2006).

t values based on robust standard errors clustered by education type. Grades only in second-stage regression; first-stage regressions separated by grade quartile.

from 10 waves of the PSID and finds no significant risk compensation within either the union or the non-union sector, but instead finds that unions provide wage insurance (lower variance) at the price of higher hours variability.

Second, with panel data we can separate earnings variation between individuals from variation for given individuals over time. With a large and long Danish panel (1984–2000), Diaz Serrano et al. (2004) separate the earnings residual in an individual (random) effect and an annual transitory shock. We take the variance of the individual effects of individuals within the same education as the permanent risk of that education and the variance of the transitory component within an education as transitory risk, using 75 educations.[10] If consumption smoothing holds, there should be no compensation for transitory risk, if individuals know their ability we expect no compensation for permanent risk. We insert the values in the wage equation for the pooled panel and we report the results in Table 4. The compensations for permanent and for transitory risk are both highly

Table 4. Wage Compensation for Transitory and Permanent Shocks.

Denmark[a] 1984–2000	Risk	Skewness
Permanent	0.332	−0.048
	−17.9	−17.84
	0.039	−0.01
Transitory	1.572	4.183
	−6	−8.74
	0.047	0.012
USA[b] 1979–2000		
Using residual variation		
Permanent	0.001	0.076
	−0.99	−1.32
Transitory	0.309	−0.976
	−12.05	−11.94
Using earnings variation		
Permanent	0.01	0.002
	−1.92	−1.15
Transitory	0.297	−0.106

Source: Raita, 2005, Tables 5.6, 5.7; Diaz Serrano et al. (2004).

[a]Controls include years of education, age, age squared and dummies for industry and occupation. Each cell contains coefficient, *t*-value in parentheses and elasticity in italics. Compensation estimated on pooled panel data.

[b]Controls included for marital status, region, some occupation dummies, IQ test score (AFQT); the data are from NLSY 1979 (1979–2000). Compensation estimated on wages in 2000.

significant, though the elasticities are quite modest in magnitude. As to skewness, compensation for the permanent component is highly significant, with the right sign. For the transitory component, however, the prediction of a negative sign is squarely rejected, with a significant positive effect. Again, the panel data estimates do not suggest an overestimation of compensation because of unobserved heterogeneity. We also have estimated the standard equation on each of the 17 years of our panel data. The average coefficient value from these 17 estimates is about equal to the estimate for the permanent component for both *R* and *K*, while the panel data estimate for the transitory component is much larger than annual average.[11] The results for the permanent component are at variance with the hypothesis that individuals know their own fixed effect and need no compensation for it; the results for transitory risk are at variance with full and costless consumption smoothing.

Comparable results are obtained with the NLSY panel for the United States, with the same risk decomposition (permanent risk from individual random effects, transitory risk from the annual transitory shocks), but with compensation for risk only tested on the wage equation for the final year (Raita, 2005). Risk and skewness are measured in education-ability cells, with two levels of education and 10 ability deciles (AFQT), resulting in 17 observations (as not all cells contain sufficient number of observations). Again one finds that risk compensation has the predicted sign, both permanent and transitory, although insignificantly so in one case. For skewness, the predicted effect for transitory shocks is found but permanent skewness has no significant effect.

Unobserved individual heterogeneity is also filtered out if we use individuals' expectations. Schweri et al. (2008) analyse data on the probability distribution of wages that Swiss students expect for themselves from different potential schooling scenarios: medians and dispersion measures elicited with the Dominitz and Manski (1996) method (see next section). Expected risk variables show a positive effect, expected skewness variables a negative effect on expected median wage. In fact, we even get similar values for the elasticities: a risk elasticity of 0.12 and a skewness elasticity of −0.011. These values are in the middle of the interval of values that we found in the empirical literature based on market data. The regression coefficients are only modestly reduced if we include individual fixed effects in the regressions.

One may have doubts that *R* and *K* properly measure the uncertainty they are meant to measure. In that respect, it is reassuring that if we use dispersion measures derived from the percentile distribution of residual earnings, the results are not essentially different (Hartog & Vijverberg, 2007). Supporting evidence is also provided by Pereira and Martins (2002). They measure risk as the difference between returns to education in the highest and the lowest decile in quantile regression. Regressing the Mincer rate of return on risk across 16 countries, they find a significant positive effect with implied elasticity of 0.2. Even though there are only 16 observations, the evidence is neatly in line with the other results we report here.

SELF-SELECTION: WHAT DO STUDENTS KNOW?

The hypothesis of risk compensation in wages is based on the assumption that supply decisions by potential students affect market wages. Students are supposed to act on the financial uncertainty they associate with an education. The estimations we presented use observed residual variances as an indicator of risk. It's by now a natural reflex of labour economists to assume a selectivity problem here, on the hypothesis that individuals are well informed on their abilities and their income prospects. Selectivity corrections are based on the assumption that students, when they take their decisions, have better information on future returns than the researcher and precisely these decisions make the observed distribution of residuals a biased estimate of the actual uncertainty: we observe realised, not potential dispersion. A proper econometric modelling and a proper estimation technique should retrieve the true dispersion that individuals base their decision on. If we just use the observed distribution of residuals, we confuse unobserved heterogeneity and risk. In fifth section, we indicated that selectivity by no means leads to unambiguous biases and that we cannot discard the results as obviously spurious. Here, we consider the issue of student information more generally.

There are very few empirical studies to inform us on this distinction between risk and heterogeneity. Chen (2008) uses the NLSY 1979–2000 and estimates wage equations and schooling choice. The wage equation contains a permanent and a transitory effect, and the schooling choice contains unobserved heterogeneity. The transitory component cannot be foreseen by the individual, but individual uncertainty on the permanent component is reduced through its correlation with unobserved heterogeneity in the schooling choice equation: the unobserved heterogeneity factors allow the individual a better prediction of the permanent effect in wages (a lower variance) than the outside observer. Chen finds that wage uncertainty (the unforeseen transitory component in wages plus the incompletely foreseen permanent component) does not deviate much from observed wage inequality. Observed residual variances in wages, for less than high school, high school, some college and college are 0.526, 0.411, 0.500 and 0.512, respectively, while calculated wage uncertainties are 0.485, 0.406, 0.497 and 0.472. That would make observed inequality a good indicator of uncertainty.[12] In an earlier version of the paper, the selectivity correction on the variance of the permanent component was shown to be negligible (Chen, 2003). Chen and Khan (2007) focus on the average effect of education on wage inequality (residual variance): college versus high school or less. OLS estimation gives a ratio of 1.08, Heckman two-stage 1.09, an IV estimate gives 0.94 and pairwise matching gives 1.29. The absolute effect is also quite small. Straightforward OLS estimation of an earnings model yields residual standard deviation of 0.397 for college and 0.370 for high school graduates, while two-stage Heckman estimation gives 0.455 and 0.445 (op. cit., Table 5 in the 2005 working paper version). Thus, correction for selectivity has very little effect.

Heckman, with several co-authors, has developed an elaborate framework to identify counterfactual distributions of earnings for various schooling choices. The method rests on the notion that if information on results that only become observable to the outsider in realised outcomes has an impact on schooling choices, it must have been in the information set of the agent when she made her choice. In a survey paper, Cunha and Heckman (2007, p. 892) conclude: 'For a variety of market environments and assumptions about preferences, a robust empirical regularity is that over 50% of the ex post variance in the returns to schooling are forecastable at the time students make their college choices'. Arcidianoco (2004) focuses on information on ability; with his econometric specification he estimates that 50–60% of the variance of an ability indicator related to major in university is noise.

Rather than extracting evidence from observed behaviour through an imposed econometric model, one might simply question individuals about their information set. We should point out that here we are *not* interested in the true risk associated with an education. What matters in our case is the *belief* of potential students on the risks they are facing, as this is what they act on. We encounter a methodological divide here. Under a strict instrumentalist approach, it's irrelevant what individuals believe: all that matters is the quality of the prediction. Alternatively, one may argue that if individuals are inevitably to base their choices on expected outcomes, one might as well study these expectations directly, as this can only improve our understanding of individuals' behaviour.[13]

The direct approach to eliciting perceptions on the risk of returns to education has been pioneered by Dominitz and Manski (1996). Their study is rather exploratory in methodology, with only 71 high school students and 39 college students, but it is very carefully executed and gives unusual insights.[14] Students are asked to answer questions in a computer-executed survey, with feedback to correct errors. First, they are asked the median salary for a given educational scenario (complete high school), with an explanation of what a median is. Next, the program calculates 75% of the median salary and asks for the probability that the student's future salary will not surpass this level, and it asks for the probability of surpassing 125% of the median, with feedback on answers that violate the rules of probability. Assuming a normal distribution of future salaries, the answers are sufficient to calculate the individual's parameters of this distribution. Students appear to have widely divergent anticipations. For example, among male high school students asked for expected median earnings at age 30 in the scenario where they will have completed a bachelor degree, the 10th decile expects $25,000 whereas the 90th decile expects $56,000. On the dispersion in their future distribution of earnings, the same groups, under the same scenario, expect interquartile ranges of $28,000 and 58,000, respectively. Perceived returns also differ widely. At age 30, the male high school students at the 10th percentile expect an earnings advantage from college of $10,000, at the 90th percentile they expect a gain of $30,000. Students were also asked to state the actual dispersion of earnings by education. Generally, they overestimate the interquartile range. Interestingly, predictions of their own median expected salary correlate positively with their perception of the actual median: 'Respondents who believe current median earnings to be high (low) tend also to expect their own earnings to be high (low)' (op. cit., p. 25).

Wolter and Weber (2004) apply the Dominitz and Manski approach to Swiss students. They also find large dispersion in expected medians (a coefficient of variation across individuals of about 0.20) and considerable uncertainty as reflected in the interquartile range. Americans' individual uncertainty is larger than actual interquartile ranges, whereas for Swiss students individual uncertainty is smaller than actual dispersion. The Swiss students are asked for individual wage expectations under two scenarios: secondary education and tertiary education. These estimates are not significantly different from actually observed medians for these groups (the mean signed error is not significantly different from zero). Most interestingly, the deviations do not differ between respondents with different actual schooling choice (students in high school, in a business college or a university of applied science), neither for men nor for women, neither for age 30 nor for age 40. This does not point at selectivity related expectations. Rather, the outcomes are compatible with all students anchoring their expectations on actually observed wages.

Schweri et al. (2008) also argue against a pervasive role for superior private information. Using another set of data on Swiss students collected with the Dominitz and Manski method, they report that individuals' expectations on the distribution parameters of earnings for specified education choices are related to individuals' perceptions on these parameters for employees already in the labour market and who have realised these choices. That is, an individual's expectations mirror just what they see in the labour market as realised outcomes. Even more interestingly, deviations between an individual's predictions for himself and his perceptions of realised market outcomes for those who have chosen the particular schooling scenario are not systematically related to variables that could reveal private information. Neither family background nor ability (secondary school grade for math) explains the differences. This is similar to results reported by Nicholson and Souleles (2001). They use survey data from students at a particular medical school in the United States to assess the formation of income expectations and their relevance for explaining the choice of medical specialty. Income expectations are strongly anchored on perceived contemporaneous incomes, without exclusively determining them. For every \$1,000 increase in the actual contemporaneous income of the specialty that the student plans to enter, the student's expectation for that specialty goes up by \$590. For every \$1,000 difference between the student's estimate of contemporaneous specialty income and actual specialty income, the student's expected income goes up by \$840. Misperceptions in actual specialty income end up almost dollar for dollar in income expectations. By contrast, the effect of 'ability' is very small: performing in the top quartile of the exam at the end of the second year in medical school only increases expected income by 5.9%.

In fact, students' perceptions of the wages associated with an education, as realised in the market, differ widely, but it's hard to identify systematic differences. Betts (1996) asks students for their perceptions of starting wages and average earnings for graduates with specific degrees and finds a coefficient of variation of about 0.2–0.3 in the distribution of beliefs across students. Students' estimates get closer to the true market wage as they progress towards graduation but both students' beliefs and estimation errors are hard to predict (R^2's below 0.06, few significant effects).

Results by Brunello, Lucifora, and Winter-Ebmer (2004) are also at variance with anticipations from the private information hypothesis. They collected information on expected earnings from university students in 10 European countries (business and economics). The expected wage premium over high school graduates at labour market entry was unrelated to any variable except age: not to parental background, not to channel of information about future earnings (university publication, career centre, special reports, press, personal communication), not to reason for choosing their selected university, not to self-assessed relative ability. The expected premium of university over high school graduation after 10 years of experience is only significantly lower for older students, women and students with longer expected time to complete the degree (and again not related to self-assessed ability). These results only refer to university students, not to those who choose not to go to university, but they do not point to systematic patterns in expected benefits, except for the effect of expected length of study, which possibly reflects an update of initial expectations during the study.

Perhaps the strongest blow to the notion of superior information about one's future position in the wage distribution is from Webbink and Hartog (2004). First-year students can predict differences in mean salaries by fields of education but they cannot predict their own starting salary after graduation, four years ahead. The correlation between an individual's starting salary after graduation predicted upon entering tertiary education and the realisation after graduation is a mere 0.06!

We conclude that direct measurement of potential students' information points to a large dispersion between individuals and to substantial perceived uncertainty by individuals on their own prospects. The large dispersion indicates that students do not all just use observed distributions for graduates already in the market as their own expected distribution. But the differences in their expectations are neither compatible with an obvious pattern of private information: they are unrelated to self-assessed ability. Even more telling: Dutch first-year students appeared unable to predict their position in the distribution of starting salaries. There is evidence, however, to support the hypothesis that students anchor their expectations on their perceptions of actual rewards in the labour market, but differ in these perceptions. This is certainly a hypothesis worthy of further investigation. Econometric modelling to extract information from observed behaviour lends more support to the relevance of self-selection, although the magnitude of the correction for private information is uncertain and not necessarily large.

SUPPORTING EVIDENCE

To consider the credibility of the results, we may consider some circumstantial evidence. First of all, we may note that compensation for risks in the labour market is well established, both for instability of employment and for health and morbidity hazards (Rosen, 1986). In fact, employer behaviour exhibits mirror effects of the risk compensation we analyse here. New graduates pose a risk for employers to the extent that they cannot accurately assess their potential productivity. But as graduates have no alternative for putting their education at work, we expect employers to shift the risk of unknown abilities to employees. Using variance and skewness of students' grades in different disciplines as indicators of employer uncertainty, we find that starting wages are lower in fields with high variance and higher in fields with high skewness (Berkhout, Hartog, & van Ophem, 2009).

More specifically, we will cite evidence that individuals care about financial risk when choosing a career, that structural parameters estimated for risk compensation are in line with estimates in life cycle consumption models and that more risk-loving workers experience higher wage growth.

Evidence that individuals care about the financial risk when choosing a labour market position is given by King (1974) and by Saks and Shore (2003). They note that with risk aversion declining in wealth, one should expect that students from wealthier backgrounds choose more risky occupations. This is precisely what they find in American data. Lazear (2005) reports that individuals are more likely to start their own business firm if the first industry in which they were employed after leaving university has high-wage variance, suggesting they select themselves into positions to match their relatively low-risk aversion. Diaz Serrano (2005) and Dohmen et al. (2005) document such selection more explicitly. Diaz Serrano measures earnings uncertainty as residual variance in Italian panel data after removing individual fixed effects and finds that earnings uncertainty correlates significantly with the stated reservation price for a lottery ticket: more risk-averse individuals have less earnings uncertainty. Dohmen et al. use a measure of individual risk attitude obtained from a survey question (validated in experimental data) and measure earnings risk as residual earnings variance by occupation. They report significant correlation between risk and individual risk attitude: more risk-averse individuals sort into jobs with less earnings variance. Negative results are reported by Kodde (1985), who uses Dutch questionnaire data on individual students' expectations. He finds no clear effects on the decision to attend university of the gap between an individual's expected highest and expected lowest earnings to be earned after completing a university education.

Belzil and Leonardi (2007) measure risk attitudes from answers on the reservation price for a hypothetical lottery. Conditional on completing senior high school (in Italy), the probability to go on to university appears to be decreasing in risk aversion, with an effect as large as that of parental education. However, conditional on junior high school the decision to attend senior high school is increasing in risk aversion. That would imply that individuals see a university education as risky and senior high school education as an insurance. Hartog and Diaz Serrano (2007) find that Spanish high school graduates are less inclined to go to university in provinces where the return to university is more risky (as measured by residual earnings variance), and that the effect is indeed mitigated by declining risk aversion. Flyer and Rosen (1997) derive that someone who in his/her life cycle anticipates to devote less time to market activity should behave as if he/she were more risk averse. Indeed they find in CPS two-digit occupation data that the coefficient of variation in women's wages correlates negatively with the percentage of women in the occupation: women flock into less risky occupations.

Shaw (1996) argues that on-the-job training is a risky investment and that less risk-averse individuals will invest more; hence, less risk-averse individuals should have higher wage growth. She measures risk attitudes from the share of wealth held in risky assets and from direct survey questions. Indeed, less risk-averse individuals have higher wage growth. If the share of financial wealth invested in risky assets increases from the sample mean of 0.1 to 0.4, the share of human capital devoted to investment in creating new human capital would also increase fourfold. The three-year growth rate of the wage would then increase from 6.6% to 7.8%, that is, an increase by 18%. We can use some of her results to calculate that compensation for earnings risk as emphasised in this chapter has an elasticity of about 0.5: moving from the class of above-average risk takers to the class of average risk takers, residual log wage variance falls by 50% while the average wage falls by 30%, moving to the class of no-risk takers, residual log wage variance falls by 70%, while the average wage falls by 40%. Shaw's results provide strong evidence in favour of our approach. Her results are not based on *assumed* risk-taking behaviour; they hold for individuals who differ in stated risk attitudes. Individuals who indicate that they take more financial risk in order to obtain larger gains have higher average wage and higher residual wage variance. The same relationship holds in growth rates: less risk-averse individuals have higher wage growth rate and higher variance of residual wage growth.[15] In a replication study for the United States, Germany, Spain and Italy (Budria, Diaz Serrano, Ferrer Carbonell, & Hartog, 2009), we confirm that risk attitudes are relevant for wages (support for the original Shaw specifications is mixed though, and we find that in particular the wage level is sensitive to attitudes towards risk taking, more so than wage growth). Brown and Taylor (2005) report support for the Shaw model in British data.

Hartog and Vijverberg (2002) estimate structural parameters in wage compensation equations like (25) for US data. The estimated coefficient of relative risk aversion is 0.64 for men and 0.46 for women, which is in the low end of the interval of estimates from various sources, such as consumption-savings models, TV games and direct surveys. The coefficient of relative skewness affection is estimated at 1.03 for men and 2.18 for women, also well within the interval of results found elsewhere in structural models (e.g. using a CRRA utility function and thus directly connecting risk aversion and prudence, Hubbard, Skinner, and Zeldes (1995) take relative risk aversion at 3 and relative prudence at 4 as representing empirical findings, while Keane and Wolpin, 2001, report values of 1.5 and 2.5, respectively; generally, the range of values found in the empirical literature is very wide). The interesting observation is that the implied preference parameters are very much in line with similar values found in quite different applications, and that attitudes towards financial risk in the labour market are not fundamentally different from attitudes revealed in consumption-saving decisions. Skyt Nielsen and Vissing-Jorgenson (2006) estimate a model of educational choice for 50 Danish post-high school educations,[16] characterising returns to education from a long panel of individuals, correcting the earnings data for selectivity. They find a clear negative effect of earnings risk on choosing an education, in particular for the permanent component of the variance. They use a utility function with CRRA and estimate the coefficient at 5. This is much higher than what Hartog and Vijverberg (2002) find, with a more flexible utility function, but still easily within the wide range of commonly found values.

ALTERNATIVE EXPLANATIONS

One might conjecture that the observed relationship reflects something other than risk compensation. One argument might be that earnings distributions obey the lognormal distribution, in which a relationship between mean and variance is implied. It is well known that when a variable W has a lognormal distribution with parameters μ and σ^2, there is a linear relationship between the mean and standard deviation of W: $E[W] = \exp(\mu + 0.5\sigma^2)$ and one may write the variance of W as $\mathrm{Var}(W) = (E[W])^2 \exp(\sigma^2 - 1)$. Thus, mean and variance of W will both increase if the log variance increases, and even the relative variance (the coefficient of variation) will increase. Thus, one might argue that we only have reproduced a property of the lognormal distribution. There are several arguments to counter this interpretation. First, lognormality does not explain anything: even if we were to observe that a variable perfectly obeys a lognormal distribution, we still want to know why this is so. Risk compensation might be precisely the argument. Second, lognormality is not an iron law and statistical tests often reject it (as we show in Hartog & Vijverberg, 2002 for our type of data). Third, in Diaz Serrano et al. (2004), we find risk compensation in earnings also if we measure risk as the intertemporal variation in earnings from panel data; in this case there is even less reason to believe that we just reproduce an iron law of distribution. Fourth, a reasonable model of schooling choices and resulting earnings distributions by education does not imply a necessarily positive relationship between mean and variance. Suppose, schooling just slices off successive segments of an ability distribution and transforms ability monotonically into marketable skills. Then, mean income by schooling will increase, but dispersion measures will depend on ability dispersion within the segments and the schooling transformation function; such a model may easily exhibit earnings variance declining in schooling level. Finally, the most compelling counterargument is that it would require skew also to be positively related to the mean, as skew for a lognormal variable equals $(2 + \exp\sigma^2)\sqrt{\exp\sigma^2 - 1}$. However, we consistently find a negative relationship.

Could it be that an underlying skill price effect drives the result? If earnings emerge as the reward for a skill, with the price of the skill determined in the labour market, an increase in the market price of the skill, with stable underlying skill distribution, will increase both mean and variance of earnings. But if so, the third moment of the earnings distribution should also go up.

Tournament theory (Lazear & Rosen, 1981) also implies a relationship between mean and variance: if shocks to performance become more important, both mean and variance of wages will be affected. With risk-neutral agents, optimal effort is independent of the variance of the shocks to output;[17] increasing shock variance does not affect output or mean wage. The spread between the two wages increases as the shock variance increases.[18] Hence, as one would expect, if agents are risk neutral, with wage spread increasing and mean wage unaffected, there is no compensation for increasing risk. In case of risk-averse agents, the relationship between mean and dispersion may be positive or negative, depending on parameter values (see Appendix B).

Job search theory has a systematic explanation for the persistence of wage differences among observationally identical individuals, pointing to the cost of mobility and of searching for information. A distribution with a large dispersion presents ample opportunity to find a high wage, and one might think the theory yields the same predictions as the risk compensation model. This is not the case however: in job search models, a positive association between mean and dispersion of observed wages *may* arise, but a negative relationship is a distinct possibility. In the simplest possible model, unemployed workers sample from a wage offer distribution with a reservation wage. As Mortensen (1986, p. 864) shows, an increase in the dispersion of the wage offer distribution increases the reservation wage. If one assumes the wage offer distribution to be normal, an increase in the truncation level from a higher reservation wage will increase the mean of the observed wage distribution (realised offers), while the effect on the variance cannot be unambiguously signed.[19] Thus, this model does not unambiguously predict the observed positive relationship between mean and variance of observed wages. This basic mechanism remains in more complicated models.[20] In a more informal sense, one might point to the appreciation that individuals will have for a higher dispersion in the job offer distribution, as this will bring them higher expected wage. This would have a negative effect on mean wages, as supply increases. If the higher wage is to be realised from repeated search, after entering the labour market, and if the higher variance in the offer distribution translates into higher variance in the observed wage distribution, one may perhaps expect a lower starting wage in high variance educations, as individuals appreciate the opportunity to search in a distribution with great opportunities, and a higher mean wage after sufficient experience, when search has paid off. Thus, while in this case predictions are identical for advanced careers, the effect on early careers stages has the power to discriminate. The SEO/Elsevier data analysed in Berkhout et al. (2006) are restricted to starting wages, one to two years after graduating from tertiary education. As Table 3 above shows, starting wages respond positively to risk (variance), which does not support the merger of risk preferences and search theory. The role of skewness in search theory has not been investigated. Intuitively, one expects opposing effects: the opportunity to arrive in the high end of the distribution, by prolonged search, will push up mean earnings. But as individuals like this opportunity, they will accept a lower wage. Again, one might differentiate by career stages. At young ages, the effect of increased supply dominates and the wage will be depressed. Later, when individuals have moved up through search, the wage should be boosted. But as pointed out above, the estimated effects for starters in the labour market have no different signs.[21]

WHAT HAVE WE LEARNED, WHAT REMAINS TO BE DONE?

Our empirical results have quite convincingly shown that wages in an occupation/education relate positively to the residual variance and negatively to the residual skew of wages within that occupation/education. These results are compatible with risk-averse individuals demanding compensation for risk and willing to pay for favourable odds to obtain really high wages. We have given several supporting arguments that make this a plausible link.

The magnitudes of the elasticities are not large. Interestingly, including the risk compensation terms in the Mincer equation has generally no effect on the estimated rate of return to education. This indicates that the estimated return does not suffer from omitted variable bias if risk is ignored, counter to the suggestions of Weiss (1972), Olson, White, and Shefrin (1979) and Low and Ormiston (1991). The outcome is compatible with the finding that (residual) earnings dispersion within schooling categories has no robust standard pattern in relation to the level of schooling (schooling and risk are uncorrelated, as was demonstrated empirically in Raita (2005, chapter 4)).

Although we believe that risk compensation in wages is genuine, a true test on causality would be most welcome. However, so far we have been unable to find a natural experiment or a good instrument for risk. A relevant concern is the correlation of risk attitude with other variables that may enhance earnings. If high-risk activities attract individuals with more ambition, greater drive, lower discount rate, then the reward for these traits will show up in higher earnings that give the appearance of compensation for risk. Note, however, that this argument does not seem to hold for ability, to the extent that the methods used to control for ability are sufficient (our use of school grades, IQ measures used in some regressions, using individual expectations and including individual fixed effects as regressor).

Further reflection on the nature and proper measurement of risk will lead into deep waters. An individual about to decide on the choice of an education has to consider the consequences of the alternatives over an entire lifetime. Conceptually, one may decompose the charting of possible consequences in several stages. The first step would be to analyse the present situation: observe realised outcomes for individuals who have made particular choices in the past. The second step would be to extrapolate such outcomes into the future, possibly acknowledging the effects of observable developments and trends (e.g. the impact of high and increasing enrolment rates in particular types of education). While this is obviously a difficult task in which individuals may differ greatly in skill (or luck), the first step is not an easy one either. To learn from realised outcomes in the present labour market what the consequences of a particular choice will be for an individual that individual should know to whom he should compare himself. He should know his abilities, ambitions, drives and also his tastes, both now and in the future. He should know not only whether he is smart enough to realise a particular career but should also know how hard he wants to work when he will be in his mid-forties. And he should understand how the labour market works and distinguish between consequences under control of the individual and consequences not under control. Ideally, he should have an idea of effects on his opportunity set and consequences of choice. The opportunity set is the set of jobs that he may choose from: jobs with different characteristics that would be priced as compensating differentials and therefore generate the same utility. Within the opportunity set, a competitive and transparent labour market would have wages to equate the 'whole of the advantages and the disadvantages' of these jobs. Risk would then only relate to the distribution of opportunity sets. Wages used to test risk compensation should use a reference wage, net of these effects (i.e. the wage should be purged of the monetary compensation for disamenities, by including the disamenities in the wage regressions[22]). But if the labour market is not fully transparent, there will be less than full compensation, depending on search and mobility costs. This leaves an element of risk in the wage distribution within an opportunity set: wage differentials for identical work by identical workers that will not be erased by search and mobility, as a form of stochastic rents. In a fully detailed analysis, extending to all the possible consequences of choosing a particular education during a worker's future working life, with all kinds of decision nodes, it is not immediately obvious how one should measure risk, as the uncertain outcome of a choice, and the consequences of choices within an opportunity set.

We have argued that there are strong arguments to accept the observed residual wage distribution as the agents' source of information on risk, and that there is no reason to apply a correction for unobserved heterogeneity. Indeed, in those cases where (some) unobserved heterogeneity was accounted for (controlling for ability, using individuals' predicted wages rather than market wages), the basic conclusions were upheld. But this is a very controversial issue, which is not surprising considering the lifetime sequence of opportunity sets that choice and luck will bring to individuals. At the same time it points to a most interesting direction for further research: uncovering the information that potential students actually use when they decide on their schooling. Heckman has set a challenging standard by claiming that at least half of the ex post variance in earnings is foreseen by individuals ex ante. Direct survey information from students suggests much more ignorance. Investigating students' information sets is not only relevant for the issue tackled in this chapter, but has far wider relevance in the economics of education.[23]

NOTES

1. The basic Mincer framework leads to earnings equation ln Y_s−ln $Y_0 = r$S. The standard deviation is taken from Hartog, van Ophem, and Bajdechi (2007). That paper presents a simulation of the distribution of rates of return as a function of stochastic properties of alternative life cycle wage profiles.

2. The classic reference for human capital investment under uncertainty is Levhari and Weiss (1974). Interest in the role of risk is growing; see the *Labour Economics Special Issue on Education and Risk*, 2007.

3. After I suggested this approach to Luis Diaz Serrano for his dissertation, he dug up the early references. A referee on one of the papers discussed here noted that the same idea had been repeatedly formulated by students.

4. In Diaz Serrano, et al. (2004), we have extended the model to include permanent and transitory shocks in a longitudinal framework. In Hartog and Vijverberg (2002), we estimate parameters of the utility function in a model with new shocks at every year of experience.

5. Cochrane (2001) points out that in a lifetime welfare maximising framework, variance as such is not relevant: it's the covariance of an asset with consumption that is essential. Levhari and Weiss (1974) also stress the key importance of the covariance between marginal utility of consumption and returns to education. We still denote the residual variance of wages as risk, as we abstract from optimal consumption profiles over the life cycle.

6. If the variables in X, like industry, firm size etc., would catch perfectly compensating differentials associated with free choice, they would have to be included as the residuals would then be standardised on equal-utility wages. This assumption is too strong to accept. See discussion in ninth section.

7. Hartog and Vijverberg (2002) test for log normality and mostly reject it. Still, adding the variance reduces the bias in the estimate of the mean.

8. Johnson (1977) and McGoldrick and Robst (1996) report a higher compensation in occupations with less mobility to other occupations: lock-in effects are compensated.

9. The Moulton problem is not relevant for Johnson (1977) and King (1974), who estimated on aggregate data by occupation and for Feinberg (1981), who estimated on panel data.

10. An education is a well-defined program, with its own curriculum and its own diploma. In Europe, secondary education is often organised in separate school types (like lower vocational, or general intermediary), tertiary education is not organised by 'majors' in broad bachelors', but by discipline right from the start, for example, economics or sociology.

11. Annual averages are in Table 6 of our IZA discussion paper no. 963 (Diaz Serrano et al. 2004).

12. The numbers are not equal to those in Chen's Table 4, but have been corrected for obvious printing errors.

13. See Blaug (1980) on the Lester–Machlup controversy (chapter 7) and on Friedman's methodological stance (chapter 4).

14. McKenzie, Gibson, and Stillman (2007) underscore the value of direct measurement of expectations. They also apply the Dominitz and Manski method and find that potential emigrants from Tonga underestimate earnings in New Zealand,

probably because actual emigrants under-report to restrict transfer obligations to relatives back home.

15. The effect of the increase in the risky asset share is given in Shaw's Table 2. Changes in mean wages by risk class are given by the regression results at the bottom of page 641. Variances by risk class are given in Footnote no. 22.

16. See Footnote no. 10 for definition of an education.

17. Eq. (9) in Lazear and Rosen (1981) and page 31 in Lazear (1995).

18. Eq. (10), Lazear and Rosen (1981): increasing shock variance reduces $g(0)$.

19. See Maddala (1983, p. 365). The conditional mean M of the truncated normal distribution is positive in threshold c. The conditional variance $V = 1 - M(M-c)$ cannot be signed as M is positive in c but $M-c$ is negative, as the derivative of M to c is smaller than 1.

20. In Gautier and Moraga-Gonzales (2003), wage dispersion is non-monotonic in labour market tightness: it first increases and then decreases with increasing tightness.

21. One commentator has remarked that workers can continue searching on the job and that there is repeated sampling rather than a single draw. This would imply that risk is not properly measured by observed wage variance. However, the argument is more complex. Repeated sampling keeps chopping off the lower end of the offer distribution, with presently earned wages as threshold. If the variance of the offer distribution increases, this will increase the mean of observed wages. But as the effect on observed variance cannot even be predicted for a single draw, the effect on observed variance in this case will be even harder to predict. Hence, we cannot predict the relationship between mean and variance of observed wages.

22. As noted earlier, we did so for the United States, in Hartog and Vijverberg (2002); it left key results unaffected.

23. Nicholson and Souleles (2001) report that individually expected income is a better predictor of specialty chosen by medical students than actual income, whether contemporaneous or realised. Predicting specialty choice with actual contemporaneous average income by specialty, uncorrected for selection bias, is correct in 57.3% of the cases. Using, instead, individually expected incomes with selectivity correction for actually chosen specialty yields correct predictions in 85.6%. Using realised average incomes as predictors of future incomes yields 50.6% correct predictions, whereas using expectations on the same sub-sample gives 72.8 correct predictions. These differences are also affected by the difference between using individual expectations and group averages, with much less variation.

ACKNOWLEDGEMENT

I have benefitted from discussions in the joint UvA-VU Labour seminar, at CREB (University of Barcelona), the SOLE/IZA Transatlantic Meeting in Buch am See 2007, University of Maastricht, SUNY Binghamton, SUNY Albany and Queen's University Kingston (Ont., Canada). Comments by Jim Rebitzer, Michael Sattinger, Hessel Oosterbeek and Pieter Gautier are also gratefully acknowledged.

REFERENCES

Arcidianoco, P. (2004). Ability sorting and the returns to college major. *Journal of Econometrics*, *121*(1–2), 343–375.

Arrow, K. (1965). *Aspects of the theory of risk-bearing*. Helsinki: Yrjo Hahnsson Foundation.

Belzil, C., & Leonardi, M. (2007). Can risk aversion explain schooling attainments? Evidence from Italy. *Labour Economics*, *14*(6), 957–970.

Berkhout, P., & Hartog, J. (2006). *Starting wages respond to employer risk*. Working Paper. University of Amsterdam.

Berkhout, P., Hartog, J., & van Ophem, H. (2009). *Starting wages respond to employer risk*. Discussion Paper Tinbergen Institute 09.071/3. Amsterdam (revision and extension of Berkhout and Hartog, 2006).

Berkhout, P., Hartog, J., & Webbink, D. (2006). *Risk compensation under worker heterogeneity*. Working Paper. Universiteit van Amsterdam, published in *Southern Economic Journal*, *76*(3), 762–790.

Betts,, J. R. (1996). What do students know about wages?. *Journal of Human Resources*, *31*(1), 27–56.

Blanchard, O. J., & Fisher, S. (1989). *Lectures on macroeconomics*. Cambridge, MA: MIT Press.

Blaug, M. (1980). *The methodology of economics*. Cambridge: Cambridge University Press.

Brown, S., & Taylor, K. (2005). Wage growth, human capital and financial investment. *Manchester School*, *73*(6), 686–708.

Brunello, G., Lucifora, C., & Winter-Ebmer, R. (2004). The wage expectations of European business and economics students. *Journal of Human Resources*, *39*(4), 1116–1142.

Budria, S., Diaz Serrano, L., Ferrer Carbonell, A., & Hartog, J. (2009). *Risk attitude and wage growth: Replication and reconstruction*. IZA discussion paper. Bonn.

Card, D. (1999). The causal effect of education on earnings. In: O. Ashenfelter & D. Card (Eds.), *Handbook of labor economics* (Vol. 3A). Amsterdam: North-Holland (Chapter 30).

Carroll, C. (2001). A theory of the consumption function, with and without liquidity constraints. *Journal of Economic Perspectives*, *15*(3), 23–45.

Chen, S. (2003). *Does college attendance reduce wage volatility?* Discussion paper. SUNY-Albany, NY.

Chen, S. (2008). Estimating the variance of wages in the presence of selection and unobserved heterogeneity. *Review of Economics and Statistics*, *90*(2), 275–289.

Chen, S., & Khan, S. (2007). *Estimating the causal effect of education on wage inequality using IV methods and sample selection models*. Working Paper. SUNY-Albany, NY.

Cochrane, J. (2001). *Asset pricing*. Princeton, NJ: Princeton University Press.

Cunha, F., & Heckman, J. (2007). Identifying and estimating the distributions of ex post and ex ante returns to schooling. *Labour Economics, Special Issue: Education and Risk*, *14*(6), 870–893.

Davis, S., & Willen, P. (2000). *Occupation-level income shocks and asset returns: Their covariance and implications for portfolio choice*. NBER Working Paper no. 7905. Boston, MA.

Diaz Serrano, L. (2000). *Human capital, progressive taxation and risk aversion*. Ph.D. dissertation, Universitat Rovira i Virgil, Spain.

Diaz Serrano, L. (2005). On the negative relationship between labor income uncertainty and homeownership: Risk aversion versus credit constraints. *Journal of Housing*, *14*(2), 109–126.

Diaz Serrano, L., & Hartog, J. (2006). Is there a risk-return trade-off across educations? Evidence from Spain. *Investigaciones Economicas*, *30*(2), 353–380.

Diaz Serrano, L., Hartog, J., & Skyt Nielsen, H. (2004). *Compensating wage differentials for schooling risk in Denmark*. Discussion Paper Maynooth/Amsterdam/Aarhus, an earlier version was published as IZA DP 963 in 2003; revision 2007; published in *Scandinavian Journal of Economics*, *110*(4), 2009.

Dohmen, T., Falk, A., Huffman, D., Sunde, U., Schupp, J., & Wagner, G. G. (2005). *Individual risk attitudes: New evidence from a large representative experimentally validated survey*. IZA discussion paper no. 1730. Bonn.

Dominitz, J., & Manski, C. (1996). Eliciting student expectations of the return to schooling. *Journal of Human Resources*, *31*, 1–26.

Feinberg, R. M. (1981). Earnings-risk as a compensating differential. *Southern Economic Journal*, *48*, 156–163.

Flyer, F., & Rosen, S. (1997). The new economics of teachers and education. *Journal of Labor Economics*, *15*(1, Part 2), S104–S139.

Garrett, T. A., & Sobel, R. S. (1999). Gamblers favor skewness, not risk: Further evidence from United States' Lottery games. *Economics Letters*, *63*, 85–90.

Gautier, P., & Moraga-Gonzales, J.L. (2003). *Strategic wage setting and coordination frictions with multiple applications*. Working Paper. Amsterdam.

Golec, J., & Tamarkin, M. (1998). Bettors love skewness, not risk, at the horse track. *Journal of Political Economy*, *106*(1), 205–225.

Gollier, C. (2001). *The economics of risk and time*. Cambridge, MA: MIT Press.

Hartog, J., & Diaz Serrano, L. (2007). Earnings risk and demand for higher education. *Journal of Applied Economics*, *X*(1), 1–28.

Hartog, J., van Ophem, H., & Bajdechi, S. (2007). Simulating the risk of investment in human capital. *Education Economics*, *15*(3), 259–275.

Hartog, J., Plug, E., Diaz Serrano, L., & Vieira, J. (2003). Risk compensation in wages – A replication. *Empirical Economics*, *28*, 639–647.

Hartog, J., & Vijverberg, W. (2002). *Do wages really compensate for risk aversion and skewness affection*? IZA discussion paper no. 426. Bonn.

Hartog, J., & Vijverberg, W. (2004). *On compensation for risk aversion and skewness affection in wages*. Working Paper. University of Amsterdam, revision of Hartog and Vijverberg (2002); shorter version in *Labour Economics, Special Issue on Education and Risk*, *14*(6), 938–956 (2007).

Hartog, J., & Vijverberg, W. (2007). Schools, skills and risk. *Economics of Education Review*, *26*(6), 758–770.

Hubbard, R., Skinner, J., & Zeldes, S. (1995). Precautionary saving and social insurance. *Journal of Political Economy*, *103*(2), 360–399.

Jacobs, B., Hartog, J., & Vijverberg, W. (2008). Self-selection bias in estimated wage premiums for earnings risk. *Empirical Economics*, *37*(2), 271–286.

Johnson, W. (1977). Uncertainty and the distribution of earnings. In: F. Juster (Ed.), *The distribution of economic well-being* (pp. 379–396). Cambridge, MA: Ballinger for NBER.

Keane, P., & Wolpin, K. (2001). The effect of parental transfers and borrowing constraints on educational attainment. *International Economic Review*, *42*(4), 1051–1103.

King, A. G. (1974). Occupational choice, risk aversion and wealth. *Industrial and Labor Relations Review*, 586–596.

Kodde, D. (1985). *Microeconomic analysis of demand for education*. Ph.D. thesis, Erasmus University Rotterdam.

Lazear, E.. (1995). *Personnel economics*. Cambridge, MA: MIT Press.

Lazear, E. (2005). Entrepreneurship. *Journal of Labor Economics*, *23*(4), 649–680.

Lazear, E., & Rosen, S. (1981). Rank-order tournaments as optimal labor contracts. *Journal of Political Economy*, *89*(5), 841–864.

Levhari, D., & Weiss, Y. (1974). The effect of risk on the investment in human capital. *American Economic Review*, *64*(6), 950–963.

Low, H. (2005). Self-insurance in a life-cycle model of labour supply and savings. *Review of Economic Dynamics*, *8*(4), 945–975.

Low, S., & Ormiston, M. (1991). Stochastic earnings functions and risk. *Southern Economic Journal*, *57*(4), 1124–1132.

Ma, X. (2005). *Research on the risk of individual investment in education – Using the urban Chinese in the 1990s as an example*. Ph.D. dissertation, Peking University.

Maddala, G. (1983). *Limited-dependent and qualitative variables in econometrics*. Cambridge: Cambridge University Press.

McGoldrick, K. (1995). Do women receive compensating wages for earnings risk?. *Southern Economic Journal*, *62*, 210–222.

McGoldrick, K., & Robst, J. (1996). The effect of worker mobility on compensating wages for earnings risk. *Applied Economics*, *28*, 221–232.

McKenzie, D., Gibson, J., & Stillman, S. (2007). A land of milk and honey with streets paved with gold: Do emigrants have over-optimistic expectations about incomes abroad? IZA discussion paper no. 2788. Bonn.

Mincer, J. (1974; reprinted 1993). *Schooling, experience and earnings*. Aldershot UK: Gregg Revivals.

Moore, M. J. (1995). Unions, employment risks, and market provision of employment risk differentials. *Journal of Risk and Uncertainty*, *10*(1), 57–70.

Mortensen, D. (1986). Job search and labor market analysis. In: O. Ashenfelter & R. Layard (Eds.), *Handbook of labor economics* (Vol. 2). Amsterdam: North-Holland (Chapter 15).

Moulton, B. R. (1986). Random group effects and the precision of regression estimates. *Journal of Econometrics*, *32*, 385–397.

Murphy, K., & Topel, R. (1985). Estimation and inference in two-step econometric models. *Journal of Business and Economic Statistics*, *3*, 88–97.

Nicholson, S., & Souleles, N. (2001). *Physician income expectations and specialty choice*. NBER Working Paper no. 8536. Cambridge.

Olson, L., White, H., & Shefrin, H. (1979). Optimal investment in schooling when incomes are risky. *Journal of Political Economy*, *87*(3), 522–539.

Palacios-Huerta, I. (2003). An empirical analysis of the risk properties of human capital returns. *American Economic Review*, *93*(3), 948–964.

Pereira, P., & Martins, P. (2002). Is there a return-risk link in education? *Economics Letters*, *75*(1), 31–37.

Pratt, J. (1964). Risk aversion in the small and in the large. *Econometrica*, *32*, 122–136.

Raita, S. (2005). *The risk of investment in human capital*. Ph.D. thesis, Tinbergen Institute Universiteit van Amsterdam.

Rosen, S. (1986). The theory of equalizing differences. In: O. Ashenfelter & R. Layard (Eds.), *Handbook of labor economics* (Vol. 1). Amsterdam: North-Holland (Chapter 12).

Saks, R., & Shore, S. (2003). *Risk and career choice*. Paper presented at the AEA Meetings, San Diego, January 2004.

Schweri, J., Hartog, & Wolter, S. (2008). *Do students expect compensation for wage risk?* Working Paper. University of Amsterdam.

Shaw, K. L. (1996). An empirical analysis of risk aversion and income growth. *Journal of Labor Economics*, *14*(4), 626–653.

Skyt Nielsen, H., & Vissing-Jorgenson, A. (2006). *The impact of labour market risk on education choices: Estimates and implied risk aversion*. Working Paper. Aarhus/Northwestern.

Tsiang, S. C. (1972). The rationale for mean-standard deviation analysis, skewness preference and the demand for money. *American Economic Review*, *62*(3), 354–371.

Webbink, D., & Hartog, J. (2004). Can students predict their starting salary? Yes! *Economics of Education Review*, *23*(2), 103–113.

Weiss, Y. (1972). The risk element in occupational and educational choices. *Journal of Political Economy*, *80*(6), 1203–1213.

Wolter, S., & Weber, B. (2004). *Returns to education: Are students' expectations rational?* Working Paper. Swiss Coordination Center for Research in Education, Aarau, Switzerland.

APPENDIX A: RISK COMPENSATION IN LEVHARI AND WEISS (1974)

Eq.(5) in Levhari and Weiss (1974), in their notation, reads

$$E\left\{\frac{\partial U}{\partial c_1}\left[f_\lambda - (1+r)y_0\right]\right\} = 0$$

or

$$\frac{E(\partial U)/(\partial c_1)f_\lambda}{y_0 E(\partial U)/(\partial c_1)} = 1 + r$$

Subtracting $E(f_\lambda)/y_o$ on both sides, and using $E(xy) = E(x)E(y) + \text{cov}(x,y)$, we can write

$$\frac{Ef_\lambda}{y_0} = 1 + r - \frac{\text{cov}((\partial U)/(\partial c_1), f_\lambda)}{y_0 E(\partial U)/(\partial c_1)}$$

Kodde (1985, chapter 7) shows, using a second-order Taylor expansion around $E(\mu)$ that we may write

$$\begin{aligned}\text{cov}\left(\frac{\partial U}{\partial c_1}, f_\lambda\right) &= \frac{\partial^2 U}{\partial c_1^2}\text{f}_\mu \text{f}_{\lambda\mu}\sigma^2 - \left|\frac{\partial^3 U}{\partial c_2^3}\text{f}_\mu^2 \text{f}_{\lambda\mu\mu}\right. \\ &\quad \left. + \frac{\partial^2 U}{\partial c_2^2} f_{\mu\mu} f_{\lambda\mu\mu}\right|\sigma^4/4\end{aligned}$$

where σ^2 is the variance of μ. Assuming $f_{\lambda\mu\mu} = 0$, as Levhari and Weiss (1974) implicitly do, we can write

$$\begin{aligned}E\frac{f_\lambda}{y_0} &= 1 + r - y_0 \frac{\partial^2 U/\partial c_1^2}{E\partial U/\partial c_1}\text{f}_\mu \text{f}_{\lambda\mu}\frac{\sigma^2}{y_0^2} \\ &= 1 + r + \rho \text{f}_\mu \text{f}_{\lambda\mu}\frac{\sigma^2}{y_0^2}\end{aligned}$$

where ρ is relative risk aversion evaluated at expected values. Thus, with risk aversion positive, and $f_{\lambda\mu}$ positive as assumed by Levhari and Weiss, under uncertainty the expected return on human capital surpasses the Mincer rate by a term that is proportional to risk aversion and relative variance.

APPENDIX B: MEAN AND DISPERSION IN THE TOURNAMENT MODEL (LAZEAR & ROSEN, 1981)

Under risk aversion, equilibrium condition (23) in Lazear and Rosen (1981) can be written as

$$\mu = \frac{1}{C'(\mu)} \frac{V}{1 + a\sigma^2} \quad \text{with} \quad a = sC''\Pi > 0$$

Totally differentiating and rewriting yields

$$\frac{d\mu}{d\sigma} = -\frac{2a\sigma\mu/(1 + a\sigma^2)}{1 + \mu C''(\mu)/C'(\mu)} < 0$$

This holds because $C' > 0$ and $C'' > 0$ by assumption. One might also write the equilibrium condition as

$$\mu C'(\mu) = \frac{V}{1 + a\sigma^2}$$

With the LHS increasing in μ, an increase in σ^2 has to be matched by a decrease in μ.

The equilibrium wage dispersion, according to Footnote (9) in Lazear and Rosen (1981) obeys

$$C'(\mu) = wb\sigma^{-1} \text{ with } w = w_1 - w_2 \text{ and } b = 1/\sqrt{2\Pi}$$

Totally differentiating this condition (to μ, w and σ) yields,

$$\frac{dw}{d\sigma} = \frac{\sigma}{b}\left\{C''(\mu)\frac{d\mu}{d\sigma} + wb\sigma^{-2}\right\}$$
$$= \frac{\mu C''(\mu)}{b}\left\{\varepsilon_\sigma^\mu + \frac{1}{\mu C''(\mu)/C'(\mu)}\right\}$$

where ε_σ^μ is the elasticity of μ to σ. Thus

$$\frac{dw}{d\sigma} > 0 \quad \text{if} \quad \varepsilon_\sigma^\mu > -\left[\frac{C''(\mu)}{C'(\mu)}\mu\right]^{-1}$$

that is, if the elasticity of effort is between zero and the inverse of what might be called relative effort aversion. The elasticity is endogenous, characterising the dislocation of equilibrium effort. If we substitute from Eq. (1) above, we can derive

$$\frac{\mathrm{d}w}{\mathrm{d}\sigma} = \frac{C'(\mu)}{b}\left\{1 - \frac{2a\sigma^2\mu C'(\mu)}{1 + \mu C''(\mu)/C'(\mu)}\frac{1}{V}\right\}$$

This is ambiguous in sign, depending on exogenous parameter values.

CHAPTER 5

WORKERS' MOBILITY AND THE RETURN TO EDUCATION, EVIDENCE FROM PUBLIC AND PRIVATE SECTORS

Yuval Mazar

ABSTRACT

This chapter examines whether changes in return to education affect workers' mobility between jobs. Employee panel data are used to study staff movement from the public sector to the private sector or vice versa from 1995 to 2005. It is found that in line with the situation in other advanced economies, the wage structure in the public sector in Israel is more compressed than that in the private sector, for employees with similar characteristics and in general, and that the difference widened during the period reviewed. Hence, the findings support the contention that the public sector compensates employees less for their skills than does the private sector. In addition, it is found that during that period the return to education increased in the private sector by about 1 percentage point more than in the public sector. In an analysis of those who switched from one sector to the other, our findings imply that if the return to education changed at the same rate in both sectors, the probability of highly educated workers moving from the public sector to the private sector would be 5 percent lower, and the probability of highly educated workers moving from the private sector to the public sector would be 2 percent higher.

Research in Labor Economics, Volume 33, 175–208

ISSN: 0147-9121/doi:10.1108/S0147-9121(2011)0000033008

Keywords: Workers' Mobility; Return to Education; Wage-Structure's Differences between the Private and Public Sector; Quintiles Regressions Models (QRM)

JEL classifications: J31; J38; J45; J62; H83

INTRODUCTION

This chapter[1] makes a contribution to the literature by dealing empirically with the question of whether, and to what extent, workers' incentives of switching jobs are affected by changes in the return to education.

In the framework of this chapter, a unique set of panel data has been used, which includes employees who left the public sector and those who entered it. The data for these employees have enabled me to examine the selection processes for both exits from and entrances to posts in the public sector.

Beggs and Chapman (1988) analyzed public-sector employees at the level of clerks in Australia and found that employees with a high level of ability displayed a higher probability of leaving the public sector. They ascribed this finding to the more concentrated wage distribution in the public sector than in the private sector in Australia.

Kats and Kruger (1991, 1993) provided supplementary evidence showing that when a correction for the differences in the distribution of education and experience between the sectors is introduced, there is less inequality in income among public sector employees than among private sector employees.

Dahl (2002) found by exploiting migration's data between U.S. states that relative state-to-state migration flows of college versus high-school educated individuals respond strongly to differences in the return to education and amenities across states. His calculation implies that 3.9 percent of the college educated men moved in response to a higher return in another state, which it accounts for 9.6 percent of the migration of college-educated men.

Using data from the 10-yearly census and regular population surveys undertaken in the United States, Borjas (2002) documented the differential shifts that occurred in the wage structure of the public and private sectors between 1960 and 2000. He found that the wage differential between similar employees in the public and private sectors was relatively constant for men during this period but declined significantly for women. He also found that the variance of wages in the public sector rose relative to that in the private sector before 1970, when employment in the public sector expanded rapidly. Since 1970, there has been a relatively significant compression of wage distribution in the public sector. He claimed that the various developments of wage structure in the two sectors constituted an important factor determining the selection of employees between the sectors, and as a result of the relative wage compression the public sector found it increasingly difficult to attract and retain able employees.

Using a cohort of young employees, Fougère and Pouget (2003) found that when all the observed characteristics are equal the employees with the lowest wage in the private sector were also those whose probability of being unemployed was the highest. Conversely, it appears that the entrance examinations for the public sector select those individuals who have the greatest potential for earning a high wage in the private sector. Fougère and Pouget (2003) provided further evidence of the excess supply of employees seeking work in the French public sector.

Lucifora and Meurs (2004) analyzed wage determination in the private and public sectors by means of microeconomic data from France, the United Kingdom, and Italy. In contrast with the traditional methods, which focus on parametric ways of estimating the wage differential in the public sector, they used both non-parametric methods and quantile regressions to analyze wage-distribution between the sectors. They showed that the (hourly) wage differential between the public and private sectors was sensitive to the selection of percentile, and that the premium pattern changed with both gender and skill level. They found that in all the countries studied the public sector employed a greater number of low-skilled employees than the private sector, whereas the reverse applied for better educated employees; they also found that these trends were more pronounced among women.

Bargian and Melly (2008) estimated the wage differential in the French public sector for the period 1990–2002, for both the mean and the various percentiles of the wage distribution, for men and women separately. They found that the wage premium in the public sector (for women), or the 'penalty' (for men), was essentially a result of selection. After taking unobserved heterogeneity into account, only small wage differences remained between the sectors over time; thus, the differences reflected specific public policy and the pro-cyclical nature of wages in the private sector. In the final event, the difference in the long run was zero. They also found that the relative compression of the wage distribution in the public sector was derived in part also from unobserved characteristics. These results were explained by the fact that the public sector manages to attract better employees at the lower end of the distribution, partly due to non-financial advantages (including job security), but does not manage to keep the most productive employees at the top. This is often explained by the fact that governments are motivated by competitive considerations to a lesser extent than is the private sector, and also have a greater tendency towards justice and fairness in wage arrangements. This is expressed in higher wages than the market level at the lower end of the wage distribution and more modest wages at the higher end in the public sector. Employees at the lower end of the wage distribution in the public sector are those who were positively selected by this sector. At the top of the wage distribution are employees with the highest potential wage (and possibly also with the least risk-avoidance) who choose the private sector by self-selection. Several findings tend to bear out these opinions.

Ghinetti and Lucifora (2008) studied wage determination in the public and private sectors by means of microeconomic data from France, the United Kingdom, and Italy, taken from ECHP 2001. They showed that the wage distribution differed widely between the private and the public sectors. As a result the premium on the public-sector wage changed as the employee rose or fell in the wage distribution. In France, the United Kingdom, and Italy the premium on the public-sector wage is higher for employees with a low level of education, whereas the reverse is true for better educated employees. These trends are particularly evident in the services sector. Additional results indicated that if an employee with specific characteristics is transferred exogenously from the public to the private sector he loses welfare (wage), and this is greater for employees with a low level of education, as for them job security is more significant.

Gould and Moav (2008) reviewed the effect of inequality in the period from 1995 to 2004 on the incentive to emigrate from Israel to the United States on the basis of the observed and unobserved characteristics of working men in Israel. In their article they distinguished between general skills which are relatively easily transferred and specific skills which are less easily transferred. They found a non-monotonic U-shaped correlation between an employee's skills, defined by his residual wage, and the probability of emigration, and a positive correlation between an employee's education level and the probability of emigration.

The rest of the article is organized as follows: Part 2 contains an analysis of the environment and data sources, including their advantages and disadvantages; Part 3 gives a statistical account of the data, including an examination of the difference between the way the two sectors reward employees; Part 4 details some estimations of the return to education during the period; Part 5 presents stylized facts about the probability of leaving a sector during the period; Part 6 provides statistical analysis using appropriate regressions; and Part 7 consists of the conclusion.

THE DATA

The data series used here is a representative random sample of the entire population, and is a panel sample that is unique to Israel. The employees were taken from Israel's 1995 population census and linked to income-tax employer–employee data for the period 1996–2005 (the link was affected with the aid of Israel's Central Bureau of Statistics). The data included all Israeli citizens who responded to the 'expanded questionnaire' that was administered to 20 percent of households in 1995 in such a way as to be representative of the general population. The population census is the most extensive source of demographic and socio-economic data on the population in Israel.

The relatively large number of observations makes it possible to analyze different groups of employees separately and reliably. An employee was defined as an individual who works in one of the sectors on the basis of the principal industry: the uniform classification of principal industries to the four-digit level. It was assumed that if an employee were defined as working in the public sector on the basis of the four-digit classification in 1996, he also worked in the public sector in 1995, according to a three-digit classification. This refers to a very small number of observations. To adjust for temporary shifts of employees from one sector to the other, the following two main periods were defined:

I. 'First period', 1995–1997
II. 'Second period', 2003–2005

An employee was defined as working in a given sector if he was employed in that sector for at least two years in a specific period. The employee's wage was calculated only on the basis of his wage in the sector in which he was employed.

The data enable us to compare employees who left the public sector with those who remained in it, as well as to compare those who left the private sector with those who remained in it, to examine selection in leaving. Employees who left a given sector were not compared with those in the sector to which they moved.

To give these comparisons significance, the study refers solely to employees who were aged between 30 and 50 years in 1995 and had worked at least 25 hours a month in 1995. The sample does not include full-time military personnel or self-employed persons, meaning that the data about labour income are reliable. Since the focus of this chapter is to determine the selection of workers in terms of their education and wages, I restrict the statistical analysis (see section 'Statistical Tests') to males who have stronger attachment to labour market compared to females.

The data file has several drawbacks:

1. I do not have data showing whether the employee was dismissed or resigned from his post.

2. The definition of the sector in which an employee works, even though this has been done to the four-digit level for the first time in Israel, is not 100 percent accurate. This means that the employee may be defined as working in the public sector but in effect works in the private sector, and vice versa. Although this occurrence is fairly rare, the issue should be taken into account. In addition, the organization within which employees work may have been privatized. In a situation of this kind, we will not have the transition of employees between sectors even though this has in fact occurred. Note that this refers to a negligible number of observations.
3. There is no data on the education of employees after 1995. For this reason we have focused on employees who are more than 30 years of age, assuming that most of the investment in human capital is made at earlier ages. Similarly, there is no data on the hours worked by employees after 1995, and hence we have concentrated solely on employees who worked at least 25 hours a month in 1995.
4. The data are a balanced panel data, as workers who did not work at the second period are excluded from the data. The share of these workers is about 19 percent, 22 percent from the private sector workers and 15 percent from the public sector workers. It is known that the selection out from the labour market is negatively correlated with workers' productivity. This is to say that the analysis of the sub-population in this chapter does not represent the whole population at the labour market but only the population which is better labour-market-tied.
5. A negligible share of the workers have worked in the same sector at the first and the second period but changed their sector at least twice during the period – about 1 percent.

DESCRIPTIVE STATISTICS AND AN EXAMINATION OF THE DIFFERENCE BETWEEN THE SECTORS IN EMPLOYEES' PAY

Throughout the period reviewed, 1995–2005, there was no significant change in the relative shares of the public and private sectors; the public sector accounted for 36 percent, with 50 percent of women and 25 percent of men. Table 1 gives the mean and standard deviations of the main variables used in the analysis of the two sectors in 1995. The table refers solely to the population selected from the total census population (the table for the entire population is available from the author).

Table 1. Descriptive Statistics.

			Men		Women	
	Public	Private	Public	Private	Public	Private
No. of observations	33,617	59,227	12,063	38,239	21,554	20,988
Monthly wage	5,083	5,195	6,526	5,837	4,276	4,023
Standard deviation	3,011	3,428	3,472	3,629	2,361	2,651
Hourly wage	39.4	33.0	41.3	34.8	38.3	29.7
Standard deviation	21.0	22.7	22.6	23.5	20.0	20.7
Years of education	14.3	12.7	13.9	12.5	14.5	13.0
Standard deviation	3.17	3.15	3.55	3.34	2.92	2.74
Family size	4.4	4.2	4.5	4.4	4.3	4.0
Married	0.88	0.88	0.92	0.92	0.86	0.81
No. of months worked in a year	11.6	11.5	11.7	11.5	11.5	11.4
No. of hours worked in a month	135.0	164.8	164.9	176.5	118.2	143.3
Standard deviation	46.7	41.8	43.8	39.6	39.4	36.9
Jewish	0.93	0.91	0.88	0.87	0.95	0.98
New immigrant	0.10	0.19	0.10	0.18	0.10	0.20
Secular	0.98	0.99	0.95	0.99	1.00	1.00
Born in Africa or Asia	0.14	0.15	0.14	0.14	0.13	0.13
Born in America or Europe	0.26	0.24	0.26	0.29	0.27	0.36
Women	0.64	0.36				

Several stylized facts may be inferred from the table:

- As is the case in most other countries, women are over-represented in the public sector.
- The average monthly wage in both sectors is similar even though the monthly wage is higher in the public sector for both men and women. This is the result of the higher monthly wage among men.
- The scatter, as measured by the standard deviation, of both the monthly and the hourly wage is higher in the private sector.
- Both men and women, but especially women, work fewer hours in the public sector.
- The hourly wage is higher in the public sector for both men and women, and for both of them together. This also reflects the higher average level of education in the public sector.
- In the public sector the hourly wage of men was 8 percent higher than that of women, whereas in the private sector it was 17 percent higher. This is the case despite the fact that the ratio between years of education is similar in both sectors, being higher among women in both sectors.

Since the wage distribution in general, and wage variance in particular, is not similar in both sectors, a comparison of the mean wage (conditional and non-conditional) cannot provide a full picture of the differences in the way they reward employees. Moreover, if the distribution changes over time, limiting the analysis to the first moment is even more problematic. As a result, it is necessary to analyze the differences in wages between the two sectors by means of techniques which expose the differences throughout the distribution, taking into account the fact that these differences exist.

We begin by presenting the monthly wage distribution of the two sectors with the aid of a non-parametric Kernel density. The illustrations are given in Fig. 1 separately for each period (the first and the second). The main statistics of the distribution are presented at the end of each illustration.

The presentation of the distribution in both sectors over time emphasizes the fact that the wage distribution in the public sector is more condensed than that in the private sector, and over time the difference in the scatter between the two sectors has increased. Thus, for example, the difference between the standard deviation of the wage log throughout the period is 6.5 and 11.9 points for the first period and the third period, respectively.

Studies undertaken elsewhere in the world show that in most of the developed and developing countries the wage distribution is more equitable in the public than in the private sector.[2] This is expressed in a more compressed structure of wages, whether conditional or not, and almost certainly in a lower return to the individual's skill level. In view of the differences in the wage distribution and scatter between the sectors, several studies have criticized the accepted approach which is based on analyzing the mean conditional wage only. The use of quantile regression methods[3] (QRM) makes it possible to analyze the entire wage distribution, while the marginal effect of the independent variables on the dependent variables could be different at different points of the wage distribution.

These results may also be interpreted as the effect of the different distribution of unobserved wage factors, for a given series of employees' characteristics, at different points of the wage distribution. The analytical framework chosen here for the estimation is based on the quantile regression methodology developed by Koenker and Bassett (1978) and applied in the context of wage equations by Chamberlain (1994), Poterba and Rueben (1994), Buchinsky (1994, 1997), and others.

Fig. 2 describes the public premium across the percentiles with and without occupation control separately for women and men. The negative slope in the figure presents the decrease of the public wage premium with workers' wage percentile. As it is seen, the negative slope is not sensitive to the regressions' definitions: with or without occupations' control. However, the positive public premium for men over all wage percentiles is changed to negative premium when submitting the regressions without less educated workers.

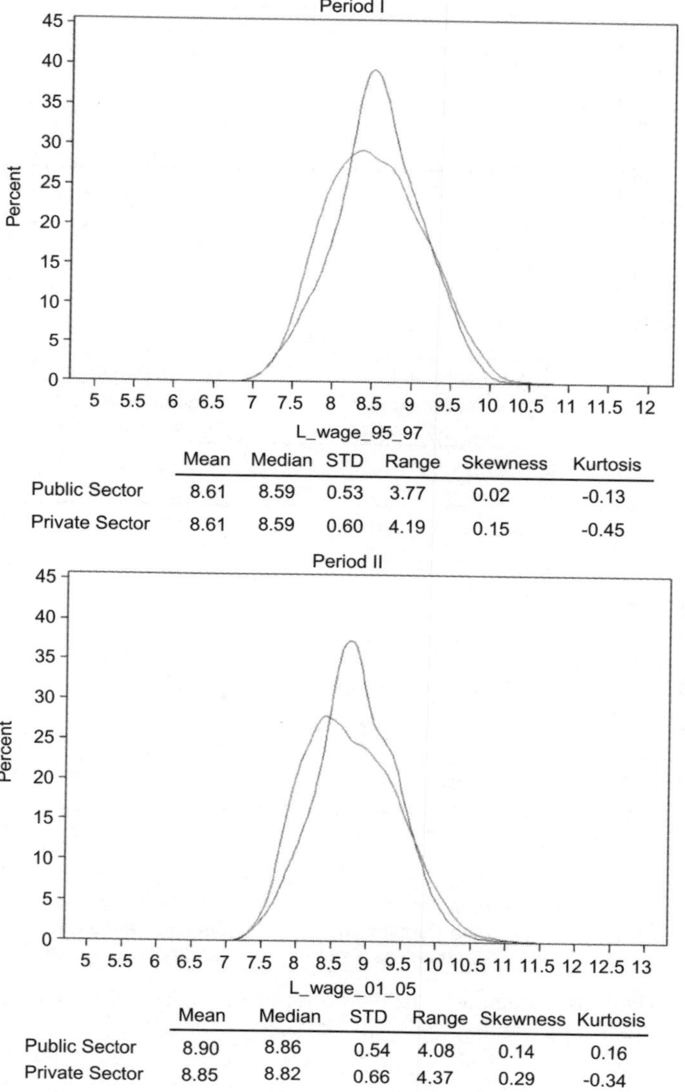

Period I

	Mean	Median	STD	Range	Skewness	Kurtosis
Public Sector	8.61	8.59	0.53	3.77	0.02	-0.13
Private Sector	8.61	8.59	0.60	4.19	0.15	-0.45

Period II

	Mean	Median	STD	Range	Skewness	Kurtosis
Public Sector	8.90	8.86	0.54	4.08	0.14	0.16
Private Sector	8.85	8.82	0.66	4.37	0.29	-0.34

Fig. 1. Distribution of log monthly wage in the public and the private Sectors. *Note*: There are two lines in each illustration, the upper one representing the wage distribution in the public sector and the lower one representing the wage distribution in the private sector.

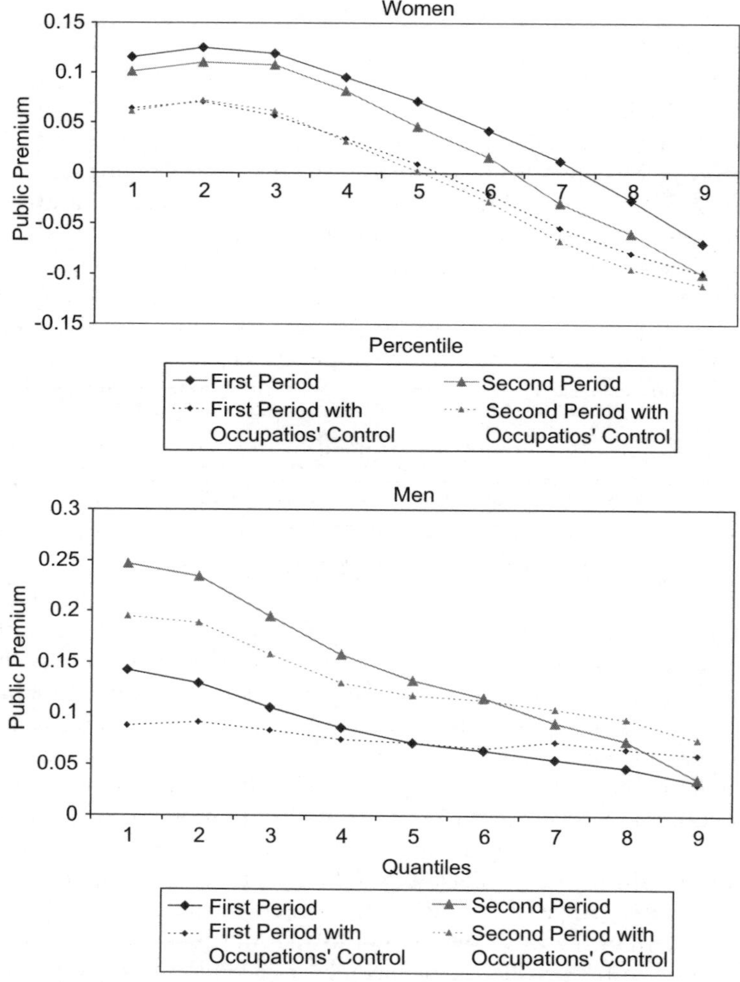

Fig. 2. The wage premium in the public sector throughout the wage percentiles.

A comparison of the two sectors' reward systems is not without its problems. The greater the difference between the sectors with regard to their activity, and the smaller the substitutability between them with regard to the provision of a service, the harder it is to compare the two sectors, so it is preferable to concentrate on smaller groups of employees. Since most physicians, nurses, teachers, policemen, and members of the legal system work in the public sector, while most salesmen, insurance employees, engineers, and tradesmen work in the private sector, a comparison of the wage distribution of all employees would be erroneous and misleading. Fig. 3 describes the proportion of employees in each sector in each of the nine principal occupations (according to the one-digit definition of Central Bureau of Statistics [CBS] (in Israel)), for men and women separately. The proportions are an average of the entire period reviewed.

The difference in occupational frequency between the two sectors is particularly evident among women: most of the women who are employed in the public sector have a university degree or work in the liberal professions (nurses) in contrast to those who are employed in the private sector, where most of them are secretaries. Most of the men who are employed in the public sector also have an academic degree or work in the liberal professions, but in the private sector most of them are employed in manufacturing and the services sectors.

THE RETURN TO EDUCATION

Fig. 4 depicts the development of average monthly wage in the private and public sectors during 1995 to 2005. This is done separately for highly educated workers (more than 14 years of schooling) and less educated workers (less than 15 years of schooling), and for women and men. The figure displays that the average monthly wage of highly educated workers was higher in the private sector compared with the average monthly wage of highly educated workers in the public sector, and this gap was raised during the period, for both women and men. It also shows that the average monthly wage of less educated men was lower in the private sector compared with the average monthly wage of less educated workers in the public sector.

This pattern of the wage's growth hints that during the period the return to education in the private sector has increased rapidly compared with the return to education in the public sector. Now I will try to support this hypothesis by submitting many regressions which take into account the different observed and unobserved skills among the workers at the two sectors.

Table 2 details, separately for women and men, the estimation of the private skilled premium (PSP) derived from different specifications of Ordinary Least Squares (OLS) regressions. The specifications are differed by the explanatory variables which they control for – the row effect, and by the analyzed population – the column effect.

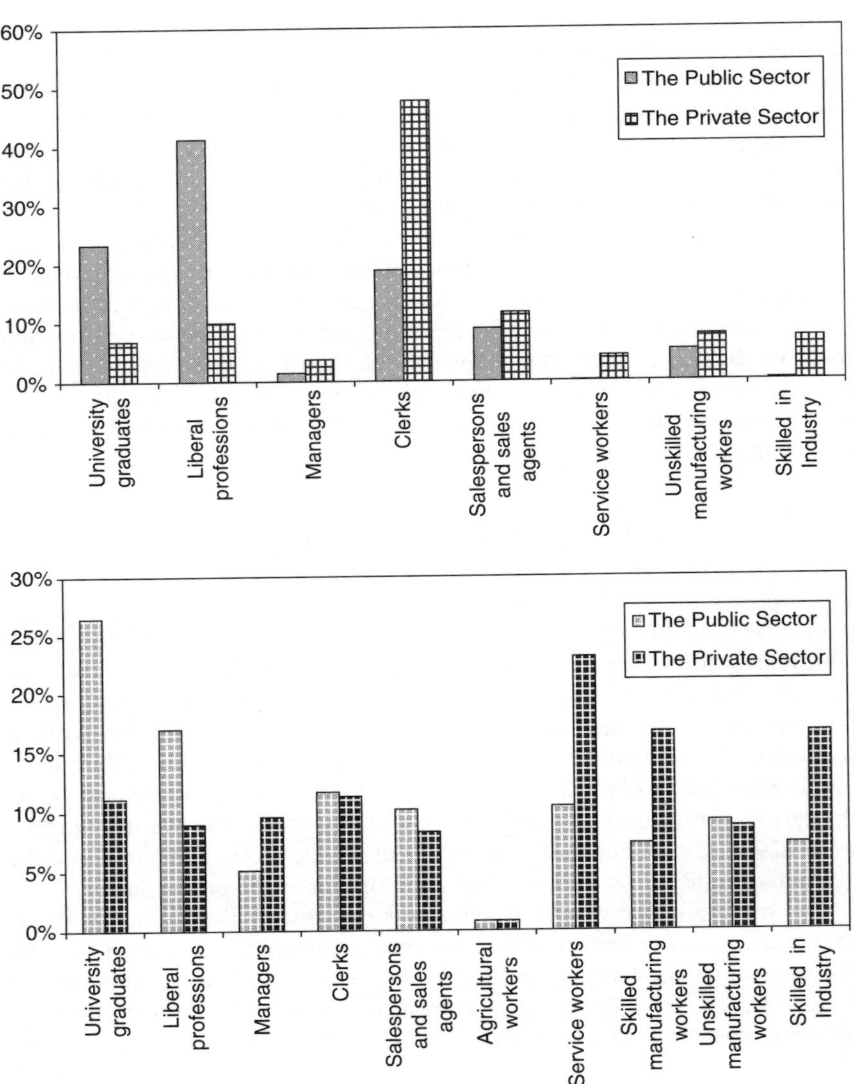

Fig. 3. Frequency of principal occupations in the private and the public sectors.

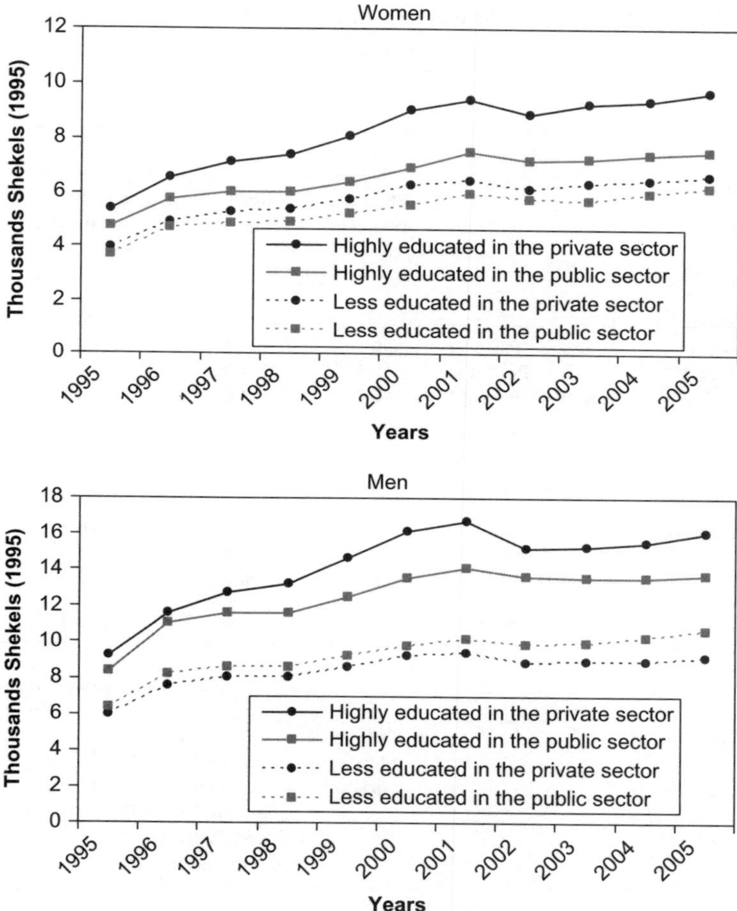

Fig. 4. The average wage in the private and the public sectors among highly educated and less educated workers.

The regression estimate is as follows:

$$w_{i,t} = X'\beta + \text{NYS} \cdot \delta_1 + Pr \cdot \delta_2 + \text{NYS} \cdot Pr \cdot \delta_3 + \varepsilon_{i,t}$$
$$t = 1996 - 2005$$

where $X =$ age, age squared, the average hours of working per month.

Table 2. The Private Skilled Premium for One Year of Schooling During the Period.

Women

	Population	A	B	C	
		Steady workers	Steady workers who have stayed at the same sector during the period	B′ + Fixed age during the period	Average
Independent variables X'	Period I	−0.3	−0.9	−1.8	
	Period II	−0.1	−0.0	1.4	
	Period II−Period I	**0.2**	**0.9**	**3.1**	**1.4**
X' + occupations	Period I	0.1	0.1	−1.0	
	Period II	0.2	0.2	1.2	
	Period II−Period I	**0.1**	**0.1**	**2.1**	**0.8**
X' + occupations + initial wage	Period I	0.2	0.2	−0.1	
	Period II	0.7	0.8	1.2	
	Period II−Period I	**0.5**	**0.6**	**1.3**	**0.8**
	Average	**0.3**	**0.6**	**2.2**	1.0

Men

	Population	A	B	C	
		Steady workers	Steady workers who have stayed at the same sector during the period	B′ + Fixed age during the period	Average
Independent variables X'	Period I	3.3	3.3	3.0	
	Period II	3.5	4.4	5.0	
	Period II − Period I	**0.2**	**1.1**	**2.1**	**1.1**
X' + occupations	Period I	2.7	2.7	2.2	
	Period II	2.7	2.7	3.8	
	Period II − Period I	**−0.0**	**−0.0**	**1.6**	**0.5**
X' + occupations + initial wage	Period I	1.2	0.9	0.7	
	Period II	1.7	1.7	1.9	
	Period II − Period I	**0.4**	**0.7**	**1.2**	**0.8**
	Average	**0.2**	**0.6**	**1.6**	0.8

NYS is the number of years of schooling, which means that δ_1 is the return to education. Pr is a dummy variable for working at the private sector, which means that δ_3 is the PSP estimation and its values are detailed in Table 2.

Above all, it can be seen that PSP increases during the period in most specifications for both genders. The discrepancy of the results is lower for men compared with women. The occupations' control diminishes the increase in PSP, whereas the effect of the initial wage's control is not monotonous even if, on average, it raises the increase in PSP. Most of the time the increase in PSP is reinforced when the population analyzed is only workers who have not changed their sector during the whole period (column B). When the age of the workers is fixed during the period, which means only workers at ages between 30 and 45 for each year are chosen, the increase in PSP is obviously reinforced. The average increase in PSP from the first period to the second period is 0.8 percent and 1.0 percent for men and women, respectively.

The raise in PSP during the period is robust for other checks, among them checking only workers with full-time position or restricting the examination to the sub-population, analyzed in section 'Statistical Tests', by the multivariable regressions.

Another specification is to use a dummy variable for highly educated workers instead of the number of years of schooling; this variable gets 1 if a worker has 15 years of schooling at least and 0 otherwise. Table 3 presents the estimate of the interaction variable of PSP using the dummy variable of highly educated workers and the private sector.

The regression estimate is as follows:

$$w_{i,t} = X'\beta + \text{HEW} \cdot \delta_1 + \text{Pr} \cdot \delta_2 + \text{HEW} \cdot \text{Pr} \cdot \delta_3 + \varepsilon_{i,t}$$
$$t = 1996 - 2005$$

where HEW is the dummy variable for highly educated workers.

The results are at the same direction as the raise in PSP derived from using years of schooling instead. The average value of the raise at the interaction variable (6.8) during the period is the same for both genders and it approximately equals to the increase in PSP (1.0 and 0.8) multiplied by the difference at the average number of years of schooling among highly educated workers and less educated workers (6 years). Like the previous specification, the main result is robust to other specifications or population's definitions.

Table 3. The Private Skilled Premium for Highly Educated Workers During the Period.

Women

	Population	A	B	C	
		Steady workers	Steady workers who have stayed at the same sector during the period	B′ + Fixed age during the period	Average
Independent variables X'	Period I	−5.5	−8.5	−13.5	
	Period II	−1.8	−2.9	3.3	
	Period II−Period I	**3.7**	**5.6**	**16.8**	**8.7**
X' + occupations	Period I	−2.9	−2.9	−8.6	
	Period II	0.5	0.5	3.9	
	Period II−Period I	**3.4**	**3.4**	**12.5**	**6.4**
X' + occupations + initial wage	Period I	0.4	−0.2	−1.6	
	Period II	4.6	3.9	5.5	
	Period II−Period I	**4.2**	**4.1**	**7.1**	**5.1**
	Average	**3.8**	**4.3**	**12.2**	6.8

Men

	Population	A	B	C	
		Steady workers	Steady workers who have stayed at the same sector during the period	B′ + Fixed age during the period	Average
Independent variables X'	Period I	10.7	8.7	6.5	
	Period II	16.5	16.3	20.3	
	Period II − Period I	**5.8**	**7.6**	**13.7**	**9.0**
X' + occupations	Period I	2.7	2.7	−1.4	
	Period II	6.9	6.9	8.7	
	Period II − Period I	**4.2**	**4.2**	**10.1**	**6.2**
X' + occupations + initial wage	Period I	2.9	1.1	0.2	
	Period II	7.3	5.8	7.0	
	Period II − Period I	**4.4**	**4.7**	**6.8**	**5.3**
	Average	**4.8**	**5.5**	**10.2**	6.8

Using panel data, which it controls for the individuals' effects, supports the main conclusion that PSP increased significantly during the period and the increase in PSP was an exogenous occurrence (by workers' view). This argument is particularly accurate after controlling for the initial wage of the workers at period *t*. Here, the initial wage of the workers is used as a proxy for the workers' invariant skill.

One can charge that the increase in PSP is mainly caused by workers' different skills between the sectors; namely the gap between the unobserved skills between highly educated workers and less educated workers is bigger in the private sector compared to the public sector and this gap may be reflected by increase in PSP during the years. If it is correct, PSP should also increase as a function of workers' age. I have checked this argument and found that PSP does not increase with workers' age.

Other can charge that the increase in PSP is a result of a raise in hours of working per month, which was characterized especially by the highly educated workers in the private sector.[4] I exploited other data source (the Israeli Annual Income Surveys) of the same period and found that a relative increase in hours of work among the highly educated workers in the private sector, which may explain the phenomena, had not occurred.

So how can we explain the increase in PSP during the period?

This question is not at the core of this chapter, but I believe that the increase in PSP can be ascribed to the globalization progress, which raises the share of the export and import in GDP during the period. Export share in GDP was 30 percent in 1995 and 43 percent in 2005. Import and especially export are done mainly by the private sector and the raise at their share in GDP impacts especially the private sector employment.

EMPLOYEES' TRANSITIONS BETWEEN THE TWO SECTORS

Fig. 5 describes the empirical probability of leaving the public sector for the private sector, and vice versa, throughout the period, for each group separately (classification into sub-periods is available from the author).

It is possible to draw several conclusions:

- Five percent of private sector employees left that sector for the public sector in the course of the 1995–2005 decade, whereas 7 percent moved in the opposite direction.

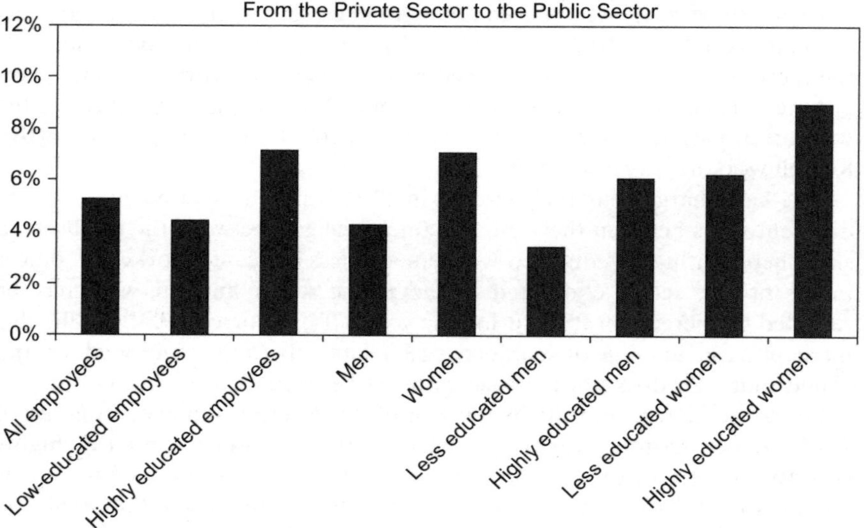

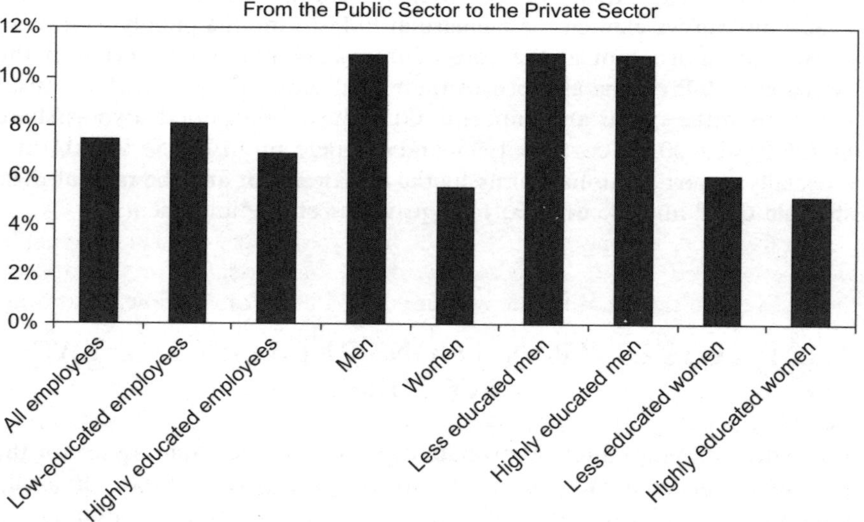

Fig. 5. The empirical percentage of workers who have changed a sector during the period.

- Men left the public sector more than women, and women left the private sector more than men.
- Highly educated employees tended to leave the private sector more than less educated ones, and this applies to both men and women. There is no significant difference by level of education in the tendency to leave the public sector.

STATISTICAL TESTS

To examine if the changes documented related to the return to education (see section 'Descriptive Statistics and an Examination of the Difference Between the Sectors in Employees' Pay') has affected employees' decisions differently whether leaving or remaining in a sector, some statistical checks were made.

Four multinomial regressions were submitted (separately for men and women), where the dependent variable includes 10 options (a vector with 10 years: 1996–2005) of whether a worker has left a sector in a specific year. This procedure estimates the marginal odds ratio of highly educated workers compared with less educated workers to leave in each period, given their cumulative probability of leaving during the whole period.

The explanatory variables are age, dummy variable for highly educated worker, and wage. I transformed workers' wage to a discrete variable by using the appropriate percentile wage of each worker. The percentile wage was calculated after controlling for age, sector and education.

Fig. 6 depicts the marginal effect of highly educated workers leaving a sector compared with less educated workers; this is relative to the ratio at the first year of the examination, in our case – 1996. For example, according to Fig. 6, for men, the probability of highly educated workers leaving the public sector compared with less educated workers during the year 2000 was doubled relative to the same ratio during year 1996.

Fig. 6 suggests that the changes at the return to education affected mostly the decision of men and particularly increased the probability of highly educated workers leaving the public sector compared with less educated workers. It also suggests that the changes decreased the probability of highly educated workers leaving the private sector compared with less educated workers, but it seems that the impact about the workers who have worked at the private sector was much weaker. The goal of the next section is to provide statistical evidence to these suggestions and to quantify the effect of the change in the return to education on the decision to leave a sector.

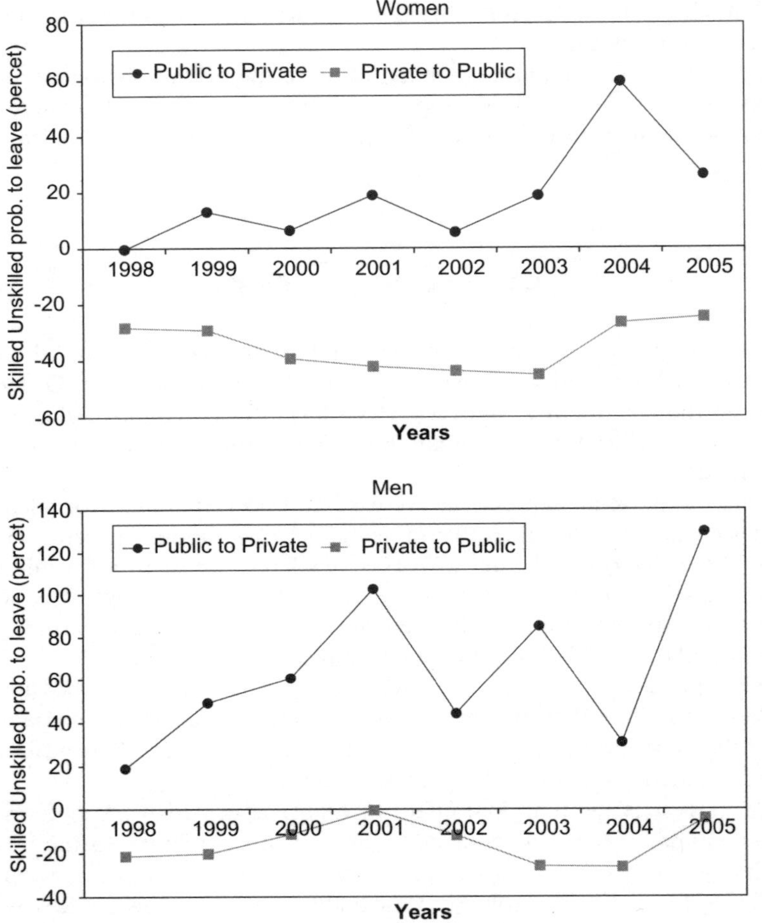

Fig. 6. The probability ratio of highly educated workers to less educated workers to switch a sector.

To test the selection in leaving I used particularly the following six different models (all models are Probit regressions):

I.

$$D_{i,t+1,t} = \beta_0 \mathrm{Educ}_i + \beta_1(S_i) + \beta_3 X_i + \delta\theta_j + \varepsilon_{i,j}$$

II.

$$D_{i,t+1,t} = \beta_0 \text{Educ}_i + \beta_1(S_i) + \beta_2(S_i^2) + \beta_3 X_i + \delta\theta_j + \varepsilon_{i,j}$$

III.

$$D_{i,t+1,t} = \beta_0 \text{Educ}_i + \beta_1(S_i) + \beta_2(S_i^2) + \beta_3 X_i + \gamma_1 \cdot \text{Educ}_i \cdot \text{RTE}_{j,t}^{\text{Pb}} + \gamma_2 \cdot \text{RTE}_{j,t}^{Pr} + \delta\theta_j + \varepsilon_{i,j}$$

IV.

$$D_{i,t+1,t} = \beta_0 \text{Educ}_i + \beta_1(S_i) + \beta_2(S_i^2) + \beta_3 X_i + \gamma_1 \cdot \text{Educ}_i \cdot \text{RTE}_{j,t+1}^{\text{Pb}} + \gamma_2 \cdot \text{RTE}_{j,t+1}^{Pr} + \delta\theta_j + \varepsilon_{i,j}$$

V.

$$D_{i,t+1,t} = \beta_0 \text{Educ}_i + \beta_1(S_i) + \beta_2(S_i^2) + \beta_3 X_i + \delta\theta_j + \gamma_1 \text{Educ}_i(\text{RTE}_{j,t+1}^{\text{Pb}} - \text{RTE}_{j,t}^{\text{Pb}}) + \gamma_2 \text{Educ}_i(\text{RTE}_{j,t+1}^{Pr} - \text{RTE}_{j,t}^{Pr}) + \varepsilon_{i,j}$$

VI.

$$D_{i,t+1,t} = \beta_0 \text{Educ}_i + \beta_1(S_i) + \beta_2(S_i^2) + \beta_3 X_i + \delta\theta_j + \gamma \cdot \text{Educ}_i((\text{RTE}_{j,t+1}^{\text{Pb}} - \text{RTE}_{j,t}^{\text{Pb}}) - (\text{RTE}_{j,t+1}^{Pr} - \text{RTE}_{j,t}^{Pr})) + \varepsilon_{i,j}$$

D_i, representing the decision of employees to move to the other sector, is a binary variable. S_i is the employee's skill level as represented by his residual wage after correcting using Heckman method (Heckman, 1979, 1990). An employee's skill includes two kinds of skills: one is a *general skill* which is relatively easily transferred and a *specific skill* which is less easily transferred (Gould & Moav, 2008). The parameters $\text{RTE}_{j,t}^{\text{Pb}}, \text{RTE}_{j,t}^{Pr}$ are the return to education at time t in each occupational group j in the public and the private sector, respectively; θ_j is a dummy variable for occupation; and index t represents the period.

Below is a brief summary of the hypotheses.

- The prediction regarding β_0 is ambiguous. On the one hand, the greater demand for white-collar employees in the public sector is consistent with a positive coefficient. On the other hand, the higher return to education in the private sector is consistent with a negative coefficient; and vice versa if the estimated equation is leaving the public sector. As a result, the net effect is not clear.[5] I also checked another set of the same models with a non-linear effect of the number of years of schooling, i.e. I added the square of the number of years of schooling as an explanatory variable.

- Since the return to unobserved characteristics is higher in the private sector as measured by the Mean Squared Errors (MSEs) in Mincer regressions or by the negative slope of the public sector premium in QRM regressions (Fig. 2), we will expect a negative sign of β_1 if the estimated equation is the probability of leaving the private sector. However, if the estimated equation is the probability of leaving the public sector, the prediction regarding β_1 is ambiguous: if the effect of the employee's *general skill* is stronger than that of the *specific skill*, we will expect a positive sign, and vice versa.
- The main parameters of interest are the γ. If the changes in PSP, which are described in section 'The Return to Education', have increased the probability of highly educated workers leaving the public sector (the private sector) for the private sector (the public sector), then in model V we will expect a negative (positive) sign for γ_1 and a positive (negative) sign for γ_2. In model VI, we will expect a positive (negative) sign for γ_2 if we estimate the probability of leaving the private sector (the public sector).

Estimation of the Probability that Employees Will Move From One Sector to the Other

Tables 4 through 9 present the estimations of the interesting parameters of models I through VI for employees in the 30– 45 age group. The classification by occupation is undertaken in accordance with the specifications in Table A.1. In order to increase the reliability of the tests, occupations with a low representation in a given sector have been removed from the sample regression. Lawyers, chemists, biologists, and service workers have been removed from the examination.

I use three different patterns to examine the robustness of the results: (1) the bench line pattern (Tables 4 and 7); (2) a model with non-linear effect related to the number of years of schooling (Tables 5 and 8); (3) the bench line pattern just for workers whose wage has increased to at least 5 percent during the period (Tables 6 and 9). The last pattern is submitted because there is no data about hours of working after 1995 and I do not want that workers who have changed their position, especially those who have changed their position from full time to part time position, would bias the estimation.

Table 4. The Probability of Men Moving from the Private to the Public Sector During 1995– 2005.

	(1)	(2)	(3)	(4)	(5)	(6)
RW	−0.0313**	−0.0288**	−0.0291**	−0.0291**	−0.0289**	−0.0288**
	[0.0035]	[0.0031]	[0.0032]	[0.0031]	[0.0032]	[0.0031]
RW Square		0.0122*	0.0129*	0.01302*	0.0126*	0.0126*
		[0.0060]	[0.0056]	[0.0056]	[0.0056]	[0.0059]
NYS	0.0028*	0.0028*	−0.0044*	−0.0032	0.0036**	0.0030**
	[0.0011]	[0.0012]	[0.0021]	[0.0022]	[0.0008]	[0.0010]
NYS*RTE_ Private_t			0.0977*			
			[0.0327]			
NYS*RTE_ Public_t			0.0846			
			[0.0581]			
NYS*RTE_ Private_t +1				0.0741		
				[0.06795]		
NYS*RTE_ Public_t +1				0.06126		
				[0.1008]		
NYS*D_RTE_ Private					−0.1752**	
					[0.0552]	
NYS*D_RTE_ Public					0.1436	
					[0.1277]	
NYS*D_D_RTE_ Pub-Pri						0.0631**
						[0.0066]
X						
Fixed effects for Occu.						
N	17,263	17,263	17,263	17,263	17,263	17,263
Pseudo R^2	0.0345	0.0357	0.0376	0.0372	0.0368	0.0364

X is the workers' features: age, age square, number of hours worked per month, married, religion, origin (born in Israel or born in Europe or America or born in Asia or Africa) and total years cited in Israel.

RW is the workers' residual wage, which is defined as the unexplained residual from OLS regression where its dependent variable is the workers' monthly wage and the dependent variables are *X*. The regressions were submitted with Heckman correction for being employed in the private sector or the public sector. The Heckman method uses five ordinal groups of hours of working, town of living and total income except wage as instrument variables for being worked in the private sector or the public sector.

NYS is the workers' number of years of schooling; RTE_Private_t is the return to education in occupation *j* in the private sector at the first period; RTE_Public_t is the return to education in occupation *j* in the public sector at the first period; RTE_Private_t + 1 is the return to education in occupation *j* in the private sector at the second period; RTE_Public_t + 1 is the return to education in occupation *j* in the public sector at the second period; D_RTE_Private is the gap between the second period and the first period at the return to education in occupation *j* in the private sector; D_RTE_Public is the gap between the second period and the first period at the return to education in occupation *j* in the public sector; D_D_RTE_Pub-Pri is the difference between them (public minus private).

*,**,***Statistically significant at 1%, 5% and 10% respectively.

Table 5. The Probability of Men Moving from the Private to the Public Sector During 1995– 2005: Non-linear Effect for the Number of Years of Education.

	(1)	(2)	(3)	(4)	(5)	(6)
RW	−0.0315***	−0.0289***	−0.0291***	−0.0291***	−0.0290***	−0.0290***
	[0.0036]	[0.0032]	[0.0032]	[0.0032]	[0.0032]	[0.0032]
RW Square		0.0120**	0.0129**	0.0127**	0.0124**	0.0124**
		[0.0059]	[0.0056]	[0.0056]	[0.0055]	[0.0058]
NYS	−0.0035*	−0.0035*	−0.0067**	−0.0061***	−0.0015	−0.0026
	[0.0020]	[0.0020]	[0.0023]	[0.0019]	[0.0021]	[0.0020]
NYS Square	0.0002**	0.0002**	0.0001	0.0002**	0.0002**	0.0002**
	[0.0001]	[0.0001]	[0.0001]	[0.0001]	[0.0001]	[0.0001]
NYS*RTE_Private_t			0.0797**			
			[0.0343]			
NYS*RTE_Public_t			0.0658			
			[0.0502]			
NYS*RTE_ Private_t+1				0.0605		
				[0.0714]		
NYS*RTE_ Public_t+1				0.0424		
				[0.1020]		
NYS*D_RTE_Private					−0.1380***	
					[0.0552]	
NYS*D_RTE_Public					0.1041	
					[0.1022]	
NYS*D_D_RTE_ Pub-Pri						0.0575***
						[0.0045]
X						
Fixed effects for Occu.						
N	17,263	17,263	17,263	17,263	17,263	17,263
Pseudo R^2	0.0357	0.0369	0.0376	0.0377	0.0375	0.0373

*,**,*** Statistically significant at 1%, 5% and 10% respectively.

Table A.1 in the appendix depicts the estimation of the *interest variables* in the regressions and the workers' frequency in each occupation. As expected, there is a very strong and positive correlation between the right to education (RTE) estimations in each occupation and the discrepancy of years of schooling; this correlation is stronger in the private sector.

Analysis of the Results of the Regressions: Men

Transitions from the Private Sector to the Public Sector

The average effect of the employee's skill level is negative, but the squared effect is positive. Both parameters are stable, robust and highly significant.

Table 6. The Probability of Men Moving from the Private to the Public Sector During 1995– 2005: Just Workers Whose Wage Has Increased During the Period.

	(1)	(2)	(3)	(4)	(5)	(6)
RW	−0.0383***	−0.0331***	−0.0331***	−0.0332***	−0.0331***	−0.0330***
	[0.0055]	[0.0053]	[0.0051]	[0.0052]	[0.0053]	[0.0053]
RW Square		0.0137***	0.0145***	0.0145***	0.0141***	0.0140***
		[0.0049]	[0.0047]	[0.0049]	[0.0048]	[0.0048]
NYS	0.0025**	0.0024**	−0.0037	−0.0021	0.0036**	0.0027**
	[0.0010]	[0.0011]	[0.0025]	[0.0024]	[0.0007]	[0.0009]
NYS*RTE_Private_t			0.0794**			
			[0.0324]			
NYS*RTE_Public_t			0.0820			
			[0.0580]			
NYS*RTE_Private_t + 1				0.0463		
				[0.0621]		
NYS*RTE_Public_t + 1				0.0638		
				[0.0880]		
NYS*D_RTE_Private					−0.2114***	
					[0.0618]	
NYS*D_RTE_Public					0.1117	
					[0.1131]	
NYS*D_D_RTE_Pub-Pri						0.0548***
						[0.0064]
X						
Fixed effects for Occu.						
N	12,504	12,504	12,504	12,504	12,504	12,504
Pseudo R^2	0.0345	0.0495	0.0510	0.0505	0.0505	0.0500

*,**,*** Statistically significant at 1%, 5% and 10% respectively.

Table 7. The Probability of Men Moving from the Public to the Private Sector During 1995– 2005.

	(1)	(2)	(3)	(4)	(5)	(6)
RW	−0.0992***	−0.0755***	−0.0754***	−0.0765**	−0.0758**	−0.0754**
	[0.0270]	[0.0315]	[0.0319]	[0.0312]	[0.0322]	[0.0318]
RW Square		0.0551***	0.0551***	0.0557***	0.0551***	0.0551***
		[0.0153]	[0.0148]	[0.0149]	[0.0151]	[0.0152]
NYS	0.00297	0.00278	0.0029	−0.0117	0.0019	0.0026
	[0.0032]	[0.0032]	[0.0145]	[0.0031]	[0.0113]	[0.0036]
NYS*RTE_ Private_t			0.1444**			
			[0.0593]			
NYS*RTE_ Public_t			−0.2220			
			[0.3110]			
NYS*RTE_ Private_t +1				0.3781*		
				[0.2003]		
NYS*RTE_ Public_t +1				−0.1492		
				[0.1815]		
NYS*D_RTE_ Private					−0.0534	
					[0.0577]	
NYS*D_RTE_ Public					0.2203*	
					[0.1215]	
NYS*D_D_RTE_ Pub-Pri						−0.0499***
						[0.0184]
X						
Fixed effects for Occu.						
N	5,644	5,644	5,644	5,644	5,644	5,644
Pseudo R^2	0.0716	0.0761	0.0777	0.0781	0.0771	0.0750

*,**,*** Statistically significant at 1%, 5% and 10% respectively.

We can use these parameters in calculating the predicted probability of workers with different skills (residual wage) to leave the private sector. The average of the predicted probability of workers in lowest 10th of the residual wage is 0.069, but this probability is 0.029 at the highest 10th (Tables 4–6).

The number of years of schooling has in average positive effect on the decision to leave the private sector, but the squared effect is also significant (Table 5), and in this specification with non-linear effect the linear effect has changed its sign to negative. Taking both effects into account, it is estimated that till 9 years of schooling adding one year of schooling decreases the probability of leaving the private sector, but beyond 9 years another year of

Table 8. The Probability of Men Moving from the Public to the Private Sector During 1995– 2005: Non-linear Effect for the Number of Years of Education.

	(1)	(2)	(3)	(4)	(5)	(6)
RW	−0.0959***	−0.0729**	−0.0722**	−0.0729**	−0.0731**	−0.0725**
	[0.0267]	[0.0312]	[0.0319]	[0.0315]	[0.0312]	[0.0315]
RW Square		0.0532***	0.0529***	0.0532***	0.0532***	0.0530***
		[0.0153]	[0.0149]	[0.0153]	[0.0148]	[0.0154]
NYS	−0.0234***	−0.0228***	−0.0152	−0.0341***	−0.0225***	−0.0253***
	[0.0052]	[0.0051]	[0.0098]	[0.0034]	[0.0049]	[0.0047]
NYS Square	0.0009***	0.0008***	0.0008***	0.0009***	0.0008***	0.0010***
	[0.0001]	[0.0001]	[0.0001]	[0.0001]	[0.0001]	[0.0001]
NYS*RTE_ Private_t			0.0902			
			[0.0638]			
NYS*RTE_ Public_t			−0.3345			
			[0.2330]			
NYS*RTE_ Private_t +1				0.4601***		
				[0.0699]		
NYS*RTE_ Public_t +1				−0.4100***		
				[0.1084]		
NYS*D_RTE_ Private					0.0220	
					[0.0481]	
NYS*D_RTE_ Public					0.1160	
					[0.1040]	
NYS*D_D_RTE_ Pub-Pri						−0.0554***
						[0.0139]
X						
Fixed effects for Occu.						
N	5644	5,644	5,644	5,644	5,644	5,644
Pseudo R^2	0.0759	0.0802	0.0810	0.0822	0.0804	0.0799

*,**,*** Statistically significant at 1%, 5% and 10% respectively.

schooling increases it. The average predicted probability of workers with less than 13 years of schooling leaving the private sector is 0.03, and for highly educated workers it is about 0.045.

No correlation is found between the return to education in each sector at the second period interacted by workers' years of schooling. A positive correlation is found between the return to education in the private sector interacted by workers' years of schooling at the first period and the decision to leave the private sector. This result is unexpected and cannot be

Table 9. The Probability of Men Moving from the Public to the Private Sector During 1995– 2005: Just Workers Whose Wage Has Increased During the Period.

	(1)	(2)	(3)	(4)	(5)	(6)
RW	−0.0787***	−0.0517*	−0.0508*	−0.0515*	−0.0519*	−0.0516*
	[0.0208]	[0.0260]	[0.0260]	[0.0257]	[0.0260]	[0.0263]
RW Square		0.0505***	0.0497***	0.0503***	0.0505***	0.0505***
		[0.0145]	[0.0139]	[0.0142]	[0.0144]	[0.0145]
NYS	0.0060***	0.0060***	0.01673*	−0.0006	0.0057***	0.0061***
	[0.0020]	[0.0019]	[0.0100]	[0.0064]	[0.0023]	[0.0023]
NYS*RTE_ Private_t			0.1094**			
			[0.0488]			
NYS*RTE_ Public_t			−0.4395			
			[0.2417]			
NYS*RTE_ Private_t +1				0.3977**		
				[0.1529]		
NYS*RTE_ Public_t +1				−0.3563		
				[0.1569]		
NYS*D_RTE_ Private					0.0048	
					[0.0372]	
NYS*D_RTE_ Public					0.1095	
					[0.1111]	
NYS*D_D_RTE_ Pub-Pri						−0.0247*
						[0.0133]
X						
Fixed effects for Occu.						
N	4,563	4,563	4,563	4,563	4,563	4,563
Pseudo R^2	0.0889	0.0963	0.0986	0.0989	0.0965	0.0959

*,**,*** Statistically significant at 1%, 5% and 10% respectively.

supported by the theory. However, the effect of the difference between the RTE in each sector at time *t* is not significant (this specification does not appear in this chapter) and it weakens the last result.

The interaction between workers' years of schooling and the difference between the RTE within the *private sector* between the second and the first period (according to model V) is negative as expected and robust. Hence, an increase in RTE within the private sector during the period decreases the probability of leaving it as a function of workers' years of schooling. The boundary of the estimation is quite large: between −0.14 and −0.21. However, the interaction between workers' years of schooling and the difference between the RTE within the *public sector* between the second and the first period is not significant.

The analysis of the interaction variable (according to model VI) shows that a larger increase in the return to education in the private sector than in the public sector caused less educated employees to move from the private to the public sector, as hinted also by Fig. 6. The boundary of the parameter (0.055–0.063) indicates that a 1 percentage point rise in the yield difference on education between the private and the public sectors leads to a decline of 0.06 percentage points in the proportion of employees leaving the private sector for each year of education. This result, which is the main result of this section and this chapter, is robust also for checking only workers who have worked at full-time position in the first period; and it is also robust when excluding the teachers' occupation from the analysis which its RTE in the private sector looked quite weird (Table A.1).

Take into account the gap in schooling between highly educated workers and less educated workers in the private sector is 5.9 years and the increase at the rate of return to education during the period is about 0.8. Multiplying 0.8, 5.9 and 0.06 implies that due to the raise in PSP the probability of highly educated workers leaving the private sector was 0.3 percentage points lower compared with a situation without increase in PSP during the period. Given the empirical probability of highly educated workers leaving the public sector during the period (0.061), it can be concluded that 5 percent of the highly educated workers did not leave the private sector for the public sector due to the increase in PSP. While much of the variation in switching sector choices remains unexplained, the robust effect of the return differentials in explaining switching supports a Roy model of comparative advantage.

Transitions from the Public Sector to the Private Sector

As in the opposite direction analysis, the average effect of the employee's skill level is negative and the squared effect is positive. Both parameters are stable, robust and highly significant. The average predicted probability of workers leaving the public sector for the private sector in lowest 10th of the residual wage is 0.19, but this probability is estimated to be 0.09 at the highest 10th. However, the squared effect is much stronger and more robust compared with the reverse direction and it is reflected by positive selection, respected to the residual wage, of the top 5 percentiles of the public sector workers (Tables 7–9).

The number of years of schooling has in average positive effect on the decision to leave the private sector, but the squared effect is also significant (Table 8) and in the specification with the non-linear effect the linear effect has changed its sign to negative. Taking both effects into account it is estimated that till 15 years of schooling adding one year of schooling decreases the probability of leaving the public sector, but beyond 15 years another year of schooling increases it.

A positive correlation is found between the return to education in the private sector interacted by workers' years of schooling at the first period and the decision to leave the private sector. This result is fitting the prediction but its significance is low and it is not robust. The positive correlation between the return to education in the private sector interacted by workers' years of schooling at the second period and the decision to leave the private sector is stronger and robust. The assessed elasticity is between 0.38 and 0.46. Another model which does not appear in this chapter is of the difference between the RTE within each sector at the second period, which is very significant and its sign fits the theory.

The interaction between workers' years of schooling and the difference between the RTE within *the private sector or the public sector* between the second and the first period (according to model V) is not significant.

The analysis of the interaction variable (according to model VI) shows that a larger increase in the return to education in the private sector than in the public sector caused highly educated employees to further move from the public to the private sector, as hinted also by Fig. 6. The boundary of estimation is between 0.024 and 0.055, which indicates that a 1 percentage point rise in the yield difference on education between the private and the public sectors leads to a raise of 0.04 percentage points in the proportion of employees leaving the private sector for each year of education. As in the opposite direction analysis, this result is robust also for checking only workers who have worked at full-time position at the first period, and it is also robust after excluding the teachers' occupation from the analysis.

Take into account the gap in schooling between skilled and unskilled employees in the private sector is 5.9 years and the increase at the rate of return to education during the period is about 0.8. Multiplying 0.8, 5.9 and 0.04 implies that due to the raise in PSP the probability of highly educated workers leaving the public sector is 0.18 percentage points higher compared with a situation without increase in PSP during the period. Given the empirical probability of highly educated workers leaving the public sector during the period (0.109), it can be concluded that 1.7 percent of the highly educated workers left the public sector for the private sector due to the increase in PSP. As in the reverse direction analysis, much of the variation in switching sector choices remains unexplained, but the robust effect of the return differentials in explaining switching supports a Roy model of comparative advantage.

CONCLUSIONS

This study compared the development of the wage in the public and the private sectors using panel data for employees between 1995 and 2005. It was found that during this period the differences in the wage distribution between the two sectors were intensified, primarily due to changes in the wage distribution in the private sector, among them a higher increase in the return to education. In addition, it was found that the public sector gives greater positive rewards to employees who are at the lower end of the wage distribution than does the private sector, and gives negative rewards (i.e. punishment) to employees who are situated at the upper end. This is similar to the picture that can be seen in developing countries where the differences in wage distribution between the two sectors have been studied.

The study also examined whether, in view of these changes, the public sector has succeeded in maintaining the quality of its employees. Assuming that the number of years of schooling constitutes a good index of the quality and productivity of the workforce, the answer is unclear. The tendency to move from the private to the public sector, and also from the public to the private sector, increased with years of schooling of male employees. In addition, a significant positive correlation was found between the differential increase in the return to education in both sectors and men's education, on the one hand, and their tendency to leave their jobs, on the other. In analyzing those who switched from one sector to the other, our findings imply if the return to education had not changed at different rates between sectors, the probability of highly educated workers leaving the public sector for the private sector would be 5 percent lower and the probability of highly educated workers leaving the private sector for the public sector would be 2 percent higher.

NOTES

1. This chapter constitutes a continuation of a previous article that discussed a similar subject (Mazar, 2011) but uses a wider, more up-to-date database. In common with the previous chapter, this chapter endorses, albeit to a limited extent,

the selection hypothesis regarding employees who leave the public and private sectors, but unlike the previous chapter, this chapter focuses on wage structure and the movement of skilled versus unskilled workers between the sectors. Finally, because of the wealth of data, the descriptive section of this study is deeper.

2. The articles by Bender (1998, 2003) and Gregory and Borland (1999) contain reviews of this literature.

3. The standard regression method (OLS) is based on estimating the given conditional mean y (wage log, for example) as a linear function of individual characteristics (e.g. vector X for the public sector: $Q^q(y|X) = X^T\beta^q + \text{Public} \cdot \delta^q$. Instead, the methodology of the quantile regression assumes that it is not the mean but the qth percentile of the conditional wage distribution which is the linear function of the employee's characteristics): $Q^q(y|X) = X^T\beta^q + \text{Public} \cdot \delta^q$ (Ghinetti & Lucifora, 2008).

4. As I have noted, I have not data about hours of working after 1995.

5. The demand for highly educated workers is greater in the public sector than in the private sector, largely because of the different mix of occupations in each sector. As a result, employees in the public sector have more years of education than those in the private sector (14.3 and 12.7, respectively, in 1995). Consequently, the average hourly wage in the public sector is higher.

ACKNOWLEDGEMENTS

I would like to thank Kobi Braude and Eric Gould for their helpful advice, as well as the other members of the Research Department for their useful comments. I am also grateful to the employees of the Central Bureau of Statistics – Anat Katz, Orly Forman and David Gordon.

REFERENCES

Bargian, O. & Melly, B. (2008). Public sector pay gap in France: New evidence using panel data. IZA Discussion Paper No. 3427.

Beggs, J. J., & Chapman, B. J. (1988). Labor turnover bias in estimating wages. *Review of Economics and Statistics*, *70*(1), 117–123.

Bender, K. A. (1998). The central government-private sector wage differential. *Journal of Economic Survey*, *12*, 177–220.

Bender, K. A. (2003). Examining equality between public- and private-sector wage distributions. *Economic Inquiry*, *41*, 62–79.

Borjas, G. J. (2002). The wage structure and the sorting of workers into the public sector. NBER Working Paper 9313.

Buchinsky, M. (1994). Changes in the U.S. wage structure 1963–1987: Application of quantile regression. *Econometrica*, *62*, 405–458.

Chamberlain, G. (1994). Quantile regression, censoring and the structure of wages. In: C. A. Sims (Ed.), *Advances in econometrics: 6th world congress* (Vol. 1). Cambridge, MA: MIT Press.

Dahl, G. B. (2002). Mobility and the return to education: Testing a Roy model with multiple markets. *Econometrica*, *70*(6), 2367–2420.

Fougère, D. & Pouget, J. (2003). Les Déterminants Economiques de L'entrée dans la Fonction Publique. *Economie et Statistique*, 369.370, 15.48. [English version: "Who Wants to Be a 'Fonctionnaire'? The Effects of Individual Wage Differentials and Unemployment Probabilities on the Queues for Public Sector Jobs. mimeo, CREST-INSEE.]

Ghinetti, P. & Lucifora, C. (2008). Public sector pay gaps and skill levels: a cross-country comparison," paper prepared for the project "Privatisation and marketisation of services – social and economic impacts on employment, labour markets and trade unions." [Unpublished manuscript].

Gould, E., & Moav, O. (2008). When is "Too Much" inequality not enough? The Selection of Israeli emigrants. CEPR Discussion Paper 6955.

Gregory, R. G., & Borland, J. (1999). Recent developments in public sector labor markets. In: O. Ashenfelter & C. David (Eds.), *Handbook of Labor Economics 3(C)*. Amsterdam: North-Holland.

Heckman, J. (1979). Sample selection bias as a specification error. *Econometrica*, *47*, 153–161.

Heckman, J. (1990). Varieties of selection bias. *American Economic Review*, *80*(2), 313–318.

Kats, L., & Kruger A. (1991). Changes in the structure of the wages in the public and private sectors. *Research in Labor Economics*, JAI Press, 12.

Koenker, R., & Bassett, G. (1978). Regression quantiles. *Econometrica*, *46*, 33–50.

Lucifora, C., & Meurs, D. (2004). The public sector pay gap in France, Great Britain and Italy. IZA Discussion Paper 1041.

Mazar, Y. (2011). Self-selection of employees moving between the public and private sectors. *Israel Economic Review*, *9*(1).

Poterba, J., & Rueben, K. (1994). The distribution of public sector wage premia: Evidence using quantile regression methods. NBER Working Paper 4734.

APPENDIX

Table A.1. Database for the Regressions.

Public Sector	*N*	Wage_95_97	Wage_03_05	Schooling	STD	RTE_1	RTE_3
All	5,058	7,612	10,060	14.4	3.2	0.042	0.044
Engineers	285	10,596	15,541	16.8	2.0	0.026	0.031
Physicians	411	10,987	14,953	18.0	2.0	0.040	0.060
Economists	98	8,292	11,979	17.4	2.5	0.025	0.005
Teachers	755	7,032	8,817	16.8	2.9	0.051	0.062
Managers	340	10,242	14,221	14.9	2.7	0.041	0.061
Free occupations	1,193	6,667	8,573	14.5	2.4	0.049	0.039
Clerks	742	6,555	8,826	12.7	2.4	0.030	0.030
Professionals	1,234	7,456	9,785	11.6	2.1	0.029	0.030
Private Sector	***N***	**Wage_95_97**	**Wage_03_05**	**Schooling**	**STD**	**RTE_1**	**RTE_3**
All	16,783	6,495	8,029	12.9	3.1	0.044	0.051
Engineers	1,511	9,733	13,964	16.3	1.8	0.036	0.043
Physicians	139	12,229	13,721	18.3	1.9	0.042	0.056
Economists	332	10,151	14,985	16.4	1.9	0.006	0.003
Teachers	37	8,914	11,491	16.5	3.3	0.121	0.067
Managers	2,098	12,319	14,074	14.5	2.5	0.072	0.082
Free occupations	1,840	7,716	10,162	14.1	2.1	0.044	0.051
Clerks	2,368	6,639	8,374	12.9	2.4	0.061	0.065
Professionals	8,458	4,792	5,738	11.3	2.8	0.033	0.041

CHAPTER 6

FOREGONE EARNINGS FROM SMOKING: EVIDENCE FOR A DEVELOPING COUNTRY

Michael Lokshin and Kathleen Beegle

ABSTRACT

This chapter estimates the negative effect of smoking on earnings in the context of a developing country. Using data from the 2005 Albania Living Standards Measurement Survey, models are estimated by parametric and semi-parametric methods to account for the effect of observable and unobservable characteristics that could affect individual smoking decisions and earnings. Information on the smoking behaviour of parents is used to address the endogeneity of the smoking decision. The results show that, after controlling for observed individual characteristics and parental education and taking into account unobserved heterogeneity in personal characteristics, smoking is found to have a substantial negative impact on earnings. The main results are robust to a range of alternative specifications. On average, smokers' earnings are 19–23 percent lower than the earnings of similar non-smokers.

Keywords: Smoking; wages; earnings

JEL classifications: D10; J31; J70

Research in Labor Economics, Volume 33, 209–238

ISSN: 0147-9121/doi:10.1108/S0147-9121(2011)0000033009

INTRODUCTION

In 2000, about one out of three adults, or 1.1–1.2 billion people worldwide, smoked (WHO, 1999). The number of smokers was forecasted to grow to around 1.3 billion by 2010 (FAO, 2003). The vast majority of the world's smokers (82 percent) live in developing countries where, in sharp contrast to developed countries, the consumption of tobacco is on the rise. Tobacco control is increasingly seen as a public health priority, motivating campaigns such as the World Health Organization's Tobacco Free Initiative as well as country-specific tobacco control campaigns. These efforts are justified not only on grounds related to adverse effects of smoking on health, but also, more generally, on economic grounds.[1]

Estimates of the economic costs of smoking tend to reflect costs associated with increased premature death and healthcare costs related to smoking-induced chronic diseases. In addition to these pathways, there is a third category of costs that has been considered: the earnings and wage reductions associated with smoking. The literature on the relationship between smoking and labour market performance is limited and based on data from Western Europe and the United States. Berger and Leigh (1989) and Levine, Gustafson, and Valenchik (1997) investigate the effect of smoking on wages using data from the United States. Drawing on data from Germany, Heineck and Schwarze (2003) examine whether smoking affects the earnings of employees 25–55 years old. Depending on the model specification, this study finds that the estimated losses in earnings for smokers range from 2 to 8 percent compared to non-smokers.

Several studies examine the simultaneous effect of alcohol and smoking on earnings. Controlling for the endogeneity of drinking and smoking, Van Ours (2004) finds that the wages of smokers are 10 percent lower than the wages of non-smokers in the Netherlands. Auld (2005) estimates a model of drinking, smoking and wages using a sample of employed Canadian men. After accounting for the endogenous nature of the decision to use alcohol and tobacco and their simultaneous effects on wages, he reports that smokers have wages about 30 percent lower than that of non-smokers.

The limited set of studies of the wage or earnings consequences of smoking consistently shows significant negative effects. However, these results are restricted to high-income settings; estimates of the economic costs of smoking in developing countries are non-existent to our knowledge. This paper addresses this gap in the literature by estimating the economic losses related to the negative effect of smoking on earnings in a developing country, namely Albania, where 60 percent of adult males and 18 percent of females smoked in 2002 and the number of smokers has been increasing rapidly over the last decade (WHO, 2002a). Rates of smoking among Albanian adults are comparable to rates in other transition economies and among developing countries in other regions.[2]

Using recent household survey data, we study the impact of smoking on men's earnings with three approaches. We estimate a conventional two-stage least squares model. We also estimate a system of three equations: the smoking decision (never having smoked and current smokers) and two separate earnings equations, one for smokers and one for non-smokers. We produce two estimates of this system, one by a full information maximum likelihood (FIML) model and one by a semi-parametric local instrumental variables (LIV) model, both methods control for the effects of observed and unobserved characteristics that may be correlated with earnings and the smoking status of men. We introduce new instrumental variables to identify the causal effect of the smoking decision on earnings. The results show that smoking has a substantial negative impact on earnings. On average smokers' earnings are 19–23 percent lower than the earnings of similar non-smokers. Although these negative effects are private costs of smoking, they provide motivation for the potential policy relevance of tobacco control initiatives for developing countries if they are due to adverse and unrealized health effects.

The structure of this chapter is as follows. The methodology and empirical approach are discussed in the second section. The data are discussed in the third section. The fourth section presents the empirical results and conclusions are drawn in the last section.

METHODOLOGY AND EMPIRICAL SPECIFICATION

Several theories have been proposed to explain the lower earnings associated with smoking. We discuss four of these theories which are related to health effects, costs to employers, discrimination, and individual preferences.

First, the adverse health implications of smoking could affect a worker's productivity and, therefore, labour market outcomes. Even for the young workers, smoking is associated with lower physical endurance (Levine et al., 1997) and a higher incidence of respiratory infections (Conway & Cronan, 1992; Hoad & Clay, 1992). The higher incidence of respiratory diseases among young smokers and more serious illnesses at older ages can result in lower productivity and higher absenteeism (Bertera, 1991). In addition, smoking may lead to more breaks during the workday or otherwise interfere with job performance.

Second, employers may face higher costs to hire a smoker. The cost of medical insurance for smokers is higher (Bertera, 1991). In turn, larger health insurance claims would reflect negatively on earnings of smokers, as employers are unwilling to pay for all or part of the costs of employing smokers.[3] At the same time, workers who are aware of the negative consequences of smoking might select themselves into occupations that provide better health coverage, accepting lower earnings in exchange. The cost of a smoking worker to his employer could also rise given the need for additional facilities for smokers that would increase air cooling, heating, and ventilation cost, increased fire hazard and fire insurance premiums, and smoke pollution leading to larger cleaning and maintenance costs (Center for Health Promotion and Publications, 2000).

Discrimination against smokers is another potential reason for differences in earnings between smokers and non-smokers driven by the effect of secondhand smoke on other employees and on customers. Statistical discrimination may also exist if employers assume that smokers are less productive based on the average health effects of smoking.[4]

A fourth theoretical consideration would be that smoking is a proxy for some personal characteristics that could affect earnings. In the 'Rational Addiction Theory' (Becker & Murphy, 1988), the decision to smoke is based on a comparison of the present and future costs and benefits of smoking (Chaloupka, 1991; Becker, Grossman, & Murphy, 1994). The costs are related to the negative effects of smoking on health which are often realized only in the longer term. The perceived benefits of smoking are predominantly immediately realized and might include stimulation, enhancement of concentration and short-term memory, weight control to a certain degree (Rohsenow et al., 2003), facilitating social interactions and relaxation (Brandon & Baker, 1991), and alleviating boredom, stress, and aggressive responses to stressful events (Senagore, 2004). By choosing the short-term benefits over the long-term costs, smokers reveal a higher rate of time preference than that of non-smokers. Fuchs (1982) suggests that smoking is therefore an indication or proxy of a high rate of time preference resulting in lower human capital accumulation and lower earnings, as evidenced by Evans and Montgomery (1994) and Lahiri and Song (2000). Likewise, smokers may have flatter earning profiles if they have a higher rate of time preference (Viscusi & Hersch, 2001).

Given these theories that link smoking to earnings, one empirical approach to measure the magnitude of this effect is to estimate an earnings equation based on a model that relates earnings with individual human capital characteristics (Mincer, 1974) modified to include smoking. In the simplest case the earning function has a form:

$$\ln W_{\text{i}} = X_{\text{i}}\beta + S_{\text{i}}\gamma + \varepsilon_{\text{i}} \tag{1}$$

where W_{i} represents monthly earnings of individual i, X_{i} is a vector of exogenous individual characteristics, S_{i} is dummy variable of the individual smoking status, ε_{i} is an i.i.d., mean-zero error term, and β is a vector of parameters. In this specification, parameter γ could be interpreted as the effect of smoking on earnings.

Although differences in observable characteristics of smokers and non-smokers can be controlled for by a standard regression approach, the presence of unobservable factors affecting both smoking and earnings would lead to the endogeneity of S_{i} in (1). As a result of such endogeneity, the estimated effect of smoking on earnings would be biased.[5] Smokers may differ from non-smokers in some unobserved dimensions that are correlated with earnings. As noted above, the rate of time preference is one possible trait that is unobserved to the analyst and its omission biases estimates in (1). We address these potential biases using three methods with instrumental variables: a standard two-stage least square (2SLS) regression, an FIML method switching regression approach (e.g. Lee, 1978), and a semi-parametric LIV method (e.g. Heckman & Vytlacil, 2000).

The 2SLS model is appealing because the previous studies noted above use 2SLS to estimate the effect of addictive behaviour on earnings and the 2SLS produces an easily interpreted measure of the effect of smoking: γ in (1). On the other hand, 2SLS assumes that the effect of personal characteristics on earnings is linear and independent of smoking status. In addition, the 2SLS model treats the binary indicator for smoking status as a continuous variable that could lead to a bias in predicting the probabilities of smoking.

These assumptions in 2SLS can be relaxed by the simultaneous estimation of two earnings equations, one for smokers and another for non-smokers, and an equation for the smoking status. The resulting model can be expressed as:

$$\begin{aligned} S_{\text{i}} &= 1[Z_{\text{i}}\eta + u_{\text{i}}] \\ \ln \quad W_{\text{i}}^{1} &= X_{\text{i}}^{1}\beta_1 + \varepsilon_{1\text{i}} \quad \text{observed if } S_{\text{i}} = 1 \text{ (smokes)} \\ \ln \quad W_{\text{i}}^{2} &= X_{\text{i}}^{2}\beta_2 + \varepsilon_{2\text{i}} \quad \text{observed } \textit{if } S_{\text{i}} = 0 \text{ (does not smoke)} \end{aligned} \tag{2}$$

where $1[Z_{\text{i}}\eta + u_{\text{i}}]$ is an indicator function; Z_{i} is a vector of exogenous characteristics; u_{i}, $\varepsilon_{1\text{i}}$, and $\varepsilon_{2\text{i}}$ are error terms; η is a vector of parameters; and superscript 1 identifies smokers and 2 identifies non-smokers. From (2) observed earnings can be expressed as:

$$\ln W_i = S \ln W_i^1 - (1 - S) \ln W_i^2 \tag{3}$$

The probability of an individual smoking is defined as $P(Z) = Pr(S = 1|Z = z)$, which can also be interpreted as a propensity score. Taking expectations of (3), it is easy to show (Heckman, Urzua & Vytlacil 2006) that:

$$E(\ln W|X = x,\ P(Z) = z) = \beta_1 x + ((\beta_1 - \beta_2)x)p + K(p)$$

where

$$K(p) = E(u|P(Z) = p) + E(\varepsilon_1 - \varepsilon_2|S = 1, P(Z) = p)p \tag{4}$$

Then the expected impact of smoking on earnings for individuals with observed characteristics X and unobserved characteristics V can be expressed as:

$$E(\ln W^1 - \ln W^2|X = x,\ V = v) = x(\beta_1 - \beta_2) + E(\varepsilon_1 - \varepsilon_2|V = v) \tag{5}$$

where $V_i = F_u(u_i)$, F_u is a cumulative distribution function of u, and V is distributed uniformly. Heckman and Vytlacil (2000) call the expectation in (4) the marginal treatment effect (MTE(x, v)) and show that:

$$\text{MTE}(x, v) = \left.\frac{\partial E(Y|X, P)}{\partial P}\right|_{X=x,P=v} = \left.\frac{\partial(X\beta_2 + PX(\beta_2 - \beta_1) + K(P))}{\partial P}\right|_{X=x,P=v}$$
$$= X(\beta_1 - \beta_2) + K'(P) \tag{6}$$

From (5) conventional treatment parameters can be constructed, such as average treatment effect (ATE), average treatment on the treated (ATT) and average treatment on the untreated (ATU) as weighted averages of the MTE for the corresponding sub-populations, as proposed by Heckman and Vytlacil (2000, 2005).

The interpretation of the results depends on how we model the counterfactual. There is no consensus on the choice of the comparison group in the literature on smoking and earnings. The majority of the literature compares earnings of current smokers with everybody else (Lye & Hirschberg, 2004; Van Ours, 2004; Heineck & Schwarze, 2003). Levine et al. (1997) compare wages of smokers with those who quit smoking. The main goal of our study is to evaluate the component of the economic costs of smoking related to the effect of smoking on earnings. We define the economic costs of smoking as measured by the higher wage earnings of smokers had they never started smoking. In terminology of impact evaluation, the impact of smoking on earnings is defined as the ATT where the treatment group is composed of smokers and the ideal counterfactual would be non-smoking smokers – someone with the same demographic and risk profile (e.g. Manning, Keeler, Newhouse, Sloss, & Wasserman, 1991; Sloan, Ostermann, Conover, Taylor, & Picone, 2004). Our data do not allow us to construct such an ideal counterfactual, so we use as the counterfactual to smokers the group of those who have never smoked.[6] In the general case, the ATT can be derived from (6) as:

$$\mathrm{ATT}(x) = E(\ln W^1 - \ln W^2 | x, S = 1) = \int_0^1 \mathrm{MTE}(x, v) h_{\mathrm{TT}}(x, v) \mathrm{d}v$$

where

$$h_{\mathrm{TT}}(x, v) = \left[\int_v^1 f(p|X = x) \mathrm{d}p \right] \frac{1}{E(P|X = x)} \tag{7}$$

We estimate MTE(x,v) and ATT(x) using both parametric and semi-parametric techniques. Assuming that (X, ε_1, ε_2, and u) are i.i.d., and ε_1, ε_2 and u have, conditional on X, a joint normal distribution with mean zero and positive definite covariance matrix, (6) can be estimated by FIML. One of the problems with FIML estimation is its reliance on a normality assumption for the distribution of the error terms ε_1, ε_2 and u in (2). To relax this assumption we use the semi-parametric LIV method developed by Heckman and Vytlacil (2000, 2005) and Carneiro, Heckman and Vytlacil (2006).

In the parametric FIML model, the effect of smoking on the earnings of smokers (ATT) is derived by comparing the expected earnings of smokers with the earnings they would receive had they been non-smokers or quitters. The expected earnings of a smoker can be expressed as:

$$E(\ln W_{\mathrm{i}}^1 | X_{\mathrm{i}}^1, S = 1) = \beta_1 X_{\mathrm{i}}^1 + \rho_1 \sigma_1 \frac{\phi(\eta Z_{\mathrm{i}})}{\Phi(\eta Z_{\mathrm{i}})} = \beta_1 X_{\mathrm{i}}^1 + \rho_1 \sigma_1 \lambda(Z_{\mathrm{i}} | S = 1) \tag{8a}$$

and the expected counterfactuals earnings as:

$$E(\ln W_{\mathrm{i}}^2 | X_{\mathrm{i}}^1, S = 0) = \beta_2 X_{\mathrm{i}}^1 + \rho_2 \sigma_2 \lambda(Z_{\mathrm{i}} | S = 1) \tag{8b}$$

where σ_1 and σ_2 are variances of the error terms in the earnings equations; ρ_1 and ρ_2 are the coefficients of correlation between ε_1, ε_2 and u; and λ is the inverse Mills ratios.

Estimation of the semi-parametric LIV model involves several steps. First the propensity score *P*(*Z*) is estimated assuming a probit model for the selection equation in (2). From (4) we compute residuals that retain only the unobserved heterogeneity:

$$R = \ln W - [X\beta_1 + PX(\beta_1 - \beta_2)]. \tag{9}$$

Then, *K*(*P*) is obtained from a nonparametric (local quadratic polynomial) regression of *R* on *P* and derive *K'*(*P*) in (6) from this estimation.

Both FIML and LIV models are identified through non-linearities and the stronger identification condition which requires that *Z* contains at least one variable that is correlated with smoking status *S* and is uncorrelated with individual earnings.

Identification Strategy

Several studies use instrumental variables for identifying the effect of smoking and alcohol consumption on wages. Lye and Hirschberg (2004) control for endogeneity of smoking and alcohol consumption by the two-step Heckman (1979) correction. The paper does not discuss the identification conditions, but seems to rely on identification by the functional form. Such an approach could be problematic due to the 'weak instrument bias' (Staiger & Stock 1997). The instrumental variables in Van Ours (2004) are the indicators for having a partner and an early start of smoking. Auld (2005) uses religion and the price of tobacco. Heineck and Schwarze (2003) use such variables as 'strong religious conviction' and marital status as instruments in their 2SLS estimation.

In our view, it is hard to justify the validity of these instruments for identification of the effect of smoking on earnings. Empirical research has consistently shown that, on average, married men have substantially higher wages than otherwise similar unmarried men, the so-called 'marriage wage premium' phenomenon (e.g. Cornwell & Rupert, 1997; Daniel, 1991; Gray, 1997). Early start of smoking would be an invalid instrument if length of smoking exposure directly affects earnings through health; long-term adverse effects of teenage smoking on health are well documented in the medical literature (e.g. CDC, 1994). The price of tobacco could also be a problematic instrument because of the addictive nature of smoking (see footnote 5). Moreover, the price reflects both supply and demand factors, confounding its validity as an instrument. Using community price data, we find that the local price of cigarettes does not predict smoking probabilities for men in Albania. Finally, it is difficult to argue that religious beliefs, while affecting the individual's probability to smoke, have no effect on earnings given the extensive literature that demonstrates the opposite (e.g. Nigel, 1984). Indeed, Van Ours (2004, p. 11) concludes that '... *it is difficult to find good instrumental variables*' and Heineck and Schwarze (2003, p. 8) state that their '... *identifying instruments ... perform poor[ly] in the first stage*' of 2SLS regression.

Our identification strategy relies on two variables about smoking behavior of the respondent's parents.[7] We had an opportunity to introduce these variables in the questionnaire specifically for the purpose of using them as instruments in the current analysis. We argue that parental smoking is correlated with the likelihood of smoking and has no direct impact on individual's earnings.[8] The effect of parental smoking on offspring tobacco use is well established in the literature (e.g. Andrews, Hops, Ary, Tildesley, & Harris, 1993; Pedersen & Lavik, 1991). Smoking parents present a model of smoking behavior to their children, who are therefore at increased risk of tobacco use when adults (Fagan, Brook, Rubenstone, & Chenshu, 2005).

Perhaps the strongest argument against the validity of the instruments is the adverse health effects of secondhand smoke that could affect the productivity of children of smoking parents. Although there exists an extensive literature on the short-term effects of secondhand smoke on health we are unaware of any study that demonstrates the direct impact of the secondhand smoke when a child on future labour productivity in adulthood.

Smoking could also be an indication of certain personal traits of a parent, potentially unrelated to smoking, that could influence outcomes of her children (e.g. schooling attainment, motivation, etc.), which, in turn, affect the children's future earnings.[9] For example, the rate of time preference might be transferred from parents to their children genetically or acquired in early childhood. Then the observed lower earnings of smokers relative to non-smokers could be caused by a higher rate of personal time preference of smokers that was acquired from their parents. Omitting these measures could potentially invalidate our instruments. We partially address this by including education of parents in our model – the only additional parental information available in the data. The rate of time preference of parents would be reflected in their educational achievements, thus clearing our instruments from the component potentially correlated with respondents' earnings. The educational achievements of parents are quite similar between smokers and those who never smoked, indirectly lending support to our chosen instrument.

Nevertheless, given the limitations of our data, we can never be sure that our instruments capture all unobserved characteristics of parents that could be correlated with the respondents' labour market outcomes. Thus, our estimates could reflect not only the direct effect of smoking on earnings but also the effects of these unobservables. We realize these potential weaknesses of our instruments and suggest that they are at least as valid as those used in previous studies on smoking in high-income countries. To ascertain the validity of our instruments we conduct a wide range of diagnostics tests.

DATA AND DESCRIPTIVE STATISTICS

The data for our analysis come from the fourth round of Albania Living Standard Measurement Survey (ALSMS) conducted in April–July 2005 by the Albanian Institute of Statistics with technical support from The World Bank. The ALSMS uses a two-stage stratified clustered sample of 3,640 households and is representative at the national, urban, rural, and regional levels.[10] The ALSMS collects information on the characteristics of household members (demographics, labour market activities, education, health) and the household's access to social services. The questionnaire also gathers information on individual and household income and consumption expenditures as well as ownership of assets. A special section on ALSMS collects information about individual smoking behavior including whether the respondent smokes on a daily basis or is an ex-smoker, age at which the respondent started smoking, number of cigarettes smoked per day, and whether the respondent's father and mother ever smoked.

For the purpose of the current analysis we restrict our sample to employed prime-age adults 25–60 years of age. By the age of 25 most adults in Albania have completed their education and are actively involved in the labour market. An individual is considered to be employed if he worked in a permanent job in the week preceding the survey or was absent from his permanent job due to vacation or illness. The sample excludes employers, self-employed, and individuals working in a household farm because earnings are not reported for these group of respondents. Individual wage earnings including bonuses are measured as net monthly payments from employment.

Forty percent of males and about 5 percent of females age 25–60 have ever smoked; 32 percent of males and less than 4 percent of females in the sample categorize themselves as current smokers.[11] These numbers are comparable with other studies of smoking in Albania. In the population-based survey in

2002, 38 percent of adult males and 18 percent of females in the capital Tirana smoked (Shapo, Gilmore, Coker, McKee, & Shapo, 2003). IMF (2006) reports that, according to 2002 ALSMS survey, 31 percent of Albanian men smoked. Because of the small proportion of female smokers in the sample, our analysis focuses only on working males.

The left panel of Fig. 1 graphs the results of a non-parametric regression (running-line least-squares) of the proportion of smokers by age. The incidence of smoking is increasing with the age of the respondent. Less than 20 percent of 25-year-old men are current smokers. The proportion of smokers increases sharply with age and plateaus at about 38 percent at 35 years of age.

The right panel of Fig. 1 shows the relationship between monthly (log) earnings and the age of the respondents. On average, non-smokers earn about 26,300 lek (3.27 in thousands in logs) per month relative to 24,290 lek per month (3.19) for smokers (8.3 percent difference). Both groups have an inverted U-shaped age–earnings profile. Earnings of younger males increase and reach a maximum at age 35 and decline for older workers. Earnings of

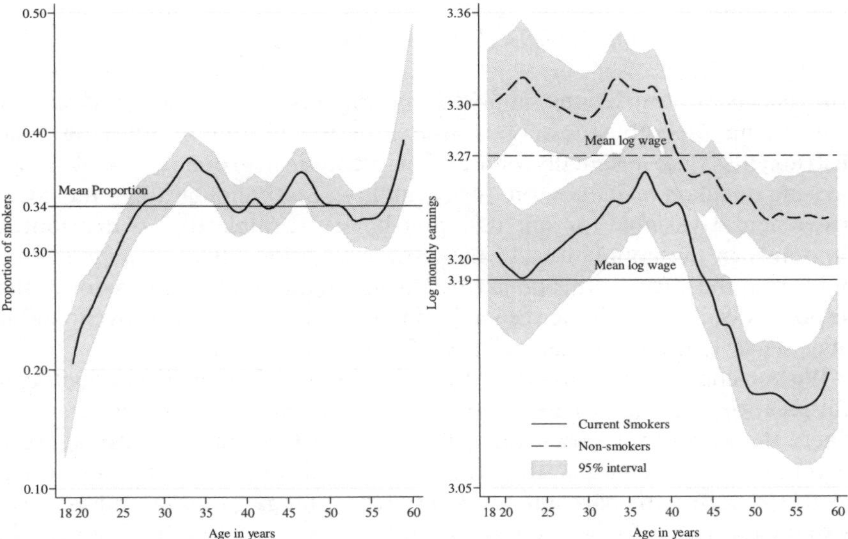

Fig. 1. Proportion of smokers and average log monthly earnings for smokers and non-smokers by age. Sample of working males 25–60 years of age.

non-smokers are higher than earnings of smokers for all age groups, with the largest gap observed for workers 35–50 years of age.

RESULTS

To estimate the effect of smoking as described in the second section, the dependent variables in the regressions are the log of monthly earnings for male smokers and men who never smoked, and a binary indicator capturing whether a man is a current smoker or has never smoked. Table 1 shows the descriptive statistics for the dependent and explanatory variables separately for smokers, those who never smoked, and quitters. The variables include human capital characteristics: age (squared and cubed), educational level, foreign languages spoken, and religious affiliation; socio-demographic characteristics of the household: household size and household composition variables; 36 district dummies to capture conditions of the local labour markets; and a dummy for the type of locality (urban or rural). Parental education is included as an indicator of familial background that could affect motivation or productivity. Finally, total hours worked last month are included.

Instruments: Relevance and Exclusion

The exclusion restrictions imposed on the instruments are crucial for considering the robustness of measures of the impact of smoking. The instruments were originally chosen on theoretical grounds and here we present ancillary evidence on their validity. Methodologically, the ideal instrumental variable for our case is a binary variable that is distributed randomly in the population. In the 2SLS estimation, the first stage is then built from the effect of this binary treatment on the smoking behavior of the respondents. This could be seen as a classic intent-to-treat approach, and it suggests several tests on the validity of our instruments.

We consider the plausibility of the exclusion restrictions by conducting a 'falsification' exercise where we examine the earnings of women, a group where the instrument varies, but there are almost no smoking respondents. Given the valid concern that there are other omitted variables which correlate both with parental smoking and earnings of adult children, we would expect that for women, who rarely smoke, parental smoking would be significantly associated with lower earnings in the reduced form. Table A.1 shows the OLS estimation results for Albanian women; there is no

Table 1. Summary Statistics for Sample of Working Men.

	Smokers		*Never Smokers*	
	Mean	Standard Error	Mean	Standard Error
Log monthly earnings	3.186	0.511	3.273	0.543
Monthly earnings/10,000	28.061	20.282	28.393	17.533
Mother ever smoked	0.065	0.247	0.040	0.197
Father ever smoked	0.701	0.458	0.506	0.500
Age in years	40.506	10.147	39.609	10.851
Marital status				
Single	0.123	0.329	0.190	0.393
Married	0.856	0.352	0.808	0.394
Divorced	0.005	0.072	0.001	0.031
Widowed	0.011	0.102	0.000	0.000
Religious beliefs				
Muslim	0.821	0.384	0.791	0.407
Christian Orthodox	0.077	0.267	0.094	0.292
Christian Catholic	0.049	0.216	0.074	0.261
Bektashian	0.037	0.189	0.033	0.180
Other religions	0.016	0.125	0.008	0.088
Education				
Primary	0.425	0.495	0.350	0.477
Secondary general education	0.193	0.395	0.228	0.420
Vocational education, 2–3 years	0.026	0.160	0.029	0.169
Vocational education, 4–5 years	0.230	0.421	0.212	0.409
University diploma	0.125	0.331	0.181	0.385
Speaks English	0.028	0.165	0.064	0.244
Speaks Italian	0.058	0.234	0.083	0.277
Speaks Greek	0.079	0.270	0.090	0.287
Hours worked per week	46.525	9.959	46.558	9.786
Household characteristics				
Household size	4.917	1.803	4.864	1.600
Share of children 0–6 years[a]	0.079	0.126	0.074	0.126
Share of children 7–14 years	0.162	0.177	0.148	0.175
Share of elderly	0.064	0.119	0.072	0.124
Urban household	0.666	0.472	0.677	0.468
Education of the father				
Primary	0.489	0.500	0.462	0.499
Secondary general education	0.244	0.430	0.211	0.408
Vocational education, 2–3 years	0.127	0.333	0.114	0.318
Vocational education, 4–5 years	0.046	0.209	0.068	0.251
University diploma	0.095	0.293	0.145	0.353
Education of the mother				
Primary	0.548	0.498	0.546	0.498
Secondary general education	0.214	0.411	0.201	0.401
Vocational education, 2–3 years	0.116	0.320	0.091	0.288

Table 1. *(Continued)*

	Smokers		*Never Smokers*	
	Mean	Standard Error	Mean	Standard Error
Vocational education, 4–5 years	0.026	0.160	0.036	0.187
University diploma	0.095	0.293	0.126	0.332
Number of observations	569		1019	

Note: Shares of children and elderly are the proportions in the household, e.g., in a household of size 10 with 2 elderly the share of elderly is 0.2.
[a]The sample for this table contains observations with all non-missing values for the variables listed in the table, which is this sample used for all estimations in this chapter.

significant correlation between earnings and parental smoking. Thus, at least for women, these instruments do not seem to capture some omitted variables that would otherwise explain earnings differentials and would result in inconsistency in the 2SLS. The coefficients on maternal education dummies indicate that women whose mothers had vocational education or university degree have higher earnings relative to women with less educated mothers (not presented). This suggests that conditional on own education, parental education is picking up some of the effects of unobservable parental characteristics.

Turning to the earnings of men, the key result from the first stage of the 2SLS model is the joint significance of the instrumental variables for smoking. The Sargan's (1958) test of over-identifying restrictions fails to reject (χ^2 *P*-value of 0.643) the null hypothesis that our excluded instruments, mother's and father's smoking status, are uncorrelated with the error term and are correctly excluded from the earnings equation. The F-statistic on the excluded instruments (22.35) indicates that the first-stage estimates have strong predictive power, in other words, our instruments are not weak (Staiger & Stock, 1997). The Cragg–Donald test of weak instruments further confirms the power of our instruments: The Cragg–Donald statistic of 46.74 rejects (with at least 99 percent confidence) the hypothesis that our system is only weakly identified. This result could be interpreted as another test for the presence of the weak instruments (Stock & Yogo, 2002).

Main Results

Table 2 presents the results of the OLS and 2SLS regressions of the effect of smoking on earnings.[12] According to the OLS regression, smoking decreases

Table 2. OLS and 2SLS Estimations of the Effect of Smoking on Earnings of Men.

Monthly Earnings	OLS		2SLS			
			First Stage		*Second Stage*	
	Coefficient	Standard Error	Coefficient	Standard Error	Coefficient	Standard Error
Instrument: *Father smoked*			0.100*	0.056		
Instrument: *Mother smoked*			0.157***	0.025		
Current smoker	−0.049*	0.026			−0.267*	0.152
Respondents who never smoked	Reference Category					
Age	0.099**	0.048	0.109**	0.047	0.122**	0.051
Age squared/100	−0.266**	0.125	−0.281**	0.123	−0.325**	0.132
Age cubed/10,000	0.217**	0.105	0.226**	0.103	0.264**	0.110
Marital status						
Single	Reference Category					
Married	0.098*	0.056	0.046	0.056	0.111*	0.057
Divorced/Widowed	−0.324	0.257	0.405	0.254	−0.228	0.266
Religious beliefs						
Muslim	Reference Category					
Christian Orthodox	0.033	0.048	−0.045	0.047	0.025	0.048
Christian Catholic	−0.004	0.059	−0.123**	0.058	−0.035	0.062
Bektashian	−0.037	0.073	0.028	0.072	−0.036	0.073
Other religions	−0.037	0.118	0.248**	0.117	0.015	0.124
Education						
Primary	Reference Category					
Secondary general education	−0.007	0.034	−0.080**	0.033	−0.026	0.036
Vocational education, 2–3 years	0.057	0.076	−0.034	0.075	0.044	0.076
Vocational education, 4–5 years	0.101***	0.034	−0.044	0.034	0.091***	0.035
University diploma	0.340***	0.042	−0.103**	0.041	0.313***	0.046
Speaks English	0.288***	0.066	−0.083	0.065	0.272***	0.067
Speaks Italian	0.082	0.051	0.019	0.051	0.084	0.052
Speaks Greek	0.187***	0.046	−0.022	0.045	0.181***	0.046
Log hours worked per week	0.401***	0.053	0.013	0.053	0.402***	0.053
Household characteristics						
Log household size	−0.151	0.178	−0.027	0.177	−0.170	0.179
Log household size squared	0.052	0.058	0.015	0.058	0.059	0.059
Urban household	0.025	0.030	−0.013	0.030	0.022	0.030
Share of children 0–6 years	−0.231*	0.127	−0.138	0.125	−0.258**	0.128
Share of children 7–14 years	0.054	0.089	−0.011	0.087	0.050	0.089
Share of elderly	−0.182	0.114	0.076	0.113	−0.181	0.114
Constant	0.415	0.645	−1.101*	0.638	0.214	0.661

Table 2. *(Continued)*

Monthly Earnings	OLS		2SLS			
			First Stage		*Second Stage*	
	Coefficient	Standard Error	Coefficient	Standard Error	Coefficient	Standard Error
F-statistic for excluded instruments ($P > F$)			22.35	(0.000)		
Sargan overidentification test χ^2 and P-value			0.215	(0.643)		
R^2	0.254		0.100		0.159	
Number of observations	1588		1588			

Note: * is significant at 10% level; ** at 5% level; *** at 1% level. Regressions also include a complete set of geographic dummy variables for the 38 districts and a set of dummy variables reflecting educational achievement of the mother and father of the respondent.

male earnings by 4.8 percent (standard error (SE) of 0.025); this result is comparable to what was shown in Fig. 1.[13] Given concerns that smoking does not randomly occur among men in Albania, the results on the probability of smoking are discussed first. The results are presented in the first two columns of Table 3.

The probability of smoking is positively and significantly related to whether the father of the respondent smoked. This first stage of the 2SLS also finds that maternal smoking is a stronger predictor of the respondent's smoking than father's smoking habits which is consistent with the fact that the majority of respondents grew up with smoking fathers, whereas female smoking is less socially acceptable. The coefficients on mother's and father's smoking habit are jointly significant. Older individuals are more likely to smoke relative to younger respondents. The prevalence of smoking is lower among Catholics and significantly higher among atheists relative to men of other religions. Men with less than primary education are more likely to smoke compared to better educated men. The estimation also reveals some regional differences of the incidence of smoking among working men.

From the second stage of the 2SLS estimation, we find that the earnings reduction associated with smoking is larger when smoking is treated as an endogenous variable. Smokers suffer a 23.4 percent earnings reduction

Table 3. FIML Estimation of the Switching Regression Model for Men.

	Probability to Smoke		*Earnings of Smokers*		*Earnings of Never Smokers*	
	Coefficient	Standard Error	Coefficient	Standard Error	Coefficient	Standard Error
Instrument: *Father smoked*	0.297*	0.144[a]				
Instrument: *Mother smoked*	0.450***	0.079[a]				
Age	0.324*	0.139	0.080	0.094	0.136*	0.061
Age squared/100	−0.805*	0.363	−0.197	0.241	−0.375*	0.160
Age cubed/10,000	0.635*	0.303	0.145	0.197	0.314*	0.135
Marital status						
Single			Reference Category			
Married	−0.004	*0.153*	0.049	0.080	0.162*	0.074
Divorced/Widowed	0.874	*0.810*	−0.506	0.332	0.457	0.520
Religious beliefs						
Muslim			Reference Category			
Christian Orthodox	−0.160	0.141	0.103	0.085	−0.017	0.059
Christian Catholic	−0.378*	0.174	−0.147	0.116	−0.013	0.073
Bektashian	0.168	0.204	0.058	0.113	−0.077	0.096
Other religions	0.644*	0.325	0.073	0.177	−0.007	0.177
Education						
Primary			Reference Category			
Secondary general education	−0.237*	0.096	−0.001	0.061	−0.031	0.044
Vocational education, 2–3 years	−0.096	0.215	0.031	0.126	0.054	0.094
Vocational education, 4–5 years	−0.148	0.096	0.055	0.054	0.108*	0.046
University diploma	−0.305*	0.119	0.214*	0.081	0.335***	0.055
Speaks English	−0.303	0.202	0.792***	0.143	0.145*	0.077
Speaks Italian	0.021	*0.149*	−0.022	0.087	0.111*	0.064
Speaks Greek	−0.044	0.131	0.044	0.079	0.243***	0.057
Log hours worked per week	0.007	0.152	0.358***	0.084	0.424***	0.067
Household characteristics						
Log household size	−0.206	0.501	−0.449	0.284	−0.003	0.232
Log household size^2	0.079	0.164	0.135	0.091	0.011	0.077
Urban household	−0.039	0.085	0.064	0.050	0.003	0.038
Share of children 0–6 years	−0.246	0.356	0.096	0.204	−0.460**	0.161
Share of children 7–years	0.014	0.248	0.196	0.144	−0.006	0.112
Share of elderly	0.353	0.327	−0.113	0.195	−0.150	0.142
Constant	−4.475*	1.888	0.545	1.321	−0.072	0.803

Table 3. *(Continued)*

	Probability to Smoke		*Earnings of Smokers*		*Earnings of Never Smokers*	
	Coefficient	Standard Error	Coefficient	Standard Error	Coefficient	Standard Error
$\sigma_{1,2}$			0.485	0.080	0.479	0.015
$\rho_{1,2}$			0.703*	0.350	0.242**	0.109
LR test of independent equations						
χ^2 $(P>\chi^2)$	3.995**	0.012				
Number of observations	1588					

Note: * is significant at 10% level; ** at 5% level; *** at 1% level. Regressions also include a complete set of geographic dummy variables for the 38 districts and a set of dummy variables reflecting educational achievement of the mother and father of the respondent.
[a]Joint significance of coefficients at 10% level.

(bootstrapped SE of 9.8) compared with non-smokers. These large losses are comparable to the estimates by Auld (2005) who finds a 30 percent earnings loss for smokers in Canada but are higher than the effects found in studies of smoking in the United States and the Netherlands. The results show a positive selection bias into smoking as found in other studies (e.g. Auld, 2005 and Van Ours, 2004). Levine et al. (1997) show mixed evidence of positive selection, but find no evidence of negative selection. If the instruments are taken as valid, OLS results underestimate the negative earnings effect of smoking.[14]

The results of the FIML estimation of the switching regression model (2) are shown in Table 3.[15] The log-likelihood test of independence is rejected in favour of joint dependence of the error terms in system (2). The Hausman over-identification test (Hausman, 1983) confirms the validity of our instruments with a 5 percent significance level.

Conditional on other covariates, we expect that when a characteristic is associated with higher (lower) earnings, the association for non-smokers will be as high (low) or higher (lower) than for their counterparts who smoke. This is generally the case. Married non-smoking males earn significantly more than single non-smokers, whereas marital status of smokers has no effect on earnings. The relationship between earnings and education of non-smokers is stronger (i.e. the earnings–education profile is steeper) than that for smokers. Ability to speak English is associated with a significant earnings premium for both groups. Knowledge of Italian and Greek, however, is beneficial in terms of higher earnings only for non-smokers. Overall there is a stronger dependence between earnings and productive human capital characteristics for non-smokers than for smokers. That could support the hypothesis about the differences in the discount rates between smoking and non-smoking individuals (Evans & Montgomery, 1994).

In the FIML estimation, the effect of smoking on earnings is simulated using estimates of the parameters of (4) and (5). For every smoking respondent, his expected earnings conditional on being a smoker is estimated and compared with predicted earnings conditional on not smoking. An average smoker experiences a 22.5 percent reduction in his earnings due to smoking (bootstrap SE 9.2). The results are not statistically different from the earnings reduction associated with smoking derived from the 2SLS estimates.[16] Moreover, the effect of smoking on earnings is similar across age groups and for respondents residing in rural and urban locations. Yet, there is evidence that the smoking penalty is lower for men with higher education: conditional on other characteristics, earnings of smokers with a university diploma are 17 percent lower than their non-smoking counterparts.

The difference in earnings estimated by the LIV model for smokers relative to non-smokers is somewhat lower: a 19.2 percent reduction (bootstrap SE 6.4).[17] The ATTs calculated for the different groups of smokers demonstrate that, similar to the FIML estimations, earnings of smokers with university degree is about 16.3 percent lower compared with non-smokers. There are no significant differences in the effect of smoking by age or location.

Several alternative econometric specifications for model (2) are examined in order to assess the robustness of our results. The effect of smoking using a specification that includes the occupational dummies is estimated. These variables could be endogenous in the earnings equation and so the results of this estimation should be interpreted with caution. Again, the results are largely unchanged; after controlling for occupational choice, an average smoker earns 26.3 percent less than a non-smoker according to the FIML estimation and 20.0 percent less according to the semi-parametric LIV estimation.[18] Likewise, when measures of self-reported health status are included the results are largely unchanged.[19]

The estimates in Tables 2 and 3 suggest that religious beliefs are strongly associated with the decision to smoke but not with earnings conditional on smoking. We estimate model (2) using religious affiliation as an additional instrument. Although this could be a questionable instrument, it has been used as such in previous research (e.g. Auld, 2005), and so affords comparability. Using these instruments, the reduction in earnings due to smoking is 24 percent for the FIML estimator and 18.8 percent for the LIV estimator. Finally, the results in 2SLS, FIML and LIV estimations remain basically the same when parental education is excluded from the set of covariates. This is consistent with the fact that the difference in parental education between smokers and non-smokers is similar (Table 1). In sum, these different specifications produce comparable (and statistically similar) estimates of the individual earnings losses due to smoking.

Causal Relationship Between Smoking and Earnings

In the main findings, we show a large negative impact of smoking on earnings for Albanian men. Ideally, we would also try to explain the pathways of this effect. As noted by Levine et al. (1997) and faced in our study, it is very difficult to disentangle which channels drive the negative earnings impact of smoking. Some pathways seem less plausible in this context, such as higher health insurance costs and discrimination. The lack of an age gradient suggests that time preferences do not fully explain the earnings reduction we find. Here we explore the health impact of smoking: that smoking-related morbidities make smokers less healthy resulting in lower labour productivity and lower earnings. We explore this from the perspective of a dose–response relationship whereby the magnitude of the negative impact of smoking on earnings should increase with the intensity of smoking, such as the number of years smoking and the number of cigarettes smoked per day.

Based on an exposure argument, one would expect a weaker effect of smoking on earnings for young individuals who have recently started smoking. To test this hypothesis we stratified our sample in two groups of younger (age 18 to 34) and older males (age 35 to 60), since onset of smoking seems to stabilizes in the mid-30s (Vakeflliu, Argjiri, Peposhi, Agron, & Melani, 2002). The simulations based on FIML and LIV estimations demonstrate no significant differences in the effect of smoking on earnings between the younger and older smokers.[20] However, age-specific smoking-related traits may offset any exposure effects. The study by Ryan, Zwerling, and Jones (1996) found that smokers have elevated rates of accidents, absence, discipline, and firing relative to non-smokers and that these rates decline with job tenure. This would offset any small health consequences (and lower earnings impact) of smoking for younger workers. So, the lack of difference by age groups does not eliminate health effects that are driving the lower earnings for smokers.

Another assumption of the dose–response relationship is that the causal effect of smoking on earnings would be the largest for current smokers relative to never smokers and somewhat smaller for former smokers relative to never smokers. There are fewer quitters in the data set (95 men) and, perhaps more importantly, we have no information on when the individual quit. So, we are not able to explore this avenue with these data.

Finally, we attempt to explore information on the average number of cigarette smokers report smoking and number of years smoking. These data are heavily heaped since the response codes are categorical (number of packs and, for years smoking, five-year intervals). In both cases we have insufficient variation to adequately explore this in the ALSMS.

CONCLUSIONS

For working prime-age men in Albania, this study shows that earnings of smokers are significantly lower than earnings of individuals who never smoked. The simple comparison indicates an 8 percent earnings advantage for non-smokers relative to smokers. Controlling for the differences in observable characteristics in an OLS regression, the negative effect of smoking among men persists but is reduced to 4 percent. Taking the differences in observable and unobservable characteristics of smokers and non-smokers into account through 2SLS, FIML and semi-parametric LIV estimators, the earnings penalty for smoking is statistically and economically large: smokers experience earnings reductions of 19–23 percent. The large earnings reduction caused by smoking is robust to several specifications and controls for occupation and intensity of smoking. While better educated smokers have a slightly lower earnings penalty, there are otherwise no differences by other characteristics (such as age and location). Of course, the validity of these results depends on a set of assumptions about the instrumental variables employed. We assess these assumptions in a variety of ways and find support for them. In terms of underlying pathways of this impact, due to data limitations, including the lack of or limited data on morbidities, absenteeism, and intensity of smoking, we cannot empirically study to what extent each of the competing hypotheses contributes to the large earnings reduction from smoking. One exception is the lack of an age gradient in the earnings penalty which suggests that time preferences cannot fully explain the earnings reduction.

These results suggest that there are large private economic costs of smoking in low-income settings. Some caveats to this analysis should be mentioned. First, the sample is restricted to employed males. Employment is likely to be endogenous to smoking: if smokers are more likely than non-smokers to exit the labour force, for example due to poor health caused by smoking, then our estimates of the earnings differential between smokers and non-smokers may be biased. The results may underestimate the actual effect of smoking on earnings as a result of this bias. Second, excluding women may result in an incomplete computation of the societal cost of smoking if the earnings effects of smoking differ between men and women. Finally, the policy implications of this work will depend on the nature of the private earnings losses we study. This hinges on a better understanding of the causal pathway such as whether this negative effect is due to health effects which are underestimated by smokers.

NOTES

1. The WHO estimates that tobacco is the second major cause of death worldwide and the fourth most common risk factor for disease worldwide. The gross health care cost of smoking for developing countries is estimated to be as high as 1.1 percent of GDP (Jha & Chaloupka, 2000). The economic costs associated with losses in productivity because of smoking could be at least as large and be disproportionately incurred by the poor (The World Bank, 1999).

2. The smoking rates for men and women, respectively, in Eastern Europe are as follows: Bulgaria 49% and 24%; Croatia 34% and 32%; Macedonia 40% and 32%; Poland 44% and 25%; Romania 62% and 25%; Slovakia 55% and 30%; Slovenia 30% and 20%; Serbia and Montenegro 52% and 42%; Ukraine 51% and 19 (WHO, 2002b). The smoking rates for men and women, respectively, for the most populous developing countries include: Bangladesh 54% and 24%; Brazil 38% and 29%; China 67% and 4%; India 29% and 3%; Indonesia 59% and 4%; Pakistan 36% and 9% (WHO, 2002b).

3. The argument about the higher costs of health insurance for employers might not be relevant for Albania where only a small percentage of firms offer health insurance coverage (Nurl & Tragakes, 2002).

4. Heineck and Schwarze (2003) report that in Germany discrimination against smokers is more moderate than in the United States where social norms make smoking less acceptable as reflected in state-level bans against smoking in public spaces. A similar case can be made for Albania where smoking prevalence is even higher and where there are no restrictions against smoking.

5. The reverse causality of the effect of wages on smoking is partly mitigated by the evidence of the addictive nature of smoking. Lance, Akin, Dow, and Loh (2004) report a price elasticity of cigarette consumption for China and Russia to be in the range of 0 to −0.15, compared to −0.40 in the United States. This low elasticity

demonstrates the strong addiction of consumers to cigarettes. Developing countries often lack defined regulations on production of cigarettes. As a result, cigarettes in these settings are likely to have higher nicotine content and to be more addictive on average than in developed countries.

6. Alternative counterfactuals can also be framed. Perhaps the most obvious alternative would be to evaluate the economic costs of smoking as measured by the increased wages for smokers if they quit. In this case the counterfactual of smokers is the group of quitters. However, no convincing instruments were found in our data to identify the decision to quit or continue smoking. Also, there are few quitters in the sample. One could also assess the change in earnings associated with never-smokers who begin to smoke. These counterfactuals reflect future benefits of anti-smoking campaigns, whereas our chosen counterfactual measures the costs of smoking in terms of current productivity losses.

7. In related work, Cawley, Markowitz and Tauras (2004) use mother's weight as an instrument for own weight in their estimation of the impact of own weight on smoking initiation of adolescents. They acknowledge that maternal weight may be correlated with maternal smoking. Maternal smoking, which is omitted, may in turn increase the probability of the adolescent smoking.

8. MacDonald and Shields (2001) use similar instruments in the analysis of the impact of alcohol use on occupational attainments in England. Here these instruments are discussed in the context of probability of being a current smoker with the caveat that the instruments are arguably stronger for identification of non-smokers who have never smoked as opposed to quitters.

9. We know of no study confirming this multi-level effect of parental smoking on children's future earnings. In addition, the influence of these factors on future productivity may be less pronounced in Albania, where more than 60 percent of respondents grew up with smoking parents.

10. For further information on a survey design and sample frame see: http://www.instat.gov.al/

11. The low proportion of smoking women may be an underestimate of the actual prevalence of female smoking, as in Albania smoking is not seen as being socially acceptable for women and, therefore, women may be reluctant to admit they smoke (IMF, 2006). Nevertheless, it is important to note that the prevalence of female smoking has been increasing over time. According to WHO (2004), the proportion of females who smoked on a regular basis more than doubled in Albania from 1990 to 2000.

12. Wu-Hausman (Wu, 1973, 1978) F-test for endogeneity of smoking status in the 2SLS is $F(1,1519) = 2.13$; $P\text{-value} = 0.1044$. We also estimate the same specification in Table 2 with log hourly wages as a dependent variable rather than earnings. The results of this estimation are almost identical to those in Table 2.

13. In both OLS and 2SLS estimations, the percent change in earnings of smokers relative to non-smokers is calculated as: $\%\Delta = 100 \times (\exp(\gamma) - 1)$, where γ is a coefficient on the smoking dummy in (1). Likewise, the standard error of the percent change is computed by boot strapping and is not the standard error reported on the coefficient of smoking from the regressions.

14. The standard error on the current smoker coefficient in the OLS estimation is considerably smaller compared with the 2SLS estimate, although this is to be expected given the increase in the coefficient from the OLS to 2SLS.

15. The estimation of the switching regression model and simulation are based on the FIML algorithm implemented as Stata program *movestay* (Lokshin & Sajaia, 2004). For comparison, the FIML results for the un-identified model are presented in Table A.2 and show a small earnings effect of smoking, 5.1 percent, which is comparable to the results of the OLS estimate.

16. Likewise, we compare the estimated effects of smoking on earnings from the FIML model to those of OLS for the two subsamples of smokers and non-smokers (not presented here), which is analogous to comparing the 2SLS and OLS estimates. Again, we find that OLS results understate the negative effect of smoking on earnings by the same magnitude as the 2SLS and OLS comparison.

17. Estimation of the LIV model is implemented as Stata program *liv* (Lokshin & Umapathi, 2009).

18. All results discussed in the text but not presented are available from the authors upon request.

19. Other measures of health (such as physical or mental health indicators) are not available in these data. Several recent studies report an association between smoking and higher risk of unemployment through smoking-related diseases and higher rates of work accidents in Western Europe and the US (e.g. Ryan et al., 1996; Montgomery, Cook, Bartley, & Wadsworth, 1998; Leino-Arjas, Liira, Mutanen, Malmivaara, & Matikainen, 1999; Jusot, Khlat, Rochereau, & Serme, 2008). Such selection of healthier smokers (compared with unhealthy smokers) into the labour force would suggest that the findings here on the effect of current smoking status on earnings are attenuated. However, in our sample, we do not find that smokers are less likely to work. The percentage of men who are working is high (above 80 percent) and not statistically different between smoking and non-smoking men over 30 years old. Among younger workers (up to 30 years old), non-smokers are less likely to be working.

20. These findings also address possible selectivity issues in the sample of men who are working. Worse health due to smoking may drive smokers out of the labour force, so examining the sample of younger workers (for whom health effects may not yet appear) may address such selection concerns.

ACKNOWLEDGEMENT

We thank Martin Ravallion, Jed Friedman, Jishnu Das, and Gero Carletto, and two anonymous referees for useful and constructive comments.

REFERENCES

Andrews, J. A., Hops, H., Ary, D. V., Tildesley, E., & Harris, J. (1993). Parental influence on early adolescent substance use: Specific and nonspecific effects. *Journal of Early Adolescence*, *13*(3), 285–310.

Auld, M. (2005). Smoking, drinking, and income. *Journal of Human Resources*, *40*(2), 505–518.

Becker, G., Grossman, M., & Murphy, K. (1994). An empirical analysis of cigarette addiction. *American Economic Review*, *84*(3), 396–418.

Becker, G., & Murphy, K. (1988). A theory of rational addiction. *Journal of Political Economy*, *96*, 675–700.

Berger, M., & Leigh, J. (1989). The effects of smoking and being overweight on current earnings. *American Journal of Preventive Medicine*, *5*(1), 8–14.

Bertera, R. (1991). The effects of behavioral risks on absenteeism and health-care costs in the workplace. *Journal of Occupational Medicine*, *33*(11), 1119–1123.

Brandon, T. H., & Baker, T. (1991). The smoking consequences questionnaire: The subjective expected utility of smoking in college students. *Psychological Assessment*, *3*, 484–491.

Carneiro, P., Heckman, J., & Vytlacil, E. (2006). Understanding what instrumental variables estimate: Estimating average and marginal returns to schooling. The University of Chicago Working Paper.

Cawley, J., Markowitz, S., & Tauras, J. (2004). Lighting up and slimming down: The effects of body weight and cigarette prices on adolescent smoking initiation. *Journal of Health Economics*, *23*(2), 293–311.

Center for Disease Control and Prevention (CDC). (1994) *Preventing tobacco use among young people: A report of the surgeon general*, the United States.

Center for Health Promotion and Publications. (2000). *The dollar (and sense) benefits of having a smoke-free workplace*. Lansing, MI: Michigan Tobacco Control Program.

Chaloupka, F. (1991). Rational addictive behavior and cigarette smoking. *Journal of Political Economy*, *99*, 722–734.

Conway, T., & Cronan, T. (1992). Smoking, exercise, and physical fitness. *Preventive Medicine*, *21*, 723–734.

Cornwell, C., & Rupert, P. (1997). Unobserved individual effects, marriage and the earnings of young men. *Economic Inquiry*, *35*(2), 285–294.

Daniel, K. (1991). *Does marriage make men more productive*? mimeo, University of Chicago.

Evans, W. & Montgomery, E. (1994). Education and Health: Where There's Smoke There's an Instrument. NBER Working Paper 4949.

Fagan, P., Brook, J., Rubenstone, E., & Chenshu, Z. (2005). Parental occupation, education, and smoking as predictors of offspring tobacco use in adulthood: A longitudinal study. *Addictive Behaviors*, *30*, 517–529.

FAO, X. (2003). *Projections of tobacco production, consumption and trade to the year 2010*. Rome, Italy: Food and Agriculture Organization of the United Nations.

Fuchs, V. (1982). Time preference and health: an exploratory study. In: V. R. Fuchs (Ed.), *Economic aspects of health* (pp. 93–120). Chicago, IL: University of Chicago Press.

Gray, J. (1997). The fall in men's return to marriage: Declining productivity effects or changing selection? *Journal of Human Resources*, *32*(3), 481–504.

Hausman, J. (1983). Specification and estimation of simultaneous equations models. In: Z. Griliches & M. Intriligator (Eds.), *Handbook of econometrics*. Amsterdam: North Holland.

Heckman, J. (1979). Sample selection bias as a specification error. *Econometrica*, *47*(1), 153–161.

Heckman, J., Urzua, S., & Vytlacil, E. (2006). Understanding instrumental variables in models with essential heterogeneity. *The Review of Economics and Statistics*, *88*(3), 389–432.

Heckman, J., & Vytlacil, E. (2000). Local instrumental variables. In: C. Hsiao, K. Morimune & J. Powells (Eds.), *Nonlinear statistical modeling: Proceedings of the thirteenth international symposium in economic theory and econometrics: Essays in Honorof Takeshi Amemiya* (pp. 1–46). Cambridge: Cambridge University Press.

Heckman, J., & Vytlacil, E. (2005). Structural equations, treatment, effects and econometric policy evaluation. *Econometrica, 73*(3), 669–738.

Heineck, G. & Schwarze, J. (2003). Substance Use and Earnings: The Case of Smokers in Germany. Discussion Paper 743, IZA, Germany.

Hoad, N., & Clay, D. (1992). Smoking impairs the response to a physical training regime: A study of officer cadets. *Journal of the Royal Army Medical Corps, 138*, 115–117.

International Monetary Fund. (2006). Albania: Poverty reduction strategy paper – Annual progress report." IMF Country Report No. 06/23, IMF, Washington, DC.

Jha, P., & Chaloupka, F. (2000). *Tobacco control in developing countries*. New York: Oxford University Press.

Jusot, F., Khlat, M., Rochereau, T., & Serme, C. (2008). Job loss from poor health, smoking and obesity: A national prospective survey in France. *Journal of Epidemiology and Community Health, 62*(2), 332–337.

Lahiri, K., & Song, J. (2000). The effect of smoking on health using a sequential self-selection model. *Health Economics, 9*, 491–511.

Lance, P., Akin, J., Dow, W., & Loh, C. (2004). Is cigarette smoking in poorer nations highly sensitive to price? Evidence from Russia and China. *Journal of Health Economics, 23*, 173–189.

Lee, L. (1978). Unionism and wage rates: A simultaneous equations model with qualitative and limited dependent variables. *International Economic Review, 19*, 415–433.

Leino-Arjas, P., Liira, J., Mutanen, P., Malmivaara, A., & Matikainen,, E. (1999). Predictors and consequences of unemployment among construction workers: Prospective cohort study. *British Medical Journal, 319*, 600–605.

Levine, P., Gustafson, T., & Valenchik, A. (1997). More bad news for smokers? The effect of cigarette smoking on wages. *Industrial and Labor Relations Review, 50*, 493–509.

Lokshin, M., & Sajaia, Z. (2004). Maximum-likelihood estimation of endogenous switching regression models. *STATA Journal, 4*(3), 227–234.

Lokshin, M. & Umapathi, N. (2009). *Estimation of treatment effects under heterogeneity: Stata module*. mimeo, The World Bank.

Lye, J., & Hirschberg, J. (2004). Alcohol consumption, smoking and wages. *Applied Economics, 36*, 1807–1817.

MacDonald, Z., & Shields, M. (2001). The impact of alcohol use on occupational attainment in England. *Economica, 68*, 427–454.

Manning, W., Keeler, E., Newhouse, J., Sloss, E., & Wasserman, J. (1991). *The costs of poor health habits*. Cambridge, MA: Harvard University Press.

Mincer, J. (1974). *Schooling, experience, and earnings*. Brookfield, VT: Ashgate Publishing.

Montgomery, S., Cook, D., Bartley, M., & Wadsworth, M. (1998). Unemployment, cigarette smoking, alcohol consumption and body weight in young British men. *European Journal of Public Health, 8*, 21–27.

Nigel, T. (1984). The effects of religion and denomination on earnings and the returns to human capital. *Journal of Human Resources, 19*(4), 472–488.

Nurl, B. & Tragakes, E. (2002). *Health care systems in transition: Albania*. Report 4(6) of European Commission on Health Care Systems, Copenhagen.

Pedersen, W., & Lavik, N. (1991). Role modeling cigarette smoking: Vulnerable working class girls? A longitudinal study. *Scandinavian Journal of Social Medicine, 19*(2), 110–115.

Rohsenow, D., Abrams, D., Monti, P., Colby, S., Martin, R., & Niaura,, R. (2003). The smoking effects questionnaire for adult populations. Development and psychometric properties. *Addictive Behaviors, 28*, 1257–1270.

Ryan, J., Zwerling, C., & Jones, M. (1996). Cigarette smoking at hire as a predictor of employment outcome. *Journal of Occupational and Environment Medicine*, *38*, 928–933.

Sargan, J. (1958). The estimation of economic relationships using instrumental variables. *Econometrica*, *26*, 393–415.

Senagore, A. (2004). Smoking cessation. In: A. Senagore (Ed.), *Encyclopedia of surgery: A guide for patients and caregivers*. Farmington Hills, MI: Gale.

Shapo, L., Gilmore, A., Coker, R., McKee, M., & Shapo, E. (2003). Prevalence and determinants of smoking in Tirana city, Albania: A population-based survey. *Public Health*, *117*(4), 228–236.

Sloan, F., Ostermann, J., Conover, C., Taylor, D., & Picone, G. (2004). *The price of smoking*. Cambridge, MA: MIT Press.

Staiger, D., & Stock, J. (1997). Instrumental variables regression with weak instruments. *Econometrica*, *65*(3), 557–586.

Stock, J. & Yogo, M. (2002). Testing for weak instruments in linear IV regression. NBER Technical Working Paper 284.

The World Bank. (1999). *Curbing the epidemic: Governments and the economics of tobacco control*. Washington, DC: The World Bank.

Vakeflliu, Y., Argjiri, D., Peposhi, I., Agron, S., & Melani, A. (2002). Tobacco smoking habits, beliefs and attitudes among medical students in Tirana, Albania. *Preventive Medicine*, *34*, 370–373.

Van Ours, J. (2004). A pint a day raises a man's pay; but smoking blows that gain away. *Journal of Health Economics*, *23*(5), 863–886.

Viscusi, K., & Hersch, J. (2001). Cigarette smokers and job risk takers. *Review of Economics and Statistics*, *83*(2), 269–280.

World Health Organization. (1999). *Making a difference, world health report 1999*. Geneva, Switzerland.

World Health Organization. (2002a). *European country profiles on tobacco control, 2001*. Copenhagen, Denmark: WHO Regional Office for Europe.

World Health Organization. (2002b). *The tobacco atlas*. Geneva, Switzerland: WHO.

World Health Organization. (2004). European health for all statistical database. Available at: http://www.who.dk/

Wu, D. (1973). Alternative tests of independence between stochastic regressors and disturbances. *Econometrica*, *41*, 733–750.

APPENDIX

Table A.1. OLS Estimation of Earnings Equation for Women.

	Non-smoking women		All Women	
	Coefficient	Standard Error	Coefficient	Standard Error
Instrument: *Father smoked*	0.076	0.060	0.073	0.059
Instrument: *Mother smoked*	0.000	0.025	−0.009	0.025
Age	0.035	0.061	0.046	0.061
Age squared/100	−0.071	0.164	−0.105	0.164
Age cubed/10,000	0.050	0.142	0.083	0.142
Marital status				
Single		Reference Category		
Married	0.024	0.052	0.022	0.050
Divorced/Widowed	−0.097	0.071	−0.144	0.101
Religious beliefs				
Muslim		Reference Category		
Christian Orthodox	0.046	0.038	0.049	0.038
Christian Catholic	0.058	0.066	0.106	0.065
Bektashian	−0.006	0.072	0.037	0.070
Other religions	−0.048	0.096	0.030	0.307
Education				
Primary		Reference Category		
Secondary general education	−0.011	0.040	0.001	0.040
Vocational education, 2–3 years	−0.053	0.063	−0.033	0.063
Vocational education, 4–5 years	0.062	0.038	0.089**	0.038
University diploma	0.374***	0.043	0.387***	0.043
Speaks English	0.240***	0.053	0.240***	0.052
Speaks Italian	0.061	0.055	0.069	0.054
Speaks Greek	0.387***	0.087	0.341***	0.082
Log hours worked per week	0.123**	0.061	0.112*	0.062
Household characteristics				
Log household size	−0.089	0.132	−0.080	0.128
Log household size squared	0.011	0.050	0.014	0.049
Urban household	0.012	0.038	0.020	0.038
Share of children 0–6 years	−0.203	0.143	−0.207	0.142
Share of children 7–14 years	−0.084	0.089	−0.073	0.089
Share of elderly	−0.069	0.097	−0.089	0.095
Constant	1.604**	0.743	1.502**	0.747

Table A.1. *(Continued)*

	Non-smoking women		All Women	
	Coefficient	Standard Error	Coefficient	Standard Error
F-test of joint significance of maternal education dummies	$F(4,737)=3.46$; $P>F=0.008$		$F(4,763)=3.87$; $P>F=0.006$	
F-test of joint significance of paternal education dummies	$F(4,737)=0.95$; $P>F=0.043$		$F(4,763)=0.71$; $P>F=0.588$	
Adjusted R^2	0.429		0.377	
Number of observations	805		831	

Note: * is significant at 10% level; ** at 5% level; *** at 1% level. Regression also includes a complete set of geographic dummy variables for the 38 districts and a set of dummy variables reflecting educational achievement of the mother and father of the respondent.

Table A.2. FIML Estimation of the Switching Regression Model for Men.

	Probability to smoke		Earnings of smokers		Earnings of non-smokers	
	Coefficient	Standard Error	Coefficient	Standard Error	Coefficient	Standard Error
Instrument: *Father smoked*	0.225*	0.114	−0.030	0.088	0.140	0.122
Instrument: *Mother smoked*	0.475***	0.073	0.065	0.067	−0.016	0.041
Age	0.315**	0.140	0.107	0.099	0.145**	0.062
Age squared/100	−0.798**	0.363	−0.267	0.255	−0.403**	0.162
Age cubed/10000	0.632**	0.303	0.203	0.210	0.340**	0.136
Marital status						
Single			Reference Category			
Married	0.141	0.160	0.060	0.095	0.165**	0.075
Divorced/Widowed	0.809	0.678	0.061	0.271	0.508	0.529
Religious beliefs						
Muslim			Reference Category			
Christian Orthodox	−0.037	0.136	0.086	0.084	−0.038	0.058
Christian Catholic	−0.383**	0.174	−0.180	0.116	−0.022	0.074
Bektashian	0.155	0.204	0.080	0.119	−0.074	0.097
Other religions	0.748**	0.329	0.120	0.184	−0.011	0.179

Table A.2. *(Continued)*

	Probability to smoke		Earnings of smokers		Earnings of non-smokers	
	Coefficient	Standard Error	Coefficient	Standard Error	Coefficient	Standard Error
Education						
Primary			Reference Category			
Secondary general education	−0.260***	0.095	−0.016	0.064	−0.028	0.045
Vocational education, 2–3 years	−0.113	0.215	0.063	0.132	0.056	0.095
Vocational education, 4–5 years	−0.142	0.095	0.036	0.056	0.114**	0.045
University diploma	−0.298**	0.119	0.201**	0.082	0.337***	0.055
Speaks English	−0.290	0.201	0.739***	0.151	0.134*	0.078
Speaks Italian	0.020	0.147	−0.008	0.090	0.111*	0.064
Speaks Greek	−0.054	0.130	0.046	0.081	0.246***	0.057
Log hours worked per week	0.021	0.151	0.381***	0.088	0.418***	0.067
Household characteristics						
Log household size	0.239	0.527	−0.360	0.303	−0.026	0.233
Log household size squared	−0.054	0.171	0.104	0.096	0.016	0.077
Urban household	−0.021	0.084	0.059	0.051	0.002	0.038
Share of children 0–6 years	−0.477	0.360	0.091	0.229	−0.448***	0.163
Share of children 7–14 years	−0.095	0.249	0.198	0.152	0.012	0.112
Share of elderly	0.276	0.324	−0.119	0.201	−0.166	0.141
Constant	−4.805**	1.875	−0.044	1.395	0.039	0.813
$\sigma_{1,2}$			−0.732***	0.039	−0.665***	0.149
$\rho_{1,2}$			0.289	0.230	0.898**	0.394
LR test of independence equations χ^2 $(P > \chi^2)$	4.943**	0.014				
Number of observations	1588					

Note: * is significant at 10% level; ** at 5% level; *** at 1% level. Regressions also include a complete set of geographic dummy variables for the 38 districts and a set of dummy variables reflecting educational achievement of the mother and father of the respondent.

CHAPTER 7

THE IMPACT OF WORKER EFFORT ON PUBLIC SENTIMENT TOWARD TEMPORARY MIGRANTS

Gil S. Epstein and Alessandra Venturini

ABSTRACT

Temporary and circular migration programs have been devised by many destination countries and supported by the European Commission as a policy to reduce welfare and social costs of immigration in destination countries. In this chapter, we present an additional reason for proposing temporary migration policies based on the characteristics of the foreign labor-effort supply. The level of effort exerted by migrants, which decreases over their duration in the host country, positively affects production, real wages, and capital owners' profits. We show that the acceptance of job offers by migrants results in the displacement in employment of national workers. However, it increases the workers' exertion, decreases prices, and thus can counter anti-immigrant voter sentiment. Therefore, the favorable sentiment of the capital owners and the local population toward migrants may rise when temporary migration policies are adopted.

Keywords: Migration; exertion of effort; contracted temporary migration

JEL classifications: J23; J61

Research in Labor Economics, Volume 33, 239–261

ISSN: 0147-9121/doi:10.1108/S0147-9121(2011)0000033010

INTRODUCTION

Migration is a never-ending problem in modern society. The debate on the best immigration policy has been ongoing since the colonial period and grew increasingly intense in the last century when the destination countries began to impose controls on immigration.

The core issue in this debate is finding the appropriate policy with which to favor a positive effect of immigration, at least in the destination countries. Should policies be more open or more restrictive, should they be selective or otherwise?

There are three main arguments backing this choice: *The first* is the effect of foreigners on the labor market in the destination country. Are migrants competing with natives in the labor market or are they complementary? Should policies be more restrictive or should they be more open? Should the migrants be skilled or unskilled? The empirical literature from Europe, the USA, Canada, and Australia finds little evidence of wage competition and employment competition. The debate continues, but it is centered on the econometric techniques that enable better measurement of the foreign effect and better control for the endogeneity of migration location.[1] *The second* line of reasoning starts after the conclusion of the first. Even if migrants are not strong competitors in the labor market, they use the welfare system, in some countries more than the natives do. Some authors have even suggested the existence of "welfare shopping" whereby migrants locate and where the welfare system is more generous (Borjas, 1999), but significant evidence of this does not exist, with the exception of the findings by De Giorgi and Pellizzari (2011). In countries where welfare systems are more generous, especially in Europe, evidence indicates a greater foreign population on welfare. This is the case in Germany, the United Kingdom, and Sweden.[2] Such welfare usage declines if the migrants' characteristics are taken into account (Barrett & McCarthy, 2008; Pellizzari, 2011).[3] This result is supported by the many empirical studies conducted on wage and employment assimilation.[4] *The third* line of argument stresses the difficult and limited social assimilation of foreigners: even the second generation seems unable to integrate into the social life of the destination country. Both the "melting pot" (Glazer & Moynihan, 1970) and the "bumpy line" theories of assimilation (Gans, 1979, 1996) questioned the previous positive view of the immigrant integration process, and the "segmented assimilation paradigm," developed by Portes and Zou (1993), put an end to them: it interpreted social upgrading either as specific and occasional individual action or as an organized group activity that is not always successful. These three arguments have given new support for a temporary migration policy that may solve the difficulties of integrating foreigners economically and socially, and possibly reduce to some extent their welfare costs and competition in the labor market.

New emphasis has been given within the European Commission (2007) to the proposal of circular migration policies. These seemingly repropose the temporary migration policies adopted in North Europe until the oil price increase of 1973 and the beginning of the recession, but in fact they represent a new vision of the international mobility pattern. Temporary migration will not only solve competition, economic, social integration, and welfare costs in the destination countries but will also favor the economic growth of sending countries by reducing brain drain and contrasting the negative effects of remittances, which frequently create a subsidized economy and reduce the labor force participation rate and the future growth path (see, e.g., Newland & Agunias, 2007; Venturini 2008).

In this chapter, we suggest another reason for pursuing temporary migration. This is based on an efficient use of human resources by the employer and a maximization of the utility of consumers. Whereas Dustmann and Weiss (2007) analyze the incentives for migrants to adopt short-stay migration plans, we analyze their labor productivity and the implications of the employer's maximizing decisions and for the consumers consumption levels, which will both be in favor of short stopover.

On the political economic side, studies on immigration policy investigate voters' attitudes toward immigrants (see, e.g., Benhabib, 1996; Hillman & Weiss, 1999; Mazza & van Winden, 1996).[5] Such studies require an underlying basis that explains why a voter may support or object to immigration. One basis, which identifies personal gains and losses from immigration, is the standard full-employment model of international trade and factor movements (see Kai-yiu Wong, 1995). Alternatively, all members of a local population may benefit when immigration reduces the domestic per capita tax burden for the financing of collective goods. Or, more generally, there may be benefits for the local population when immigration expands the domestic tax base, and, for example, allows the public financing of intergenerational transfers that might otherwise be unsustainable because of demographic imbalance in the local population (see Bonin, Raffelhüschen, & Walliser, 2000; Hillman, 2002; Lee & Miller, 1998; Storesletten, 2000). Epstein and Hillman (2003) consider employed workers who pay taxes, which finance income transfers to the unemployed, and find that immigrants initially displace national workers from the unemployment pool. The real wage declines because of immigration, but the probability of a local worker being employed increases. Although employed workers finance income transfers to the unemployed, immigration, within designated bounds, increases the expected utility of local workers. Since employers benefit from immigration, there are immigration policies that are mutually beneficial to all voters, whether they are local employees or employers, although employers will want more immigrants than workers.

In this chapter, we take a different view by looking at the effort exerted by migrants during their stay or work in the host country. We suggest a possible interpretation of why migrants, at least in the initial period in the host country, exert more effort than the local population. When immigrants arrive in the host country, they may accept jobs that entail long hours of work. For example, female immigrants employed in family services frequently work around the clock. This implies that migrants' working hours are uncertain and that they enjoy little freedom and free time. The longer they stay in the destination country, the more they are reluctant to accept such jobs. They prefer normal hours with leisure time. A similar pattern is apparent in other types of service jobs. In addition, migrants in agriculture accept long working hours, and may be willing to perform the heaviest tasks in the industrial sector. Not only are they willing to work overtime but also very flexible and willing to accept last-minute changes. The results of our chapter have a similar flavor to those presented by Galor and Stark (1991). Their chapter builds on the idea that migrants consider the possibility of eventually returning to their (low-wage) country of origin, and thus may have an incentive to work harder in the (high-wage) country of destination. Our chapter does not consider this incentive. If we would add this incentive, our results would even be further enhanced.

We consider an efficiency wage model to analyze the choice of local workers and migrants regarding the exertion of effort in the workplace. The level of effort affects the consumption patterns of both groups. When determining their level of consumption, individuals take into account the price of consumption. Upon arrival, immigrants evaluate the weighted average between the local price level and the price level in their home country.[6] With time, the weight of the price level in the home country decreases and it converges to the local price level. Therefore, the consumption patterns and the effort exerted merge with those of the local population.

The application of high effort and low consumption patterns has two different effects on the local population. Higher effort decreases the employment of the local population; however, a decrease in patterns of consumption by migrants increases the benefits for the local population.

Over time, both consumption patterns and the exertion of effort converge to those of the local population. Therefore, the sentiment of capital owners and the local population toward migrants may change when temporary migration policies are adopted. Under such policies, the temporary migrants will enter the country for a short period of time, exert a high level of effort in the workplace, and at the same time decrease the cost of consumption for the local population. These temporary migrants would leave at the end of the period and be replaced by new temporary migrants.[7]

In second section, we present some evidence on the variables at the heart of the model. The model is described in third section. The consumption pattern of immigrants is specified in fourth section. In fifth section, we determine the equilibrium wage and the level of effort exerted in the case of homogeneous or heterogeneous human capital with or without inelastic supply of immigrants. Sixth section analyzes the implications of the efforts supplied by immigrants on the local labor and products. The chapter concludes with some policy implications.

PUZZLING EMPIRICAL EVIDENCE

Our chapter is motivated by some stylized facts. More specifically, research indicates two contradictory behaviors: when arriving in the host country migrants have low consumption levels and large saving. With time consumption increases, remittances decrease and the savings decrease. On the other hand, the effort invested by the migrant is higher initially and declines as the migrants become more integrated into the destination economy. Our model tries to understand this contradictory by considering the migrants' attitudes toward prices in both the home and host countries.

The first one is that in the initial phase of migration foreigners have a very limited consumption in the destination country, very large saving, and large amount of remittances which they send back to the origin country. As migration goes on, however, consumption in the destination country increases, remittances decrease, and the savings become more similar to the natives.

There is a large amount of empirical evidence that shows that the amount of remittances declines as the migrant becomes more integrated into the country of destination and decreases with family reunification (Carling, 2008; Funkhouser, 1995; Galor & Stark, 1990; Poirine, 1997). The reduction in the remittances, and the increase in the consumption in the destination countries, is frequently related to the reunification of the family but also to the more general assimilation process, where the assimilation in the consumption pattern prevailing in the destination country plays an important role.

De Voretz and Vadean (2005) point out that in Canada the migrants' remittances decline as the duration of residence in the host country increases. There are, however, differences among communities and the migration policies play an important role because if family reunification is allowed and favored from the commencement of the migration pattern, the amount of remittances sent back is reduced and their decline as well. The same is found in the Eastern European countries by Mansoor and Quillin (2006)[8] and in Europe by Holst, Schäfer, and Schrooten (2010) for women migrants. The evidence, regarding the decline in remittances, is very well recorded.

Less evidence exists regarding consumption and saving behavior of the migrants in the destination country. The evidence stresses an increasing pattern of consumption and a declining one for savings. Kumku (1989) found in Germany a high saving rate for Turkish immigrants in their first few years, and Kirdar (2009) found that the saving rate decreases with age in Germany. More specifically, Bauer and Sinning (2005), using GSOEP, show that in 2001 in Germany the saving rate of temporary migrants was larger than the saving rate of permanent migrants (0.072 vs. 0.050) and the savings plus the remittances rate is higher for the temporary migrants than for the permanent ones (0.10 vs. 0.066). In Sinning (2007) using the same data, it was established that temporary migrants save on average 16.7% more and send 20.6% more other transfers to their home country than permanent migrants. Similarly, Piracha and Zhu (2007) find that among the migrants there are larger savings and remittances relative to the locals and this is interpreted as an insurance against an uncertain future. These savings decline as the integration in the destination country become more formalized.

For Italy, Speciale and Barigozzi (2009) find that the consumption of immigrants with higher permanence in the host country dominates the one with lower permanence. Migrants are not different from other consumers and are affected by the reference group and by emulating behavior (Maurer & Meier, 2008).

The second empirical evidence is that the effort invested in the work is higher initially and declines as the migrants become more integrated into the destination economy.

The idea, that the initial effort of the migrant is bigger, belongs to the general perception of the foreign worker behavior (Schaeffer, 1995). Unfortunately, the information on the individual productivities is very rare. A proxy for this would be the amount of hours spent at the workplace. There does exist evidence regarding the number of hours worked. Kahanec and Shields (2010), using the GSOEP, observe a reduction in hours worked as migrant tenure increases. Temporary migrants work on average 15 hours per week more than permanent ones. This behavior is reported for the USA labor market where Lonzano (2010) finds that the probability of a migrant working long hours decreases significantly after five years being in the USA.

Cortes (2004) finds that in the USA refugees, with more permanent migration prospects, work 14% less than the more temporary economic migrants. A preliminary research by Reyneri (2011) on the Italian market indicates similar results. Also, in Italy total hours worked by migrants decrease after five years by at least 10%, and the reduction is even larger for some groups: Moroccans reduce their contribution to production by 29% after five years, Bulgarian and Romanians by 25%, and South Americans by 20%.[9]

These two behaviors seem contradictory because when migrants increase consumption in the destination country, where prices are higher, we would expect an increase in working hours to gain extra money, and a relaxation of their budget constraints, while instead we observe a reduction in effort and hours worked on the job that seem irrational.

With the model below, we provide an interpretation of this puzzling behavior of the migrants that is very rational if regarded in term of real wage and the consumption basket that the migrant can afford.

THE MODEL

Consider a population that consists of owners of capital and workers. Workers consist of N_L nationals and N_F immigrants. All workers are risk neutral and averse to effort and have the same level of productivity.[10] The utility of the workers, $U(.)$, is a function of consumption, C: $U(C)$. As commonly assumed in such cases we assume that $U(C) = C$. Consumption is time consuming. To simplify, we assume that, on average, each unit of consumption needs one unit of time. Each worker has a total of T units of time to consume. However, if a worker exerts effort at the workplace he has less time to consume (one could give this many explanations, for example, the more effort exerted at the workplace gives the worker less strength to consume/expend at the end of the day, or the more time/effort spent at the workplace, leaves less time for consumption). Denote the effort exerted at the workplace by e and the price of an average unit of consumption equals P. Therefore, the constraint facing the worker that emerges is $P(T - e) \leq w_N$, where w_N is the nominal wage of the worker. As the worker's objective is to maximize his utility (consumption), he/she will always set the total cost of consumption to equal the wage: $P(T - e) = w_N$. If the worker exerts minimum amount of effort at the workplace ($e = e_L$), then his/her utility will equal $U(C, e = e_L) = (w_N)/(P) - e_L$; however, if the worker does exert effort at a higher level ($e = e_H$) the workers utility will equal $U(C, e = e_H) = (w_N)/(P) - e_H$. Namely, exerting effort decreases the consumption level. As the effort at the workplace increases, the worker will be able to consume fewer products as a result of the time restriction. We therefore obtain, as assumed by Shapiro and Stiglitz (1984), Epstein and Hillman (2003), and others, that the utility is separable and linear in private consumption that is provided through expenditure of a real wage w ($w = w_N/P$ where w_N is the nominal wage and P is the price level) and in the level of effort e,

$$U(w, e) = w - e \tag{1}$$

To simplify we assume that effort is dichotomous, it either equals e_L or $e_H > 0$.[11] We always exert effort, whether employed or unemployed. Thus, under this assumption $e = e_L$ is the minimum level of effort exerted by the worker. An unemployed worker receives benefits of w_o from the state and exerts the minimal level of effort ($e = e_L$). Welfare payments are the same for nationals and immigrants (immigrants are legal).

A worker has a probability p of becoming unemployed for exogenous reasons that do not depend on the employer. All workers maximize present discounted utility, with a rate of time preference $r > 0$. The model is set in continuous time. The only choice that a worker makes is selection of effort $e \in (e_L, e_H)$. A worker, who does not shirk, performs at a customary level of effort for the job, e_H, receives the wage w, and retains his or her job until he or she exogenously becomes unemployed. Employers imperfectly monitor effort. Workers, who shirk ($e = e_L$), are detected and fired with probability per unit of time q. $V_e(s,j)$ and $V_e(n,j)$ are expected lifetime utilities of an employed worker of type j (immigrant or local) when shirking (s) and when not (n). V_u is the expected lifetime utility of an unemployed person.[12] For a shirker,

$$rV_e(s,j) = w - e_L - (p + q)(V_e(s,j) - V_u) \tag{2}$$

And for a nonshirker,

$$rV_e(n,j) = w - e_H - p(V_e(n,j) - V_u) \tag{3}$$

From (2) and (3):

$$V_{\mathrm{e}}(s,j) = \frac{(w - e_{\mathrm{L}}) + (p + q)V_{\mathrm{u}}(j)}{r + p + q} \tag{4}$$

and

$$V_{\mathrm{e}}(n,j) = \frac{(w - e_{\mathrm{H}}) + pV_{\mathrm{u}}(j)}{r + p} \tag{5}$$

No shirking takes place if and only if $V_{\mathrm{e}}(s,j) \leq V_{\mathrm{e}}(n,j)$, that is,

$$w - e_{\mathrm{L}} \geq rV_{\mathrm{u}}(j) + \frac{(r + p + q)}{q}\Delta e_{\mathrm{H}} \tag{6}$$

Such that $\Delta e_{\mathrm{H}} = e_{\mathrm{H}} - e_{\mathrm{L}}$.

Production functions are given by $\tilde{f}(\bar{K}, L_{\mathrm{L}}z_{\mathrm{L}} + L_{\mathrm{H}}z_{\mathrm{H}})$. $\bar{K}$ is the available capital and $L_{\mathrm{L}}z_{\mathrm{L}} + L_{\mathrm{H}}z_{\mathrm{H}}$ is the amount of labor normalized by the effort exerted and the human capital level of the workers.

$$z_i = f\left(h_N e_i \frac{L_N}{L_N + L_F} + h_F e_i \frac{L_F}{L_N + L_F}\right) \quad i = L, H \tag{7}$$

L_{L} workers exert the minimum amount of effort e_{L}, and L_{H} workers exert the effort at the level of e_{H}. The incomes of owners of capital (or employers) increase when the number of workers who are employed increase.[13] Demand for workers is given by the value of the marginal product, and is a decreasing function of the wage w. Equilibrium is defined as an outcome when owners of capital, taking as given wages and employment levels at the other firms, find it optimal to offer the going wage rather than a different wage, that is, there is a Nash equilibrium in wages paid by employers.

It is assumed that all workers receive the same wages; that is, we are considering a pooling equilibrium where all workers, local and migrants receive the same wages. Thus, the sole variable determining employers' decisions is the disciplining of employed workers through V_{u}, the expected utility of an unemployed worker.

Since all unemployed workers receive the same welfare benefits w_{o}, V_{u} is common to all employees. An unemployed person's utility is thus independent of the identity of his or her previous employer. Hence

$$rV_{\mathrm{u}}(j) = w_0 - e_{\mathrm{L}} + k_j(V_{\mathrm{e}}(j) - V_{\mathrm{u}}(j)) \tag{8}$$

where k_j is the rate at which workers who are unemployed find jobs and $V_e(j)$ is the expected utility of an employed worker of type j, which in equilibrium equals $V_e(n,j)$. Substituting (8) into (4) and (5), we obtain

$$rV_e(j) = \frac{(w - e_H)(k_j + r) + (w_o - e_L)p_j}{k_j + p_j + r}$$

and (9)

$$rV_u(j) = \frac{(w - e_H)k_j + (w_o - e_L)(r + p_j)}{k_j + p_j + r}$$

Then, substituting (9) into (6), we determine that worker j will not shirk if

$$w \geq w_o + \Delta e_H + \frac{\Delta e_H}{q}(k_j + p_j + r) \tag{10}$$

while $\Delta e_H = e_H - e_L$.

As we stated above we are concerned with a pooling equilibrium, thus the wages for the natives and the local workers are identical. Notice that while we are assuming the same wages migrants are identical and the same holds for the local population. Thus, all workers in each group act in the same way: either invest high effort or low effort. The condition in (8) specifies two different conditions: one for the local population ($j = N$) and other for the immigrants ($j = F$). Thus, the probability of losing a job and finding a job depends on the worker's status: local worker or migrant. In equilibrium, the probability of finding a job will be k_j that may differ for the two types of workers.

THE DYNAMICS OF THE MODEL

We assume that both the local and the migrants earn the same income w.[14] In industrialized countries, wages are often determined by type of jobs and employers cannot easily discriminate on the remuneration given to workers. On the contrary, workers are free to be more productive or less productive. Thus, in principle, there is no wage discrimination between locals and migrants.

As assumed above real wages are thus defined as $w = w_N/P$. It is important to note that wages in equilibrium, paid by the employers, are in nominal terms. Moreover, to simplify matters we assume that prices in the host country are constant. The price level, which is used to normalize the wages, differs between the local and foreign workers. Denote by P_N the national price index and by P_F the prices in the migrant's home country (to simplify we assume that there is only one type of migrant coming from the same original home[15] country and thus all discount wages with the same price level). Moreover, we consider migrants who come from a country with a lower price level than the host country.

Immigrants, when entering the host country, have little or no knowledge of the host country and its cost of living. Over time this information is revealed to the immigrant.[16] Many migrants send a lot of their income to their families as remittances. Therefore, cost of living for the migrants, the price level at which they discount the nominal wages, will be the price level at their home country. However, as the migrant stays longer in the host country, they will start adopting the lifestyle of the local population and obtain more information regarding the cost of living in the host country. Therefore, the older migrants (those with a longer tenure in the host country) put a higher weight on the local price index when making calculations regarding the real wages. The price level by which the migrant normalizes his wage is a function of three parameters: the price level at the home country, the price level in the host country, and the weight assigned by the immigrants to each of the prices. The weight is therefore a function of the time the migrant has already spent in the host country and is given by the following function:

$$P_f = \alpha(t)P_{\mathrm{N}} + (1 - \alpha(t))P_{\mathrm{F}} \tag{11}$$

where $0 \leq \alpha(t) \leq 1$ and $(1 - \alpha(t))$ are, respectively, the weights assigned to the local price level and to the home country's price level, and t denotes the length of time that the migrant has spend in the host country. It is assumed that $(\partial\alpha(t))/(\partial t) \geq 0$ and $t > t, \alpha(t) = 1$. Namely, with time the migrant puts a larger weight on the local price level and a smaller one on the price at the home country.[17] Moreover, it is assumed that if the migrant spends a sufficient amount of time in the host country, he/she will use the host country's price level only to normalize his wages.[18] We can conclude therefore that even though all migrants (and the local workers) earn the same nominal wages, the newly arrived migrants earn a different real wage than those who have arrived before them.[19]

One should note that the weight applied to the price level, in the country of origin and in the host economy, may be endogenous to the migration strategy and expected consumption patterns. While the assumption made in the model, that the value placed on the country of origin's price level decreases, it may well be that it rather depends on the strategy applied (temporary, permanent, permanent with remittances, etc). One may think that these values are constant within these groups but, in a world with a degree of uncertainty about time spent in the host country, more and more people realize that their intentions are more permanent than temporary. Such a change of weight would not affect the results presented. Moreover, the results presented in (10) are given for each migrant as a function of the time spent in the host country.

POSSIBLE EQUILIBRIUMS

Let us now return to the equilibrium wage and to the level of effort exerted by the different workers.

As the price level at which the migrants discount their wages is lower than that of the local workers, the real wage received by the local workers is lower than that received by the migrants (and the real wages received by the newly migrants is higher than that of the migrants that arrived earlier). As the migrants stay longer in the host country, their real wages starts converging to the wages of the local population. If the wages in equilibrium are set so that the local worker will exert a high level of effort, e_{H}, then it is clear that the migrants will also exert a high level of effort. However, if the wages are set in equilibrium so that the local workers exert a low level of effort, e_{L}, then it may well be the case that the migrants will exert a high level of effort.

Assume that in the absence of foreign workers the wage is set such that the local workers exert a high level of effort. Denote the number of workers employed in equilibrium as L_N^0. The profits of the capital

$$\pi(L_N^0) = \tilde{f}(\bar{K}, L_N^0 z)P_x^0 - C(L_N^0 w^0) \tag{12}$$

where $\bar{K}$ is the capital level, total output is given by $\tilde{f}(\bar{K}, Lz)$, the price of the product by P_x^0 equilibrium wage w^0, and total cost of production $C(L_N^0 w^0)$.

When migrants enter the country, the equilibrium wage level will change as a result of the changes in the individuals willing to work (and as a result the price level of the products will also change). Thus, the wage, which will encourage a high level of effort from the local population, will decrease (see Epstein & Hillman, 2003). Therefore, if the firms continue to pay wages that will stimulate a high level of effort from the local population, then the migrants will also exert a high level of effort.

Fixed and Equal Human Capital

In this section, we assume that human capital is equal and fixed for all the workers. So we can concentrate on the worker's productivity as a function their effort.

Now let us consider three different equilibriums with both native workers and migrants: a both the migrants and the native population are exerting a high level of effort, b the native population is exerting a low level while the migrants are exerting a high level, and c all workers are exerting a low level of effort:

Case 1a. Wages are set at w^1, both the local and migrants exert a high level of effort,

$$\pi(L_N^1, L_F^1) = \tilde{f}(\bar{K}, (L_N^1 + L_F^1)e_{\mathrm{H}})P_x^0 - C((L_F^1 + L_N^1)w^1) \tag{13}$$

Case 1b. Wages are set at w^2, the local population exerts a low level of effort, e_{L} and the migrants exert a high level, e_{H},

$$\pi(L_N^2, L_F^2) = \tilde{f}(\bar{K}, L_N^2 e_{\mathrm{L}} + L_F^2 e_{\mathrm{H}})P_x^0 - C((L_F^2 + L_N^2)w^2) \tag{14}$$

Case 1c. Wages are set at w^3, both the local and migrants exert a low level of effort,

$$\pi(L_N^3, L_F^3) = \tilde{f}(\bar{K}, (L_N^3 + L_F^3)e_{\mathrm{L}})P_x^0 - C((L_F^3 + L_N^3)w^3) \tag{15}$$

where $w^0 > w^1 > w^2 > w^3$ and, of course, the number of workers employed in equilibrium in all three cases are not identical. All three equilibriums are possible. We wish to consider the second case where wages have dropped as a result of migration, and in equilibrium, the level of effort of the foreign population is higher than that of the local population. As assumed above, all workers receive the same nominal wages. Therefore, the local population receives, in real terms, a lower wage than the migrants. However, the employer receives a higher level of effort at the same nominal wage level. It is obvious that case b may well be an equilibrium outcome. However, we must note that the profits of the firm and the level of exertion are a function of time.

A Fully Inelastic Supply of Immigrants

Assume that the number of migrants is fixed in the economy, then over time Case 1b will converge into Case 1a or Case 1c: $\pi(L_N^2, L_F^2) \to \pi(L_N^1, L_F^1)$ or $\pi(L_N^2, L_F^2) \to \pi(L_N^3, L_F^3)$. Namely, it is not clear whether the migrants are increasing the average level of effort exerted or decreasing it. The reason for this is that over time the migrants' real wages converge on that of the native population. As the real wages converge, the level of efforts extracted by the workers also converge as well as their productivity. At the same time the labor force has increased, the wages have dropped and thus the wages may drop to a level such that both groups exert a high or low level of effort.

We conclude therefore that,

Migrants may well exert a higher level of effort than the local population. However, with time, the level of effort exerted by the migrants and the local population will converge.

Notice that the effort exerted by the worker is a function of the unemployment level. If we consider, in addition, that migrants do not know, on their arrival, the level of employment and unemployment, and that over time this knowledge is revealed to them, then this new knowledge will affect their effort invested at the workplace.[20] Their efforts will converge over time and become equal to that of a local worker. Thus, if we incorporate, directly into the model above, this lack of information about the unemployment level, it would only enhance the results presented above.

Constant Inflow of Immigrants

As a direct result, the longer the migrants are in the host country, the more they appear like the local population. Therefore, over time, the employers will employ the newcomers instead of the old migrants and the local population. The rate at which the hiring and firing occurs will depend on the costs and rate at which the effort of the migrants changes over time.[21]

Heterogenous Human Capital

Let us consider the case where human capital is an important component of total workers productivity. Assume that immigrants and the local population have only two types of human capital: high, h_H, and low, h_L. The total productivity can thus be written as follows: $z(h, e)$ and the production function can be written as follows: $\tilde{f}(\bar{K}, Lz(h, e))$. We assume therefore that human capital and effort exerted at the workplace can be substitutes. Namely if a worker with low human capital increases his effort at the workplace, he will be identical to a worker with high human capital with low exerted effort. Let us consider the following cases:

a. Natives and foreigners have the same level of productivity, $z(h, e)$. As described above, the migrants' real wages decrease over time and as a result the workers may exert less effort at the workplace. If the migrants exert less effort, then this will not be compensated by an increase in human capital as the employers will fire the foreigners and employ recently arrived migrants or the local population.

b. If the human capital of the foreigners and natives are equal to each other and at a low level, and at the same time, the effort invested by the foreigners is higher than that of the local population: $en_L < ef_H$, then foreigners productivity level will be higher than that of the local population: $z_f(h, e) > z_n(h, e)$. In this case, the employer will prefer to hire foreigners in the first period. If in the second period the effort of the foreigners declines without any increase in human capital, then the employer will be indifferent as to employing natives or second period foreigners, but he will prefer first period immigrants. If on the other hand, the human capital of the foreigners increase over time, while the effort of others is reduced such that it compensates for the reduction in exerted effort, then the employers will also prefer foreigners in the second period.

THE LOCAL WORKERS AND THE EMPLOYERS

As defined above, the utility of the workers is given by

$$\begin{aligned} U(C) &= C \quad \text{s.t.} \\ P(T-e) &\leq w_{\mathrm{N}} \\ C &= P(T-e) \end{aligned} \tag{16}$$

Total consumption of the workers is a function of the level of effort exerted by the workers.

e Denotes the aggregate demand as $D(e_{f,}, e_n, P)$, namely the demand for the products is a function of the effort exerted by the different groups and the price of the products. Moreover, as the levels of exerted effort increase, the demand for the products decreases. Let us denote the supply by $S(z_n, z_f, P)$, namely the supply is a function of the productivity levels of the different groups and the price level (which in equilibrium is a function of the wage level). It is clear that as the level of productivity increases the supply increases.

We now consider the effect, which changes in the effort exerted by the different groups, has on the equilibrium, quantity, and prices. In equilibrium, the quantity demanded equals the quantity supplied. Let us consider the following situation under which both the local and the migrant workers exert the same effort: $e_n = e_l = e$ and $z_n = z_l = z$. In this case

$D(e,e,P) = S(z,z,P)$ and we obtain that the quantities and prices in equilibrium equal:

$$q_b^l + q_b^n = q_b^*; p_b^* \tag{17}$$

where q_b^j and p_b^j are the quantities and the prices group $j=n,\ l$ in equilibrium. q_b^* and p_b^* denote the total quantity and price at equilibrium.

Case 1. Both the local population and the migrants have the same level of productivity, while the migrants invest more effort than the local population: $e_n < e_f^1$ and $z_n = z_l = z$. After migration denote the new quantities and prices as q_1^j and p_1^j In this case we would obtain that

$$q_1^f < q_b^f; q_1^n > q_b^n \quad q_1^* < q_b^* \\ \text{and} \\ p_1 < p_b^* \tag{18}$$

As the immigrants spend more effort at the workplace we can see from (16) that the immigrants will have a lower consumption level. This will decrease the total demand for products, which will, in turn, decrease the price of the products. As the price level decreases, the demand of the local population will increase.

Case 2. Now let us take this one step further. Let us assume that the above analysis is true for second year immigrants. Here the employers decide to replace the second year immigrants with those newly arrived. In this case we will obtain $e_n < e_f^1 < e_f^2$ and $z_n < z_2$. The supply will increase as the employers have more efficient workers. As the newly arrived immigrants exert more effort at the workplace, the demand for them will decrease relative to that of the second year immigrants. At the same time, the demand for the local population will increase as the price level has increased and therefore the real wage increased.

The local workers benefits: *The local workers are better off; their real wages have increased as has their consumption. It is true that maybe some of them are worse off as they have been replaced by newly arrived migrants; however, this is not clear as the decrease in prices has increased the quantity demanded. The unemployed are also better off as their real unemployment benefits have increased.*

The capital owners' benefit: *Each firm sees as given the wages and the price level and it is assumed that each firm is small and has no market power. Thus, the capital owners benefit from replacing an "older" migrant with a "newly" arrived one.*

The reason for this result is that the employer will receive a better worker, who extracts more effort in the workplace and earns the same wage as the "older" migrant. At the firm level, the price of the product is given and thus his profits increase. However, in equilibrium it is not clear if the firms' profit increases or decreases, as real wages increase and production increases. It is clear that for each firm it is optimal to replace its "older" migrant with the newly arrived migrant.

CONCLUDING REMARKS AND POLICY IMPLICATIONS

In this chapter, we have provided a rationale for the newly arrived legal migrants to exert more effort than the local population.[22] Moreover, new migrants exert more effort than the "older" ones and invest a higher level of effort, but over time, the level of effort exerted by the local population and the migrants converges.

Fundamentally, if immigrants have the same human capital as the natives, firms prefer new immigrants to "older" immigrants, and if they are able to fire "older" immigrants and employ new ones, they will do so. This implies that employers will always prefer newly arrived migrants.[23] On the other hand, as shown above, the local population may also benefits from newly arrived migrants. However, both the local population and the employers gain disutility from migrants who stay too long in the host country. The policy that will achieve this situation will be to *limit the time the migrants can stay in the host country and replace migrants with newly arriving migrants. This policy is a temporary migration policy.*

Such a temporary migration policy will benefit both the employers and the workers. Under this policy, migrants will enter the host country for a given period of time. At the end of the period, the migrants will return to their home country. If the host country still needs migrant workers, the old workers will be replaced by the newly arrived migrants exerting a high level of effort.

The rational for a temporary migration policy derives not from the welfare costs, nor from social or labor market competition, but from the profit maximization choice of the employer and the benefit to the final consumer. The same rationale applies to the more recent circular migration policy in which the repetition of temporary migration spells with the consumption focused in the origin country could reproduce the effort and the productivity behavior described above.

The question is how such a policy can be implemented? The way to implement such a policy is to create a *contracted* temporary migrant policy, which limits the period of time that the migrants can stay in the host country. When migrants leave the host country, new migrants will enter, and these will exert a high level of effort in the workplace.

Theoretically, one new migrant should enter every day and one should leave. However, training migrants and teaching them the new jobs entail costs. Moreover, also to be considered are the transportation costs, which may well fall on the capital owners. Thus, the policy should also take account of the costs of changing migrants and calculate the optimal time that a migrant should stay in the host county. Temporary contracted migration has many problems; the main one is ensuring that legal migrants will leave the host country on the conclusion of their contracts. There are many ways to ensure that they do so (see Epstein et al. (1999) and chapter 7 in Boeri, Gordon, and McCormick (2002)). Temporary migration may well benefit the sending country because the temporary migrants are likely to increase their human capital in the host country and thus return to the home country with greater human capital.[24]

Note that the capital owners will benefit from migration. Their level of benefit will be a function of the length of the contract. On the other hand, however, the native labor force, which will be unemployed as a result of such a policy, will be harmed. Yet the **native population**, or better the **native consumers** (which include the unemployed), will prefer to have a large turnover of migrants with a higher effort and lower consumption.

The favorable sentiment of capital owners and the local population toward migrants may arise when temporary migration policies are adopted. *If such policies are adopted, the level of effort extracted from migrants is optimized, prices decrease, real wages increase, and welfare grows.*

NOTES

1. The debate was first dominated by the Borjas (1994), Filer (1992), and Card (2005) puzzle namely that in a cross-spatial analysis the complementary of immigrants may be induced by the internal mobility of natives from an increasing migration and declining wage area to a nonincreasing immigration area. The latter area is contaminated by the former labor market affect and conceals the negative impact of immigrants in the first

area. Then, to overcome this weakness, the debate shifted to the skill-cell approach in a production function model with mixed results by Borjas (2003) and Ottaviano Peri (2006).

2. See, for example, Castronova, Kayser, Frick, and Wagner (2001) and Riphan (2004) for Germany, Barrett and McCarthy (2008) for the United Kingdom, and Hansen and Lofstrom (2003) for Sweden.

3. On general problems of the welfare state, see Hans-Werner Sinn (1995).

4. See, for example, Dustmann and Fabbri (2005) for the United Kingdom and Venturini and Villosio (2008) for Italy.

5. Epstein and Nitzan (2006) consider the role of interest groups in the determination of migration quotas.

6. We are assuming that migrants come from countries with lower price levels. We elaborate on this later in the paper. The value applied to the price level in the country of origin and in the host economy may be endogenous to the migration strategy and expected consumption patterns (temporary, permanent, permanent with remittances, etc). We discuss this later on.

7. On other benefits and costs of temporary migration and on optimally creating such a policy, see Epstein, Hillman, and Weiss. (1999) and Boeri, Hanson, and McCormick (2002). For a more general analysis of permit and temporary contracts, see Venturini (2004, pp. 208–219).

8. See for instance in the Mediterranean case Venturini (2004) and see also Kirdar 2008.

9. Reyneri, 2011, Preliminary results on the hours worked by migrants, mimeo.

10. For the sake of our analysis, assuming that the level of productivity of the migrants is lower would only enhance our results.

11. One could also imagine that migrants, when they arrive, do not consume leisure – they do not go to the cinema or have family meetings – thus their upper boundary of the effort devoted to work is higher (see Venturini, 1997).

12. The disutility, of immigrants of being unemployment, is not considered here. Usually migrants are unhappy being unemployed because they risk expulsion, the loss of legal residency permits, etc. The introduction of the disutility of immigrant's unemployment status will only enhance the results.

13. Because of diminishing marginal product of labor.

14. If wages could differ between the local population and migrants, then the migrants would have a higher wage (a higher cost to be unemployed); however, the local populations' reservation wages would be higher than that of the migrants. Therefore, in equilibrium we would obtain that both groups would have more or less the same wages.

15. If we would assume more than one country of origin, the main results would not change.

16. It may also be the case the speed and level of information revealed to the migrant is a function of the size of the network of the foreign local population from the same origin.

17. The migrants' decision on allowances has the same effect as described above. Migrants, as soon as they arrive in the destination country, remit a lot of their income to their home country, evaluating part of their income with respect to the price of the country of origin. The more they stay in the destination country the less they remit and the more they consume in the destination country. This myopic behavior is, however, adopted also by foreigners who do not remit. Italian engineers, going to Geneva (SW) in order to work at the CERN, have the same attitude

regarding their wages. They evaluate it by Italian prices at the beginning and they work night and day. They do not send money home, but they feel that their wages are very high. The more they stay in destination country, and the more they have a normal life in the host country, the more they consider their wages in purchasing power terms to be not so high, and thus reduce their effort.

18. Since we are analyzing migration of low-skilled workers, we assume that the price level in the home country is lower than that of the host country: $P_N > P_F$. Given (12), it is clear that over time the price level that the migrant uses in the normalization of his wages approaches that of the host country: $P_f \rightarrow P_N$.

19. However, two migrants with the same time duration, the first with the family at home and the second reunified by the family could make a different effort.

20. The information level can also be a function of the size of the existing network at the time of arrival of the migrants into the host country. The reason for this is that as the size of the network increases the new migrant may receive more information and adapt more easily to the local population.

21. Low exertion of effort, if not accompanied by a return home, will increase the unemployment rate among immigrants staying a long period of time in the host country. Looking at the data on first- and second-generation migrants, there is evidence of this correlation. In France in 1993 the unemployment rate among natives was 10%, while among foreigners it was 20.6%; moreover, the unemployment rate among the natives aged under 25 years old was 25.2%, while among foreigners of the same age it was 32.3%. In the Netherlands in the same period of time, the unemployment rate was 5.7% among natives and 19.6% among foreigners, and respectively 9.8% and 25% among young natives and foreigners. In Germany, the unemployment rate was 4.9% and 12.7% for all natives and foreigners, while for the population aged under 25 it was 4.8% and 14.1%, respectively (see Böhning 1995).

22. Our model considers only legal immigration. With regard to illegal immigration, see, for example, Djaji™ (1997). For a perspective on efficiency wages with illegal immigration in a dual labor market model, see Carter (1999).

23. If the migrant invests in the specific human capital of the country of destination, his productivity increases and thus counteracts the decline of his productivity imputed to the reduction in effort. The final result is not clear: the two forces can be of different strength. However, many jobs filled by migrants do not need any human capital investment and there is no increase in productivity.

24. See also the economic case for broad benefits from immigration based on the human capital upgrading of domestic unskilled labor made by Schmidt, Stilz, and Zimmermann (1994) and the positive effect of reducing child labor in the host country (see Epstein & Kahana, 2008).

ACKNOWLEDGMENT

Gil S. Epstein is grateful for the support of the Adar Foundation. We are grateful to the referees and to the editor for their useful and constructive comments.

REFERENCES

Arad, R. W., & Hillman, A. L. (1979). The collective good motive for immigration policy. *Australian Economic Papers, 18*, 243–257.

Barrett, A., & McCarthy, Y. (2008). Immigration and welfare programmes: Exploring the interactions between immigrant characteristics, immigrant welfare dependence and welfare policy. *Oxford Review Economic Policy, 24*(3), 542–559.

Bauer, T., & Sinning, M. (2005). *The saving behaviour of temporary and permanent migrants in Germany*. IZA discussion paper no. 1632. Bonn, IZA.

Benhabib, J. (1996). On the political economy of immigration. *European Economic Review, 40*, 1737–1743.

Boeri, T., Gordon, H., & McCormick, B. (2002). *Immigration policy and the welfare system*. Oxford University Press.

Böhning R. W. (1995). Labour market integration in Western and Northern Europe. Which way are we heading? In R. W. Böhning & R. Zegers de Beijl (Eds.), *The integration of migrant workers in the labour market: Policies and their impact. I.L.O.* Employment Department, International Migration Papers, no. 8.

Bonin, H., Raffelhüschen, B., & Walliser, J. (2000). Can immigrants alleviate the demographic burden? An assessment with generational accounting. *Finanzarchiv, 57*, 1–21.

Borjas, G. (1994). The economics of immigration. *Journal of Economic Literature, 32*, 1667–1717.

Borjas, G. (1999). Immigration and the welfare magnets. *Journal of Labour Economics, 17*(4, Part 1), 607–637.

Borjas, G. (2003). The labour demand curve is downward sloping: Reexamining the impact of immigration in the labour market. *Quarterly Journal of Economics, 118*, 1335–1374.

Card, D. (2005). Is the new immigration really so bad? *Economic Journal, 115*, F300–F323.

Carling, J. (2008). The determinants of migrant remittances. *Oxford Review of Economic Policy, 24-3*, 582–599.

Carter, T. J. (1999). Illegal immigration in an efficiency wage model. *Journal of International Economics, 49*, 385–401.

Castronova, E., Kayser, H., Frick, J., & Wagner, G. (2001). Immigrants, natives and social assistance: Comparative take-up under comparable circumstances. *International Migration Review, 35*(3), 726–748.

Cortes, K. E. (2004). Are refugees different from economic immigrants? Some empirical evidence on the heterogeneity of immigrant groups in the United States. *Review of Economics and Statistics, 86*(2), 465–480.

Djaji™, S. (1997). Illegal immigrants and resource allocation. *International Economic Review, 38*, 97–117.

Dustmann, C., & Fabbri, F. (2005). Immigrants in the British labour market. *Fiscal Studies, 26*(4), 423–470.

Dustmann, C., & Weiss, Y. (2007). *Return migration: Theory and empirical evidence*. CREAM discussion paper series no. 2/07. UCL, London, CREAM.

Epstein, G. S., & Hillman, A. L. (2003). Unemployed immigrants and voter sentiment in the welfare state. *Journal of Public Economics*, 1641–1655.

Epstein, G. S., Hillman, A. L., & Weiss, A. (1999). Creating illegal immigrants. *Journal of Population Economics, 12*(1), 3–21.

Epstein, G. S., & Kahana, N. (2008). Child labor and temporary emigration. *Economics Letters, 99*(3), 545–548.

Epstein, G. S., & Nitzan, S. (2006). The struggle over migration policy. *Journal of Population Economics*, *19*(4), 703–723.

European Commission. (2007). On circular migration and mobility partnership between the European Union and third countries. COM(2007), final Bruxelles, 16 May.

Filer, R. (1992). The effect of immigrant arrival on migratory patterns of native workers. In: G. J. Borjas & R. Freeman (Eds.), *Immigration and the work force*. Chicago, IL: University of Chicago Press.

Funkhouser, E. (1995). Remittances from international migration. *The Review of Economic and Statistics*, *77*(1), 137–146.

Galor, O., & Stark, O. (1990). Migrants' savings, the probability of return migration and migrants' performance. *International Economic Review*, *31-2*, 463–467.

Galor, O., & Stark, O. (1991). The probability of return migration, migrants' work effort, and migrants' performance. *Journal of Development Economics*, *35*(2), 399–405.

Gans, H. (1979). Symbolic ethnicity: The future of ethnic groups and cultures in *America. Ethnic and Racial Studies*, *2*(1), 1–20.

Gans, H. (1996). Second-generation decline. Scenarios for the economic and ethnic futures of the post-1965 American immigrants. In: N. Carmon (Ed.), *Immigration and integration in post-industrial societies. Theoretical analysis and policy-related research* (pp. 65–85). Basingstoke: Macmillan.

De Giorgi, G., & Pellizzari, M. (2011). Welfare migration in Europe. *Labour Economics*, *16*(4), 353–363.

De Voretz, D., & Vandean, F. (2005). A model of foreign-born transfers: Evidence from Canadian micro data, IZA D.P. 1714.

Glazer, N., & Moynihan, D. (1970). *Beyond the melting pot*. Cambridge, MA: MIT Press.

Hansen, J., & Lofstrom, M. (2003). Immigrants assimilation and welfare participation: Do immigrants assimilate into or out of welfare?. *Journal of Human Resources*, *38*(1), 74–98.

Hillman, A. L. (2002). Immigration and intergenerational transfers. In: H. Siebert (Ed.), *Economic policy for aging societies*. Berlin: Springer.

Hillman, A. L., & Weiss, A. (1999). A theory of permissible illegal immigration. *European Journal of Political Economy*, *15*, 585–604.

Holst, E., Schäfer, A., & Schrooten, M. (2010). *Gender, transnational networks and remittances: Evidence from Germany*. SOEP paper no. 296. SOEP, DIW, Berlin.

Kahanec, M., & Shields, M. (2010). *The working hours of immigrants in Germany: Temporary versus permanent*. IZA discussion paper no. 4735. Bonn, IZA.

Kirdar, G. M. (2008). Labor market outcomes, savings accumulation, and return migration. *Labour Economics*, *16*(4), 418–428.

Kirdar, G. M. (2009). *Source country characteristics and immigrants' migrant duration and saving decisions*. MPRA paper no. 13322. MPRA, University of Munich, Germany

Kumku, E. M. (1989). The saving behaviour of migrant workers: Turkish workers in W. Germany. *Journal of Development Economics*, *30*, 273–286.

Lee, R. D., & Miller, T. W. (1998). The current fiscal impact of immigration and their descendants: Beyond the immigrant household. In: J. P. Smith & B. Edmonston (Eds.), *The immigration debate* (pp. 183–205). Washington, DC: National Academy Press.

Lonzano, F. A. (2010). Understanding the workweek of foreigner born workers in the United States. *Review Economic Household*, *8*, 83–104.

Mansoor, A., & Quillin, B. (2006). *Migration and remittances, Eastern Europe and the former Soviet Union*. The World Bank.

Maurer, J., & Meier, A. (2008). Smooth it like the "Joneses?" Estimating peer-group effects in intertemporal consumtion choice. *Economic Journal*, *118*(527), 454–476.

Mazza, I., & van Winden, F. W. (1996). A political economy analysis of labor migration and income distribution. *Public Choice*, *88*, 333–363.

Newland, K., & Agunias, D. (2007). *How can circular migration and sustainable return serve as development tools*? Background paper for the first meeting of the Global Forum on Migration and Development (GFMD), Bruxelles, July 9–11.

Ottaviano, G. M., & Peri, G. (2006). *Rethinking the effects of immigration on wages*. NBER Working Paper no. W12497.

Pellizzari, M. (2011). *The use of welfare of migrants in Italy*. Bonn, IZA D.P. 5617.

Piracha, M., & Zhu, Y. (2007). *Precautionary saving by natives and immigrants in Germany*. IZA discussion paper no. 2942. IZA Bonn.

Poirine, B. (1997). A theory of remittances as an implicit family loan arrangement. *World Development*, *25-4*, 589–611.

Portes, A., & Zou, M. (1993). The new second generation: Segmented assimilation and its variants among post-1965 immigrant youth. *The Annals of the American Academy of Political and Social Sciences*, *530*, 74–96.

Reyneri, E. (2011). *Preliminary results on the hours worked by migrants*. Mimeo.

Riphan, R. (2004). Immigration participation in social assistance programs. *Applied Economics Quarterly*, *50*(4), 329–362.

Schaeffer, P. V. (1995). The work effort and the consumption of immigrants as a function of their assimilation. *International Economic Review*, *36*(3), 625–642.

Schmidt, C. M., Stilz, A., & Zimmermann, K. F. (1994). Mass migration, unions, and government intervention. *Journal of Public Economics*, *55*, 185–201.

Shapiro, C., & Stiglitz, J. (1984). Equilibrium unemployment as a worker discipline device. *American Economic Review*, *74*, 433–444.

Sinn, H.-W. (1995). A theory of the welfare state. *Scandinavian Journal of Economics*, *97*, 495–526.

Sinning, M. (2007). Determinants of saving and remittances: Empirical evidence from immigrants in Germany. *Review of Economics and Household*, *9*(1), 45–67.

Speciale, B., & Barigozzi, M. (2009). *Immigrant's legal status, permanence in the destination country and the distribution of consumption expenditure*. ECARES Working Paper no. 2009-019. ULB, Brussels, ECARES.

Storesletten, K. (2000). Sustaining fiscal policy though immigration. *Journal of Political Economy*, *108*, 300–323.

Venturini, A. (1997). L'offerta differenziale dello straniero. *Economia Politica, annoXIV, no. 2*, 257–282.

Venturini, A. (2004). *Post war migration in Southern Europe: An economic approach*. Cambridge, MA: CUP.

Venturini, A. (2008). *Circular migration as an employment strategy for Mediterranean countries*. CARIM/RSCAS ASN no 39.

Venturini, A., & Villosio, C. (2008). Assimilation of migrants in recent immigration countries: The Italian experience. *OXREP*, *23*(4), 518–542.

Wong, K-y. (1995). *International trade in goods and factor mobility*. Cambridge: MIT Press.

CHAPTER 8

MIGRANT NETWORKS, MIGRANT SELECTION, AND HIGH SCHOOL GRADUATION IN MÉXICO

Alfonso Miranda

ABSTRACT

This chapter enquires whether family migration experience affects the probability of high school graduation of children once unobserved heterogeneity is properly accounted for. Bivariate dynamic random effects probit models for cluster data are estimated to control for the potential endogeneity of education and migration outcomes of elder members of a family in a regression for the education and migration of younger children. Correlation of unobservables across migration and education decisions as well as within groups of individuals such as the family are explicitly modeled. Results show that children from households headed by a migrant are less likely to graduate from high school than children from households headed by a non-migrant. However, as the number of migrants in the family increase, a larger number of migrants in the family is associated with a higher probability of graduation from high school in México. Negative migrant selection in unobservables is detected.

Keywords: Migration; education; bivariate dynamic random effects probit

JEL classifications: F22; I21; J61; C35

Research in Labor Economics, Volume 33, 263–306

ISSN: 0147-9121/doi:10.1108/S0147-9121(2011)0000033011

INTRODUCTION

In recent years, there is an increasing interest in learning whether international migration has impacts on poverty, accumulation of human and physical capital, economic growth, and development in source countries (see, for instance, World Bank, 2006). The México-USA is a leading case of interest because in the last two decades the flow of labor from México to the United States reached unprecedented numbers.[1] In addition, the amount of remittances sent by Mexican expatriates to their families in México increased steadily and became, without doubt, a nonnegligible source of income.[2]

The present chapter intends to shed some light about the relationship between México-USA migration flows and the accumulation of human capital in México.

The relationship between migration and education in México is complex. Most Mexican migrants cross the US border illegally and in their quest they walk through the Arizona desert or swim at various points of Rio Grande, where there is a good chance of drowning or dying of dehydration (see, for instance, Hanson, 2006; Massey, 2007). Many have access to a broad network of relatives and/or friends with previous migration experience that are a valuable source of advice and contacts in the United States for finding a job upon arrival. Because of the dangers involved, Mexican migrants are predominantly men who start migrating, in many cases before marriage, following the steps of their parents. Females tend to follow parents rather than husbands (Cerrutti & Massey, 2001) and the movement of young children is limited.[3] Even in the most recent years, the simultaneous move of a whole household is a rare phenomenon (see, e.g., Sana & Massey, 2005). Before changes on the border enforcement introduced in late 1980s, the typical migrant was a temporary/seasonal worker seeking to accumulate savings in the United States and then returning home. In the 2000s, however, this cyclical movement of labor was disrupted by the tightening of the border and more and more migrants stay permanently in the United States once they have successfully crossed it (Massey, 2007). Most Mexican migrants send money (remittances) back home to help their families in México.

These remittances are often used to finance the education of children left behind in México, including post-compulsory education. This option is particularly attractive for youngsters who have no plans to emigrate to the United States and education offers them an opportunity to improve their standard of life at the home country. The story, however, does not end there. If an individual plans to leave México, then using remittances to finance his/her education in México is only rational if qualifications prove to be broadly portable across the two countries.[4] In contrast, if observable qualifications are non-portable, rational prospective migrants will behave in a forward looking fashion and drop out school early to avoid wastage of valuable resources (a similar argument is put forward by McKenzie & Rapoport, 2006). Finally, if qualifications are "noisily" portable, then a zero effect of migrant networks on education at the source country may be observed. Clearly, because crossing the border is difficult, some of the people subject to the incentive will eventually arrive to the United States and some will remain in México. Hence, the effect of migration experience within the family on the education in the source country is ambiguous and empirical investigation is needed.

Understanding the impact that portability of qualifications across borders may have on the incentives that children from migrant households face to study in México is a difficult task that requires high-quality longitudinal data that follows people moving both legally and/or illegally across México and the United States. These kinds of data are currently unavailable.[5] In the meantime one can try to have an initial approximation to the topic.

The present chapter tries to contribute a study on these issues. In particular, the study intends to give an initial answer to the following questions: Are children from households headed by a parent with México-USA migration experience less or more likely to graduate from high school? Conditional on the migration and education status of the family head, does migration and education outcomes of an immediately elder sibling affect the migration and education decisions of a younger child? Conditional on the migration and education status of the family head and the immediately elder sibling, do total number of migrants and high school graduates in the family affect the migration and education decisions of a child? Clearly, the answer to these questions have key relevance in the understanding of how international migration may affect the accumulation of human capital in developing countries.

The main previous two pieces of work in the topic are contributed by McKenzie and Rapoport (2006) and Hanson and Woodruff (2003). Both pieces of work look at whether children from migrant households complete more (or less years) of education in México and use instrumental variables (IV, hereafter) techniques for the analysis. Hanson and Woodruff find that 10 to 15-year-old girls from migrant households attend nearly one extra year of education, but only for those with a less-educated mother. No conclusive effect for boys is obtained. On the contrary, McKenzie and Rapoport (2006) find that migration reduces schooling attendance and attainments of 12 to 18-year-old boys and of 16 to 18-year-old girls.

The present chapter adds to the literature in two ways. First, it looks at preparatory education (high school) rather than primary and secondary education. This is important because most migrants start their quest to the north aged 15 or more and the most relevant choice is whether to wait and study high school or drop out school upon finishing secondary school (which since 1993 became compulsory for all children in México). Second, the chapter explicitly recognizes that unobservable heterogeneity that affects migration can also affect education, and that such correlation may occur either (or both) at the individual or the family level. A leading example of this type of unobserved heterogeneity is cognitive skill. If smarter pupils are better at school and more likely to find better paid jobs upon graduation, then people with high IQ are less likely to migrate because the returns to education are higher in México than in the United States (see, for instance, Borjas, 1994). Similarly, a low IQ may imply performing bad at school and having more incentives to move to the American side where unqualified jobs are better paid (see, for instance, Borjas, 1994). Hence, heterogeneity on cognitive skills can create correlation between migration and education outcomes at the individual level. Moreover, if variation in IQ within the members of a given family is lower than between families in the population as a whole, then unobservables affecting migration and education will also be correlated at the family level.

Accounting explicitly for potential correlation of unobservables affecting migration and education outcomes at the family level is important because, if present, the education and migration outcomes of the family head and other members of the family are *endogenous* in an equation intending to investigate the effect of those variables on the education of children.[6] This endogeneity problem is known as the initial conditions problem in dynamic models (see, for instance, Heckman, 1981) and is important because the correlation between education and migration outcomes of the members of a kin can be driven by unobserved heterogeneity at the family level rather than by true state dependence; with the latter implying that actions taken by parents and elder siblings truly affect the decisions of younger children. This true state dependence is what the researcher is interested because, if present, it implies a causal relationship.

Taking care of the initial conditions problem is also important because the family head may have born to a family of migrants (graduates) himself/herself. As a consequence, the researcher cannot really observe the true beginning of the dynamic process. In this context, single equation IV strategies that instrument for migration of the family head (household) in an equation for the education outcomes of the children are likely to fail unless the instrument can be agued to affect the migration outcome of the family head but not the migration status of his/her children and, at the same time, not to be correlated with unobservables at the family level. The present work addresses these issues by estimating bivariate dynamic random effects probit models (BDPM). Results show that children from households headed by a migrant are less likely to graduate from high school than children from households headed by a nonmigrant. However, as the number of migrants in the family increase, a larger number of migrants in the family is associated with a higher probability of graduation from high school in México. Negative migrant selection in unobservables is detected.

DATA

Data from the Mexican Migration Project (MMP) are used. The MMP is a pooled cross-section of migrant communities located throughout México, which are collected by a joint group of researchers at Princeton University and Universidad de Guadalajara.[7] Every year, from 1982 to 2009, members of the MMP team survey a random sample of 200 households in 2–5 communities in México to gather a new cross section. Such cross section is then added to the pool. Current files, the MMP124 database, contain information at individual and community level in 124 localities.

The communities surveyed by the MMP are not selected at random. As a consequence, the data may not be argued to be national or state representative. Instead, the MMP124 is representative of the population in the 124 communities that are included in the study. Very importantly, selected communities are chosen on the basis that they have some, though not necessarily long-lasting, migrant tradition. Across the years, the MMP team has managed to survey communities in many regions of the country and with different sizes, from small rural towns to large cities.[8] Moreover, there has been some effort to select communities so that there is enough variation in terms of economic activity – from small places that specialize in mining, fishing, and farming, to large urban areas that are highly diversified.

National representative surveys commonly contain too few observations of migrant individuals to allow meaningful statistical analysis (CONAPO, 2000). As a consequence, there is always a need to over-sample areas with migrant tradition if useful numbers of migrants are to be obtained. Moreover, it is well-documented that migrants do not come at random from all the geographical areas of México. Instead, they cluster intensively in the states and areas covered by the MMP124 (CONAPO, 2000). Hence, if a trend is not present in the MMP124 data, it will hardly appear in a national representative survey. From this point of view, using the MMP124 to perform exploratory analyses of México-USA migration issues is well justified and a number of influential papers in the field have used the survey (see, for instance, Delechat, 2001; Durand, Kandel, Parrado, & Massey, 1996).

The MMP124 has characteristics that made it an important source of information for the study of migration. First, and substantively, it is the only México-USA migration survey that covers long-term migrants. In particular, information about the head of the household and all her/his sons and daughters is gathered, independently of the current location or household membership status of the latter individuals. This implies that data for all sons and daughters are available even if some of them formed their own households and emigrated to the United States – and have not come back – many years before the survey. Further, an individual's emigration event is recorded regardless of her/his legal status in the United States. Date and destination of every legal or illegal border crossing in an individual's life history is carefully documented. The other two major surveys about México-USA migration, the ENADID and the MXLFS, do not cover long-term emigrants.[9]

The MMP data, however, is particularly weak for studying education. The only dimension of education that is known is the total number of years of education. There is no record of the date of first enrollment, schooling interuptions, grade retention, or date in which individuals last attended school. The MMP team did not apply any type of cognitive skills test or recorded the distance, at the time each child went to school, from the household to the nearest primary, secondary, or preparatory school. There is knowledge of a large number of characteristics of the community. Unfortunately, as it is discussed later on, community characteristics are likely to affect education as much as migration.

Importantly, the MMP does not collect information about the place where individuals went to school at any stage of their compulsory or post-compulsory education. Hence, the researcher cannot set apart individuals that attended school in México from those who attended school in the United States. Data on the number of Mexican migrants under the age of 18 is scarce. However, according to the DHS Office of Immigration Statistics (2009), during the second half of the 2000s children under the age of 17 represented 9.6% of all apprehensions in the border in 2005. The figures for 2006, 2007, and 2008 are 9.3%, 8.9% and 8.2%, respectively. These figures agree with the statistics generated in México. In particular, tabulations of the author using data from the *Encuesta Nacional de la Dinámica demográfica* (ENADID) 2006 show that only 3% of people with migration experience are aged 10 or less, 5% are aged 15 and less, and 12% are aged 17 and less. Hence, children migrating at an early age and attending school in the United States should be a relatively minor issue. This is, however, a potential source of bias that the reader should keep in mind when qualifying the results.

The present study is based on information for 12,430 women and 12,402 men collected in 5,940 families in 70 rural and urban communities throughout México between 1997 and 2008.[10] Individuals are clustered in families. Within a family the MMP124 gives information about the age (year, but not month nor day of birth) of each member. Since the focus of the chapter is high school graduation, only individuals aged 18 or over at the time of the survey are included in the sample. These figures exclude data from 285 individuals in 83 households where the eldest son/daughter migrated (for the first ever time) to the United States before or in the same year the household head did his/her first ever trip across the border – data for the whole household was dropped. Excluding these observations is important to avoid the threat of reverse causality as the study intends to find the effect of migration status of the family head on the migration and education outcomes of his/her children. Hence, one should ensure that migration of the family head occurs always before migration of the children. These 83 households represent 1.4% of the total number of households and 6.4% of the total number of migrant households. Therefore, according to the data, children migrating before (or simultaneously) than parents is a fairly rare phenomenon. The MPP does not record the year individuals left the school permanently. As a consequence, it is not possible to do the same filtering of problematic cases for the education variable. However, it is hard to foresee that a large proportion of parents may graduate from high school after their children do. Obviously, there will be some cases of parents going back to school after retirement, but the number of such cases must be quite limited given that only a small proportion of people in old generations of Mexicans completed studies beyond primary school.

Given that migration year is known for all members of the family, the researcher can establish the correct order of migration of all siblings – and can know whether or not they migrated together. For the case of the education variable, unfortunately, the ordering based on year of graduation from high school is not available. As a consequence if the researcher is interested in estimating a dynamic model – where the migration and education decisions of elder members of the family affect the choices of younger members – then the best the researcher can do is to order siblings by age and suppose that age

Table 1. Descriptive Statistics.

Variable	Description	Observation	Mean	Standard Deviation	Minimum	Maximum
Individual characteristics						
sex	= 1 if female	24,832	0.50	–	0	1
C1820	= 1 if aged between 18 and 20 years (control group)	24,832	0.12	–	0	1
C2125	= 1 if aged between 21 and 25 years	24,832	0.21	–	0	1
C2630	= 1 if aged between 26 and 30 years	24,832	0.20	–	0	1
C3135	= 1 if aged between 30 and 35 years	24,832	0.16	–	0	1
C3640	= 1 if aged between 30 and 35 years	24,832	0.13	–	0	1
C41p	= 1 if aged 36 and older	24,832	0.18	–	0	1
usmigra	= 1 if ever migrated to the United States	24,832	0.18	–	0	1
prepa	= 1 if completed high school	24,832	0.28	–	0	1
raildis	Distance from rail line in 1900 in state of birth, 000s km	24,832	0.10	0.18	0	1.46
Head of household						
hsex	= 1 if female	5,940	0.19	–	0	1
HC3050	= 1 if aged between 30 and 50 years (control group)	5,940	0.33	–	0	1
HC5160	= 1 if aged between 51 and 60 years	5,940	0.15	–	0	1
HC61p	= 1 if aged 61 and older	5,940	0.52	–	0	1
hnchild	No. of children ever born	5,940	5.28	2.87	1	19
usmigra	= 1 if ever migrated to the United States	5,940	0.20	–	0	1
prepa	= 1 if completed high school	5,940	0.10	–	0	1
raildis	Distance from rail line in 1900 in State of birth, 000s km	5,940	0.10	0.18	0	1.48

Table 1. (*Continued*)

Variable	Description	Observation	Mean	Standard Deviation	Minimum	Maximum
Community						
urban	= 1 if urban community	70	0.44	–	0	1
urate	Unemployment rate at United States main destination 1990–2000	70	6.60	1.74	3.44	11.28
Birthplace (base México city and environs)						
DF	= 1 if born in México City and environs (control group)	30,772	0.25	–	0	1
North	= 1 if born in north	30,772	0.27	–	0	1
Center	= 1 if born in center	30,772	0.14	–	0	1
CenterP	= 1 if born in center Pacific	30,772	0.21	–	0	1
South	= 1 if born in south	30,772	0.13	–	0	1
Survey year (base 1997)						
1997	= 1 if collected in year 1997 (control group)	30,772	0.07	–	0	1
1998	= 1 if collected in year 1998	30,772	0.16	–	0	1
1999	= 1 if collected in year 1999	30,772	0.07	–	0	1
2000	= 1 if collected in year 2000	30,772	0.08	–	0	1
2001	= 1 if collected in year 2001	30,772	0.12	–	0	1
2002	= 1 if collected in year 2002	30,772	0.10	–	0	1
2003	= 1 if collected in year 2003	30,772	0.07	–	0	1
2004	= 1 if collected in year 2004	30,772	0.11	–	0	1
2005	= 1 if collected in year 2005	30,772	0.02	–	0	1
2006	= 1 if collected in year 2006	30,772	0.07	–	0	1
2007	= 1 if collected in year 2007	30,772	0.08	–	0	1
2008	= 1 if collected in year 2008	30,772	0.05	–	0	1

ordering broadly agrees with migration and high school graduation ordering. Obviously this potentially introduces the problem of reverse causality because in the data some young siblings may precede his/her elder siblings in migrating to the United States. Hence, the dynamic models estimated in the next section should be taken with due care. The problem, however, is expected to be relatively small because, as it was discussed in the Introduction, historically Mexican migration is initiated by the father and then sons follow when they reach an age in which they are strong enough to cross the México-USA border illegally. This somehow resembles a waiting-to-migrate queue process that is largely determined by birth order.

The MMP124 contains information on whether individuals have ever migrated to the United States (usmigra = 1) and on whether they graduated from high school (prepa = 1). These are the two dichotomous dependent variables of interest in the present analysis. Eleven percent of women and 26% of men have migrated to the United States at least once. Similarly, 30% of females and 27% of males are high school graduates. Hence, females migrate much less intensively than males and have better odds of graduating from high school.

Migrants are clearly less educated (see Tables 2 and 3). Among women, 23% of the migrants are graduates compared to the 30% of non-migrants. Similarly, among men, only 16% of migrants are graduates whereas 31% of nonmigrants are graduates. Hence, male migrants successfully finish preparatory school at a rate that is nearly a half of the nonmigrant population. The same trend is observed when looking at the distribution of migrants and graduates among households heads. Notice that, among household heads, only 10% of the sample are high school graduates and, whithin the migrants, only 6% are graduates. Table 1 contain additional summary statistics and a description of the variables used in the study.

ECONOMETRIC ISSUES

Dynamic bivariate random effects probit models for cluster data are used for the analysis.[11] Denote by M_{ji} the variable that takes on 1 if, by the time of the survey, the i-th member of the j-th family has emigrated to the United States at least once and zero otherwise. Similarly, E_{ji} indicates whether the i-th member of the j-th family graduated from high school ($E_{ji} = 1$) or not ($E_{ji} = 0$) by the time of the survey. Within families, and to avoid any ambiguity, heads are given the $i = 0$ index. Families can have a different number of members – excluding the singleton family – and the head may or may not be in a union. No data for the spouse of the household head is used for the analysis.

Dynamic Equations

A latent variable framework is the natural approach. Let M^*_{ji} and E^*_{ji} be two latent continuous variables. The econometrician does not observe M^*_{ji} and/or E^*_{ji}. Instead, two dichotomized variables, M_{ji} and E_{ji}, are available. It is supposed that the high school dummy is generated according to the following data generating process

$$\begin{aligned} E^*_{ji} = {} & \boldsymbol{x}^e_{ji}\boldsymbol{\beta}^e \\ & + \delta_{11}E_{j,0} + \delta_{12}M_{j,0} \\ & + \delta_{13}E_{j,i-1} + \delta_{14}M_{j,i-1} \\ & + \delta_{15}ES_{j,i} + \delta_{16}MS_{j,i} + f^e_j + u^e_{ji} \end{aligned} \tag{1}$$

with $E_{ji} = 1$ if $E^*_{ji} > 0$ and zero otherwise, $i = \{1 \ldots I_j\}$ and $j = \{1 \ldots, J\}$. Notice that the education outcome of the family head within the j-th family (initial observation) is indexed by zero, $i = 0$. Vector $\boldsymbol{x}^e_{ji}$ represents a set of observed characteristics that can vary at the individual, family, and community levels. Elements of $\boldsymbol{x}^e_{ji}$ are assumed to be strictly exogenous and $\boldsymbol{\beta}^e$ denotes a conformable coefficient vector – including the constant term. Similarly, $\boldsymbol{\delta}_1 = \{\delta_{11}, \ldots, \delta_{16}\} \in \mathbb{R}^6$ represent coefficients on the migration and education outcomes of the family head ($E_{j,0}$ and $M_{j,0}$), the immediately elder sibling ($E_{j,i-1}$ and $M_{j,i-1}$), and the stock of migrants and high school graduates up to the i-th member ($ES_{j,i}$ and $MS_{j,i}$).[12] Here, MS_{ji} and ES_{ji} are a measure of an individual's access to family migration and education networks net of the effect of the outcomes of the family head and the immediately elder sibling. Finally, variables f^e_j and u^e_{ji} are random heterogeneity terms. One term, f^e_j, varies at the family level while the other term, u^e_{ji}, varies at the individual level. The equation for the migration dummy is

$$\begin{aligned} M^*_{ji} = {} & \boldsymbol{x}^m_{ji}\boldsymbol{\beta}^m \\ & + \delta_{21}E_{j,0} + \delta_{22}M_{j,0} \\ & + \delta_{23}E_{j,i-1} + \delta_{24}M_{j,i-1} \\ & + \delta_{25}ES_{j,i} + \delta_{26}MS_{j,i} + f^m_j + u^m_{ji} \end{aligned} \tag{2}$$

with $M_{ji} = 1$ if $M^*_{ji} > 0$ and zero otherwise. Following Alessie, Hochguertel, and Van Soest (2004), f_j^m and f_j^e are specified to be jointly normally distributed with mean vector zero and covariance matrix $\mathbf{\Sigma}_f$:

$$\mathbf{\Sigma}_f = \begin{bmatrix} \sigma_m^2 & \rho\sigma_m\sigma_e \\ \rho\sigma_m\sigma_e & \sigma_e^2 \end{bmatrix}$$

In a similar fashion, u_{ji}^m and u_{ji}^e are jointly normal with mean vector zero and covariance matrix $\mathbf{\Sigma}_u$:

$$\mathbf{\Sigma}_u = \begin{bmatrix} 1 & \rho_u \\ \rho_u & 1 \end{bmatrix}$$

To close the model it is assumed that f_j^h and u_{ji}^h are independent, for $h=(m,e)$. Further, f_j^h and u_{jk}^h are serially uncorrelated for every j and k. The assumption that u_{jk}^h is serially uncorrected is natural as, conditional on everything that make the members of a family alike, there is no reason to believe that individual shocks within a family should be correlated. The assumption that f_j^h is not serially correlated is more substantial. The requirement is that the random effects at the family level are uncorrected across all families in the sample. This requirement is not very restrictive in the context of urban communities where there is a large number of households. In the case of small rural communities, however, the assumption may prove unrealistic. In the present application, there is only one community belonging to a municipality with population of less than 5,000. So, the assumption is probably sensible.

The model implies the following relationships. M_{ji}^* and M_{jk}^*, $k \neq i$, are correlated within the j-th family through the random term f_j^m. However, no such correlation exist among individuals who belong to different families. Intra-family clustering is also induced between E_{ji}^* and E_{jk}^* by the random term f_j^e. Also, at the family level, correlation between E_{ji}^* and M_{jk}^* for all i and k that belong to the j-th family is induced by correlation between f_j^e and f_j^m. Finally, at the individual level, correlation between M_{ji}^* and E_{ji}^* is created by the correlation between u_{ji}^m and u_{ji}^e. We say that there is true state dependence if $\delta=(\delta_{11},\ldots,\delta_{26})\neq 0$.

Initial Conditions

Estimation of Eqs. (1) and (2) by simple OLS or probit models (either univariate or bivariate) treating M_{j0}, E_{j0}, $\mathrm{M}_{j,i-1}$, $\mathrm{E}_{j,i-1}$, MS_{ji}, and ES_{ji} as exogenous variables will produce inconsistent estimators because migration and education outcomes of different members within the j-th family are correlated through the common family level unobserved terms f_j^m and f_j^e.[13] This is particularly important because the head of the household might have been originated in a family of migrants and/or high school graduates. So, the researcher does not really observe the true beginning of the dynamic process. To address the problem one needs to explicitly model the *initial conditions* M_{j0} and E_{j0}. Once M_{j0} and E_{j0} are carefully modeled, the endogeneity of $\mathrm{M}_{j,i-1}$, $\mathrm{E}_{j,i-1}$, MS_{ji}, and ES_{ji} will also be addressed because, given f_j^m and f_j^e, for the i-th individual in the j-th family $\mathrm{M}_{j,i-1}$, $\mathrm{E}_{j,i-1}$, MS_{ji}, and ES_{ji} are a deterministic function of the outcomes generated by Eqs. (1) and (2) up to the $(i-1)$-th individual and will be exogenous as long as all the distributional assumptions hold. To solve the initial conditions problem here the strategy suggested by Heckman (1981) is used. Namely, a model for the reduced-form marginal probability of M_{j0} and E_{j0} given f_j^e and f_j^m is specified. Hence, two further equations are needed:

$$\mathrm{E}_{j0}^* = z_{j0}^e \gamma^e + \lambda_{11} f_j^e + \lambda_{12} f_j^m + v_{j0}^e \tag{3}$$

$$\mathrm{M}_{j0}^* = z_{j0}^m \gamma^{\mathbf{m}} + \lambda_{21} f_j^e + \lambda_{22} f_j^m + v_{j0}^m \tag{4}$$

with $\mathrm{E}_{j0}=1$ if $\mathrm{E}_{j0}^*>0$ and $\mathrm{M}_{j0}=1$ if $\mathrm{M}_{j0}^*>0$ and zero otherwise. As usual, z_{j0}^e and z_{j0}^m represent vectors of explanatory variables that can vary at the individual, family, and community level. Coefficients $\lambda = (\lambda_{11}, \lambda_{12}, \lambda_{21}, \lambda_{22}) \in \mathbb{R}^4$ represent free parameters (*factors loadings*) that allow any type of correlation among E_{j0}^*, M_{j0}^*, E_{ji}^*, and M_{ji}^*. We suppose that v_{j0}^h is uncorrelated with v_{jk}^h for every j and k. As usual, v_{j0}^e and v_{j0}^m are jointly normal with mean vector zero and covariance matrix Σ_v:

$$\Sigma_v = \begin{bmatrix} 1 & \rho_v \\ \rho_v & 1 \end{bmatrix}$$

Equations (1) and (2) can be estimated by simple univariate probit models if $\lambda=(\lambda_{11}, \lambda_{12}, \lambda_{21}, \lambda_{22})=0$ (or random effects univariate probit models to gain efficiency). If $\lambda_{11}\neq 0$ and $\lambda_{22}\neq 0$ but $\lambda_{12}=\lambda_{21}=0$, then univariate dynamic random effects models will be enough to obtain consistent and efficient estimators. However, if either $\lambda_{12}\neq 0$ or $\lambda_{21}\neq 0$, then the full bivariate random effects dynamic probit model will be needed to obtain consistent estimators.

Identification and Control Variables

Technically the model is identified through functional form (see Heckman, 1978). However, in the absence of exclusion restrictions identification may be "tenuous" (in the context of the multinomial probit model see Keane, 1992). Hence, specifying exclusion restrictions to help identification is a good practice.

Using information from the MMP survey, one can identify the main US city/urban area destination of each community in the sample between 1990 and 2009. Similarly, local area unemployment rates in the United States are available from the Bureau of Labor Statistics (BLS). Hence, it is possible to obtain an average unemployment rate (urate) between 1990 and 2009 for each local area reported by the BLS and match such information with the MMP data. The unemployment rate is an indicator of the labor market characteristics of the main US city/urban area destination of the MMP communities included in the sample.

Variable urate enter the migration equations but are excluded from the schooling equations. Clearly, unemployment rate at the community's main US destination is a good indicator of how difficult it is for new immigrants to find a job at arrival. The higher urate is the less attractive migration will be for prospective migrants. This variable is unlikely to affect education decisions in México and, if they do, it is exclusively through their impact on migration. We use, therefore, this variable to impose exclusion restrictions to help identification.

Following Woodruff and Zenteno (2007), community migrant networks are controlled by exploiting variation in an individual's degree of access to historical migrant networks. Given that historical migration may be endogenous in system (1)–(4), a proxy that is unlikely to be correlated with all $f^{(\cdot)}$, $u^{(\cdot)}$, and $v^{(\cdot)}$ is used instead. In particular, access to community migrant networks is approximated by the distance from the capital of the state in which an individual was born to the nearest station on the north/south rail lines in the early 1900s, raildis.[14]

As indicated by Woodruff and Zenteno (2007), the rationale behind the use of raildis as a proxy for historical migration and, therefore, as a proxy for current access to community migrant networks is that during the first two decades of the 20th century a large number of Mexican workers were recruited to work in the south of the United States. Given the lack of important population centers nearby the border and other more efficient means of transport, American contractors went down the existing Mexican north/south railway route hiring Mexican citizens along the way. Also, between 1910 and 1921, the north/south railway played a central role in moving troops during the Mexican revolution. When either the *villista* or the federal army went through a population nearby the railway, they would stop to get supplies and force young men in town to join the army (see Taibo II, 2006, for an excellent narrative and extensive historical reference of the movement of troops along the rails during the Mexican revolution and the implications for towns, villages, and cities that were nearby). As a response to this menace, many men and families fled to the north using the railway as soon as they had news it was safe to do so. Part of this displaced population went as far as to the south of the United States.

Proximity to the railway in early 1900s in México gave, therefore, reasons and opportunities to Mexican citizens to migrate to the United States. These early movements of labor and displaced population helped to accumulate experience and contacts in the United States that were used upon the end of the Second World War to send new waves of migrants. There are, as a consequence, good reasons to suggest that raildis is correlated with current access to community migrant networks. In contrast, no reasons lead us to believe that raildis should be correlated with other current community characteristics that may affect education and migration in the present day. One can reasonably sustain, therefore, that raildis is neither correlated with family level random effects $f^{(\cdot)}$ nor with individual level error terms $u^{(\cdot)}$ and $v^{(\cdot)}$. Hence, it is reasonably justified to use raildis to impose one further exclusion restriction in system (1)–(4), as raildis is likely to affect migration but not directly education. As a consequence raildis enters migration equations but is excluded from education equations.

Justifying credible exclusion restrictions for the education equations is harder. The MMP data are a set of pooled cross sections and there is no longitudinal dimension to exploit. One could try cohort effects together with changes in compulsory education law. For instance, in 1993 the Mexican Constitution was changed to make secondary school compulsory for all Mexican children. This implied a shift from six to nine years of compulsory education. There are two problems with this strategy. First, there is no geographic variation as the change in the law came into force at the same time in all states and municipalities across Mexico. Second, Mexico has gone through a series of economic booms and crises since 1950s. Therefore, hoping to identify the effect of changes in compulsory education law through simple cohort effects is overoptimistic. Relevant dates of economic and social turmoil include 1976 and 1982 (debt crisis), 1986 (oil price crisis), 1994 (Zapatista outbreak and Mexican peso crisis), 2001 (September 11), to count just the few most relevant. Clearly, any of these events may have had impact on both education and migration.

The MMP collects a series of characteristics of the communities it surveys. There is knowledge, for instance, about the number of primary, secondary, and preparatory schools in the municipality where the community is located at the time of the survey. And there is even information on the date the first school of each type was open for the first time. One could argue that these variables are good candidates to impose exclusion restrictions. A potential threat to this strategy, however, is that the education policy of the Mexican government may react (increasing or decreasing supply) to the intensity of migration in each state and municipality. Moreover, in many instances clubs and associations of migrants finance, in association with local authorities, a number of public infrastructure projects in the community. This includes building schools, roads, and irrigation in the municipality. From this point of view, it is hard to justify that the number of schools, or even the date it were open, in the community are independent of the migration phenomenon. Other characteristics of the community collected by the MMP, such as quality and type of land available in the community, prices of land, agricultural production, and number of factories, are all subject to the same criticism.

Forcing an exclusion restriction using a variable that truly affects both migration and education is, in the present context, the highest risk. Hence, in the hope of helping identification, the researcher can compromise the consistency of the estimators. Given that there are already some identified exclusion restrictions for migration, the best strategy is then to leave unspecified exclusion restrictions for the education equations and rely partly on identification by functional form. This is an important limitation of the study that the reader should keep in mind when qualifying the results. Despite the lack of an exclusion restriction for education, the model is still identified. In fact, if one specifies exclusion restrictions for the initial conditions then there is no need for any additional exclusion restrictions (see Arulampalam, Booth, & Taylor, 2000; Stewart, 2007).[15]

Notice that the approach taken here is better than just ignoring the endogeneity of the migration and education status of the family head and previous family members (i.e., ignoring the initial conditions problem). A remark is guaranteed. The endogeneity of E_{j0} in system (1) and (2) can be caused by two different reasons. First, because $\lambda_{11} \neq 0$ and E_{j0} is a function of f_j^e. This the usual initial condition problem in an univariate setting. Second, because $\lambda_{12} \neq 0$ and E_{j0} is a function of f_j^m. This is the "cross" state dependence in unobservables at family level that one gains by recognizing the need of fully accounting for the bivariate nature of migration and education decisions. Parallel reasoning applies to M_{j0}. Notice that if $\lambda_{12} \neq 0$, the initial conditions problem of M_{j0} in the E_{ji} regression cannot be dealt with using univariate dynamic random effects probit models. An IV strategy will not produce consistent estimators unless the instrument can be agued to affect only the migration outcome of the family head and, at the same time, not to be correlated with unobservables at the family level. The bivariate dynamic probit allows the researcher to relax the first requirement – that is, can have a variable that affects migration of parents and children but not their education – because it models explicitly the initial conditions.

To help the identification of the initial conditions one can exploit the fact that parents and children belong to different cohorts of age. Hence, a different set of age cohort dummies are created for heads of household and their children. Given that only 10% of the heads are high school graduates, the age cohorts of the household heads were generated such that the cell size of graduates in each cohort does not become too small.

Other explanatory variables include sex, age, and the total number of children the head ever had. Dummies for rural/urban classification of the surveyed communities as well as birthplace, region, and survey year are also included. Variables such as income, labor participation status, and wage are not included in the list of explanatory variables because they are very likely to be endogenous and the MMP does not contain information on characteristics that can be used as valid instruments. Hence, Eqs. (1)–(4) should be seen as a reduced-form model and the reader should take due care when interpreting results.

Estimation Strategy

The model is estimated by maximum simulated likelihood (see, for instance, Train, 2003). The contribution of the *j*-th family to the likelihood is

$$L_j = \int\int \Phi_2(q_{1j0}w_{11}, q_{2j0}w_{12}, q_{1j0}q_{2j0}\rho_v) \times \prod_{i=1}^{I_j} \Phi_2(q_{1ji}w_{21}, q_{2ji}w_{22}, q_{1ji}q_{2ji}\rho_u) g(f^e, f^m, \Sigma_f)\ \mathrm{d}f^e \mathrm{d}f^m \quad (5)$$

where $g(.)$ represents the bivariate normal density of the family random effects, $q_{1,ji} = 2E_{ji} - 1$, and $q_{2,ji} = 2M_{ji} - 1$. Finally, w_{11} and w_{12} are the right-hand side of Eqs. (3) and (4) excluding u^e_{ji} and u^m_{ji}, respectively. Variables w_{21} and w_{22} are defined in the same fashion using Eqs. (1) and (2).

Two uncorrelated Halton sequences of dimension R are first obtained. Then, random draws from density $g(.)$ are simulated using the Halton sequences, a Cholesky decomposition, and the inverse cumulative normal distribution. Next, for each draw (which is a two-dimension vector), the conditional likelihood of the j-th family is evaluated. Finally, an average of the R simulated conditional likelihoods is taken. This average is the contribution of the j-th family to the overall simulated likelihood – an approximation of the double integral in Eq. (5). Halton sequences have been shown to achieve high precision with fewer draws than uniform pseudo-random sequences because they have a better coverage of the [0,1] interval (for more on this topic see Train, 2003).

Maximum simulated likelihood is asymptotically equivalent to ML as long as R grows faster than $\sqrt{N}$ (Gourieroux & Monfort, 1993). Following Alessie et al. (2004) maximization is performed on the basis of BHHH algorithm. At convergence, numerical second derivatives are obtained to calculate the Eicker–Huber–White community clustered robust (sandwich estimator) covariance matrix.

EMPIRICAL RESULTS

In what follows Eicker–Huber–White community clustered robust standard errors (sandwich estimator) are always reported and used to perform hypothesis tests. For all random effects models estimated by maximum simulated likelihood 400 Halton draws were used. In all cases, adding more Halton draws did not produce significant changes in log-likehood, standard errors, or coefficients.

Main Results

Let the discussion start by presenting briefly results from simple pooled probit models fitted by sex on the sample of sons and daughters of the family head (see Table 4). In these regressions the migration and education status of the family head, usmigra_{j0} and prepa_{j0}, the migration and education status of the immediately elder sibling usmigra_{i-1} and prepa_{i-1}, and the stock of migrants and graduates up to the $(i-1)$-th individual MS_i and ES_i, are all treated as exogenous variables. The clustering of children within families has not been accounted for but one should still obtain consistent estimates, though not efficient, if usmigra_{j0}, prepa_{j0}, usmigra_{i-1}, prepa_{i-1},

MS_i, and ES_i are truly exogenous. According to Table 4, at 5% of significance, the migration status of the family head has no effect on the probability that his/her children will graduate from high school for either males or females. The migration status of the immediately elder sibling $usmigra_{i-1}$ has a significant positive marginal effect on the probability of high school graduation for boys but not for girls at 5% of significance. Finally, also at 5% of significance, the stock of migrants MS_i has a negative and significant marginal effect for both males and females.

Regarding migration, the migration status of the family head is found to have no bearing on the probability of migration of both boys and girls. This does not imply that no migrant network effect is found. In fact, the migration outcome of the immediately elder sibling increases the likelihood of migration by about 22 percentage points (p.p. hereafter) for the girls. In the case of boys, a t-test for the significance of the coefficient on $usmigra_{i-1}$ fails to reject the null of zero at a 5% significance level. Further, the stock of migrants increases the probability of migration by 5.4 p.p. for the females and 6.3 p.p. for males. Both marginal effects are statististically different from zero at 1%. All the probit evidence agree with, and do not add too much more than, the stylized facts that the reader can draw from the descriptive statistics reported in Tables 2 and 3. Namely, that migrants study less.

Next, Table 5 contains results from random effects dynamic probit models fitted on the sample of males. To aid qualifying empirical findings, marginal effects calculated from univariate dynamic models are tabulated alongside marginal effects on marginal probabilities obtained from the dynamic bivariate random effects probit model. The univariate regression for prepa controls for the endogeneity of $prepa_{j0}$, $prepa_{i-1}$, and ES_i but treats $usmigra_{j0}$, $usmigra_{i-1}$, and MS_i as exogenous. Similarly, the univariate regression for usmigra controls for the endogeneity of $usmigra_{j0}$, $usmigra_{i-1}$, and MS_i but treats $prepa_{j0}$, $prepa_{i-1}$, and ES_i as exogenous. Finally, the bivariate regressions addresses the initial conditions problem of $usmigra_{j0}$

Table 2. Migrants and Graduates (Sons and Daughters).

	Females						Males					
	prepa = 0		prepa = 1		Total		prepa = 0		prepa = 1		Total	
	Obs.	%	Obs.	%	Obs.	%	Obs.	%	Obs.	%	Obs.	%
usmigra = 0	7,780	70.33	3,282	29.67	11,062	100	6,334	69.10	2,833	30.90	9,167	100
usmigra = 1	1,054	77.05	314	22.95	1,368	100	2,722	84.14	513	15.86	3,235	100
Total	8,834	71.07	3,596	28.93	12,430	100	9,056	73.02	3,346	26.98	12,402	100

Table 3. Migrants and Graduates (Heads of Household).

	prepa = 0		prepa = 1		Total	
	Obs.	%	Obs.	%	Obs.	%
usmigra = 0	4,200	88.96	521	11.04	4,721	100
usmigra = 1	1,141	93.58	78	6.40	1,219	100
Total	5,341	89.92	599	10.08	5,940	100

and prepa_{j0} together and, hence, deals with the endogeneity of all the aforementioned variables. Notice that the log-likelihood between pooled probit and univariate dynamic probit models are not directly comparable because the former regressions report a figure that corresponds only to the contribution of the dynamic equation in the latter regression.

One of the most important result from the univariate models is the fact that the marginal effect of prepa_{j0} is insignificant in the prepa regression at all conventional levels of significance. In other words, no true state dependence regarding the education of the family head is detected in the education regression once unobserved heterogeneity at the family level is properly controlled for. The finding is relevant as it suggests that all the correlation between the education outcomes of parents and children is driven by unobserved factors. This is consistent with the findings from simple probit models. Interestingly, the marginal effect on the stock of graduates has opposite signs in probit and univariate dynamic models for both males and females. The results is interesting and intuitive as it suggests that as family puts effort in educating elder children, younger children get lower chances of completing high school education themselves. This is probably an indicator that children compete for resources and that families of larger size struggle more to give education to all their children and are more likely to be credit constrained when younger children grow old enough to get post-compulsory education. Notice that the probit model will conterintuitively lead the researcher to the opposite conclusion. So, clearly, accounting for the dynamics at the family level is important. However, an important challenge to the validity of this observation is the fact that the estimate for λ_{11} is zero at a 5% of significance level. So, the univariate dynamic model for prepa does not find enough evidence to reject the null hypothesis that usmigra_{j0}, usmigra_{i-1}, and MS_i are exogenous variables in the dynamic equation for prepa even though σ_e is found to be different from zero at 1% of significance. Importantly, and in agreement with the results from pooled probit, the migration status of the family head is insignificant in the prepa equation at 5% of significance.

In the case of migration, figures for the marginal effect of usmigra_{j0} in Table 5 show that boys from households headed by a migrant are around 30 p.p. more likely to migrate themselves. Hence, in this case there is evidence of true state dependence linking migrants from one generation to the next through a migrant network effect. The finding differs from those obtained from the pooled probit regression reported in Table 4 where the coefficient on usmigra_{j0} is insignificant and agree with those reported for the univariate model in Table 5. Results show, however, that the marginal effect of

Table 4. Probit Results – Marginal Effects.

	Females				Males			
	prepa		usmigra		prepa		usmigra	
Variable	ME	CRSE	ME	CRSE	ME	CRSE	ME	CRSE
usmigra_0	0.004	0.017	−0.033	0.008	0.029	0.016	−0.020	0.013
prepa_0	0.047	0.025	0.018	0.016	0.054**	0.021	−0.028	0.022
usmigra_{i-1}	0.055*	0.016	0.080	0.013	0.016	0.013	0.219*	0.015
prepa_{i-1}	0.277*	0.025	−0.018	0.010	0.272*	0.025	0.021	0.020
MS_i	−0.028**	0.012	0.063*	0.005	−0.021**	0.010	0.054*	0.008
ES_i	0.129*	0.011	−0.003	0.005	0.101*	0.013	−0.049*	0.011
C2125	0.039**	0.019	0.063*	0.014	0.048**	0.020	0.141*	0.021
C2630	0.040	0.023	0.110*	0.019	0.063*	0.018	0.209*	0.026
C3135	0.059**	0.027	0.140*	0.019	0.091*	0.025	0.235*	0.026
C3640	0.052	0.027	0.154*	0.024	0.102*	0.026	0.202*	0.033
C41p	−0.026	0.025	0.127*	0.021	0.050*	0.021	0.185*	0.031
hsex	−0.031*	0.012	0.014**	0.007	−0.036*	0.013	0.027**	0.012
hnchild	−0.033*	0.002	−0.002**	0.001	−0.030*	0.002	0.003	0.002
raildis		−0.054	0.031			0.061	−0.146*	0.061
urate		−0.007	0.004			0.008	−0.014	0.008
urban	0.094*	0.023	−0.018	0.012	0.071	0.023	−0.071*	0.022
Birthplace	Yes		Yes		Yes		Yes	
Survey year	Yes		Yes		Yes		Yes	
No. of obs.	12,430		12,430		12,402		12,402	
Log-likelihood	−5,559		−3,833		−5,569		−6,147	

Note: *(**) Significant at 1% (5%). Eicker–Huber–White community clustered robust standard errors (sandwich) are reported. Marginal effects are evaluated at the means of the explanatory variables. For dummy variables, they show the change in the relevant probability when the variable changes from 0 to 1.

Table 5. Random Effects Dynamic Probit – Marginal Effects (Males).

	Univariate Model				Bivariate Model			
	prepa		usmigra		prepa		usmigra	
Variable	ME	CRSE	ME	CRSE	ME[a]	CRSE	ME[a]	CRSE
$usmigra_0$	−0.010	0.016	0.379*	0.119	−0.175*	0.040	0.299*	0.080
$prepa_0$	0.199	0.222	−0.071*	0.020	0.134	0.127	−0.170*	0.017
$usmigra_{i-1}$	−0.016	0.011	0.085*	0.014	−0.018	0.011	0.083*	0.014
$prepa_{i-1}$	0.062*	0.019	0.022	0.019	0.062*	0.020	0.030	0.021
MS_i	0.026*	0.009	−0.020*	0.007	0.024**	0.011	−0.022*	0.008
ES_i	−0.023**	0.012	−0.029*	0.011	−0.023**	0.011	−0.031*	0.010
C2125	0.054**	0.024	0.162*	0.028	0.051**	0.022	0.158*	0.028
C2630	0.069*	0.026	0.235	0.035	0.062**	0.024	0.227*	0.034
C3135	0.083**	0.034	0.258*	0.036	0.076**	0.031	0.247*	0.035
C3640	0.058	0.032	0.200*	0.044	0.052	0.032	0.189*	0.041
C41p	−0.008	0.021	0.152*	0.035	−0.014	0.020	0.145*	0.033
hsex	−0.043*	0.014	0.079*	0.027	−0.087*	0.021	0.057*	0.019
hnchild	−0.031*	0.004	0.012*	0.003	−0.029*	0.004	0.009*	0.003
raildis			−0.157**	0.072			−0.133	0.073
urate			−0.019**	0.009			−0.021**	0.009

urban	0.114*	0.037	−0.086*	0.026	0.115*	0.035	−0.070*	0.027
Birth place	Yes		Yes		Yes		Yes	
Survey year	Yes		Yes		Yes		Yes	
Auxiliary parameters	Coeff.	CRSE	Coeff.	CRSE			Coeff.	CRSE
λ_{11}	0.263	0.166					0.381*	0.139
λ_{12}							0.848*	0.215
λ_{21}							0.413*	0.158
λ_{22}			−0.443	0.237			−0.252	0.162
σ_e	1.497*	0.139					1.633*	0.152
σ_m			0.983*	0.065			1.007*	0.068
ρ_u							−0.268*	0.045
ρ_v							−0.397	0.217
ρ							−0.123	0.075
Model information								
No. of obs.	12,402		12,402				12,402	
No. of families	5,095		5,095				5,095	
No. of Halton draws	400		400				400	
Log-likelihood	−6,783		−8,376				−15,087	

Note: *(**) Significant at 1% (5%). Eicker–Huber–White community clustered robust standard errors (sandwich) are reported.
[a]Marginal effects on marginal probabilities. For dummy variables, they show the change in the relevant probability when the variable changes from 0 to 1.

$usmigra_{j0}$ on usmigra is clearly underestimated by the pooled probit and overestimated by the univariate dynamic random effects probit.

Results from the bivariate dynamic random effects probit fitted on the sample of males adds various important insights. First, estimates for σ_e and σ_m are highly significant, so family clustering is present in both prepa and usmigra equations. Also, ρ_e, ρ_u, and ρ_v are all negative. However, only ρ_u is significantly different from zero at 5%. Hence, empirical results suggest that there is negative migrant selection in unobservables in the sense that smart people migrate less. The finding is consistent with the hypothesis put forward by Borjas (1994) around the relationship between skills and migration in the México-USA migration context.

Second, a negative and significant marginal effect of $usmigra_{j0}$ on the equation for prepa is detected and the effect is significantly different from zero at 1% (see last two columns of Table 5). Notice that this is a piece of information added by the bivariate dynamic model, as inference from pooled probit and univariate dynamic models suggest that the marginal effect of $usmigra_{j0}$ on prepa is zero. The finding implies that, once unobserved heterogeneity at individual and family level are properly controlled for, there is strong empirical evidence of true state dependance of the migration status of the household head on the education outcomes of the children. In other words, migration experience of the family head decreases the likelihood that children, boys in this case, will graduate from high school. The size of the marginal effect is economically relevant. In fact, figures in Table 4 suggest that boys from households headed by a migrant are 17 p.p less likely to graduate from high school than boys from households headed by a nonmigrant. Interestingly, the migration status of the immediately elder sibling is reported to have a negative marginal effect of −1.8 p.p. So, results suggest that having an elder migrant sibling reduces the incentives of education in México net of the effect that a migrant father has. This, again, is evidence supporting the hypothesis that children from migrant households that plan to migrate themselves tend to behave in a forward looking fashion and drop school early, probably because they cannot transfer their skills across the México-USA border. The story, however, does not end there. Results from the bivariate dynamic model in Table 5 show that the stock of migrants actually increase the probability of high school migration by around 2.4 p.p. The marginal effect is statistically significant at 5%. Clearly, this is a new piece of evidence suggesting that when the stock of migrant family members increases, children in México start to have incentives to study in the home country before migrating themselves. One could speculate that this positive effect of the stock of migrants is associated with the network of contacts in the United States getting larger and more valuable to help a relatively skilled new migrant to transfer his/her skills across the border and get a qualified job upon arrival.

The validity of the two aforementioned results are supported by the fact that the hypotheses of $\lambda_{11}=0$ and $\lambda_{12}=0$ are both rejected at 1% of significance (see auxiliary parameters panel in Table 5). Hence, there is strong evidence that all prepa$_{j0}$, prepa$_{i-1}$, ES$_i$, usmigra$_{j0}$, usmigra$_{i-1}$, and MS$_i$ are endogenous variables in the prepa equation and explain the difference between results from pooled probit, univariate dynamic random effects probit, and bivariate dynamic random effect probit. Notice that if the researcher was to, by mistake, infer on the basis of the univariate dynamic model she/he would have concluded that the education and migration status of the family head has no effect on the education outcomes of the children (boys in this case). As a consequence, it seems that recognizing all the complexities of the migration and education relationship and estimating the bivariate dynamic probit model is fundamental to do correct inference.

Regarding the migration equation, results from the bivariate dynamic model show strong empirical evidence that there is true dynamic state dependence with respect to both prepa$_{j0}$ and usmigra$_{j0}$, as the marginal effects on these two variables are significantly different from zero at 1% (see last two columns of Table 5). These findings agree with the results from univariate models. However, the advantage of using a fully blown BDPM is clear when one compares the size of the marginal effect of prepa$_{j0}$ on usmigra across the univarite and bivariate models. In fact, the marginal effect goes from −7.1 p.p. in the univariate model to −17 p.p. in the bivariate model, respectively. As a consequence, it is clear that the effect of the education of the household head on the migration of her/his male children is underestimated by the univariate model. The migrant network effect is still there in the bivariate model and results show that its size is overestimated by the univariate model.

Table 6 contains a set of Wald exclusion restriction tests that are important to qualify the results just discussed (results for males). There, the reader will find strong evidence that the age cohort dummies for the family head HC5160 and HC61p are strong predictors of migration and education outcomes in the initial conditions equations of both univariate and BDPMs. These variables are only included in the initial conditions equations and are therefore there to help identification. In fact, the null hypothesis that HC5160 and HC61p should be excluded from the initial conditions of the prepa equation in the bivariate model is rejected with a $\chi^2(2)=22.58$ and p-value $=0.000$ (see row 1, right panel, of Table 6). Similarly, the null

Table 6. Wald Exclusion Restrictions Tests (Males).

	Univariable Model						Bivariate Model					
	prepa			usmigra			prepa			usmigra		
	χ^2	DF	*p*-val	χ^2	DF	*p*-val	χ^2	DF	*p*-val	χ^2	DF	*p*-val
(1)	23.33*	2	0.000	12.59*	2	0.000	22.58*	2	0.000	15.48*	2	0.000
(2)	30.97*	5	0.000	101.59*	5	0.000	126.14*	5	0.000	103.27*	5	0.000
(3)				4.13*	3	0.126				4.20	3	0.122
(4)				12.69	2	0.002				11.76*	2	0.003
(5)										25.42*	2	0.000
(6)										631.95*	3	0.000

Note: *(**) Significant at 1% (5%). Eicker–Huber–White community clustered robust standard errors (sandwich) used to perform the tests. Null hypothesis in each row are as follows: (1) HC5160 = HC61p = 0 initial conditions; (2) C2125 = C2630 = C3135 = C3640 = C41p = 0 dynamic equation; (3) raildis = urate = 0 initial conditions; (4) raildis = urate = 0 dynamic equation; (5) $\lambda_{12} = \lambda_{21} = 0$; (6) $\rho_u = \rho_v = \rho = 0$.

hypothesis that HC5160 and HC61p should be excluded from the initial conditions of the usmigra equation is rejected with a $\chi^2(2) = 15.48$ and *p*-value = 0.000. The age cohort dummies C2125, C2630, C3135, and C3640 are highly significant in both prepa and usmigra equations, with $\chi^2(2) = 126.14$ and $\chi^2(2) = 103.27$, respectively. In both cases the null hypothesis is rejected with a significance level of 1% (see row 2, right panel, Table 6). These exclusion restrictions are good enough to help identifying the bivariate model. Unfortunately, the test for the exclusion of the instruments for migration in the initial conditions equation, raildis = urate = 0, cannot be rejected at any conventional significance level (see row 3, right panel). However, the instruments work quite well in the dynamic equation and the hypothesis that raildis = urate = 0 is easily rejected at 1% (see row 4, left panel). The relevance of the BDPM is tested by the null hypothesis that $\lambda_{12} = \lambda_{21} = 0$ and rejected at 1% (row 5, right panel). Finally, the null of $\rho_u = \rho_v = \rho = 0$ is also rejected at 1% (row 6, right panel). Further, details about estimates for the initial conditions for the sample of males are reported in Table A1.

The results for the females are different but, to avoid repetition, only the main results are highlighted. First, and fundamentally, the initial conditions problem in the prepa equation with respect to the migration status variables is, if anything, only marginally significant as the estimate for λ_{12} is 0.420

with an standard error of 0.269, which give a *t*-ratio of just 1.56 (p-val = 0.119). The estimate of λ_{12} is significant at 5% before clustering the standard errors at community level but becomes insignificant once the clustering has been taken into account. So, the relative low precision of the estimate of λ_{12} is largely due to the clustering correction. The fact that there are only 314 cases of girls from households headed by a migrant also contributes to the estimation of a relatively large standard error for λ_{12}. Similarly to the males, the bivariate model suggests that girls from households headed by a migrant are 13.5 p.p. less likely to graduate from high school than girls from households headed by a non-migrant. The effect is economically important. No true state dependence in the prepa equation with respect to prepa_{j0} is detected. Estimates for σ_e and σ_m are both significantly different from zero at 1%. So, there are unobservables at the family level present in both migration and education equations. Parameters ρ_u and ρ_v are both negative but only ρ_v is significantly different from zero. Hence, as in the case of males, there is evidence of negative migrant selection in unobservables at the individual level. However, ρ is zero at all conventional levels of significance. So, the random effects at family level entering migration and education equations are not correlated.

Regarding the migration equation true state dependence with respect to prepa_{j0} is detected but usmigra_{j0} is found to have an insignificant effect in the usmigra equation. Hence, no true migration network effect in the case of girls. This is an interesting gender effect that deserves further study. The marginal effect of prepa_{j0} is negative and implies that girls from households headed by a high school graduates are 3 p.p. less likely to migrate than girls from households headed by a non high school graduate. Notice that the negative effect of prepa_{j0} on the likelihood of migration is much lower for the case of girls than for the case of boys. This is, again, an interesting gender result that deserves further investigation.

Table 7 shows all exclusion Wald test that are relevant to qualify the results from the bivariate dynamic random effects model fitted to the females sample. Heads age cohort dummies are found to be highly significant in the initial condition equations of usmigra and marginally significant for the case of prepa (row 1). Similarly, cohort dummies for the girls in the sample are highly significant in the dynamic equation. Exclusion restriction tests of the instruments for migration in the initial conditions equation of usmigra fail to reject the null at 5% (row 2). However, the instruments for migration are highly significant in the dynamic equation for usmigra (row 4). The null of $\lambda_{12} = \lambda_{21} = 0$ is easily rejected at 1%, which gives confidence of the relevance of the bivariate dynamic model. Finally,

Table 7. Wald Exclusion Restrictions Tests (Females).

	Univariable Model						Bivariate Model					
	prepa			usmigra			prepa			usmigra		
	χ^2	DF	*p*-val	χ^2	DF	*p*-val	χ^2	DF	*p*-val	χ^2	DF	*p*-val
(1)	6.00*	2	0.050	11.41*	2	0.000	4.77	2	0.092	10.79*	2	0.005
(2)	57.91*	5	0.000	91.44*	5	0.000	90.86*	5	0.000	103.27*	5	0.000
(3)				3.61*	3	0.164				3.27	3	0.195
(4)				10.72	2	0.005				11.05*	2	0.004
(5)										9.86*	2	0.007
(6)										473.90*	3	0.000

Note: *(**) Significant at 1% (5%). Eicker–Huber–White community clustered robust standard errors (sandwich) used to perform the tests. Null hypothesis in each row are as follows: (1) HC5160 = HC61p = 0 initial conditions; (2) C2125 = C2630 = C3135 = C3640 = C41p = 0 dynamic equation; (3) raildis = urate = 0 initial conditions; (4) raildis = urate = 0 dynamic equation; (5) $\lambda_{12} = \lambda_{21} = 0$; (6) $\rho_u = \rho_v = \rho = 0$.

the hypothesis of $\rho_u = \rho_v = \rho = 0$ is easily rejected at all conventional significance levels. So, the bivariate dynamic model is substantive and adds over and above the evidence that two separate univariate dynamic models deliver. Further, details about estimates for the initial conditions for the sample of females are reported in Table A2.

Simplified Dynamic Model

One of the main drawbacks of the model in the third section and the analysis in section "Main Results" is the fact that the researcher does not observe the date in which children left school and, therefore, cannot build an exact ordering of siblings within a family according to the date they stop attending school. Because of this, an ordering based exclusively on age was argued to be a relatively good approximation of the true migration and high school graduation ordering of all siblings within the families under study. On the basis of this assumption a rich dynamic BDPM for clustered data was used for the analysis, allowing to set apart the effect that a migrant family head, an immediately elder migrant sibling, and the stock of migrant family members have on the education decisions of younger children. This approach has the drawback of introducing a potential problem of inverse causality as there is no way of ensuring that younger siblings do not precede older siblings in their migration and education decisions. This subsection, as a robustness check, presents briefly results from a model that simplifies the dynamics in the model and avoids the potential inverse causality problem. In particular, the dynamics in Eqs. (1) and (2) are simplified to:

$$\begin{aligned} E^*_{ji} &= \boldsymbol{x}^e_{ji}\boldsymbol{\beta}^e + \delta_{11}E_{j,0} + \delta_{12}M_{j,0} + f^e_j + u^e_{ji}, \\ M^*_{ji} &= \boldsymbol{x}^m_{ji}\boldsymbol{\beta}^m + \delta_{21}E_{j,0} + \delta_{22}M_{j,0} + f^m_j + u^m_{ji} \end{aligned} \tag{6}$$

with equations for the initial conditions remaining as in Eqs. (3) and (4) and all other aspects of the model the same. The new specification eliminates the dependence of the migration and education outcomes of the i-th individual upon the outcomes of the ($i-1$)-th individual and the stock of migrants and graduates up to the i-th migrant, MS_{ji} and ES_{ji}. Once these variables are eliminated from the model the ordering of siblings with respect to migration and education within the family is unnecessary as all sons/daughters are *interchangable* observations within a given panel/cluster/family from a statistical point of view and can be treated in the same manner from an econometric point of view – that is, the order observations contributed by the sons and daughters of the family head does not matter anymore. Notice, however, that the *first observation is not interchangeable* as it still represents the migration and education outcomes of the family head and still is supposed to come, always, as the first entry of the panel/cluster. In other words, a panel is always composed by two different types of observations: (A) interchangeable observations and (B) non-interchangeable observations. Type B are observations contributed by the family head and always come as the first observation of the panel. Type A are observations contributed by sons/daughters of the family head and, as long as they never take the first entry of the panel/cluster, its position in the panel/cluster is interchangeable and inconsequential. Introducing this hierarchy of the observations within a panel/cluster and simplifying the dynamic specification allows the researcher to avoid all potential problems of reverse causality.

Notice that the model is still dynamic in the sense that migration and education outcomes of the family head $M_{j,0}$ and $E_{j,0}$ are still explanatory variables of the migration and education outcomes of his/her children. And, more importantly, migration and education outcomes of the family head $M_{j,0}$ and $E_{j,0}$ are still thought to be determined in advance to the time when children take their own migration and education decisions $M_{j,i}$ and $E_{j,i}$, for $i>0$. As a consequence, the actions taken by parents are theoretically thought to have, still, a true causal effect on the decision making of children. Moreover, as before, parents and children belong to the same family and

Table 8. Random Effects Dynamic Probit – Marginal Effects (Females).

	Univariate Model				Bivariate Model			
	prepa		usmigra		prepa		usmigra	
Variable	ME	CRSE	ME	CRSE	ME[a]	CRSE	ME[a]	CRSE
$usmigra_0$	−0.039*	0.014	0.046	0.075	−0.135*	0.051	0.050	0.065
$prepa_0$	−0.019	0.160	0.006	0.012	−0.015	0.174	−0.027**	0.013
$usmigra_{i-1}$	−0.002	0.011	0.008	0.008	−0.001	0.011	0.008	0.007
$prepa_{i-1}$	0.042**	0.017	−0.015*	0.006	0.041*	0.017	−0.011	0.006
MS_i	0.032*	0.010	0.000	0.004	0.039*	0.014	−0.002	0.004
ES_i	−0.007	0.009	0.005	0.003	−0.009	0.009	0.006	0.003
C2125	0.030	0.014	0.050*	0.013	0.028	0.020	0.048*	0.013
C2630	0.022	0.160	0.094*	0.023	0.020	0.023	0.089*	0.022
C3135	0.006	0.011	0.122*	0.026	0.004	0.023	0.117*	0.026
C3640	−0.024	0.017	0.129*	0.030	−0.026	0.017	0.125*	0.029
C41p	−0.089*	0.010	0.067*	0.018	−0.089*	0.021	0.064*	0.017
hsex	−0.041*	0.012	0.014	0.014	−0.064*	0.019	0.013	0.012
hnchild	−0.031*	0.005	0.001	0.001	−0.029*	0.005	0.000	0.001
raildis			−0.044	0.023			−0.041	0.022
urate			−0.006**	0.003			−0.006**	0.003

urban	0.140*	0.038	−0.006	0.003	0.138*	0.038	−0.006	0.003
Birth place	Yes		Yes		Yes		Yes	
Survey year	Yes		Yes		Yes		Yes	
Auxiliary parameters	Coeff.	CRSE	Coeff.	CRSE			Coeff.	CRSE
λ_{11}	0.473	0.330					0.462	0.373
λ_{12}							0.420	0.269
λ_{21}							0.202	0.146
λ_{22}			0.048	0.372			0.047	0.303
σ_e	1.666*	0.159					1.727*	0.172
σ_m			0.973*	0.080			1.001*	0.082
ρ_u							−0.022	0.063
ρ_v							−0.447**	0.226
ρ							−0.057	0.091
Model information								
No. of obs.	12,430		12,430				12,430	
No. of families	5,028		5,028				5,028	
No. of Halton draws	400		400				400	
Log-likelihood	−6,699		−6,066				−12,752	

Note: *(**) Significant at 1% (5%). Eicker–Huber–White community clustered robust standard errors (sandwich) are reported.
[a]Marginal effects on marginal probabilities. For dummy variables, they show the change in the relevant probability when the variable changes from 0 to 1.

share common traits. Hence, if simple OLS or probit, random effect probits, models are used to fit Eq. (6) inconsistent estimators are obtained due to the correlation of $M_{j,0}$ and $E_{j,0}$ with the residuals through f_j^e and f_j^e. In other words, $M_{j,0}$ and $E_{j,0}$ are still endogenous variables in Eq. (6) if the *initial conditions* are not explicitly modeled. In conclusion, even though $M_{j,i-1}$, $E_{j,i-1}$, MS_{ji}, and ES_{ji} have been eliminated from the set of control variables, the model is still pretty much *dynamic*.

Tables B1 and B2 report results from these simplified models for males and females, respectively. Tables B5 and B6 give further details on the initial conditions equations. Finally, Tables B3 and B4 report all the relevant Wald exclusion tests for the significance of the instruments in the model and the relevance of the bivariate dynamic probit over and above what univariate dynamic models would deliver.

Results from the simplified model are quite similar to those obtained from the model reported in section "Main Results", which allows for more complex dynamics. For the sake of brevity here just the main findings are highlighted. In the case of boys, notice that the marginal effect of usmigra_{j0} is still negative and significantly different from zero in the prepa equation. The marginal effect of usmigra_{j0} on prepa is estimated to be -16.3 p.p., which is quite similar to the -17.5 by the model with more complex dynamics in Table 5. In the case of females, the marginal effect of usmigra_{j0} on prepa is reported to be -10.7 p.p. in the simplified model (see Table B2) and -13.5 in the model with more complex dynamics in Table 8. In both cases the marginal effect is statistically significant at 1%. Hence, even in the simplified model there is strong evidence that children from households with a migrant head are less likely to complete high school than children from households headed by a non-migrant.

As before, the bivariate dynamic probit model for clustered data adds over and above the information offered by the univariate models. In particular, the finding that the marginal effect of usmigra_{j0} on prepa is wrongly estimated to be zero by the univariate dynamic model is still found, for both males and females. That is, the researcher would be led to wrong inference if a univariate dynamic model was mistakenly used for the analysis. The relevance of the bivariate dynamic model is further highlighted by the fact that a Wald test for $\lambda_{12}=\lambda_{21}=0$ is easily rejected with a $\chi^2(2)=23.39$ (p-val $=0.000$) for males and a $\chi^2(2)=9.92$ (p-val $=0.000$) for females (see Tables B3 and B4). Moreover, for both males and females, the null of $\rho_u=\rho_v=\rho=0$ is easily rejected at 1% of significance. Hence, the bivariate dynamic model is substantial.

CONCLUSIONS

This chapter enquires whether family migration experience affects the probability of high school graduation of children once unobserved heterogeneity is properly accounted for. The chapter intends to give an initial answer to the following questions: Are children from households headed by a parent with México-USA migration experience less or more likely to graduate from high school? Conditional on the migration and education status of the family head, does migration and education outcomes of an immediately elder sibling affect the migration and education decisions of a younger child? Conditional on the migration and education status of the family head and immediately elder sibling, do total number of migrants and high school graduates in the family affect the migration and education decisions of a child?

Bivariate dynamic random effects probit models for cluster data are estimated to control for the potential endogeneity of education and migration outcomes of the elder members of a family in a regression for the education and migration of the younger children. Correlation of unobservables across migration and education decisions as well as within groups of individuals such as the family are explicitly modeled.

Findings indicate that boys from households headed by a migrant are 17 p.p. less likely to graduate from high school than boys from household headed by a non-migrant. Similarly, girls from households headed by a migrant are 13.5 p.p. less likely to graduate from high school than girls from households headed by a non-migrant. Individual unobserved heterogeneity that affects migration decisions is found to be negatively correlated with individual unobserved heterogeneity affecting education decisions. This negative correlation is statistically significant. Hence, results support the Borjas (1994) hypothesis that Mexican migrants to the United States are negatively selected in the sense that those with high cognitive skills migrate less.

The study finds strong evidence supporting the existence of migrant network effects in the México-USA flows of labor. In particular, results show that boys from households headed by a migrant are around 30 p.p. more likely to migrate themselves. No migrant network effect is detected in the case of girls. This is an interesting gender effect that deserves further study.

The findings in the present chapter have some relevant policy implications. In the past, and probably still today, the policy view of the Mexican authorities regarding the México-USA migration phenomena has been that the movement of labor from south to north brings a series of benefits, and no real costs, to México. The most obvious benefit of migration is serving as a valve that allows the release of a large proportion of the labor excess supply that the country has accumulated over decades of poor economic performance and fast demographic expansion. During the 2000s, the steep increase in remittances from Mexican expatriates in the United States to their families in México generated enthusiasm about emigration having a second, almost unexpected, positive effect in the accumulation of physical and human capital in México. In this context policy passivity, muted encouragement, and a timid intend to protect the human rights of undocumented Mexicans migrants have been, up to now, the pillars of the Mexican migration policy. The present study delivers a message of caution as it shows evidence that emigration to the United States may actually been reducing, rather than increasing, the accumulation of human capital in México. From this point of view it seems that the emigration of Mexicans to the United States has a costly and unexpected aspect that the Mexican authorities have yet to take into account in the future.

NOTES

1. México is by far the main origin country in Latin America. In fact, during the period 2000–2005 alone, México sent nearly 2 million of emigrants to the United States (UNPD, 2006).

2. Banco de México (2006) estimates that in 2005 remittances from the United States represented nearly 2.6% of the GDP of México.

3. See section on Data for a more detailed discussion of this point.

4. Under such an assumption acquiring education at the origin country is an efficient way to improve the odds of finding a highly paid job at the destination country (for more on this argument, see Vidal, 1998). This route will be particularly attractive if prospective migrants have no access to education at the destination country.

5. One would need longitudinal data that follows parents and their children from the onset of the youngsters' lives. Children and parents should be followed wherever they go, independently of the household splitting due to migration and/or divorce. Information about children during their schooling years should be carefully collected independently of where they are and who is caring for them. Over the years the survey should follow parents and children and see a good proportion of parents, and then children themselves, becoming migrants.

6. For instance, if (1) IQ is an unobserved characteristic, (2) education is positively correlated with IQ, (3) mother's IQ is correlated with children's IQ, then IQ will enter the residual in an OLS regression of children's education on mother's education. Hence, mother's education will be clearly correlated with the OLS residual term and, necessarily, it will be an endogenous variable.

7. Data files are freely available at http://mmp.opr.princeton.edu/

8. The MMP124 has collected information from all Mexican states.

9. In both cases information is collected for persons who lived in the household up to five years before the date of the survey. Anyone who left the household before that is not considered a member and no information is recorded. This is unfortunate because, most likely, many migrants do not comply with such requirements.

10. Information for household head and his/her children are used only. No data for the head spouse is included in the analysis.

11. The model outlined in the present section should be seen more in the tradition of multilevel modeling, a broadly used methodology in statistics, than in the economics tradition of panel data analysis. Multilevel methods emphasize the need to correctly model data that have a hierarchical (nested or clustered) structure exploiting informative within-cluster variation. Similarly, analysis of panel data intends to correctly model longitudinal data (i.e., data where an individual is observed at least twice) exploiting informative within-individual variation. These two traditions have many points of contact. In fact, if one acknowledges that in longitudinal data measurement occasions (level 1) are clustered within individuals (level 2), it is clear that most panel methods used in econometrics are multilevel models with a random intercept. From this point of view, multilevel modelling is a more general approach. For an excellent review on multilevel modelling see, for example, Goldstein (2003) and McCulloch and Searle (2001).

12. For all heads $\mathrm{MS}_{j0}=0$ and $\mathrm{ES}_{j0}=0$. If $M_{j0}=1$ $(E_{j0}=1)$ then $\mathrm{MS}_{j1}=1$ $(\mathrm{ES}_{j1}=1)$ and 0 otherwise. In this fashion, MS_{ji} (ES_{ji}) is increased by one unit every time the $(i-1)$-th individual in the j-th family is observed to migrate (graduated from high school). Hence, MS_{ji} and ES_{ji} are the running cumulative sums of the dependent variables M_{ji} and E_{ji} for $i>0$.

13. See footnote 6.

14. Woodruff and Zenteno calculate raildis as the distance from the capital city of each state to a stop on any of the main north/south rail lines as they existed in the early 1900s. Where the line passed through the state, as is the case in 16 states, a distance of 0 was assigned. For border states not served by the rail line and for Baja California Sur, raildis is the distance from the capital city to the border. I thank the authors for providing me with these data.

15. I would like to thank one of the anonymous referees for pointing me out this result.

ACKNOWLEDGMENT

I am grateful to Christopher Woodruff for kindly providing data on historical migration and state distance to the nearest station on the north/south rail lines in México in the early 1900s. I am also grateful to Gauthier Lanot, Wiji Arulampalam, Mark Stewart, Massimiliano Bratti, Leslie Rosenthal, Amanda Gosling, João Santos Silva, and two anonymous referees for useful comments and suggestions.

REFERENCES

Alessie, R., Hochguertel, S., & Van Soest, A. (2004). Ownership of stocks and mutual funds: A panel data analysis. *The Review of Economics and Statistics*, *86*, 783–796.

Arulampalam, W., Booth, A., & Taylor, M. (2000). Unemployment persistence. *Oxford Economics Papers*, *52*, 24–50.

Banco de México. (2006). *Informe anual 2005*. Document available at http://www.banxico.org.mx/publicaciones-y-discursos/publicaciones/informes-periodicos/anual/index.html

Borjas, G. (1994). The economics of immigration. *Journal of Economic Literature*, *32*(4), 1667–1717.

Cerrutti, M., & Massey, D. (2001). On the auspices of female migration from Mexico to the United States. *Demography*, *38*(2), 187–200.

CONAPO. (2000). Migración México-EU presente y futuro. CONAPO. Retrieved from http://www.conapo.gob.mx/

Delechat, C. (2001). International migration dynamics: The role of experience and social networks. *Labour*, *15*(3), 457–486.

DHS Office of Immigration Statistics. (2009). Apprehensions by the U.S. Border Patrol: 2005–2008. Facts Sheet.

Durand, J., Kandel, W., Parrado, E., & Massey, D. (1996). International migration and development in Mexican communities. *Demography*, *33*(2), 249–264.

Goldstein, H. (2003). *Multilevel statistical models, Kendall's library of statistics* (3rd ed.).

Gourieroux, C., & Monfort, A. (1993). Simulation-based inference: A survey with special reference to panel data models. *Journal of Econometrics*, *59*, 533.

Hanson, G., & Woodruff, C. (2003). *Emigration and educational attainment in Mexico*. Manuscript. University of California at San Diego. Document available at http://irps.ucsd.edu/assets/022/8772.pdf

Hanson, G. H. (2006). Illegal migration from Mexico to the United States. *Journal of Economic Literature*, *44*(4), 869–924.

Heckman, J. (1981). The incidental parameters problem and the problem of initial conditions in estimating a discrete time-discrete data stochastic process. In: C. Manski & D. McFadden (Eds.), *Structural analysis of discrete data with econometric applications* (pp. 179–195). MIT Press: Cambridge, MA.

Heckman, J. J. (1978). Dummy endogenous variables in a simultaneous equation system. *Econometrica*, *46*(4), 931–959.

Keane, M. P. (1992). A note on identification in the multinomial probit model. *Journal of Business & Economic Statistics*, *10*(2), 193–200.

Massey, D. (2007). When less is more: Border enforcement and undocumented migration. Testimony before the Subcommittee on Immigration, Citizenship, Refugees, Border Security, and International Law Committee on the Judiciary U.S. House of Representatives.

McCulloch, C., & Searle, S. (2001). *Generalized, linear,and mixed models. Wiley series in probability and Statistics*. New York, NY: Wiley.

McKenzie, D., & Rapoport, H. (2006). *Can migration reduce educational attainment? Evidence from Mexico*. World Bank policy research Working Paper no. 3952. Document available at http://www-wds.worldbank.org/servlet/WDSContentServer/WDSP/IB/2006/06/22/000016406_20060622151515/Rendered/PDF/wps3952.pdf

Sana, M., & Massey, D. (2005). Household composition, family migration, and community context: Migrant remittances in four countries. *Social Science Quarterly*, *86*(2), 509–528.

Stewart, M. (2007). The interrelated dynamics of unemployment and low-wage employment. *Journal of Applied Econometrics*, *22*(3), 511–531.

Taibo, P.I., II. (2006). Pancho Villa: Una Biografía Narrativa. Editorial Planeta, México

Train, K. (2003). *Discrete choice methods with simulation*. Cambridge, UK: Cambridge University Press.

UNPD. (2006). *International migration wall chart 2006*. United Nations Population Division. Manufactured in the United States. Document available at http://www.un.org/esa/population/publications/2006Migration_Chart/Migration2006.pdf

Vidal, J. (1998). The effect of emigration on human capital formation. *Journal of Population Economics*, *11*(4), 589–600.

Woodruff, C., & Zenteno, R. (2007). Migration networks and microenterprises in Mexico. *Journal of Development Economics*, *82*(2), 509–528.

World Bank. (2006). Economic implications of remittances and migration. *Global Economic Prospects*.

APPENDIX A: INITIAL CONDITIONS EQUATIONS

Table A1. Initial Conditions Equations (Males).

	Univariate Model				Bivariate Model			
	prepa		usmigra		prepa		usmigra	
Variable	Coeff.	CRSE	Coeff.	CRSE	Coeff.	CRSE	Coeff.	CRSE
HC5160	−0.114	0.066	−0.266*	0.084	−0.163	0.084	−0.286*	0.085
HC61p	−0.352*	0.073	−0.191*	0.064	−0.450*	0.095	−0.237*	0.072
hsex	−0.329*	0.075	−1.053*	0.115	−0.455*	0.107	−1.185*	0.135
hnchild	−0.140*	0.019	0.029*	0.010	−0.186*	0.032	0.036*	0.012
raildis			−0.838	0.469			−1.205	0.644
urate			−0.038	0.033			−0.028	0.039
urban	0.583*	0.123	−0.038	0.033	0.759*	0.171	−0.087	0.114
Birth place	Yes		Yes		Yes		Yes	
Survey year	Yes		Yes		Yes		Yes	

Note: *(**) Significant at 1% (5%). Eicker–Huber–White community clustered robust standard errors (sandwich) are reported.

Table A2. Initial Conditions Equations (Females).

	Univariate Model				Bivariate Model			
	prepa		usmigra		prepa		usmigra	
Variable	Coeff.	CRSE	Coeff.	CRSE	Coeff.	CRSE	Coeff.	CRSE
HC5160	−0.271**	0.132	−0.260*	0.077	−0.263	0.142	−0.275*	0.084
HC61p	−0.457**	0.187	−0.133**	0.059	−0.465**	0.214	−0.163*	0.067
hsex	−0.319*	0.105	−0.973*	0.090	−0.336*	0.125	−1.019*	0.104
hnchild	−0.147*	0.033	0.023*	0.009	−0.153*	0.040	0.026*	0.010
raildis			−0.631	0.389			−0.875	0.566
urate			−0.029	0.029			−0.025	0.032
urban	0.638*	0.183	−0.069	0.098	0.658*	0.243	−0.069	0.104
Birth place	Yes		Yes		Yes		Yes	
Survey year	Yes		Yes		Yes		Yes	

Note: *(**) Significant at 1% (5%). Eicker–Huber–White community clustered robust standard errors (sandwich) are reported.

APPENDIX B: SIMPLIFIED MODEL

Table B1. Random Effects Dynamic Probit – Marginal Effects (Males).

	Univariate Model				Bivariate Model			
	prepa		usmigra		prepa		usmigra	
	ME	CRSE	ME	CRSE	ME[a]	CRSE	ME[a]	CRSE
$prepa_{j0}$	0.247	0.228	−0.088*	0.020	0.158	0.142	−0.174*	0.018
$usmigra_{i0}$	0.009	0.014	0.382**	0.183	−0.163*	0.041	0.333*	0.103
C2125	0.053**	0.023	0.168*	0.029	0.049**	0.022	0.164*	0.028
C2630	0.064*	0.025	0.247*	0.036	0.058**	0.024	0.239*	0.034
C3135	0.076**	0.031	0.276*	0.037	0.070**	0.029	0.265*	0.035
C3640	0.047	0.028	0.226*	0.045	0.041	0.028	0.216*	0.043
C41p	−0.021	0.017	0.176*	0.035	−0.025	0.017	0.169*	0.034
hsex	−0.040**	0.013	0.075**	0.034	−0.083*	0.021	0.056*	0.022
hnchild	−0.029**	0.004	0.011*	0.002	−0.028*	0.004	0.008**	0.002
raildis			−0.166**	0.077			−0.140	0.076
urate			−0.020**	0.010			−0.022**	0.010
urban	0.113*	0.036	−0.093*	0.028	0.115*	0.035	−0.076	0.028
Birth place	Yes		Yes		Yes		Yes	
Survey year	Yes		Yes		Yes		Yes	
Auxiliary parameters	Coeff.	CRSE	Coeff.	CRSE			Coeff.	CRSE
λ_{11}	0.235	0.151					0.351*	0.137
λ_{12}							0.716*	0.198
λ_{21}							0.384*	0.144
λ_{22}			−0.311	0.293			−0.211	0.164
σ_e	1.533*	0.083					1.668*	0.111

Table B1. *(Continued)*

	Univariate Model				Bivariate Model			
	prepa		usmigra		prepa		usmigra	
	ME	CRSE	ME	CRSE	ME[a]	CRSE	ME[a]	CRSE
σ_m			1.068*	0.055			1.089*	0.052
ρ_u							−0.277**	0.041
ρ_v							−0.388	0.219
ρ							−0.122	0.070
Model information								
No. of obs.	12,402		12,402				12,402	
No. of families	5,095		5,095				5,095	
No. of Halton draws	400		400				400	
Log-likelihood	−6,799		−8,403				−15,130	

Note: *(**) Significant at 1% (5%). Eicker–Huber–White community clustered robust standard errors (sandwich) are reported.
[a]Marginal effects on marginal probabilities. For dummy variables, they show the change in the relevant probability when the variable changes from 0 to 1.

Table B2. Random Effects Dynamic Probit – Marginal Effects (Females).

	Univariate Model				Bivariate Model			
	prepa		usmigra		prepa		usmigra	
Variable	ME	CRSE	ME	CRSE	ME[a]	CRSE	ME[a]	CRSE
$prepa_{j0}$	−0.021	0.140	−0.002	0.008	−0.016	0.134	−0.029*	0.009
$usmigra_{i0}$	−0.011	0.013	0.026	0.049	−0.107**	0.046	0.035	0.049
C2125	0.026	0.019	0.047*	0.013	0.025	0.018	0.046*	0.012
C2630	0.015	0.021	0.090*	0.022	0.014	0.021	0.086*	0.021
C3135	−0.003	0.019	0.119*	0.025	−0.004	0.019	0.114*	0.024
C3640	−0.035*	0.013	0.126*	0.028	−0.035*	0.013	0.120*	0.027
C41p	−0.100*	0.020	0.065*	0.016	−0.101*	0.021	0.062*	0.016
hsex	−0.038*	0.012	0.010	0.012	−0.058*	0.018	0.010	0.011
hnchild	−0.028*	0.005	0.001	0.001	−0.027*	0.005	0.001**	0.000
raildis			−0.045**	0.023			−0.043**	0.022
urate			−0.006**	0.003			−0.006**	0.003
urban	0.140*	0.038	−0.012	0.010	0.139*	0.038	−0.009	0.010
Birth place	Yes		Yes		Yes		Yes	
Survey year	Yes		Yes		Yes		Yes	
Auxiliary parameters	Coeff.	CRSE	Coeff.	CRSE			Coeff.	CRSE
λ_{11}	0.466	0.301					0.436	0.280
λ_{12}							0.368**	0.181
λ_{21}							0.170	0.118
λ_{22}			0.168	0.284			0.101	0.253
σ_e	1.789*	0.112					1.825*	0.103
σ_m			1.027*	0.054			1.031*	0.053
ρ_u							−0.104**	0.045
ρ_v							−0.449*	0.171

Table B2. *(Continued)*

Variable	Univariate Model				Bivariate Model			
	prepa		usmigra		prepa		usmigra	
	ME	CRSE	ME	CRSE	ME[a]	CRSE	ME[a]	CRSE
ρ							0.037	0.058
Model information								
No. of obs.	12,430		12,430				12,430	
No. of families	5,028		5,028				5,028	
No. of Halton draws	400		400				400	
Log-likelihood	−6,712		−6,064				−12,764	

Note: *(**) Significant at 1% (5%). Eicker–Huber–White community clustered robust standard errors (sandwich) are reported.
[a]Marginal effects on marginal probabilities. For dummy variables, they show the change in the relevant probability when the variable changes from 0 to 1.

Table B3. Wald Exclusion Restrictions Tests (Males).

	Univariable Model						Bivariate Model					
	prepa			usmigra			prepa			usmigra		
	χ^2	DF	p-val	χ^2	DF	p-val	χ^2	DF	p-val	χ^2	DF	p-val
(1)	24.99*	2	0.000	12.33*	2	0.000	22.83*	2	0.000	15.85*	2	0.000
(2)	39.24*	5	0.000	102.02*	5	0.000	38.59*	5	0.000	105.11*	5	0.000
(3)				6.78**	3	0.079				5.69	3	0.128
(4)				12.59	2	0.000				11.82*	2	0.003
(5)										19.22*	5	0.000
(6)										23.39*	2	0.000
(7)										67.63*	3	0.000

Note: *(**) Significant at 1% (5%). Eicker–Huber–White community clustered robust standard errors (sandwich) used to perform the tests. Null hypothesis in each row are as follows: (1) HC5160 = HC61p = 0 initial conditions; (2) C2125 = C2630 = C3135 = C3640 = C41p = 0 dynamic equation; (3) raildis = raildis × hsex = urate = 0 initial conditions; (4) raildis = urate = 0 dynamic equation; (5) join significance test for raildis, raildis × hsex, and urate in initial conditions and dynamic equations; (6) $\lambda_{12} = \lambda_{21} = 0$; (7) $\rho_u = \rho_v = \rho = 0$.

Table B4. Wald Exclusion Restrictions Tests (Females).

	Univariable Model						Bivariate Model					
	prepa			usmigra			prepa			usmigra		
	χ^2	DF	p-val	χ^2	DF	p-val	χ^2	DF	p-val	χ^2	DF	p-val
(1)	6.74**	2	0.035	12.17*	2	0.000	6.96**	2	0.000	11.09*	2	0.004
(2)	74.29*	5	0.000	84.18*	5	0.000	80.20*	5	0.000	81.75*	5	0.000
(3)				30.96**	3	0.000				9.62**	3	0.022
(4)				12.17*	2	0.000				12.18*	2	0.002
(5)										27.33*	5	0.000
(6)										9.92*	2	0.000
(7)										12.02*	3	0.000

Note: *(**) Significant at 1% (5%). Eicker–Huber–White community clustered robust standard errors (sandwich) used to perform the tests. Null hypothesis in each row are as follows: (1) HC5160 = HC61p = 0 initial conditions; (2) C2125 = C2630 = C3135 = C3640 = C41p = 0 dynamic equation; (3) raildis = raildis × hsex = urate = 0 initial conditions; (4) raildis = urate = 0 dynamic equation; (5) join significance test for raildis, raildis × hsex, and urate in initial conditions and dynamic equations; (6) $\lambda_{12} = \lambda_{21} = 0$; (7) $\rho_u = \rho_v = \rho = 0$.

Table B5. Initial Conditions Equations (Males).

	Univariate Model				Bivariate Model			
	prepa		usmigra		prepa		usmigra	
Variable	Coeff.	CRSE	Coeff.	CRSE	Coeff.	CRSE	Coeff.	CRSE
HC5160	−0.114	0.066	−0.261*	0.081	−0.156	0.080	−0.285*	0.083
HC61p	−0.351*	0.070	−0.192*	0.067	−0.424*	0.089	−0.247**	0.073
hsex	−0.326*	0.073	−1.088*	0.116	−0.436*	0.104	−1.236*	0.143
hnchild	−0.137*	0.018	0.027*	0.010	−0.178*	0.030	0.035**	0.012
raildis			−1.734*	0.720			−2.185**	0.963
raildis × hsex			0.807*	0.431			0.897	0.552
urate			−0.037	0.032			−0.029	0.043
urban	0.576*	0.117	−0.076	0.097	0.733*	0.166	−0.086	0.115
Birth place	Yes		Yes		Yes		Yes	
Survey year	Yes		Yes		Yes		Yes	

Note: *(**) Significant at 1% (5%). Eicker–Huber–White community clustered robust standard errors (sandwich) are reported.

Table B6. Initial Conditions Equations (Females).

	Univariate Model				Bivariate Model			
	prepa		usmigra		prepa		usmigra	
Variable	Coeff.	CRSE	Coeff.	CRSE	Coeff.	CRSE	Coeff.	CRSE
HC5160	−0.283**	0.134	−0.035*	0.010	−0.270**	0.131	−0.275*	0.083
HC61p	−0.482**	0.192	−0.020**	0.009	−0.481*	0.182	−0.167**	0.067
Hsex	−0.324*	0.106	−0.247*	0.023	−0.333*	0.108	−1.123*	0.102
hnchild	−0.148*	0.030	0.003**	0.001	−0.153*	0.029	0.025**	0.010
raildis			−0.330*	0.117			−2.264*	0.770
raildis × hsex			0.201*	0.070			1.233*	0.475
Urate			−0.005	0.005			−0.025	0.034
urban	0.652*	0.182	−0.011	0.015	0.661*	0.201	−0.070	0.105
Birth place	Yes		Yes		Yes		Yes	
Survey year	Yes		Yes		Yes		Yes	

Note: *(**) Significant at 1% (5%). Eicker–Huber–White community clustered robust standard errors (sandwich) are reported.

CHAPTER 9

IN-WORK TRANSFERS IN GOOD TIMES AND BAD: SIMULATIONS FOR IRELAND

Olivier Bargain and Karina Doorley

ABSTRACT

In-work transfers are often seen as a good trade-off between redistribution and efficiency as they alleviate poverty among low-wage households, while increasing financial incentives to work. In the context of the recent economic downturn, they have been advocated to offset the disincentive effect of wage cuts and to cushion the negative redistributive impact of earnings losses and cuts in the minimum wage. We study this double effect for Ireland, a country deeply affected by the economic crisis, and for which existing in-work support policies are of limited scope. The employment and poverty effects of alternative policies are analysed thanks to counterfactual simulations built using a micro-simulation model, the Living in Ireland Survey 2001 and labour supply estimations. We focus on an extension of the existing scheme, the Family Income Supplement and its replacement by the refundable tax credit in force in the United Kingdom.

Keywords: Working poor; in-work support; labour supply

JEL classifications: C25; C52; H31; J22

Research in Labor Economics, Volume 33, 307–339

ISSN: 0147-9121/doi:10.1108/S0147-9121(2011)0000033012

INTRODUCTION

In-work transfers, also known as 'make work pay' (MWP) policies, have been in force for a relatively long time in three Anglo-Saxon countries: the United States, the United Kingdom and Ireland, with the Earned Income Tax Credit (EITC), the Working Tax Credit (WTC) and the Family Income Supplement (FIS) respectively. These policies consist of redistributing resources to low-wage families with working adults. Their appeal stems mainly from an interesting compromise as they allow redistribution to (working) poor families while increasing financial incentives to work for those living on traditional welfare payments. In the United States, the EITC has been extended and now represents the main redistributive transfer, while traditional social assistance has been considerably reduced with the 1996 reforms. The United Kingdom still cumulates a system of income support and tax credits including the WTC, as Ireland does with a set of specific social transfers and the FIS. In contrast to the vast literature on the United States and the United Kingdom, as reviewed in Blundell and Hoynes (2001), the Irish scheme has received little attention in the literature.[1] A first objective of this study is to evaluate the full potential of this scheme, both for redistribution and work incentives, and to compare its effects with what we know about policy reforms in the United States and the United Kingdom. This allows us to draw more general conclusions about the optimal policy design of in-work transfers, which seems important in a context where the existing schemes are continuously evolving and where interest in them has been renewed in many other countries. While the EITC has been expanded a number of times (Scholz, 1994), the UK tax credit has been extended and reformed several times since 1971.[2] Also, it is noteworthy that several continental European countries have considered or actually introduced similar schemes, both to compensate the strong disincentive effect of traditional social welfare programs and to curb unemployment.[3]

In the present context of an economic downturn, MWP policies may also take on a new role (Immervoll & Pearson, 2009). These policies represent an efficient redistributive tool in a low-unemployment context, such as that experienced before the crisis, as they allow redistribution to low-wage workers without distorting wages (as minimum wages may do). But, MWP schemes can also cushion the negative redistributive impact of earnings losses due to wage cuts during economic crises.[4] A recent article in the *Irish Times* notes that:

> In the run-up to the most swingeing budget of the 21st century, rarely a day passes without someone warning that 'the financially vulnerable' must be protected.[...] The impoverished workers have become the invisible victims of the recession, as they receive

> scant media attention. (Suzanne Kelly, 12 November 2009: 'Budget must not ignore plight of the working poor')

In addition, MWP policies may offset the disincentive effects of wage cuts and decreases in minimum wages. Such disincentives are less obvious than involuntary unemployment in the context of the severe economic downturn experienced by Ireland, but may however cumulate with it to increase the level of non-employment. The aforementioned article reports that firms have 'difficulty engaging employees despite the recession, as the social welfare package was, in some cases, more advantageous than wages'. The Combat Poverty Agency (2008) also notes that 'in the current climate, keeping people in employment is as, if not more, important than getting people out of unemployment'. This chapter thus analyses the cushioning and incentive impacts of MWP policies in a context of earnings losses.

More precisely, we suggest a comprehensive analysis of the labour supply and redistributive effects of the FIS and alternative MWP policies in Ireland, in both the pre-crisis situation and following significant wage cuts. Two main reforms are considered: the extension of the existing FIS (based on more generous payment rates, as introduced in 2008, assuming full take-up) and the hypothetical replacement of the FIS by the British WTC (the UK income support policy extended to childless households). We first analyse the effect of each alternative policy measure on employment and poverty using the tax-benefit micro-simulation model (EUROMOD) linked to the 2001 Living in Ireland Survey (LII) and a discrete choice labour supply model. We are thus able to assess the direct effects of these policies on poverty and inequality when holding market income constant, and to predict behavioural responses to policy changes and their consequences for income distribution. Interestingly, the poverty effect of the reforms is due to a mix of the direct redistributive effect and of the labour supply adjustment induced by the reforms. Secondly, we consider the relative performance of each policy in a macro-economic environment affected by cuts in earnings and in the minimum wage. In this way, we can examine how MWP policies can cushion income losses in the case of an economic downturn and alleviate possible disincentives due to lower gains to work in a recessionary scenario.

In what follows we position the chapter in the literature and outline the limits of our analysis. First of all, an interesting contribution we make is the comparison of the Irish FIS with other major MWP policies in place in the United States and the United Kingdom. Compared to the EITC and the WTC, which consist of refundable tax credits paid through the pay package, the FIS is a transfer paid by benefit agencies. This explains, in part, its relatively low take-up rate and, hence, its limited redistributive effect. Our simulations assume full take-up to evaluate the full potential of this policy, yet we also analyse the sensitivity of redistributive effects to various assumptions on the take-up level. Secondly, as in the United States and the United Kingdom, the FIS is targeted essentially at families with children. In this way, we focus particularly on the specific policy objective of reducing child poverty and we evaluate how the FIS and the WTC perform in this respect. Thirdly, our main analysis is based on counterfactual policy simulations and a structural model of labour supply is thus required. Past research has mixed quasi-experimental methods (e.g. Eissa & Hoynes, 2004; Eissa & Liebman, 1996) with more structural approaches (Dickert, Houser, & Scholz, 1995; Meyer & Rosenbaum, 2001) to analyse the effect of the EITC on incentives and redistribution.[5] Further research for Ireland should follow the same path and validate predictions stemming from structural models against natural experiments using changes in the policy parameters, and possibly the panel dimension in the LII survey. Fourthly, this study suggests one of the first simulations of how alternative tax-benefit systems perform at reducing poverty/inequality in a recessionary context (see also Feres et al., 2002, on the sensitivity of social inclusion indicators to an increase in unemployment and an increase in earnings inequality). A common, but serious limitation of our analysis is that we suggest a pure supply-side exercise. Reassuringly, labour supply estimations are based on pre-crisis data, and are thus much less affected by demand-side constraints. Yet, simulations of policy effects necessarily reflect an upper bound of the response that could be expected given the potential difficulties for workers to adjust their working time in a rationed labour market. Despite the importance of involuntary unemployment in the current recession, it is beyond the scope of this chapter to analyse the effect of these policies in a more complete partial or general equilibrium setting. In fact, the analysis of tax-benefit policies is most often confined to a supply-side analysis and rarely conducted in CGE frameworks (among exceptions, see Bovenberg, Graafland, & de Mooij, 2000 or Ballard, Shoven, & Whalley, 1985) or a partial equilibrium framework where wage variations are modelled by interacting labour demand and supply iteratively (see the recent attempt of Peichl & Siegloch, 2010).[6] Finally, MWP policies may also allow temporary flexibility on the labour market in a context of constrained labour demand. Indeed, recent public policies have suggested work sharing as a margin of adjustment for firms and the use of state transfers to secure incomes of workers forced into (or opting for) partial unemployment. MWP policies appear more useful than traditional unemployment benefits in this context as they are not based on employment history, and thus are available to anyone who passes the means test. Future studies could consider simulating unemployment shocks realistically. This may require sophisticated models of both labour demand and supply, as mentioned above, in order to provide a better assessment of a policy mix aimed at reducing unemployment levels (see the discussions in Bargain, Orsini, & Peichl, 2011; Immervoll & Pearson, 2009).

The remainder of this chapter is structured as follows. The second section discusses in-work poverty in Ireland and the third section presents the data and the empirical approach. The fourth section describes the policy reforms in detail and analyses their employment and poverty-alleviating effects. The fifth section presents the results and robustness checks. The sixth section concludes.

OUT-OF-WORK AND IN-WORK POVERTY IN IRELAND

We believe it is important to motivate our analysis by first describing the phenomenon of in-work poverty in Ireland (see also Rocks, 2008). For ease of exposition, we refer equivalently to the 'poor' or those 'at risk of poverty', defined as having an equivalised disposable income below 60% of the median. The working poor are households at risk of poverty with at least one adult member in work. We rely here on the Household Budget Survey (HBS) which allows more consistent comparisons over time than the LII.[7]

Using the 2004 HBS, simple calculations show that among all those at risk of poverty, 22% are pensioners, 51% are workless and 27% are working. In Table 1, we focus on working-age households (18–59) using two waves of the HBS. We observe that the proportion at risk of poverty is around 18% for both years of data (1999 and 2004), with a substantial share of households in work (43% in 1999 and 31% in 2004).[8] The proportion of working poor is particularly large among couples (56% of poor couples in 1999 and 44% in 2004) and is mainly composed of one-earner households. The overall decreasing trend seems to be essentially driven by this subgroup. Many factors may explain this observation. In particular, the relative proportion of two-earner couples has increased overall, at the expense of one-earner couples (not shown).[9] This is mainly due to the sharp increase in female-labour supply in the 1990s, starting from a situation of very low-female participation (see Callan, van Soest, & Walsh, 2009).

In this context, large-scale transfers to the working poor would target roughly one-third of the overall poor among working-age households. If they induce increased participation in the labour market, there is a potentially larger effect as

Table 1. Working-Age Households at Risk of Poverty: In and Out of Work.

Household type		HBS1999		HBS2004	
		Poverty (%)	In/out of work (%)	Poverty (%)	In/out of work (%)
All	All	18.5		17.6	
	In work	7.9	43	5.5	31
	Out of work	10.5	57	12.1	69
Singles	In work	0.9	21	1.0	16
	Out of work	2.3	75	2.3	74
Couples	Two-earner	0.5	56	0.6	44
	One-earner	5.8		3.1	
	No-earner		4.9		4.8

Note: At risk of poverty (i.e., equivalised disposable income below 60% median) among working-age households. Example: single parents represented 0.8 + 2.3 = 3.1 points among the 18.5% of working-age households at risk of poverty in 1999, and 75% of them were out of work.

Table 2. Working-Age Workless Poor: Breakdown.

Household type		HBS1999		HBS2004	
		Poverty (%)	Breakdown (%)	Poverty (%)	Breakdown (%)
Singles	Job seeker	0.8	25	0.8	17
	Inactive	0.9	27	0.8	16
	Not available	1.6	48	3.4	68
Single parents	Job seeker	0.2	10	0.1	5
	Inactive	1.7	74	1.9	82
	Not available	0.4	17	0.3	13
Men in couple	Job seeker	2.3	40	1.3	24
	Inactive	0.2	3	0.3	6
	Not available	3.4	57	3.7	69
Women in couple	Job seeker	0.3	4	0.3	4
	Inactive	8.4	86	5.9	81
	Not available	1.0	10	1.1	15

the workless poor may become working poor or escape poverty by cumulating earnings and in-work benefits. Table 2 gives an indication of where the margin for increased labour supply was in 1999 and 2004. Among those out of work, we show the proportion of job seekers and the proportion of inactive persons, which was 25% and 27% respectively among singles in 1999. The residual category

(48% for this example) is composed of all those unavailable for work, including students, disabled workers or those receiving a pension. A fraction of the job seekers may be seen as involuntary unemployed (classic or frictional unemployment). The reserve of labour supply is then to be found in the group of *inactive* persons, that is those who are not actively looking for a job. This is represented mainly by spouses and single mothers engaged in home duties and childcare, groups which are more likely to be affected by supply-side (dis)incentives because of low-wage prospects or high costs of work. The group of single mothers is also important due to its higher risk of poverty (Cooke & Lawton, 2008). Improving income support and work incentives for this group is therefore important.

EMPIRICAL APPROACH

In this section, we describe the data, the econometric method and the tax-benefit calculator used to simulate policy reforms and their labour supply responses.

Data, Sample Selection and Choice Set

The data are drawn from the *LII* for the year 2001. This is a representative sample containing information on household demographics, employment and income, among other things. The original sample consists of just over 11,400 individuals in 3,463 households. The reforms are simulated on the complete representative sample. Labour supply behaviour is estimated on sub-groups of couples, single men and single women (possibly with children). We select households where adults are aged between 18 and 59 and available for the labour market, that is neither disabled nor retired nor in education. The self-employed and farmers are excluded as their labour supply decisions are probably very different from those of salary workers. To further increase data homogeneity, 'extreme' households are selected out, that is very large households, those where children also work, and those who receive important levels of capital income. Descriptive statistics of the selected samples are presented in Table 3 while the distributions of actual worked hours for males and females in all three samples are depicted in Fig. 1. The pattern of hours shows strong concentrations around full-time and small concentrations around part-time activity (especially for women). In this context, a discrete choice model may offer a reasonable approximation of labour supply choices. In our baseline, we make use of a simple

Table 3. Descriptive Statistics.

	Single Men	Single Women	Men in Couple	Women in Couple
Age	38.6	37.1	40.8	38.9
Upper secondary education (%)	0.27	0.31	0.30	0.38
University education (%)	0.21	0.26	0.25	0.26
Wage rate[a]	10.5	10.0	14.9	11.3
Worked hours (including zeros)	28.6	24.2	37.7	19.1
Participation rate (%)	0.75	0.76	0.93	0.62
No. of children	0.10	0.79	1.87	
Presence of children 0–2 (%)	0.01	0.10	0.23	
Living in Dublin (%)	0.26	0.33	0.31	
No. of observations	183	168	775	

[a]Wages are in Euro/hour, calculated using earnings and worked hours for workers and predicted for non-workers. Labour supply statistics are before discretisation.

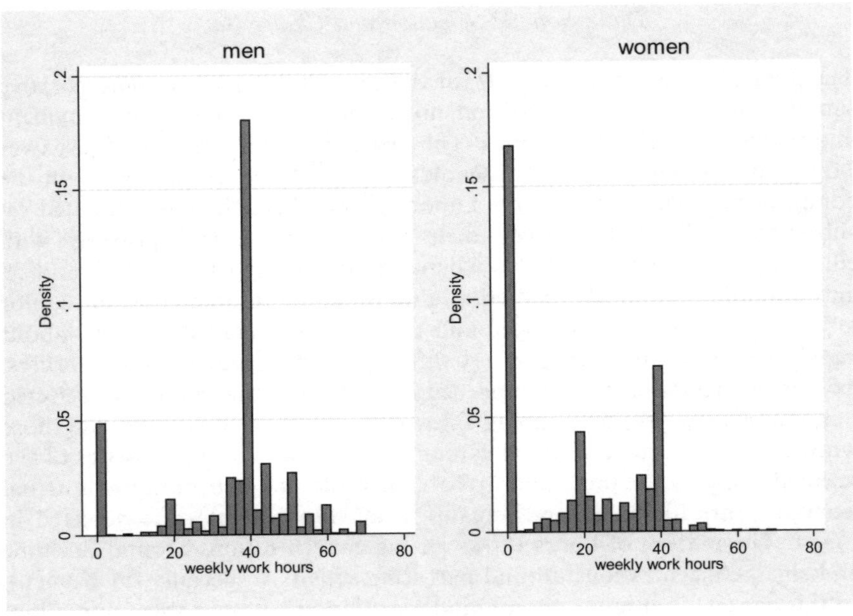

Fig. 1. Distribution of Working Time.

discretisation with $J=4$, with part-time work (20 hours/week), full-time (40), overtime (50) and non-participation (0). Bargain et al. (2011) report robustness checks for several countries, including Ireland, using a narrower discretisation with 7 and 13 choices (i.e. 0–60 hours/week with a step of 10 or 5 hours). They show that labour supply responses measured by hour and participation wage, and income-elasticities are not sensitive to the choice set.

Labour Supply Estimations

Model

We rely on a discrete choice model of labour supply (multinomial logit) estimated by simulated maximum likelihood. This approach has become relatively standard so we simply refer to van Soest (1995) and Blundell, Duncan, McCrae, and Meghir (2000). We specify consumption-leisure preferences using a quadratic utility function, that is the deterministic utility of a couple i at each discrete choice $j=1,\ldots, J$ can be written:

$$U_{ij} = \alpha_{ci}C_{ij} + \alpha_{cc}C_{ij}^2 + \alpha_{h_f i}H_{ij}^f + \alpha_{h_m i}H_{ij}^m + \alpha_{h_{ff}}(H_{ij}^f)^2 + \alpha_{h_{mm}}(H_{ij}^m)^2 + \alpha_{ch_f}C_{ij}H_{ij}^f + \alpha_{ch_m}C_{ij}H_{ij}^m + \alpha_{h_m h_f}H_{ij}^f H_{ij}^m - F_{ij} \quad (1)$$

with household consumption C_{ij} and spouses' worked hours H_{ij}^f and H_{ij}^m. The J choices in a couple correspond to all combinations of the spouses' discrete hours (here, $J=4\times 4$). Coefficients on consumption and worked hours, namely α_{ci}, $\alpha_{h_f i}$ and $\alpha_{h_m i}$, vary linearly with several taste shifters (polynomial form of age, presence of children or dependent persons, region). The term α_{ci} also incorporates unobserved heterogeneity for the model to allow random taste heterogeneity and unrestricted substitution patterns between alternatives. The fit is improved by the introduction of fixed costs of work as in Callan et al. (2009) and Blundell et al. (2000), which capture the fact that there are very few observations with a small positive number of working hours. Fixed costs of work F_{ij} also depend on observed characteristics and are expressed here in utility metric since they may correspond to actual costs (childcare) or psychological costs (leaving one's children with strangers). Note that fixed costs are only parametrically identified. That is, a very flexible utility function could pick up the gap in the distribution at low hours. This weighs in favour of relaxing usual regularity conditions on leisure/labour supply (see Heim & Meyer, 2004). More generally, as we specify utility directly, and not a labour supply function, tangency conditions are not required so we simply check the quasi-concavity of the utility function a posteriori. The only restriction to our model is the imposition of increasing monotonicity in consumption, which seems a minimum requirement for meaningful interpretation and policy analysis. For each labour supply choice j, disposable income (equivalent to disposable income in the present static framework) is calculated as a function:

$$C_{ij} = d(w_i^f H_{ij}^f, w_i^m H_{ij}^m, m_i) \tag{2}$$

of female earnings, male earnings and non-labour income m_i. Function d is approximated by numerical simulation of tax and benefit rules as explained below. Male- and female-wage rates w_i^f and w_i^m, for each household i, are calculated using observed earnings and work hours for workers, and Heckman-corrected predictions for non-workers. Because the model is non-linear, the wage rate prediction errors can be taken explicitly into account for a consistent estimation. The deterministic utility is completed by i.i.d. error terms ε_{ij} for each choice assumed to represent possible observational errors, optimisation errors or transitory situations. Under the assumption that error terms follow an extreme value type I (EV-I) distribution, the (conditional) probability for each household of choosing a given alternative has an explicit logistic form, which is a function of deterministic utilities at all choices. The unconditional probability is obtained by integrating out the disturbance terms (unobserved heterogeneity and the wage error term) in the likelihood function. In practise, this is done by averaging the conditional probability over a large number of draws, and the simulated likelihood function can be maximised to obtain all estimated parameters. The model for single individuals (with or without children) is the same as above with only one hour term and $J=4$.

Identification

It is instructive to discuss the source of variation in individual tax rates. Unobserved characteristics (e.g. being hard-working at school and, subsequently, in the labour market) may affect both wages and labour supply choices so that estimates of the wage effect in labour supply equations are biased. Ideally, exogenous variations in net wages due to tax policy changes, for instance by using several years of a panel, could be used to avoid this bias. Here, we must assume that identification is obtained thanks to non-linearities and possible discontinuities in budget constraints, due to tax-benefit policies. That is, workers with the same gross wage rate but different characteristics (family size, composition, non-labour income etc.) will face different implicit tax rates and, hence, different net wages. For a more complete discussion, please see Eissa and Hoynes (2004).

Tax-Benefit Simulations

The function d is approximated by numerical simulation of tax-benefit rules using the micro-simulation model EUROMOD. This calculator allows the computation of all social contributions, direct taxes and transfers to yield household disposable income (see Bargain, 2006). It is also used to simulate the actual and hypothetical reforms analysed in this chapter. EUROMOD is an integrated tax-benefit calculator covering the systems of EU-15 countries. We use the simulation of the 2001 Irish system combined with the LII data for the same year. The Irish module within EUROMOD exactly replicates the simulation of the Irish national model SWITCH for that year. We have also programmed the alternative functions d incorporating the different reforms and, for each of them, have simulated labour supply responses using a calibration method consistent with the probabilistic nature of the model at the individual level. It consists of drawing a set (200 draws) of $J+1$ random terms from an *EV-I* distribution for each household, which generates a perfect match between predicted and observed choices. The same draws are kept when predicting labour supply responses to a change in function d due to a reform. Averaging individual labour supply responses over a large number of draws provides robust transition matrices.[10] In the appendix, we discuss the size of the estimated elasticities and the issue of non-take-up when modelling labour supply.

POLICY DESCRIPTIONS AND SIMULATIONS

Income support already exists in Ireland but, as mentioned above, the coverage of the FIS is limited. The FIS was designed to provide cash support to low earners with families, and to thereby preserve the incentive to remain in employment in circumstances where the employee might only be marginally better off than if (s)he were claiming other social welfare payments (see Callan, O'Neill, & O'Donoghue, 1995). Publicly available estimations indicate that around one-third of potential beneficiaries actually applied for the FIS (Combat Poverty, 2008; Stephens, 2005). This very low take-up rate is even more pronounced in available data sets. For instance, in the LII, we find a take-up rate of 17% corresponding to less than 80 observations. Hence, our baseline scenario assumes no in-work support. Starting from this situation, we assess the employment and poverty effect of the FIS in 2001, if this transfer was more widely distributed and claimed (full take-up assumption). We proceed in a similar way with the other (hypothetical) reforms that we describe below.

Family Income Supplement and Extensions

The FIS is a weekly payment for families with at least one dependent child (under age 18 or 22 if in full-time education). Claimants must be working at least 19 hours per week to qualify and in a job that is expected to last at least three months. The self-employed do not qualify. The weekly hours of spouses and partners can be combined to meet this condition, which is not the case for the British WTC. Denote B the income limit, and Y the average weekly family income, which is net of taxes and social contributions and includes most transfers.[11] Then

$$\text{FIS} = max\{0, 60\%(B(n) - Y)\}$$

The income limit $B(n)$ and, therefore, the value of the benefit, vary according to the number of children n (see Table 4). For instance, it is EUR 353 per week in 2001 for a family with two children. Hence, the scheme imposes a 60% implicit marginal tax rate on net income. FIS payment is tax

Table 4. Parameters of the Family Income Supplement.

Family size	2001		2008		
	Income limit	Child increment (%)	Income limit[a]	Real increase (%)	Child increment (%)
1 child	328		474	45	
2 children	353	7.8	552	56	16.3
3 children	378	7.2	634%	68	14.9
4 children	404	6.7	735	82	16.0
5 children	436	7.9	842	93	14.5
Withdrawal rate	60%			60%	

Note: Income limits are weekly and in Euro.
Source: Citizen's Information Board and EUROMOD 2001 policy file.
[a]In 2001 prices.

free and is not counted as income when individuals are considered for a medical card.[12] This helps to reduce disincentives to seek employment.[13]

To simulate a more generous version of the FIS, we use the 2008 parameters adjusted to 2001 in real terms. As can be seen in Table 4, the base payment and the child increments have increased substantially (in real terms) in this seven-year interval. The former increased by roughly 50% while the latter doubled. We introduce this more generous FIS while holding the 2001 population constant. Note that we adjust the 2008 monetary parameters to 2001 using CPI. This reflects the fact that price uprating is traditionally used. Alternative uprating factors could be chosen, notably earnings growth, which is usually a more distributionally neutral backdrop against which policy changes can be evaluated. Note also that the change in FIS over the period is taken independently from other actual changes in the system (other tax-benefit instruments are assumed to change in line with price inflation). In particular, social welfare payments have also increased over time and at a much faster rate than prices, which would undermine some of the incentive effect of actual FIS extensions.

Working Tax Credit

We also simulate a hypothetical implementation of the British WTC. The British tax credit is certainly the most prominent in-work transfer in Europe, and, for this reason, several authors have simulated the welfare and labour supply consequences of the introduction of this system in other countries.[14] We suggest here an adaptation to the Irish context. Denote B the maximum theoretical amount, Y the net income and θ a disregard, then

$$\text{WTC} = B(n) - \max(0; 55\%(Y - \theta))$$

The WTC is for individuals who usually work 16 hours or more a week, are paid for that work and expect to work for at least 4 weeks. To qualify, adults must be either 16 or over and responsible for at least one child; or 16 or over and disabled; or 25 or over and usually work at least 30 hours a week. As we pointed out in the introduction, there is a case to be made for extending MWP benefits to childless individuals. Therefore, we slightly adapt the eligibility condition for this group in our simulations so that adults aged 16 and over are eligible whether they have a child or not. Also, we apply the same hour condition to households with and without children, that is, at least 16 hours per week.

The basic amount B is made up of different elements depending on the particular circumstances of the claimant and his/her family (basic amount plus an element for the presence of a second adult, a lone parent element, a disability element and other elements depending on the working hours). We ignore the subsidy for childcare costs which is part of the WTC scheme in the United Kingdom. The taper rate of 55% on net income corresponds to around 37% on gross income in the United Kingdom. We adjust the monetary parameters of the 2003 reform to Ireland 2001 using Eurostat estimates of PPP differentials. For those without children, the basic amount B is £127 per month in 2003 (or 194, in 2001 in our simulations) after $\theta = £422$ (643 in our simulations), and is increased by another £125 (191) for those with children. A bonus is paid to those working more than 30 hours (£52 in 2003 or 79).

RESULTS

As explained above, the baseline and the reform scenarios are simulated using the 2001 LII and the EUROMOD tax-benefit simulator for that year. The two main policy simulations, as discussed above, are the FIS with 2008 real-term parameters and the 2003 WTC with PPP-adjusted parameters. In both cases, we assume full take-up in order to assess the complete employment and redistributive potential of these reforms. We also simulate the 2001 FIS with full take-up, to be compared to a 2001 baseline situation assuming no income support. Note that the assumption of full take-up is made to compare the full potential of the reforms. We investigate below whether the distributional impacts of the different policies are sensitive to the nature of the households who may take up the transfer among all eligible households. Since labour supply estimates may also change depending on the nature of take-up behaviour, we also present a robustness check in the appendix based on various assumptions (full take-up, no take-up and actual take-up in 2001, with a joint estimation of labour supply and claiming decisions).

Budget Constraints and the Cost of Reforms

We illustrate how the main reforms impact on the budget curves of two representative households: a single-parent household (with a nine-year-old child) and a couple with two children (seven and nine-year-old children). We simulate the disposable income (original income net of all taxes and transfers for that family) obtained at different hours worked. For both family types, we assume wage rates equal to EUR 11.42 per hour in Fig. 2 (the gross hourly earnings of an Average Production Worker (APW) in Ireland in 2001) and EUR 5.96 per hour in Fig. 3 (the minimum wage in Ireland in 2001). We also assume that there is no other source of market income than earnings. The overall shape of the budget constraints is well known. In particular, there is a flat portion for low-work duration, due to the phasing-out of social benefits, leading to very high implicit marginal tax rates in this income range.[15]

For workers paid at the AWP, the graphs show a marked effect of the WTC around part-time work. FIS 2008 shows an even larger effect which continues at higher hours. For households paid at the minimum wage, the effect of the reforms is more significant, as expected. WTC and FIS 2008 substantially increase the gains to working part-time and, to a lesser extent, full-time. Hence, by increasing the gap between out-of-work welfare payments and labour income, the reforms may create incentives to participate in the labour market (Ochel, 2001). On the other hand, they flatten budget constraints or even make them downward sloping (due to the combination of high-taper rates and the withdrawal of means-tested benefits).[16] This should reduce incentives to work longer hours for those in employment or, in the case of couples, decrease participation among secondary earners. This adverse effect seems to be particularly strong with FIS 2008. This feature is common to most in-work support schemes based on household income (Blundell et al., 2000; Eissa & Hoynes, 2004).

In Table 5, we show the cost and the scope of each policy. Both budgetary costs and the number of recipients are much higher than the actual situation

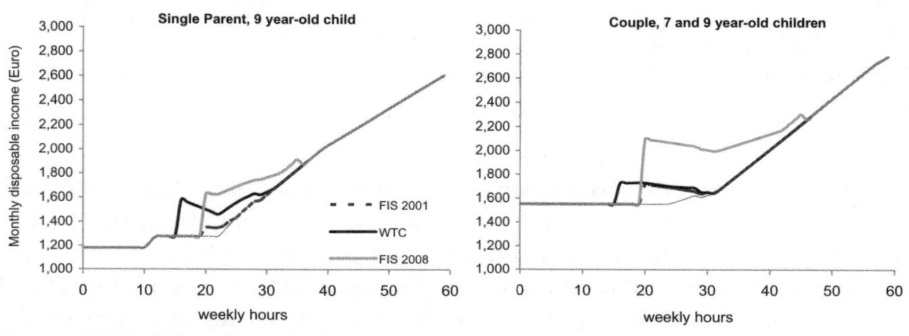

Fig. 2. Budget Constraints with Reforms (AWP).

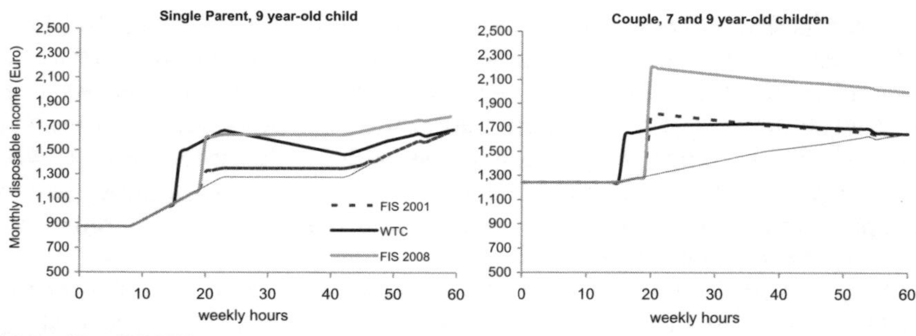

Fig. 3. Budget Constraints with Reforms (Minimum Wage).

Table 5. Cost of the Reforms.

	FIS 2001	FIS 2008	WTC
Cost (million Euro per year)[a]	102	565	256
in % GDP	0.09%	0.48%	0.22%
Cost (million Euro per year)[b]	128	769	330
in % GDP	0.1%	0.7%	0.3%
Flat tax	0.3%	1.8%	0.8%
No. of eligible household[a]	57,124	135,970	147,666
No. of eligible household[b] in proportion	62,812	159,933	164,506
of total population	5%	12%	13%
Average amount (Euro, per month)[a]	148	346	144
Average amount (Euro, per month)[b]	169	401	167

Note: We assume 100% take-up for all reforms. FIS: Family Income Supplement; WTC: 2003.
[a]With constant labour supply.
[b]After labour supply adjustment to the policy change.

in Ireland in 2001, due to the very low take-up rate that affected existing policies. In our simulation, under the full take-up assumption, the cost of the FIS 2001 is around three times the official figure (EUR 37 million), which is consistent with a take-up rate of around 33%. Costs are calculated as the change in total disposable income due to the introduction of the policy, and hence account for possible interactions between the policy and the rest of the system. We report both 'apparent' costs (ignoring labour supply adjustments) and 'real' costs (after the labour supply response).[17] The scope of the WTC is broader than that of the FIS, since it is also available to childless households, but the amount distributed is similar to FIS 2001 on average. Note that we did not attempt to make the reforms of equal cost. FIS and WTC are taken as the actual Irish and British policies, with simple time and PPP adjustments of the relevant parameters. Nonetheless, we have increased VAT in order to make each policy revenue neutral. These VAT changes are reported in Table 5 ('flat tax').

Labour Supply Effects

Table 6 presents the labour supply simulation based on the econometric model described above. We simulate the changes in average worked hours and participation rates for single men, single women and men and women in couples separately. Since positive participation effects may correspond to the take-up of a part-time job, we also express the total change in hours in terms of 'full-time equivalent' (FTE) jobs.

Even under the assumption of full benefit take-up, Table 6 shows that the FIS 2001 has a very small effect on labour supply. The FIS 2008, however, has a strong negative effect on couples, as anticipated above. Withdrawals from the labour market concern secondary earners in particular, with the participation rate of married women decreasing by 1.2 points. The hours reduction in FTE is larger than the participation effect in number of workers, which reflects the fact that there is, in addition to the response at the extensive margin, a significant decrease in work hours. This effect is strong for both women and men in couples. In contrast, the policy has a very strong positive effect on single mothers, a particularly vulnerable population (part of the 'single-women' group in Table 6). While the participation rate in this group increases by around 10 points, the FTE effect is more modest, which implies that most of the extensive response corresponds to part-time activity. Overall, the effect of the FIS 2008 on participation is positive but it is negative when considering total working time. With the WTC, the negative effect at the intensive margin (working hours) seems to dominate among couples. In contrast, a strong positive effect on the participation of single mothers can be observed. Yet the latter corresponds to a move into part-time activity, as anticipated by the budget graphs. Since the WTC is extended to childless households, we also notice a modest participation effect on single men, dominated by a reduction in work duration for those in the phase-out area of the scheme.

Table 6. Labour Supply Effects of the Reforms.

	Baseline	FIS 2001	FIS2 008	WTC
Women in couples				
Participation rate	0.609	0.607	0.597	0.607
Hours	19.6	19.4	18.7	19.4
	(0.46)	(0.47)	(0.44)	(0.47)
Participation change		−383	−3.441	−383
Hour change in FTE		−1,183	−6,775	−1,669
Men in couples				
Participation rate	0.928	0.928	0.925	0.926
Hours	38.7	38.6	37.8	38.5
	(0.50)	(0.54)	(0.49)	(0.54)
Participation change		−62	−964	−737
Hour change in FTE		−1,355	−6,827	−1,848
Single women (including lone mothers)				
Participation rate	0.732	0.748	0.829	0.803
Hours	23.7	23.9	25.7	24.2
	(1.29)	(1.15)	(1.00)	(1.03)
Participation change		1,644	9,619	7,008
Hour change in FTE		678	5,084	1,386
Single men				
Participation rate	0.757	0.757	0.757	0.764
Hours	28.2	28.2	28.2	27.6
	(1.06)	(1.06)	(1.06)	(1.11)
Participation change		0	0	696
Hour change in FTE		0	0	−1,477
Total				
Participation change		1,198	5,214	6,585
Hour change in FTE		−1,859	−8,518	−3,608

Note: We assume 100% take-up. FTE: full-time equivalent (change in number of FTE workers compared to no MWP scenario). FIS: Family Income Supplement; WTC: 2003 British Working Tax Credit. Bootstrapped standard errors for work hours are in brackets (and available from the authors for other statistics).

These results are in line with the findings of Blundell et al. (2000) for the United Kingdom, who find a mixed effect of the extension of the FC in 1999 (the WFTC reform) on employment. This was due to the combination of an increased labour market participation of lone parents, and to a lesser extent of men, partially offset by a reduction in the hours worked and a very significant drop in the participation of female secondary earners. An interesting exercise, close to that suggested here, is proposed by Brewer, Duncan, Shephard, and Suarez (2006). Using a structural model, the authors simulate the effect of completely removing the WFTC from the British system (in 2002). They find that, without any form of in-work benefit in the United Kingdom, the labour force participation of lone mothers would decrease by 11 ppt. This is of the order of magnitude of what we find for the FIS 2008 and the WTC compared to a situation with no MWP policy. Most ex post evaluations confirm this strong positive effect for single mothers. One exception is Leigh (2004) who finds a small positive effect, possibly due to a fixed effect analysis over a relatively short time period (the treatment effects of the WFTC and related reforms are identified from changes in individuals' movement into and out of work over a 15-month period). Brewer et al. (2006) also find that withdrawing the tax credit would decrease the participation of men in couples by 1.1 points and increase that of women in couples by 0.73 points.[18] The few ex post evaluations of the 1999 WFTC reform which analyse the labour supply effect for married couples actually differ slightly from these predictions. In particular, the difference-in-difference approach of Blundell, Brewer, and Shephard (2005) shows that the 1999 extension has had a small negative effect on married men and no significant effect on married mothers' employment. Yet, their robustness check suggests that there may be different trends for the treatment and control groups used (i.e. with and without children), which have not been adequately controlled for. This would imply that the negative impact of the WFTC (and combined reforms) on the employment of married women was more negative than they had estimated, which is more in line with the prediction of structural models. As for the US experience, an important lesson from the natural experiment studies is the very strong positive effect of the EITC on the employment of single women with children (Meyer, 2010). The disincentive effects in terms of working hours, as predicted by structural models, failed to materialise, however, possibly due to the difficulties for workers to freely adjust their working time (Eissa & Liebman, 1996).

Redistributive Effects

Pre-Crisis Scenarios

The upper panel of Table 7 reports poverty rates in the baseline and for the different policy scenarios. The baseline levels of the poverty headcount ratio, FGT(0), and of the intensity of poverty, FGT(1), confirm the high levels of being 'at risk of poverty' in Ireland.[19] As mentioned before, the counterfactual policy scenarios hypothetically assume 100% take-up in

Table 7. Poverty Impact of the Reforms.

	Baseline	FIS 2001	FIS 2008	WTC
Static poverty incidence				
FGT(0), poverty line = 50% median	0.174	0.170	0.166	0.169
change		*−2.5%*	*−4.9%*	*−3.2%*
FTR(0), poverty line = 60% median	0.247	0.245	0.225	0.241
change		*−0.6%*	*−8.8%*	*−2.5%*
FGT(1), poverty line = 50% median	0.0341	0.0334	0.0340	0.0337
change		*−1.9%*	*−0.2%*	*−1.1%*
FGT(1), poverty line = 60% median	0.0630	0.0620	0.0607	0.0616
change		*−1.6%*	*−3.6%*	*−2.2%*
Poverty incidence after labour supply response				
FGT(0), poverty line = 50% median	0.174	0.169	0.156	0.163
change		*−3.0%*	*−10.7%*	*−6.7%*
FTR(0), poverty line = 60% median	0.247	0.245	0.216	0.235
change		*−0.6%*	*−12.6%*	*−4.9%*
FGT(1), poverty line = 50% median	0.0341	0.0328	0.0308	0.0315
change		*−3.7%*	*−9.6%*	*−7.4%*
FGT(1), poverty line = 60% median	0.0630	0.0614	0.0564	0.0587
change		*−2.6%*	*−10.4%*	*−6.8%*
All market incomes and minimum wage cut by 10%				
FGT(0), poverty line = fixed[a]	0.265	0.262	0.227	0.252
Change compared to current baseline		−1.4%	−14.6%	−5.2%
Change compared to pre-crisis baseline	+7.6%	+6.7%	+5.1%	+7.3%

Note: We assume 100% take-up for all reforms. FIS: Family Income Supplement; WTC: 2003 British Working Tax Credit. Poverty measures are based on equivalised disposable income (using the modified OECD scale).

[a]Poverty line frozen at 60% median income of pre-crisis baseline.

order to reveal the full redistributive potential of the reforms. The upper panel assumes that gross incomes are constant, that is labour supply adjustments to the reforms are ignored. All the reforms have a modest but significant effect on headcount poverty when placing the poverty line at 50% of the median equivalised income. As expected, the FIS 2008 has the largest effect, which is almost twice the size of that of FIS 2001. With a poverty line at 60% of the median, however, the FIS 2008 has a considerably larger effect than other reforms, reflecting the fact that it benefits households just below 60% of the median in an important way. In the same way, the FIS 2008 and other policies have a moderate effect on the intensity of poverty, as measured by the poverty gap FGT(1).

Maybe more interestingly, the middle panel of Table 7 provides the change in poverty, compared to the baseline, when labour supply responses are taken into account. It turns out that the work adjustments to the FIS 2008 would double the anti-poverty effect of this measure when a poverty line of 50% of the median is considered. This effect is due to a combination of negative responses (which increase disposable income when the budget curve is decreasing because of the FIS 2008) and positive responses in the case of single mothers, a group particularly at risk of poverty. The effect of the WTC is similar to that of FIS 2008, but with around two-thirds the magnitude at a poverty line of 50% of the median, and of just over one-third at a poverty line of 60% of the median.

To put these results into an international context, the potential effect of FIS 2008 is comparable to the EITC in place in the United States in 2007. According to Meyer (2010), this policy lifted just under 4.0 million people above the poverty line (referring to the standard measure reported by the US Census), reducing the overall poverty rate by 10%. Previous versions of the US EITC in 1993 and 2002 had been estimated to lift 1 million (Scholz, 1994) and 5 million (Eissa & Nichols, 2005) people respectively above the poverty line each year. Additionally, Meyer (2010) finds that the effects of the EITC are concentrated around the poverty line. This is in line with our findings that FIS 2008 benefits households around the poverty line in an important way, such that its anti-poverty effects appear greatly amplified when compared to the other reforms. In the United Kingdom, the effect of the pre-2003 tax credit, the WFTC, is similar (Blundell et al., 2000).

After Wage Shocks

In a period of economic downturn, MWP policies may also have a role, as discussed in the introduction. In particular, they may cushion income losses caused by reduced working hours or wage cuts for those in employment. This is particularly relevant in the Irish context where wage cuts have occurred, notably in the minimum wage and in the public sector, which match the drops in expected earnings in the private sector (see Callan, Nolan, & Walsh, 2011). Here, we analyse a simple uniform cut in earnings and in the Irish national minimum wage of 10% in real terms.[20] The lower panel of Table 6 reports the results for the FGT(0) with a poverty line fixed at 60% of the median equivalised income *before the earnings losses*. In this way, we avoid possible confusion with the change specifically due to a lower median income. The last results of Table 7, which also include labour supply adjustments to policies, can be compared to the pre-crisis effects of the reforms when considering the poverty line at 60% of the median, that is the second line of the middle panel in Table 7. In the pre-crisis situation, the FIS 2008 reduces poverty by 12.6% and the WTC achieves about a half of this. When real earnings decrease by 10%, poverty increases by 7.6% in the baseline situation (compared to the 'pre-crisis' baseline when freezing the poverty line). In this case, that is with the 'current' baseline, the poverty alleviation effects of the different MWP policies are very similar to the effects in the pre-crisis situation. More interesting, we can compare poverty levels under each policy scenario (while freezing the poverty line to pre-crisis levels) to capture the cushioning effect of each policy. In this case, we notice that the wage shock is partly absorbed by the FIS 2008 since poverty increases by 'only' 5.1% compared to the baseline change (7.6%). The effect of the two other policies is more modest. With the FIS 2008, we find in particular that the drop in earnings reduces the labour supply of married women (men) by 4% (1%) and of single women (men) by 5% (4%). This is explained by the fact that work does not pay as much in our recessionary scenario, while welfare payments have not been changed. These effects are important as they add voluntary unemployment to the involuntary unemployment caused by demand-side constraints on the labour market.

Another important contribution is the effect of the suggested policies on particularly vulnerable groups. In particular, Table 8 shows that the risk of poverty among single mothers is very high in Ireland. We observe that under the full take-up assumption, the FIS 2008 has an extremely large impact as it

Table 8. Redistributive Effects of MWP Policies: Specific Groups.

	Baseline	FIS 2001	FIS 2008	WTC
Single mothers				
FGT(0), poverty line = fixed[a]	0.522	0.507	0.332	0.389
change compared to baseline		−3%	−36%	−25%
FGT(0), poverty line = fixed,[a] income cut[b]	0.562	0.529	0.342	0.415
change compared to pre-crisis baseline	+7.8%	+4.3%	+2.8%	+6.7%
Child povety				
FGT(0), poverty line = fixed[a]	0.247	0.243	0.144	0.224
change compared to baseline		−2%	−42%	−9%
FGT(0), poverty line = fixed,[a] income cut[b]	0.284	0.275	0.157	0.258
change compared to pre-crisis baseline	+15.1%	+13.3%	+9.3%	+15.3%

Note: We assume 100% take-up or all reforms. FIS: Family Income Supplement; WTC: 2003 British Working Tax Credit.

[a]Poverty line frozen at 60% median income of pre-crisis baseline.

[b]All market incomes and minimum wage cut by 10%.

could reduce poverty among single parents by 36% in absolute terms, that is when freezing the baseline poverty line at 60% of the median. These figures combine the direct effect of the transfer and the positive labour supply effect of the FIS that brings many of these single-parent households above the (frozen) poverty line.[21] The WTC would lift a quarter of single-mother households above the (frozen) poverty line in the baseline situation. In a recessionary situation, only the FIS 2001 and 2008 show interesting cushioning roles: under the FIS 2001 (2008), poverty increases by only 4.3% (2.8%) compared to the 7.8% increase in a scenario without income support (baseline change).

In-work benefits and tax credits in Ireland (FIS), the United Kingdom (WFTC) and the United States (EITC) were originally targeted at low-wage families with children since one of the policy objectives was to combat child poverty. In Ireland, the FIS is clearly viewed as an instrument for this purpose, as illustrated by recent recommendations by certain groups (the 'End Child Poverty' coalition and the OPEN network 'representing lone parents groups in Ireland') to increase the FIS. Table 8 shows that around a quarter of Irish children live in families with equivalised incomes below 60% of the median. Again, the poverty alleviation of the FIS 2008 is extremely strong, decreasing child poverty by 42%.[22] The FIS 2008 also performs well in cushioning the income loss among households with children (an increase in child poverty of 9.3% instead of 15.1% in the baseline). The WTC, on the other hand, does not particularly reduce child poverty. In the United Kingdom, policy makers have acknowledged the fact that attaining three policy objectives – increased labour supply, improved financial circumstances of low-wage workers and combating child poverty – with a single-policy instrument is a difficult task, hence the splitting of the WFTC into the WTC and the CTC. Using the WTC on its own as a reform therefore limits the anti-poverty effect of this measure.[23]

Sensitivity to Non-Take-Up

The previous analysis aims to assess the full redistributive and (dis)incentive potentials of the alternative policies under the full take-up assumption. We complement these results by investigating the sensitivity of the anti-poverty effect of each policy to non-take-up and to the nature of the non-claimants. The number of FIS recipients in the LII data set is extremely small and does not allow us to identify the claimants. Hence, we choose recipients randomly among those deemed eligible for the policy according to our simulation,

Table 9. Take-Up: Sensitivity Analysis.

		No IWB	FIS 2001	FIS 2008	WTC
Full take-up		0.241	0.238	0.218	0.234
Low take-up	5%	0.241	0.239	0.231	0.237
(confidence interval)	95%		0.241	0.237	0.240
Change	5%		−0.6%	−4.1%	−1.4%
(confidence interval)	95%		0.0%	−1.6%	−0.4%

Note: All measures are FGT(0), with poverty line frozen at 60% median income of 2001 'no IWB' scenario. Measures for low take-up are bootstrapped over 200 draws of the 33% recipients (official take-up rate) among all eligible.

using a take-up rate of 33%, which is close to the official rate for FIS in the early 2000s, that is the baseline context. We repeat this procedure to calculate the 95% confidence intervals for the poverty measures over a large number of draws. The simulation of FIS 2001 shows that the 5% bound is close to the full take-up scenario but that the 95% bound is equivalent to the baseline, that is a situation without MWP policy. In the latter case, draws include the richer among the families eligible for the FIS so that the policy has little effect. For FIS 2008 and the WTC, however, applying the 33% take-up rate randomly systematically reduces poverty compared to the baseline situation. Poverty reduction is always significant with the FIS2008, from 4.1% in the best case to 1.6% in the worst (Table 9).

CONCLUSION

Combating poverty while maintaining high-work incentives is a reasonable mix of policy objectives that has been adopted in most industrialised countries. This chapter suggests a series of simulation exercises to analyse the effectiveness of alternative 'MWP' policies in Ireland. We focus on the ability of these policies to reduce poverty in a baseline situation or when income shocks, reflecting the current economic downturn, occur. We find that a full take-up version of the existing scheme, the FIS, would significantly reduce poverty in a scenario where payments become as generous (in real terms) as in 2008. The effect is not only due to direct poverty alleviation among the working population but also to the incentive effect among certain groups at risk of poverty, in particular single-parent households. The effects are more modest when accounting for the fact that take-up is low in Ireland, particularly when compared to that of its closest neighbours, the United Kingdom. However, the FIS 2008 still has a significant effect on poverty reduction, whatever the nature of the recipients within the eligible population. Exporting the British WTC to Ireland with minor modifications also seems to generate an important redistributive effect under full take-up, yet it is smaller than that under FIS because the incentive effect among single mothers is much lower and encourages mainly part-time activity. This may not be enough to take them out of poverty.

Married women make up a significant potential margin of increased labour supply in Ireland, despite the already dramatic increase in female participation over the last few decades. Yet the policies analysed in this study have, for the most part, a disincentive effect on this group because of the means test at the household level. This is a feature of the existing FIS that we have retained for the alternative policies we investigated, but other paths to reform are possible. The trade-off, however, is that a more individualised scheme would be less targeted at low-income households. More simulations are required to assess what the most efficient policy would be in the Irish context. Looking at the other elements of the existing system is also necessary, in particular the interaction of FIS with the One Parent Family Payment.

Finally, we discuss several limitations evoked in the introduction in terms of methodology. Firstly, ex ante analyses rely on a certain number of assumptions concerning household behaviour and rationality. More systematic comparison with ex post analyses is required (see Blundell et al., 2000), although this is made difficult by the rarity of data that allows researchers to capture this effect and the problem of finding convincing control groups. Secondly, the supply-side nature of our exercise make that employment effects of the FIS and the WTC are upper bounds of what can be expected. Future research should improve our ability to model both labour supply and labour demand, especially when demand is the constraining factor. Finally, take-up is an issue in the context of the Irish FIS. Larger data sets identifying recipients and allowing an assessment of eligibility are necessary in order to measure and understand the nature of non-take-up. More qualitative studies may also reveal some of the reasons behind non-take-up and suggest further paths to reform in order to extend the scope of the FIS (see DSFA, 2008). Understanding administrative arrangements, and how WTC-style automatic (refundable) tax credits paid through the pay package could allow for a broader coverage, is also important.

NOTES

1. An early study by Callan et al. (1995) evaluates the FIS but there is currently no assessment of the labour supply effect of this policy (or its possible extensions) using econometric techniques nor any evaluation of the possible effects of alternative scenarios.

2. The British Family Income Supplement, which was the model for the Irish FIS, was introduced in the United Kingdom in 1971 and replaced in 1988 by the Family Credit (FC) which was a top-up cash payment for low-earning couples with children. The Working Family Tax Credit (WFTC), introduced in its stead in October 1999, was a refundable tax credit administered by the Inland Revenue and was more generous than the previous FC (the average monthly amount of credit increased by around 20% and the WFTC reached 1.3 million households at a cost of £5 billion, i.e. 0.6% of GDP). In 2003, a new reform split the WFTC into a refundable Child Tax Credit (CTC) to families with children, targeted at reducing child poverty, and a Working Tax Credit (WTC), which was essentially an extension of the WFTC to childless households. See the survey by Brewer (2001).

3. Small in-work support policies have been implemented in the form of refundable EITC's in France in 2001 (Stancanelli, 2008), in the Netherlands and in Belgium from 2002 to 2004 (Orsini, 2006). Exemptions from social security contributions aimed at 'making work pay' have been introduced in Germany with the 'mini-job' reform (Steiner & Wrohlich, 2005) and in Belgium after 2004. See also the surveys and international comparisons by Gradus and Julsing (2001), Martin and Grubb (2001), Pearson and Scarpetta (2002), Blundell (2000) and Duncan, Pearson, and Scholz (1994).

4. MWP policies may also act as automatic stabilisers in a credit constrained environment (see Dolls, Fuest, & Peichl, 2009, and Mabbett, 2009, on the automatic stabilisation effects of tax-benefit systems in the EU).

5. In the same way, several studies in the United Kingdom have made use of simulations to disentangle the effect of reforming family tax credits from other policy changes (e.g. Blundell et al., 2000) and to compare the result to ex-post analyses (e.g. Blundell et al., 2005; Francesconi & Van der Klaauw, 2007; Leigh, 2004).

6. Modelling the different forms of unemployment is also rarely done in the context of redistributive tax-benefit analyses. An interesting exception is Laroque and Salanié (2001), who take structural labour supply as the starting point to disentangle voluntary unemployment, minimum wage censoring and a residual category of non-employment corresponding to frictional and keynesian unemployment.

7. The HBS gathers information on household expenditures, incomes and socio-demographics for around 7,000 representative households in each wave. It has been collected for the years 1994, 1999 and 2005 and is consistently comparable over time. In contrast, LII was only collected until 2001 and is not fully comparable to the more recent EU-SILC data. Important changes (up to one point of Gini) between the LII 2001 and 2004 wave of EU-SILC are partly attributed to changes in data collection and sample reweighting methods.

8. When using EU-SILC 2005, 45.7% of those at risk of poverty are in work (Rocks, 2008). This figure is 32.6% when considering the consistently poor (income below 60% of the median and meeting at least one of eight deprivation measures).

9. One-earner couples represented 45% of all couples in 1999 and 37% in 2004, while the proportion of no-earner couples remained stable at around 11% of all couples.

10. Confidence intervals for elasticities are obtained by repetitive random draws of the preference parameters from their estimated distributions and, for each draw, by applying the calibration procedure.

11. Exceptions are child benefit, early childcare supplement, carer's allowance, guardian's payment (contributory and non-contributory), supplementary welfare allowance and foster child allowance.

12. The medical card scheme allows the holder to receive certain health services free of charge. To qualify for a medical card, your weekly income must be below a certain figure for your family size. Cash income (aside from the FIS), savings, investments and property are taken into account in the means test.

13. Generally, the payment continues for one year and is not affected by, for example, an increase in earnings or other income in the family. The means test is performed at the end of each year to determine the new payment amount for the subsequent year. We do not address administrative reforms that may affect the efficiency of in-work support policies (e.g. the form of payment, its frequency, the degree of administrative hassle to claim the benefit etc., see Duncan et al., 2003; Dilnot & McCrae, 1999/2000).

14. For instance, the simulation of the WFTC and an alternative individualised MWP policy in Finland, France and Germany (Bargain & Orsini, 2005), of the implementation of family-based and individual-based MWP policies in Southern European countries (Figari, 2009) and of a marginal EITC-style reform in the EU-15 countries (Immervoll, Kleven, Kreiner, & Saez, 2007).

15. In the case of our hypothetical budget constraints, this is made up of three components. The *Supplementary Allowance* acts as a minimum income, starting at EUR 106.65 per week for a single childless person (around EUR 464 per month). It is withdrawn at a 100% taper rate if the household has any income. The *Rent Allowance Supplement* ensures that an individual's income, after paying rent, does not fall below a minimum level. This level is the basic Supplementary Welfare for that person's circumstances minus a small amount (around EUR 10 in 2001) which is considered the minimum rent contribution the individual must make. The *Lone Parent Allowance* is a means-tested payment for men and women who are bringing children up without the support of a partner. In 2001, the first EUR 146.50 of the individual's weekly earnings was not taken into account in the means test and the withdrawal rate thereafter was 100%. Other benefits include carers allowance, disabled persons maintenance allowance, deserted wives benefit and unemployment assistance.

16. The case of a two-earner couple where one works 40 hours and the other 20 hours, both at the same minimum wage, corresponds to the point at 60 hours on the right-hand side graph of Fig. 3. It is clear for this illustration that the disposable income of the household increases when the part-time secondary earner stops working.

17. As shall be seen hereafter, the overall effect of the suggested reforms on labour supply is negative, and especially so in the case of the FIS 2008. This is in line with our expectations from inspecting the hypothetical budget constraints. In these

circumstances, the tax base decreases (efficiency loss) and in-work transfer payments increase so that the real cost is expected to be higher than the apparent cost. The difference is particularly large in the case of the FIS 2008, whose real cost increases by 35% due to labour supply responses.

18. We are not aware of any labour supply evaluation of the 2003 WTC in the United Kingdom, which would be more directly comparable with the reform simulated here. Brewer and Clark (2003) note, however, that the incentives created by the WTC are not universal. The incentive to enter work is high for the first earner in a family but lower for second earners. The benefit withdrawal rate also generates high implicit marginal taxation and, hence, hour reductions.

19. With a poverty rate of 24.5% in the FIS 2001 situation, we slightly overestimate poverty compared to official figures of around 22.1% (Nolan et al., 2002). For child poverty, our simulations are very close to the 25% found in official reports. Note that at-risk-of-poverty rates (using 60% of the median as the poverty line) are lower in the second section because we focus there on working-age households only.

20. This magnitude captures the official cuts in public sector wages of 4–5% in real terms over the 2007–2008 period, and a similar drop in the 2008–2009 period. It also coincides with the recent cut in minimum wage (11.5% in February 2011). For a specific analysis of the distributional effects of the income levies and wage cuts occurring in Ireland over the years 2008–2009, see Callan et al. (2011).

21. Note that single mothers affect the figures presented above, for the total population, by only a small amount, since this group is relatively small.

22. In comparison, Meyer (2010) notes that the EITC lifted over 2.1 million children above the poverty line in 2007 in the United States, corresponding to a 16% decrease in the child poverty rate.

23. However, the CTC in the United Kingdom replaced all child increments to welfare payments, so there was little point simulating its introduction in Ireland unless all welfare payments for those with children were cut commensurately.

24. Labour supply estimations are not reported here but are available from the authors. They show the usual results, notably the fact that children significantly decrease the propensity to work for women (both women in couples and single mothers). Taste shifters related to age are significant only for single men and women in couples. Costs of work are significantly positive for men and single women. Pseudo-R^2 are 0.26 (couples), 0.25 (single women) and 0.29 (single men).

ACKNOWLEDGEMENT

We are grateful to the Combat Poverty Agency, Dublin and the Fonds National de la Recherche, Luxembourg for financial support. We are indebted to our present and former colleagues for their invaluable contributions to the construction of EUROMOD. Simulations performed in this study rely on the Living in Ireland Survey provided by the CSO.

REFERENCES

Ballard, C., Shoven, J., & Whalley, J. (1985). General equilibrium computations of the marginal welfare costs of taxes in the United States. *American Economic Review*, *75*(1), 128–137.

Bargain, O. (Ed.), (2006). Microsimulation in action: Policy analysis in Europe using EUROMOD, *Research in Labor Economics*, (Vol. 25, pp. 165–198) North-Holland: Elsevier.

Bargain, O., & Orsini, K. (2005). In-work policies in Europe: Killing two birds with one stone? *Labour Economics*, *13*, 667–697.

Bargain, O., Orsini, K., & Peichl, A. (2011). *Every kind of people? Labor supply elasticities in Europe and the US*. IZA Discussion paper no. 5820, Institute for the Study of Labor, Bonn, Germany.

Blundell, R. (2000). Work incentives and 'in-work' benefit reforms: A review. *Oxford Review of Economic Policy*, *18*, 27–44.

Blundell, R., Brewer, M., & Shephard, A. (2005). Evaluating the labour market impact of working families tax credit using difference-in-differences. HM Revenue and Customs.

Blundell, R., & Hoynes, H. (2001). In-work benefit reform and the labour market. In: R. Blundell, D. Card & R. B. Freeman (Eds.), *Seeking a premier league economy*. Chicago, IL: University of Chicago Press.

Blundell, R. W., Duncan, A., McCrae, J., & Meghir, C. (2000). The labour market impact of the working families' tax credit. *Fiscal Studies*, *21*(1), 75–103.

Blundell, R. W., & Macurdy, T. (2000). Labor supply: A review of alternative approaches. In: O. Ashenfelter & D. E. Card (Eds.), *Handbook of labor economics*. North-Holland: Elsevier.

Bovenberg, A. L., Graafland, J. J., & de Mooij, R. A. (2000). Tax reform and the Dutch labor market: An applied general equilibrium approach. *Journal of Public Economics*, *78*, 193–214.

Brewer, M. (2001). Comparing in-work benefits and the reward to work for families with children in the US and the UK. *Fiscal Studies*, *22*(1), 41–77.

Brewer, M., & Clark, T. (2003). *The impact on incentives of five years of social security reforms in the UK*. Working Paper no. 02/14. The Institute for Fiscal Studies, London.

Brewer, M., Duncan, A., Shephard, A., & Suarez, M. (2006). Did working families' tax credit work? The impact of in-work support on labour supply in Great Britain. *Labour Economics*, *13*, 699–720.

Callan, T., Nolan, B., & Walsh, J. R. (2011). The economic crisis, public sector pay, and the income distribution. *Research in Labor Economics*, *32*, 207–225.

Callan, T., O'Neill, C., & O'Donoghue, C. (1995). *Supplementing family income*. Working Paper no. 23. ESRI Policy Research Series, Dublin.

Callan, T., van Soest, A., & Walsh, J. (2009). Tax structure and female labour supply: Evidence from Ireland. *Labour*, *23*(1), 1–35.

Cooke, G., & Lawton, K. (2008). *Working out of poverty: A study of the low-paid and the 'working poor'*. London: Institute for Public Policy Research, London.

Dickert, S., Houser, S., & Scholz, J. K. (1995). The earned income tax credit and transfer programs: A study of labor market and program participation. In: J. Poterba (Ed.), *Tax policy and the economy* (Vol. 9, pp. 1–50). Cambridge, MA: MIT Press.

Dilnot, A., & McCrae, J. (1999/2000): *The family credit system and the working families tax credit in the United Kingdom*. IFS briefing note, 3, London and OECD Economic Studies, 31, Paris.

Dolls, M., Fuest, C., & Peichl, A. (2009). *Automatic stabilizers and economic crisis: US vs. Europe*. IZA Discussion paper 4310, Institute for the Study of Labor, Bonn, Germany.

Doris, A. (2001). The changing responsiveness of labour supply during the 1990s. *Quarterly Economic Commentary*, *2001*(4), 1–14. Special Articles, Economic and Social Research Institute (ESRI).

DSFA. (2008). *Family income supplement uptake research*. Dublin: Department of Social and Family Affairs.

Duncan, A., Pearson, M. & Scholz, J. K. (2003). *Is there an emerging consensus in making work pay policies?* Paper to workshop on Internationalisation and Policy Transfer, University of Tulane, 11–12 April.

Eissa, N., & Hoynes, H. (2004). Taxes and the labour market participation of married couples: The earned income tax credit. *Journal of Public Economics*, *88*(9–10), 1931–1958.

Eissa, N., & Liebman, J. B. (1996). Labor supply response to the earned income tax credit. *Quarterly Journal of Economics*, *111*(2), 605–637.

Eissa, N., & Nichols, A. (2005). Tax-transfer policy and labor-market outcomes. *American Economic Review, Papers and Proceedings*, *95*(2), 88–93.

Feres P., Immervoll H., Lietz C., Levy H., Mantovani D., & Sutherland H. (2002). *Indicators for social inclusion in the european union: how responsive are they to macro level changes?* EUROMOD Working Paper no. EM3/02. EUROMOD at the Institute for Social and Economic Research, Essex.

Figari, F. (2009). *Can in-work benefits improve social inclusion in the southern European countries?* EUROMOD Working Papers EM4/09, EUROMOD at the Institute for Social and Economic Research, Essex.

Francesconi, M., & Van der Klaauw, W. (2007). The socioeconomic consequences of 'in-work' benefit reform for British lone mothers. *Journal of Human Resources*, *42*(1), 1–31.

Gradus, R. H. J. M., & Julsing, J. M. (2001). Comparing different European Income tax policies making work pay. OCFEB Research Memorundum 0101.

Heim, B. T., & Meyer, B. D. (2004). Work costs and nonconvex preferences in the estimation of labor supply models. *Journal of Public Economics*, *88*(11), 2323–2338.

Immervoll, H., Kleven, H. J., Kreiner, C. T., & Saez, E. (2007). Welfare reform in European countries: A microsimulation analysis. *Economic Journal*, 1–44.

Immervoll, H., & Pearson, M. (2009). *A good time for making work pay? Taking stock of in-work benefits and related measures across the OECD*. OECD Social, Employment and Migration Working Paper no. 81. OECD, Directorate for Employment, Labour and Social Affairs, Paris.

Laroque, G., & Salanié, B. (2001). Labour market, institutions and employment in France. *Journal of Applied Econometrics*, *17*, 25–48.

Leigh, A. (2004). *Optimal design of earned income tax credits: Evidence from a British natural experiment*. Mimeo, Australian National University, Centre for Economic Policy Research, Discussion Paper no. 488, Canberra.

Mabbett, D. (2009). *Fiscal stabilisers in Europe: The macroeconomic impact of tax and benefit systems*. EUROMOD Working Paper no. EM7/04, Institute for Social and Economic Research, Essex.

Martin, J., & Grubb, D. (2001). *What works and for whom: A review of OECD countries' experience of active labour market policies*. Paris: OECD.

Meyer, B. (2010). The effects of the earned income tax credit and recent reforms. *Tax Policy and the Economy*, *24*, 153–180.

Meyer, B., & Rosenbaum, D. (2001). Welfare, the earned income tax credit, and the labor supply of single mothers. *Quarterly Journal of Economics*, *116*(3), 1063–1114.

Nolan, B., Gannon, B., Layte, R., Watson, D., Whelan, C., & Williams, J. (2002). *Monitoring poverty trends in Ireland: Results from the 2000 living in Ireland survey*. Dublin: ESRI.

Ochel, W. (2001). *Financial incentives to work – conceptions and results in Great Britain, Ireland and Canada*. CESifo Working Paper no. 627, Center for Economic Studies and Ifo Institute for Economic Research, Munich.

Orsini, K. (2006). *Tax-benefits reforms and the labor market: Evidence from Belgium and other EU countries*. Center for Economic Studies Discussion papers ces0605, Katholieke Universiteit Leuven, Centrum voor Economische Studiën, Leuven.

Pearson, M., & Scarpetta, S. (2002). An overview: What do you know about policies to make work pay? *OECD Economic Studies*, *31*, 11–24.

Rocks, P. (2008). The working poor in Ireland, and analysis of EU-SILC 2005. Research Working Paper 08/09. *Combat Poverty Agency*, Dublin.

Peichl, A., & Siegloch, S. (2010). *Accounting for labor demand effects in structural labor supply models*. IZA Discussion Paper no 5350, Institute for the Study of Labor, Bonn, Germany.

Scholz, J. K. (1994). The earned income tax credit: Participation, compliance, and anti-poverty effectiveness. *National Tax Journal*, *47*(1), 59–81.

Stancanelli, E. (2008). Evaluating the impact of the French tax credit on the employment rate of women. *Journal of Public Economics*, *92*(10–11), 2036–2047.

Steiner, V., & Wrohlich, K. (2005). Work incentives and labour supply effects of the mini-jobs reform in Germany. *Empirica*, *32*, 91–116.

Stephens, R. (2005). *Universal or targeted: A comparison of poverty programmes in Ireland and New Zealand*. Dublin: The Policy Institute, Trinity College.

van Soest, A. (1995). Structural models of family labor supply: A discrete choice approach. *Journal of human Resources*, *30*, 63–88.

APPENDIX: LABOUR SUPPLY ESTIMATIONS

Estimations

Predicted elasticities are reported in Table A1.[24] With the non-linear model used, they are obtained by simulating the impact of a marginal increase in gross hourly wages on hours of work and participation. Results are in line with other findings for Ireland (Doris, 2001; Callan et al., 2009) and with the broad range of empirical findings of labour supply elasticities for other countries (see Blundell & Macurdy, 2000). We find own-wage elasticities of around 0.40 for women in couples and 0.11 for men in couples (with standard 95% confidence intervals of 0.31–0.46 and 0.08–0.13 respectively). Cross-wage elasticities of women and men in couples are −0.09 and −0.05 respectively. For single individuals, there seem to be no marked differences between men and women, with elasticities around 0.37 for men and 0.43 for women. For both single individuals and individuals in couples, we also find that most of the sensitivity of labour supply for wage rates is driven by changes in the decision to participate. Income elasticity is also simulated by

Table A1. Labour Supply Elasticities.

	Couples		Single Women	Single Men
	Female	Male		
Change in hours				
Own-wage elasticity	0.391	0.110	0.428	0.368
	(0.039)	(0.017)	(0.065)	(0.098)
Cross-wage elasticity	−0.094	−0.046		
	(0.014)	(0.007)		
Income elasticity	0.009	−0.004	−0.004	−0.025
	(0.003)	(0.001)	(0.002)	(0.004)
Change in participation				
Own-wage elasticity	0.332	0.096	0.320	0.357
	(0.036)	(0.014)		
Cross-wage elasticity	−0.065	−0.027		
	(0.036)	(0.008)		
Income elasticity	0.010	−0.003	−0.003	−0.018
	(0.003)	(0.001)	(0.001)	(0.004)

Note: Wage-elasticities (income elasticity) are calculated by predicting the change in average worked hours of incrementing wage rates (non-labour income) by 1%. Bootstrapped standard errors are in brackets.

increasing unearned income by 1% (and bottom-coding for those with zero unearned income). We find that income elasticity is marginal, as is usually reported in the literature.

Non-Take-Up

It is possible to argue that labour supply behaviour may be affected by the existing FIS for the year 2001. We have, however, seen that the number of recipients is small due to low take-up (33%), and even smaller in the LII (calculated take-up rate of 17%) due to misreporting. Also, FIS amounts in 2001 were relatively small. For a robustness check, we have verified that labour supply estimates do not vary much under different assumptions: (1) a full take-up assumption for all those deemed eligible for FIS according to our calculation, (2) a scenario where nobody takes up the FIS 2001 (this boils down to estimating the labour supply model on the 'no MWP policy' counterfactual data) and (3) a joint estimation of labour supply and take-up by adding a stigma component to the utility function. We find slightly different estimates but no fundamental differences in the simulated labour supply adjustment to the reforms.

CHAPTER 10

EXPLORING THE DETERMINANTS OF EMPLOYMENT IN EUROPE: THE ROLE OF SERVICES

Roberta Serafini and Melanie Ward

Over recent decades both Europe and the United States have experienced an increase in the share of service-related jobs in total employment. Although narrowing in all European countries, a significant gap in the share of service jobs relative to the United States still persists. The aim of the chapter is to identify the main drivers of the service sector employment share in the EU-15 as well as its gap relative to the United States. The analysis is carried out for the aggregate service sector, 4 sub-sectors and 12 service sector branches over the period 1970–2003. We find some evidence to support the hypothesis that a number of labour market regulations – such as union density and the degree of centralisation of wage bargaining – together with the mismatch between workers' skills and job vacancies, have affected Europe's ability to adjust efficiently to the reallocation of labour from manufacturing into services. Furthermore, we find significant heterogeneity in the relative weight of the various determinants of the employment share across sub-sectors and branches.

Keywords: Services; sectoral adjustment; service sector; employment share; Europe; the United States; institutions in the labour and product market; heterogeneity

JEL classifications: E24; J21; J23; J24; L80

Research in Labor Economics, Volume 33, 341–384

ISSN: 0147-9121/doi:10.1108/S0147-9121(2011)0000033013

INTRODUCTION

The literature exploring the reasons for the relatively poor employment performance of European labour markets as compared with the United States over recent decades has mainly focused on the role played by institutions (and their possible interaction with macroeconomic shocks) in affecting *aggregate* employment (see, for instance, Blanchard & Wolfers, 2000). This line of research puts little – if any – emphasis on the *sectoral* dimension. In particular, it does not explicitly take into account the transition from an industry- to a services-dominated employment structure, which has been experienced in most advanced economies. In both Europe and the United States there has been an increase in the share of service-related jobs in total employment over the past 30 years, as well as a reduction in the number of jobs in industry and agriculture. In both continents, job creation nowadays takes place almost exclusively in the service sector. Furthermore, the service sector now makes up as much as 72% of GDP in the EU-15 and 74% in the United States.

At first sight, it may not be obvious that the increase in the proportion of the workforce employed in services plays an important role in explaining Europe's employment performance – either in absolute terms or in comparison with the United States – since it has been a shared dynamic across continents and argued to reflect long-term changes mainly driven by a general improvement in living standards. However, there have also been some important differences in the employment dynamics between the two continents, which help to emphasise the key role of service sector employment in total employment and explain the different employment performances across countries. First, aggregate service sector employment has been relatively more important in the United States than in Europe, with a share over total employment which has been systematically higher since the beginning of the 1970s. Second, the pattern of employment *within* the aggregate service sector has been somewhat different in the United States. In particular, it has been higher in the sub-sectors of finance, insurance, real estate and business activities, as well as in community, social and personal services.

To demonstrate the importance of the sectoral composition of employment, Chart 1 presents what the pattern of employment growth in Europe would have been under the assumption that the weights used in computing the sectoral contributions reflected the US employment structure. Back of the envelope calculations indicate that – for given sectoral rates of growth – Europe's total employment growth would have been more than two times

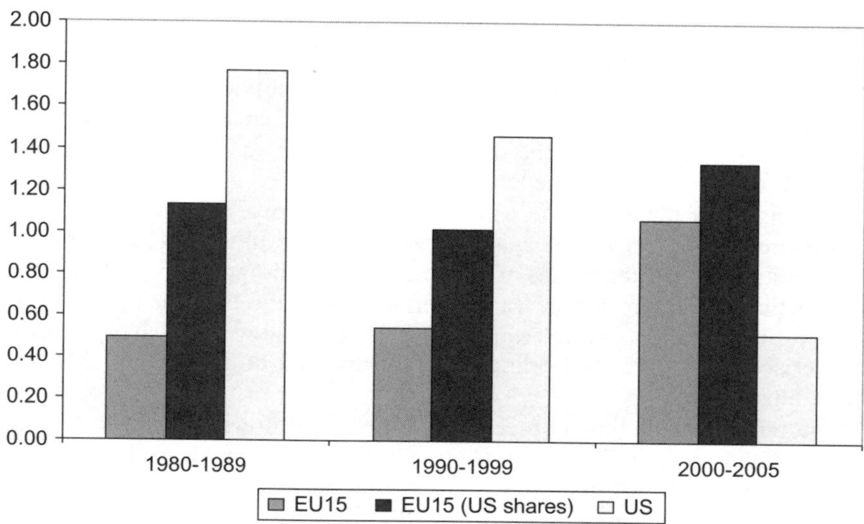

Chart 1. Total Employment Growth in the EU15 and the US (annual averages, %). *Source*: Our computation using the EUKLEMS database.

higher than the actual figures during the 1980s, and close to double during the 1990s. It follows that exploring in greater detail what the main factors driving the service employment shares in EU countries – as well as the gap relative to the United States – are key in understanding how to achieve higher employment levels in Europe.

Along with the increases in per-capita income levels, a number of explanations for the rising trend in the service sector employment share have been proposed in the economics literature. These include the slower productivity growth of services relative to manufacturing and the rise in female participation (see the literature overview for a further discussion). At the same time, it has been argued that for countries at a similar stage of development, the observed variation in the size of the service sector employment share across countries may result from differences in institutions affecting the degree of flexibility of labour and product markets. Although building on previous (theoretical and empirical) work on the topic – thereby taking into account the main determinants suggested in the literature to date – this chapter investigates a working hypothesis that in Europe, the presence of adjustment barriers may have hindered the ongoing process of sectoral reallocation of the workforce associated with the shift from manufacturing to services. In particular we investigate the role played, on the one hand, by the regulatory framework affecting labour and product market flexibility and, on the other hand, by the ability of the workforce to adjust to the sectoral change, as reflected in the mismatch between workers' skills and job vacancies on the service sector employment share. A further original contribution of the chapter is that we consider not only the determinants of the aggregate service sector in Europe, but also of its sub-sectors and branches, as well as the service sector employment gap between Europe and the United States at various levels of disaggregation. Here, we are particularly interested in learning more about the heterogeneity in the relative importance of determinants of the employment share across the service sub-sectors and branches in Europe and how this may differ to the United States.

The remainder of the chapter is organised as follows. The next section presents the main stylised facts on service employment in the EU-15 countries and the United States, with the purpose of highlighting the significant heterogeneity of employment shares across countries, and service sector branches over time and the heterogeneity of service branches, e.g. with regard to average productivity and skill levels. The key determinants of the service sector employment share discussed in the literature to date are then reviewed. We present our econometric model considering the determinants of the aggregate employment share, 4 sub-sectors and 12 branches, for 13 EU[1] countries and discuss the results. We then turn to an investigation of the determinants of the United States–European gap in employment shares. The last section concludes.

INTERNATIONAL TRENDS IN THE SERVICE SECTOR EMPLOYMENT SHARE: SOME FACTS

In 2005, the service sector contributed 72% of total nominal value added in the EU-15 and 74% in the United States, making it the largest economic sector (see Chart 2). Over time, this sector has experienced strong growth in both Europe and the United States, in contrast with a marked decline in manufacturing. From 1980 to 2005 the increase in the share of services in total nominal value added in the EU-15 was about 10 percentage points, whereas a 13-percentage point increase was observed in the United States over the same period. When looking at single European countries in the post-1990 period, the growing importance of the service sector is also

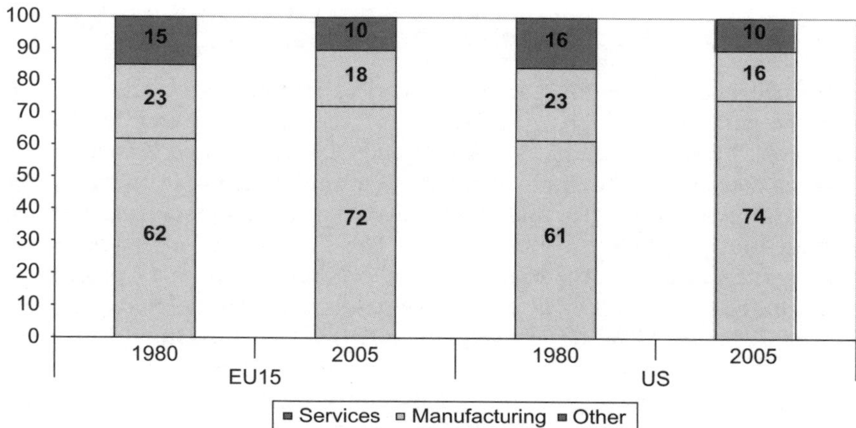

Chart 2. Value added structure in the Euro area and the USA. *Source*: Our computation using the EUKLEMS database.

Table 1. Share of Total Manufacturing and Services in Total Nominal Value-Added and in Total Employment, 1980–2003 (Annual Average Percentage Shares).

	Value-Added Shares				Employment Shares			
	Manufacturing		Services		Manufacturing		Services	
	1980–1989	1990–2003	1980–1989	1990–2003	1980–1989	1990–2003	1980–1989	1990–2003
Austria	22.4	19.9	61.5	66.6	21.2	17.3	52.1	60.1
Belgium	22.2	19.6	65.1	70.8	21.6	17.2	67.8	73.5
Denmark	18.2	16.5	68.6	71.6	19.7	17.5	66.3	71.5
Finland	25.2	23.5	56.9	64.0	22.6	19.7	56.7	65.3
France	23.1	18.5	64.3	71.1	21.3	17.0	62.5	71.0
Germany	30.0	23.6	58.9	66.8	29.5	22.9	56.8	65.3
Greece	17.5	12.9	59.6	68.1		15.5		58.2
Ireland	24.9	30.0	55.4	55.3	19.5	18.5	54.4	61.4
Italy	26.1	21.2	60.3	67.8	26.3	23.0	54.8	63.7
Luxembourg	21.4	13.0	69.8	78.4	21.4	14.7	64.4	71.9
The Netherlands	18.3	16.8	63.6	69.6	18.2	14.6	69.2	74.7
Portugal	22.5	19.2	58.5	66.1	24.6	21.4	45.7	56.9
Spain	23.9	18.4	59.2	66.1	20.9	18.4	54.6	63.2
Sweden	22.0	20.7	64.5	68.9	21.1	17.8	67.3	72.8
The United Kingdom	24.0	19.2	59.1	69.4	22.6	16.4	68.3	77.0
The United States	18.9	16.0	69.8	75.2	17.2	13.2	73.9	78.6

Source: OECD, STAN indicators database.

confirmed (Table 1), with a share of services in total value added which appears particularly high – and close to the United States level – in Denmark, France, Belgium, the Netherlands and the United Kingdom.

When considering the employment share, a similar picture of an important and growing services sector and an overall decline in manufacturing emerges in both Europe and the United States.[2] The share of service workers has steadily increased since the beginning of the 1980s, by about 17 percentage points in the EU-15 and by 11 percentage points in the United States, up to a level of 72% and 81%, respectively, in 2005 (see Chart 3). In all European countries considered, service sector employment levels are converging towards – but still lagging behind[3] – those in the United States (see Table 1). However, employment share levels appear more dispersed across countries than the value-added shares – ranging from about 57% in Portugal to 77% in the United Kingdom since the beginning of the 1990s.

Identifying the main drivers of the service employment share requires taking into account its fundamental heterogeneity. Being in fact defined as *anything but* agriculture and manufacturing, the services sector is made up of a broad range of very different activities. According to revision 3 of the International Standard Industrial Classification (ISIC), total services can be divided into four main sub-sectors: (i) wholesale and retail trade, hotels and restaurants; (ii) transport, storage and communication; (ii) finance, insurance, real estate and business services; and (iv) community, social and

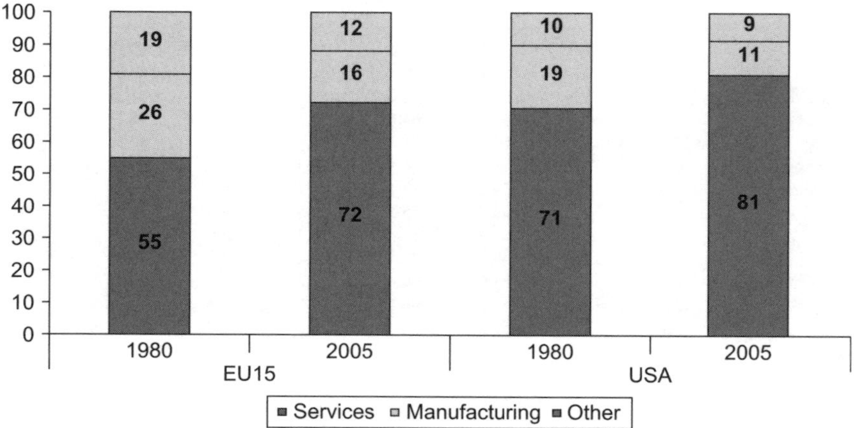

Chart 3. Employment Structure in the Euro area and the USA. *Source*: Our computation using the EUKLEMS database.

personal services.[4] Collectively, sub-sectors (i), (ii) and (iii) make up what is also known as "Business Services" sector. By going into a further level of disaggregation (see Annex 1 for details), differences appear even more evident. Branches showing low or even negative productivity growth – such as social and personal services, as well as hotels and restaurants – co-exist with the strong productivity growth of sub-sectors that make an intensive use of information and communication technology, as it is the case for financial intermediation, wholesale and retail trade, transport and storage, as well as post and telecommunications (Wölfl, 2005). Furthermore, such heterogeneity is also reflected in the mix of employment within the service sector. Financial intermediation, renting of machinery and equipment (which includes computer-related and R&D activities), education, health and social work mostly employ highly skilled workers, whereas the skill distribution appears more concentrated in the low-skilled segment in the areas of wholesale and retail trade, restaurants and hotels and transport and communication.

Table 2 shows that in both Europe and the United States, service sector employment is largest in the business services sector – particularly the sub-sectors of wholesale and retail trade, hotels and restaurants – employing on average between 32% and 50% of total employment between 1990 and 2003, and community, social and personal services, which provides between 22% and 39% of total employment. Over time, the increase in the aggregate service employment share in the post-1990 period, as compared with the previous decade, was in most countries driven mainly by the sub-sector of financial, insurance, real estate and business services, as well as by community, social and personal services. Nonetheless, these latter sectors remain the ones with the highest negative gap relative to the United States, particularly in Greece, Portugal and Spain.

Again, a breakdown of the services share in total employment into its finest classification of branch (Table 3) helps highlighting the differences relative to the United States both across sub-sectors and countries. Within business services, it is worth noting that Europe is underperforming particularly in wholesale and retail trade, in financial intermediation, as well as in the renting of machinery and equipment branches. On the contrary, the employment share in hotels and restaurants is actually higher than in the United States for all the EU-15 countries. A similar picture of a positive or very low gap with the United States is found in the transport, storage and communication sub-sector. Finally, Europe's community, social and personal services sub-sector has generally underperformed relative to the United States – largely driven by the public administration and the health

Table 2. Shares of Broad Service Sector Sub-Sectors in Total Employment, 1980–2003 (Annual Average Percentage Shares).

	Business Sector Services			Wholesale and Retail Trade, Hotels and Restaurants			Transport, Storage and Communication			Finance, Insurance, Real Estate and Business Services			Community, Social and Personal Services		
	1980–1989	1990–2003	Gap with the United States, 1990–2003	1980–1989	1990–2003	Gap with the United States, 1990–2003	1980–1989	1990–2003	Gap with the United States, 1990–2003	1980–1989	1990–2003	Gap with the United States, 1990–2003	1980–1989	1990–2003	Gap with the United States, 1990–2003
Austria	32.0	36.7	−8.2	17.9	19.4	−2.9	6.3	6.4	1.7	7.8	10.9	−7.0	20.1	23.4	−10.3
Belgium	37.0	40.7	−4.2	19.4	18.8	−3.5	6.8	6.5	1.7	10.8	15.4	−2.4	30.8	32.8	−0.9
Denmark	34.0	36.8	−8.1	17.7	18.3	−4.0	6.8	6.8	2.0	9.5	11.6	−6.2	32.4	34.7	1.0
Finland	30.5	33.1	−11.8	15.8	15.5	−6.8	7.2	7.5	2.7	7.5	10.1	−7.7	26.3	32.2	−1.5
France	34.0	37.9	−7.0	16.7	17.0	−5.3	5.8	5.9	1.2	11.5	15.0	−2.8	28.6	33.1	−0.6
Germany	32.7	37.7	−7.2	17.9	19.3	−3.0	6.0	5.7	0.9	8.8	12.7	−5.1	24.1	27.6	−6.1
Greece		35.6	−9.3		21.0	−1.3		6.8	2.0		7.8	−10.0		22.6	−11.2
Ireland	31.3	36.2	−8.7	17.6	19.8	−2.5	6.4	5.7	0.9	7.4	10.7	−7.1	23.1	25.2	−8.5
Italy	31.3	36.1	−8.8	18.8	19.8	−2.5	5.3	4.8	0.1	7.1	11.4	−6.4	23.5	27.6	−6.1
Luxembourg	42.9	50.1	5.2	21.6	20.2	−2.2	7.1	7.6	2.8	14.1	22.4	4.6	21.5	21.8	−11.9
The Netherlands	36.2	42.9	−2.0	18.0	20.0	−2.3	5.9	5.7	0.9	12.4	17.3	−0.5	33.0	31.8	−2.0
Portugal	25.5	31.4	−13.5	17.1	19.6	−2.7	3.9	3.4	−1.4	4.5	8.4	−9.4	20.2	25.5	−8.2
Spain	32.2	35.9	−9.0	19.3	21.2	−1.1	6.3	5.9	1.1	6.6	8.8	−9.0	22.3	27.3	−6.4
Sweden	29.4	33.9	−11.0	15.0	15.4	−6.9	6.8	6.9	2.1	7.6	11.6	−6.2	37.9	38.9	5.2
The United Kingdom	40.2	46.8	1.9	20.9	23.3	1.0	6.2	5.9	1.1	13.1	17.6	−0.2	28.1	30.2	−3.6
The United States	41.7	44.9	–	22.4	22.3	–	4.8	4.8	–	14.6	17.8	–	32.2	33.7	–

Source: OECD, STAN indicators database.

Table 3. Service Sector Employment Share by Branch, Relative to the United States. 2001 (Difference of Annual Average Percentage Shares).

	Wholesale and Retail Trade, Hotels and Restaurants		Transport, Storage and Communication		Finance, Insurance, Real Estate and Business Services		Community, Social and Personal Services			
	Wholesale and retail trade	Hotels and Restaurants	Transport and Storage	Post and Communications	Financial Intermediation	Real Estate, Renting of Machines and Equipment and other Business Activities	Public Administration and Defence, Compulsory Social Service	Health and Social Work	Other Community, Social and Personal Services	Private Household with Employed Persons
Belgium	−10	1	2	0	−1	−1	2	1	−1	2
Germany	−8	3	1	0	−1	−1	−5	0	0	1
Greece	−8	5	2	−1	−2	−6	−3	−5	−1	1
Spain	−8	5	1	−1	−2	−5	−3	−4	3	–
France	−9	2	1	0	−1	1	1	−1	3	–
Ireland	–	—	–	–	–	–	–	–	–	–
Italy	−8	3	0	−1	−2	−2	−4	−4	0	4
Luxembourg	−9	3	–	–	8	3	−7	−4	−1	2
The Netherlands	−6	2	1	0	−1	3	−6	2	−1	3
Austria	−8	5	2	−1	−1	−4	−5	−3	−1	−1
Portugal	−8	3	−1	−1	−2	−6	−3	−4	2	–
Finland	−11	2	2	0	−3	−3	−3	4	0	0
Denmark	−8	2	1	0	−2	−1	−3	6	0	0
Sweden	−10	1	1	0	−2	–	–	–	–	–
The United Kingdom	–	–	–	–	–	–	–	–	–	–
Euro Area[2]	−8	3	1	0	−1	−1	−3	−1	1	3
EU-15	−8	3	1	0	−1	−1	−3	−1	1	3

Source: STAN database.

and social work branches – although the gap has been narrowing over time. Belgium, Denmark, Finland, France and Sweden reversed the sign of their differential and at the end of the 1990s and experienced a large positive employment gap relative to the United States.

Summing up, data show that beyond the common trend of a systematically increasing role of services in total employment, there are substantial differences across countries and sectors. Europe's employment share is below US levels particularly in the branch of wholesale and retail trade, but also in the sub-sector of finance, insurance and business, and most branches of the sub-sector community, social and personal services. What factors might explain such differences? Are these differences due the presence of constraints that should trigger some policy reflections? Our working hypothesis, which leads us to the econometrics exercise carried out in the following sections, is that the Europe's pattern of labour allocation within services is, at least to some extent, the result of national-specific regulatory environments, and one important channel through which institutions ultimately affect aggregate employment performance.

DETERMINANTS OF EMPLOYMENT IN SERVICES: AN OVERVIEW OF THE LITERATURE

The first literature on the sectoral distribution of employment dates back to the works of Fisher (1935) and Clark (1957). Clark (1957) qualifies the movement of labour from agriculture to manufacturing, and from manufacturing to commerce and services, as 'the most important concomitant of economic progress'. More specifically, growth in the service sector is mainly explained as the result of shifting income elasticities of demand, in the process later known as the 'hierarchy of needs' (Appelbaum & Schettkat, 2001). As economies grow richer, tastes switch away from the basic needs of food and shelter towards non-material goods, including services. In other words, the increasing service employment share recorded in post-industrial economies would be the result of rising per-capita income levels.[5]

In 1967, Baumol identified the key theoretical foundation for the expansion of service sector employment – the slower productivity growth in services as compared to manufacturing.[6] According to what became later known as 'Baumol's disease', the expansion of the employment share in services relative to industry is the direct consequence of services' lower productivity performance. The theory argues that as a result of this productivity differential, if the relative level of output in industry and services is maintained, an ever increasing proportion of the labour force must be channelled to service activities. The existence of this effect leads to the 'paradox' of the service sector.[7] Baumol's model has remained one of the principle theories on service sector employment.[8] An interesting extension to this work is provided by Oulton (2003), where also the supply of intermediate service goods is considered. Oulton (2003) finds that a shift of primary inputs such as labour or raw materials from industry to intermediate service production increases the economy's productivity rate as long as the service sector has some positive productivity growth, however small.[9]

Further explanations for the increase in service sector employment may be found in the empirical literature (see also Schettkat & Yocarini, 2003). Fuchs (1980) concludes that a significant proportion of the increase in service sector employment is due to the increased labour market participation of women, the effect being driven by both income and especially substitution effects of the choice between home and market work. Erdem and Glyn (2001) find that – in both the United States and Europe – since 1973 female labour supply, rather than capital accumulation, was most important for service employment. A few papers also consider factors such as the role of international trade and outsourcing on service sector employment growth, but the evidence gathered to date is inconclusive.

In consideration of the reasons for the relatively slow service employment growth in Europe, the above contributions would suggest that productivity differences between the industrial and service sector have not been as great in Europe as in the United States or – alternatively – that the expansion in female labour supply has not been so strong. These may in fact be part of the story. However, there may be other influences playing a more important role in a European context, and which may help explain the observed differences in service sector employment shares across countries at similar stages of development. For example, any discussion of the determinants of employment within the European context needs to consider the role played by the institutional setting. A number of studies of European labour markets have identified a significant effect of labour market institutions – such as the generosity of the unemployment benefit systems, the employment protection legislation (EPL), the degree of unionisation, the level of taxation – on aggregate unemployment (see, e.g. Nickell, 1997; Elmeskov, Martin, & Scarpetta, 1998; Nickell & Nunziata, 2000; Nunziata, 2002). Bertola (2001) argues that institutional constraints – such as high non-employment benefits, legal minimum wages, centrally negotiated employment contracts, high tax wedges – may prevent the creation of low-wage jobs.[10] Others have found a positive effect of the interaction between labour market institutions and economic shocks on the European unemployment rate (see, for instance, Blanchard & Wolfers, 2000; Belot & van Ours, 2000, 2001); a survey of a number of the key hypotheses and developments in this field is provided in Bertola (2001).

This literature may be relevant for explaining the slower growth of services in Europe relative to the United States if it is the case that the institutional design in Europe has somehow prevented the setting up of new businesses and/or the flow of jobs to the service sector. According to Rogerson (2003) 'the key to understanding the deterioration of employment rates in Europe relative to the US is the failure of Europe to move workers into the service sector'. Consistent with this reading is the work by Erdem and Glyn (2001) where it is shown that after 1973, inactivity in Europe rose much more than in the United States for men and fell much less for women – accounting for two-thirds of the relatively slow employment growth in Europe. They argue that service sector employment acted like a 'sponge' – persistently expanding more where labour supply had been plentiful. This implies that where female labour market participation within Europe was inhibited through institutional rigidity, then relatively limited growth in service sector employment may also have resulted.

Previous empirical studies exploring the determinants of service sector employment have focused on the possible role played by a number of variables, for the aggregate, as well as – in the attempt to draw a comprehensive picture – its sub-sectors. In particular, based on the analysis of a sample of OECD countries from 1984 to 1998 in four service sub-sectors, OECD (2000) finds that the employment share in services is mainly affected by per-capita income, the size of the welfare state and by female participation.[11] The same study identifies a significant role of some labour market institutions, namely the strictness of employment protection legislation and the degree of centralisation of wage bargaining. Estimation is carried out by selecting a core model and then testing the significance of additional determinants. The same approach is followed in Messina (2005), where the focus is a sample of 27 OECD countries from 1970 to 1998 (5-year averages). As in OECD (2000), Messina finds a positive impact of per-capita income and the size of the public sector on the service sector employment share, together with the productivity gap between services and manufacturing, the rate of investment, the degree of urbanisation, and the administrative burden on the creation of new firms. In contrast to OECD (2000), Messina finds that female participation does not play a significant role in service sector employment. The same applies to the employment protection legislation; however, other indicators of labour market institutions – notably, the degree of unionisation and of wage setting coordination – are found to be significant determinants of the services employment share.

Table 4 shows how this chapter compares with these previous studies. In particular, while essentially following the same logic of the empirical contributions discussed earlier, the analysis has been extended in three directions. First, the panel estimation is here carried out for the total service sector in Europe as well as for its breakdown to the second digit of the ISIC classification; this amounts to a total of 4 sub-sectors and 12 branches. Given the heterogeneity of the service sector, this more disaggregated analysis aims at providing further insights into the determinants of the employment share for certain segments of the total service sector. Second, we analyse the possible role played by a broader set of labour and product market institutions in helping or hindering the reallocation of the employment both to and within the service sector. Third, we consider whether these factors may have partially driven the gap between the European and the United States employment share, as shown in the last section of the chapter.

ECONOMETRIC ANALYSIS OF THE SERVICE SECTOR EMPLOYMENT SHARE IN EUROPEAN UNION COUNTRIES

Empirical Model

In order to study the impact of macro-economic and institutional factors on the service sector employment share we estimate a simple panel data model for an unbalanced sample of 13 EU countries, over the period from 1970 to 2003 (depending on the specification) using annual data taken from the OECD Structural Analysis (STAN) database. We consider the following reduced form model:

$$y_{it} = c + \beta x_{it} + u_{it} \quad i = 1,2\ldots N \quad t = 1,2\ldots T_i \tag{1}$$

$$u_{it} = \alpha_i + \varepsilon_{it} \tag{2}$$

Table 4. Main Results from Empirical Work on the Determinants of the Employment Share in Europe.

Countries	OECD (2000)	MESSINA (2003)	THIS PAPER
	OECD Countries	Panel Estimate on (a Maximum of) 27 OECD Countries	Panel Estimate on (a Maximum of) 13 EU Countries
Sample	1984–1998, annual data	1970–1998, five year averages. T = 6 for most countries (unbalanced)	1970–2003, annual data
Sectors	Total services and 4 service sub-sectors (Elfring's criteria)	Total services and 4 service sub-sectors (ISIC)	Total services, 4 service sub-sectors and 12 branches (up to second digit of ISIC). Gap between Europe and the US
Model	Generalised least squares (GLS) estimates for random-effects (unbalanced) model	Feasible generalised least squares (FGLS) estimates for random-effects (unbalanced) model	Feasible generalised least squares (FGLS) estimates for random-effects (unbalanced) model, allowing autocorrelation in the error term
Dependent variable	Number of employees in service activities as a share of total employment	Number of employees in service activities as a share of total employment	(1) Number of employees in service activities as a share of total employment (2) Employment share gap between the United States and Europa
Independent variables	GDP per capita***	GDP per capita** (GDP per capita)^2**	GDP per capita*** Cycle***
	Relative price of services	Productivity differential**	Productivity services/ manufacturing***
	Size of the welfare state***	Government consumption**	Government consumption***
		Investment (World Development Indicators 2001)**	
	Earnings compression (ratio of the 10th to the 90th percentiles of the earning distribution, OECD)	Urbanization (World Development Indicators 2001)**	
	Female participation rate***	Female employment share	Female participation rate
		Trade ratio (manufacturing trade balance/services trade balance)	

Table 4. *(Continued)*

Countries	OECD (2000)	MESSINA (2003)	THIS PAPER
	OECD Countries	Panel Estimate on (a Maximum of) 27 OECD Countries	Panel Estimate on (a Maximum of) 13 EU Countries
		Exports of natural resources, % of GDP (World Development Indicators 2001)	
		Union density (Nickell and Nunziata 2001)**	Union density**
	Co-ordination and centralisation (OECD)**	Wage setting co-ordination (Nickell and Nunziata 2001)**	Centralisation*
	Tax wedge for a married working couple relative to the tax wedge of a one earner married couple	Earnings compression (ratio of the 50th to the 10th percentile of the earnings distribution, Barro and Lee (2001)	Centralisation^{2}*
	Average tax wedge	Replacement ratio (Nickell and Nunziata 2001)**	
		Secondary education (percentage of secondary school completed in total population, Barro and Lee 2000)	Educational attainment
	EPL	EPL (Nickell and Nunziata 2001)	EPL regular contracts
			EPL temporary contracts
	Product market regulation (summary index)	Administrative regulations on startups (Nicoletti, Scarpetta, & Boylaud, 1999)**	Administrative regulations on start ups
			Vacancies to unemployment ratio**

Note: ***statistically significant at the 1% level, **statistically significant at the 5% level and * statistically significant at the 10% level. This levels of significance refer to aggregate services.

where the error term ε_{it} is assumed to be normally distributed and such that

$$E(\varepsilon_{it}) = E(\alpha_i) = 0$$
$$E(\varepsilon_{it}^2) = \sigma^2 \; E(\alpha_{it}^2) = \sigma_\alpha^2 \; E(\alpha_i \varepsilon_{jt}) = 0 \quad \forall i, j, t$$
$$E(\varepsilon_{it}\varepsilon_{js}) = 0 \text{ if } t \neq s \text{ or } i \neq j$$
$$E(\alpha_i \alpha_j) = 0 \text{ if } i \neq j$$

N is the number of countries (up to 13 EU countries) and T_i the sample length in country i. The left-hand side variable y_{it} is the $((T_1 + \ldots + T_N) \times 1)$ vector of employment shares,[12] whereas x_{it} is the $((T_1 + \ldots + T_N) \times K)$ matrix of macro-economic and institutional determinants. The country-specific effect α_i is assumed to be randomly distributed across the cross-sectional units, as confirmed by the results of the Hausman's (1978) test. The model was first estimated by feasible generalised least square (FGLS).[13] However, the diagnostic statistics on residuals confirmed the presence of autocorrelation.[14] An alternative specification allowing autocorrelation in the error term was therefore estimated. In particular, it is assumed that:

$$\varepsilon_{it} = \rho \varepsilon_{it-1} + \eta_{it} \tag{3}$$

where $|\rho| < 1$ and η_{it} independent and normally distributed with

$$E(\eta_{it}) = 0$$

and

$$E(\eta_{it}^2) = \sigma^2$$

The model was estimated for the aggregate service sector, each service sector sub-sector and each branch separately using the GLS estimator proposed by Baltagi and Wu (1999).

Following the same logic of the empirical contributions discussed previously, we aim at quantifying the impact of a set of macro-economic and institutional determinants on the employment share in European countries. Annex 2 provides the detailed list of variables' definitions and data sources. A first set of macro-variables whose coefficients turned to be broadly significant and stable across specifications could be identified. Such a 'core' model not only includes GDP per capita as well as the productivity gap between manufacturing and services, but also an additional term capturing short-run fluctuations which may be indeed an important component of the employment share's dynamics. In order to explain differences in service employment shares across countries at similar income levels and productivity growth rates, the role of other, potentially relevant, determinants is also analysed. In particular, the model includes real government consumption, as a measure of exogenous internal demand; in many EU countries the size of the welfare state is in fact particularly important and a large contribution to service employment growth comes from social services which are largely provided or subsidised by the government. Therefore, the level of government expenditure, which increased in Europe from around 35% in 1970 to close to 50% in 2004, may be one of the main drivers of employment in services. Furthermore, the marketisation of household production may have also contributed to the expansion of service sector employment, although previous literature has generally found its role to be less important within a European context. We therefore consider the rate of female participation as an additional variable to capture this effect, showing the estimates of the core model including female participation every time the coefficient of the latter happens to be significant.

As a further step, we focus on the possible role played by labour and product market regulations. We do so by estimating a number of alternative specifications, in which the core model is augmented by including a wide range of indicators which are meant to capture different dimensions of countries' institutional setting.[15] At the outset, it should be noted that ideally taking services' heterogeneity properly into account would require sector-specific indicators of labour and product market regulations. Unfortunately, although data have become more accurate, the available indicators are still provided at an aggregate level. That may entail some unavoidable automatism in carrying out the econometrics, which we try to mitigate when interpreting the results by reflecting on the inherently different nature of the various sub-sectors and branches. Bearing these limitations in mind, no pre-selection of indicators on institutions have been made, letting data speak and assuming that every dimension of the regulatory environment may potentially play a role.

First, two dimensions of union activity – namely the degree of wage centralisation and union density – are considered. The first is intended to capture the level at which wage bargaining takes place. Some literature argues that highly centralised unions may be more concerned about issues of national inflation and competitiveness, which may result in restrained wage changes. Highly decentralised wage bargaining may also result in more restrained wage changes with wages more closely linked to labour productivity, or concerns over firm competitiveness, playing a stronger role in wage decisions. On the contrary, whereas centralised unions may not be able to capture sector specific rents, unions may be more successful at a sectoral level in translating monopoly rents and productivity increases into wages. This suggests the hump shape relationship between union centralisation and wages described in Calmfors and Driffil (1988). We therefore include a centralisation-squared term in our analysis to test the concavity of the effect of the degree of wage bargaining centralisation on the service sector employment share. At the same time, it can be argued that the greater the degree of union density the higher is the proportion of national employment that may be affected by wage bargaining decisions, and hence potentially the stronger the impact on service sector employment.[16] Furthermore, two additional measures of hiring and firing restrictions, namely the national employment protection legislation (EPL) for regular contracts and for temporary contracts, are also included in the analysis since a relatively strict legislation may in practice hamper the process reallocation of labour across sectors, thus having a potentially significant impact on the of the employment share in services. Moving to product market institutions, following Lopez-Garcia (2003) the presence of start-up costs (in particular, administrative burdens on the creation of new companies) may increase the cost of entering the market (especially by small-/medium-sized enterprises) and hinder services' growth in Europe vis-à-vis the United States, thereby creating bottlenecks in the process of shifting the sectoral composition of production from manufacturing to services.

Finally, one may argue that a reason for Europe's inability to absorb workers released from agriculture and industry could be found in the degree of mismatch between labour supply and job vacancies associated with the growing role of services. Over recent decades, there has been a change in the composition of the workforce – by qualification and skill-level associated with the change in the sectoral composition of production. Two additional explanatory variables are therefore introduced with the aim to test the hypothesis of a lack in the flexibility of labour supply in Europe, in particular in its ability to match the skills of the workforce with the skill requirements of the service sector in response to a sectoral shift. The first is a general measure of the ability of the labour market to match labour supply and demand – the vacancies to unemployment ratio. This measure provides a synthetic measure of labour market matching and picks up the effect of fluctuations in the business cycle, as well as changes in the production structure affecting the characteristics of labour demand and changes in the composition of the labour force.[17] The second variable is an indicator of educational attainment, since an economy with a relatively large endowment of skilled labour might be expected to employ a relatively higher share of its workers in knowledge-/skill-intensive services sector.

Results: Determinants of the Employment Share in the Aggregate Service Sector

Results for the aggregate service sector in Europe are presented in Table 5. When controlling for the business cycle, the strong positive correlation between the employment share and per-capita income is confirmed. Thus, as European economies have grown richer, the demand for services, and thus the employment share in this sector has increased. Our results also confirm that a decrease in productivity in services relative to manufacturing is associated with a higher service employment share. Following Baumol (1967) this suggests that slower productivity in services relative to manufacturing increased the service employment share in Europe, although this effect was smaller than the effect of per-capita incomes rising. Results support the hypothesis that countries with larger governments have a greater proportion of the workforce in services – public sector expenditure being found to have had a positive and significant impact on the service sector employment share in Europe over the period considered.[18] However, labour market participation of women seems to have played a less important role in the driving of the service employment share in Europe. This is in contrast to the findings of studies investigating the determinants of the employment share in the United States (e.g. Erdem & Glyn, 2001) and may be explained by still relatively low – although increasing – level of female participation in Europe.

With regard to the role of institutions in the determination of the aggregate service sector employment share (see the remaining columns of Table 5), there is some evidence that institutions matter. Wage bargaining systems have also had an effect on growth of the European employment share in services. Our results regarding the degree of union density generally show a negative effect of the rate of national union density on the service sector employment share, which is strongly significant. Recalling that institutional variables are measured at the national, rather than sectoral level, and the relatively low presence of unions in services as compared to manufacturing, this result suggests that countries with more union prevalence devote more of their economy's employment to manufacturing and less to services. Finally, the centralisation variable and its square reveal a significantly U-shaped relationship between the level of national wage bargaining and the total services employment share suggesting that employment in services is highest in fully centralised or decentralised systems. We find that neither the OECD indicator of product market regulation[19] (which includes both the administrative burdens on start-ups

Table 5. The Determinants of the Employment Share in Europe: Total Services, Panel Regression.

Total Services (ISIC 50-99)	Core	Core + Female Participation	I	II	III	IV	V	VI	VII
Constant	2.889	3.048	3.055	2.823	2.96	2.728	3.263	3.207	2.883
	[0.000]	[0.000]	[0.000]	[0.000]	[0.000]	[0.000]	[0.000]	[0.000]	[0.000]
GDP per capita	0.434	0.456	0.387	0.426	0.435	0.464	0.363	0.372	0.435
	[0.000]	[0.000]	[0.000]	[0.000]	[0.000]	[0.000]	[0.000]	[0.000]	[0.000]
Cycle	−0.027	−0.028	−0.019	−0.027	−0.028	−0.027	−0.022	−0.023	−0.027
	[0.000]	[0.000]	[0.000]	[0.000]	[0.000]	[0.000]	[0.000]	[0.000]	[0.000]
Productivity gap	−0.106	−0.111	−0.12	−0.107	−0.109	−0.105	−0.098	−0.097	−0.106
	[0.000]	[0.000]	[0.000]	[0.000]	[0.000]	[0.000]	[0.000]	[0.000]	[0.000]
Government consumption	0.144	0.173	0.164	0.141	0.149	0.187	0.088	0.09	0.144
	[0.000]	[0.000]	[0.000]	[0.000]	[0.000]	[0.000]	[0.001]	[0.001]	[0.000]
Female participation		−0.033							
		[0.165]							
Vacancies			−0.005						
			[0.048]						
Education				0.016					
				[0.262]					
Union density					−0.021				
					[0.038]				
Centralisation						−0.042			
						[0.062]			
Centralisation^2						0.006			
						[0.075]			
EPL regular contracts							−0.007		
							[0.226]		
EPL temporary contracts								0.001	
								[0.661]	
Barriers									0.001
									[0.655]
Observations	334	287	181	334	319	256	218	218	334
Number of countries	13	13	9	13	13	11	13	13	13
R^2 within	0.946	0.948	0.933	0.946	0.951	0.957	0.89	0.891	0.946
R^2 between	0.462	0.404	0.487	0.472	0.481	0.257	0.48	0.455	0.461
R^2 Global	0.665	0.575	0.611	0.67	0.666	0.551	0.556	0.537	0.664

Note: *p*-values in parentheses.

and regulatory and administrative opacity) nor the variables capturing the strictness of employment protection legislation are significant.[20]

On the contrary, the mismatch indicator given by the vacancies to unemployment ratio is found to have a significant negative impact on the aggregate employment share.[21] This variable supports the hypothesis that a lack of flexibility in European labour supply in Europe, in particular its inability to match the skills of the workforce with the skill requirements of the service sector, e.g. in response to a sectoral shift have inhibited the growth of the service sector employment share.

Zooming In: Results by Sub-Sector and Branch

This section focuses on a more detailed discussion of the econometric results by sub-sector and particularly branch. Results are presented in Tables 6–9. Given the heterogeneity of the service sector, this analysis aims to provide some further insights to the determinants of the employment share for certain segments of the total service sector. Furthermore, this more disaggregated analysis allows the consideration of more astute questions, which may be relevant to some branches, but not others. For example, the analysis of particular branches, such as financial intermediation and real estate activities, may be especially interesting and important against the background of the financial crisis and consideration of whether large job losses in these sectors might be easily reabsorbed into the labour market. Moreover, an analysis of a group of branches, such as those providing mainly public sector services, may reveal some information, e.g. regarding the employment implications of private versus public provision.

We have argued earlier that the demand for services is income elastic, thus as incomes rise, so does employment in the aggregate services sector. However, this effect might be expected to differ across sub-sectors and branches. For example, some services may represent inferior goods (e.g. land and water transport), others luxuries (such as recreational, cultural and sporting activities, the employment of domestic staff and research and development) and the effect of increasing GDP per capita can be expected to have a differing impact on the employment share for these services. Furthermore, structural changes affecting many countries, such as the ageing of the European population, may support decreased demand and thus employment in some services (such as the provision of education for the young), and increased demand and employment for others (such as health care). Results for sub-sector and branch support both of these hypotheses. They show that when controlling for the business cycle, richer countries have a greater proportion of employment in the finance, insurance real estate and business services sub-sector, particularly in the branch of renting of machinery/equipment and other business activities,

Table 6. The Determinants of the Employment Share in Europe: Sub-Sector 1, Wholesale and Retail Trade, Restaurants and Hotels, Panel Regression.

	Wholesale and Retail Trade; Restaurants and Hotels			Wholesale and Retail Trade; Repairs		Hotels and Restauraants	
	(ISIC 50-55)			(ISIC 50-52)		(ISIC 55)	
	Core	I	II	Core	I	Core	I
Constant	2.579	2.79	2.674	2.507	2.655	1.882	2.213
	[0.000]	[0.000]	[0.000]	[0.000]	[0.000]	[0.000]	[0.000]
GDP per capita	0.165	0.14	0.182	0.104	0.078	0.191	0.177
	[0.000]	[0.000]	[0.000]	[0.003]	[0.035]	[0.005]	[0.010]
Cycle	−0.004	−0.003	−0.007	0.002	0.005	−0.012	−0.013
	[0.210]	[0.497]	[0.095]	[0.568]	[0.240]	[0.094]	[0.079]
Productivity gap	−0.046	−0.045	−0.02	−0.048	−0.05	−0.257	−0.239
	[0.023]	[0.028]	[0.369]	[0.035]	[0.032]	[0.000]	[0.000]
Government consumption	0.018	0.034	−0.031	0.022	0.054	0.016	0.002
	[0.634]	[0.389]	[0.498]	[0.612]	[0.247]	[0.825]	[0.984]
Union density		−0.054			−0.045		−0.092
							[0.003]
		[0.001]			[0.015]		[0.003]
Centralisation			−0.097				
			[0.038]				
(Centralisation)^2			0.016				
			[0.034]				
Observations	328	313	250	275	262	262	249
Countries	13	13	11	12	12	12	12
R^2 within	0.453	0.481	0.405	0.246	0.265	0.795	0.793
R^2 between	0.098	0.006	0.048	0.001	0.112	0.11	0.048
R^2 global	0.038	0.118	0.047	0.043	0.114	0.027	0.153

Note: *p*-values in parentheses.

and in community social and personal services, including health, other community social and personal services; as shown in Annex 1, many luxury-type or high-demand services belong to these sub-sectors and branches. Similarly, richer countries have a smaller proportion of employment in transport and storage.

The results in Tables 6–9 also suggest that while some sub-sectors can be characterised by Baumol's cost disease, other sectors have productivity growth rates which exceed those in manufacturing and the productivity differential between manufacturing and services may not have such a strong

Table 7. The Determinants of the Employment Share in Europe: Sub-Sector 2, Transport, Storage and Communication, Panel Regression.

	Transport and Storage and Communications		Transport and Storage		Post and Telecommunications	
	(ISIC 60-64)		(ISIC 60-63)		(ISIC 64)	
	Core	Core	I	II	Core	I
Constant	2.27	2.484	3.17	2.549	−0.818	−0.876
	[0.000]	[0.000]	[0.000]	[0.000]	[0.009]	[0.005]
GDP per capita	−0.055	−0.097	−0.219	−0.115	0.177	0.209
	[0.035]	[0.010]	[0.000]	[0.003]	[0.007]	[0.002]
Cycle	0.001	−0.003	0.012	−0.002	0.007	0.004
	[0.696]	[0.528]	[0.070]	[0.611]	[0.423]	[0.616]
Productivity gap	−0.116	−0.085	−0.188	−0.086	−0.207	−0.195
	[0.000]	[0.000]	[0.000]	[0.000]	[0.000]	[0.000]
Government	0.071	−0.088	−0.022	−0.082	0.558	0.577
consumption	[0.089]	[0.086]	[0.744]	[0.105]	[0.000]	[0.000]
Vacancies			−0.009			
			[0.084]			
Barriers				−0.011		
				[0.071]		
Observations	328	221	118	221	221	217
Number of countries	13	11	7	11	11	11
R^2 within	0.356	0.181	0.458	0.164	0.536	0.518
R^2 between	0.358	0.096	0.232	0.178	0.678	0.669
R^2 global	0.117	0.037	0.242	0.091	0.616	0.598

Note: *p*-values in parentheses

effect on the employment share in services. Differences in productivity across service sector branches can depend on whether the respective services produce for final demand or intermediate production (see e.g. Oulton, 2003). Strong productivity growth and a high commitment to the production of intermediate goods can result in a strong indirect and positive impact of productivity in services on productivity in other sectors of the economy, and the economy as a whole. Price and income elasticities can be expected to correspondingly vary across sub-sector and branch and there may be differences according to whether a service is exposed to intensive competition, or whether service production is more locally or regionally orientated (Wölfl, 2006). Branches which are more subject to actual or potential competition, for example from international markets, as in the case of financial and business services or telecommunications services, are

Table 8. The Determinants of the Employment Share in Europe: Sub-Sector 3, Finance, Insurance, Real Estate and Business Services, Panel Regression.

	Finance, Insurance, Real Estate and Business Services						Financial Intermediation		Real Estate Activities	Renting of M&EQ and Other Business Activities	
	(ISIC 65-74)						(ISIC 65-67)		(ISIC 70)	(ISIC 71-74)	
	Core	I	II	III	IV	V	Core	I	Core	Core	I
Constant	0.474	−0.363	1.132	0.159	1.786	1.494	0.635	2.305	2.292	−0.97	−0.91
	[0.143]	0.336	[0.001]	[0.646]	[0.000]	[0.000]	[0.072]	[0.000]	[0.000]	[0.043]	[0.049]
GDP per capita	0.947	0.877	0.886	1.014	0.771	0.815	0.231	−0.24	−0.327	1.486	1.542
	[0.000]	[0.000]	[0.000]	[0.000]	[0.000]	[0.000]	[0.002]	[0.002]	[0.000]	[0.000]	[0.000]
Cycle	−0.05	−0.049	−0.049	−0.052	−0.036	−0.038	−0.016	0.009	−0.005	−0.063	−0.07
	[0.000]	[0.000]	[0.000]	[0.000]	[0.000]	[0.000]	[0.054]	[0.304]	[0.661]	[0.000]	[0.000]
Productivity gap	−0.282	−0.278	−0.322	−0.238	−0.367	−0.365	−0.115	−0.074	−0.777	−0.314	−0.31
	[0.000]	[0.000]	[0.000]	[0.000]	[0.000]	[0.000]	[0.000]	[0.001]	[0.000]	[0.000]	[0.000]
Government consumption	0.099	0.062	0.142	0.136	0.007	0.022	0.051	−0.059	0.622	−0.079	−0.084
	[0.142]	[0.350]	[0.034]	[0.035]	[0.936]	[0.796]	[0.585]	[0.549]	[0.000]	[0.385]	[0.402]
Education		0.171									
		[0.000]									
Union density			−0.115								−0.065
			[0.000]								[0.079]
Centralisation				−0.131							
				[0.028]							
$(\text{Centralisation})^2$				0.02							
				[0.037]							

EPL regular contracts					−0.038 [0.042]						
EPL temporary contracts						0.004 [0.520]		−0.012 [0.067]			
Observations	341	341	326	263	218	218	260	189	192	192	184
Countries	13	13	13	11	13	13	12	12	10	10	10
R^2 within	0.943	0.944	0.955	0.949	0.875	0.877	0.315	0.233	0.884	0.972	0.973
R^2 between	0.334	0.347	0.441	0.132	0.386	0.336	0.347	0.165	0.066	0.355	0.436
R^2 global	0.598	0.605	0.648	0.461	0.493	0.456	0.268	0.035	0.003	0.523	0.589

Note: *p*-values in parentheses.

Table 9. The Determinants of the Employment Share in Europe: Sub-Sector 4, Community, Social and Personal Services, Panel Rregression.

	Community Social and Personal Services (ISIC 75-99)				Public Administration and Defence; Compulsory Social Security (ISIC 75)	Education (ISIC 80)					Health and Social Work (ISIC 85)		Other Community, Social and Personal Services (ISIC 90-93)		Private Households with Employed Persons (ISIC 95)		
	Core	Core + Female Participation	I	II	Core	Core	Core + Female Participation	I	II	III	Core	Core + Female Participation	Core	I	Core	I	III
Constant	2.233	2.648	2.244	2.191	2.36	1.31	2.917	2.164	1.769	1.307	0.75	−0.836	1.611	2.142	3.888	5.951	1.55
	[0.000]	[0.000]	[0.000]	[0.000]	[0.000]	[0.000]	[0.000]	[0.000]	[0.000]	[0.000]	[0.030]	[0.244]	[0.000]	[0.000]	[0.017	[0.001]	[0.397]
GDP per capita	0.327	0.347	0.34	0.337	−0.133	0.24	0.373	0.041	0.118	0.264	0.429	0.346	0.35	0.297	−0.126	−0.281	0.462
	[0.000]	[0.000]	[0.000]	[0.000]	[0.016]	[0.000]	[0.000]	[0.571]	[0.098]	[0.000]	[0.000]	[0.000]	[0.000]	[0.000]	[0.673]	[0.370]	[0.123]
Cycle	−0.028	−0.026	−0.029	−0.028	−0.005	−0.028	−0.025	−0.017	−0.021	−0.028	−0.035	−0.027	−0.035	−0.036	−0.043	−0.036	−0.034
	[0.000]	[0.000]	[0.000]	[0.000]	[0.423]	[0.000]	[0.001]	[0.008]	[0.001]	[0.000]	[0.000]	[0.000]	[0.000]	[0.000]	[0.067]	[0.153]	[0.145]
Productivity gap	−0.222	−0.238	−0.223	−0.222	−0.334	−0.299	−0.305	−0.304	−0.298	−0.3	−0.297	−0.308	−0.305	−0.318	−0.335	−0.349	−0.365
	[0.000]	[0.000]	[0.000]	[0.000]	[0.000]	[0.000]	[0.000]	[0.000]	[0.000]	[0.000]	[0.000]	[0.000]	[0.000]	[0.000]	[0.002]	[0.001]	[0.001]
Government consumption	0.372	0.468	0.377	0.37	0.528	0.374	0.606	0.342	0.339	0.398	0.45	0.597	0.081	0.055	−0.598	−0.514	−0.201
	[0.000]	[0.000]	[0.000]	[0.000]	[0.000]	[0.000]	[0.000]	[0.000]	[0.000]	[0.000]	[0.000]	[0.000]	[0.269	[0.502]	[0.041]	[0.105]	[0.521]
Female participation		−0.08					−0.31					0.167					
		[0.036]					[0.000]					[0.072]					
Union density														−0.067		−0.478	
														[0.032]		[0.022]	
EPL regular contracts								−0.043									−0.282
								[0.002]									[0.062]
EPL temporary contracts									0.009								
									[0.069]								
Barriers				0.009													
				[0.070]													
Observations	334	287	327	334	233	233	194	172	172	227	233	194	233	222	166	159	117
Countries	13	13	13	13	11	11	11	11	11	11	11	11	11	11	8	8	8
R^2 within	0.883	0.909	0.893	0.885	0.689	0.784	0.829	0.632	0.6	0.801	0.874	0.89	0.905	0.896	0.356	0.462	0.521
R^2 between	0.611	0.624	0.607	0.612	0.145	0.29	0.45	0.551	0.414	0.316	0.715	0.818	0.029	0.05	0	0.132	0.019
R^2 global	0.68	0.682	0.68	0.681	0.24	0.508	0.669	0.543	0.426	0.539	0.569	0.686	0.118	0.306	0.001	0.17	0.008

Note: *p*-values in parentheses.

likely to experience greater downward pressure on prices, forcing firms to increase their level of productivity. These sectors are also strongly involved in the production of intermediate goods. For example, more than half of transport and communications services are used as intermediate inputs, which the share for final demand is only about 20%. Finance, insurance, real estate and business are also characterised by a share of intermediate goods production of around 50%. Correspondingly the results in Table 6–9 show that within these sub-sectors and particularly the branches of transport and storage, financial intermediation and real estate activities, the productivity differential between services and manufacturing has a far smaller effect on the employment share.

In contrast, service sub-sectors with a more domestic or local orientation, such as service provision in the community, social and personal services sub-sector, are likely to face less competition, and thus less pressure to increase productivity. Community, social and personal services provides an example of a 'traditional' service sub-sector, with about 80% of output aimed at final consumption and only about 10% serving intermediate demand. A high share of final demand in output is also found in hotel and restaurant services. In these sectors, productivity is lower and the effect of the productivity differential has a larger effect on the employment share, in-line with Baumol's argument. Furthermore, results for the community, social and personal services sub-sector stress the importance of the government expenditure in this sector, whereas the relatively large magnitude of the effect on the productivity gap is also suggestive of the lower productivity of employment. Thus government seems to specialise in the provision of services which are particularly labour intensive. Public provision could also be associated with a greater employment-intensity than private provision of the *same* services, thus suggesting a lower efficiency of public versus private service provision; however, this hypothesis cannot be tested directly with our data.

Results for the core determinants of the employment share by sub-sector generally stress the important, but relatively smaller role of retailing, in-line with developments in both employment and productivity in Europe than found for the United States. Instead, producer and social services play a significantly stronger role in the determination of aggregate service sector employment. Furthermore, the increase in female participation is only found to have played a significant role in the determination of the European employment share in some braches of the latter sector.[22]

Moving to consideration of the institutional variables, one might be interested in the hypothesis of whether, on the back of the financial crisis, large numbers of unemployed workers in key sectors such as financial intermediation and real estate activities can be easily reabsorbed into the labour market. Results in Table 8 show that for the sub-sector of finance, insurance, real estate and business services, as a whole, the impact of institutional variables is found to be relatively large and significant. Particularly high degrees of union density, centralisation and stringent employment protection legislation have inhibited employment growth in this sector. However, the generally high skill level of the labour force in this sub-sector – here proxied by the average years of schooling – has had a positive and significant impact on the employment share and is likely to also support the re-employment of unemployed labour from this sub-sector.

Other interesting results to mention include a relatively strong negative effect of union density in wholesale and trade, and hotels and restaurants. This result supports Gordon's (1997) suggestion that wage compression introduced by unions in Europe has cut back jobs in the lower end of the skill distribution within European service sectors. Furthermore, there is further evidence that the employment share is highest in fully centralised or decentralised systems. Other institutions are found to have only limited effects in selected branches. For example, strict product market regulation is found to have inhibited the expansion of employment in services within transport and storage, and relatively strict national EPL on regular contracts has a significantly negative effect on service sector employment in education.

AN INVESTIGATION OF THE SERVICE SECTOR EMPLOYMENT SHARE GAP: EUROPE VIS-À-VIS THE UNITED STATES

Understanding the main factors driving the gap in service sector employment between Europe and the United States is one of the focal concerns of policy makers in achieving higher employment levels in Europe. This section turns to this gap for a closer consideration of whether macroeconomic determinants or the institutional framework might have played a stronger part in explaining the differential service employment share.

We base this analysis on the following equation

$$Y_{\mathrm{US}_t} - Y_{\mathrm{EUR}_{it}} = \alpha + \eta(X_{\mathrm{US}_t} - X_{\mathrm{EUR}_{it}}) + \gamma_{it} \quad t = 1 \ldots T_i \text{ and } i = 1 \ldots N \tag{4}$$

with

$$\gamma_{it} = v_i + r_{it}$$

and

$$r_{it} = \delta r_{it-1} + \sigma_{it}$$

The model is again estimated using the GLS estimator proposed by Baltagi and Wu (1999). N denotes the number of countries and T_i the sample length in country i. The left-hand side variable $Y_{\mathrm{US}_t} - Y_{\mathrm{EUR}_{it}}$ is a $((T_1 + \ldots + T_N) \times 1)$ vector of the difference in the employment share between the United States and each of the EU-15 countries for which data are available. The left-hand side variable $(X_{\mathrm{US}_t} - X_{\mathrm{EUR}_{it}})$ is a $((T_1 + \ldots + T_N) \times K)$ matrix of the difference in the same macro-economic and institutional determinants – as considered in model (1) earlier – between the United States and each European country.

We test the significance of the same alternative specifications presented earlier, for the aggregate service sector and the four main sub-sectors, with the exclusion of the specifications including the degree of centralisation of wage bargaining and the vacancy to unemployment ratio, due to the unavailability of comparable data for the United States.[23] Tables 10–12 present the results of this investigation. A first notable finding is the significant and stable contribution of a number of our core set of variables to the US–European service sector employment share gap. Differentials in the levels of GDP per capita and government consumption contribute strongly and positively to the positive US–European employment share gap in the aggregate service sector and three of the main sub-sectors and negatively and significantly to the negative US–European employment share gap in transport and storage sub-sector. This result highlights the importance of economic growth for job creation. It supports the hypothesis that stronger increases in per-capita income and public consumption levels in Europe relative to the United States over the recent decade have helped to decrease the employment share gap in the aggregate service sector between the two continents. Furthermore, this result emphasises the importance of particularly the finance and community service sub-sectors in closing this gap.

The US–European gap in productivity between manufacturing and services is also found to be a significant determinant of the employment share gap, although less important in terms of its magnitude than per-capita income or government consumption differentials. It negatively contributes to the positive employment share gap in the aggregate service sector, and in the social and personal services sub-sector. This result indicates that the

Table 10. The Determinants of the United States–Europe Employment Share Gap. Total Services, Panel Regression.

	Total Services (ISIC 50-99)						
	Core	Core + Female Participation	I	II	III	IV	V
Constant	0.196	0.199	0.196	0.189	0.143	0.163	0.196
	[0.000]	[0.000]	[0.000]	[0.000]	[0.000]	[0.000]	[0.000]
GDP per capita	0.128	0.167	0.129	0.142	0.135	0.15	0.124
	[0.022]	[0.004]	[0.021]	[0.012]	[0.014]	[0.008]	[0.028]
Cycle	−0.004	−0.005	−0.004	−0.005	−0.002	−0.002	−0.004
	[0.176]	[0.126]	[0.177]	[0.069]	[0.458]	[0.440]	[0.215]
Productivity gap	−0.04	−0.049	−0.04	−0.045	−0.022	−0.017	−0.04
	[0.013]	[0.007]	[0.014]	[0.007]	[0.231]	[0.352]	[0.013]
Government consumption	0.214	0.244	0.214	0.206	0.194	0.199	0.215
	[0.000]	[0.000]	[0.000]	[0.000]	[0.000]	[0.000]	[0.000]
Female participation		−0.073					
		[0.006]					
Education			0.0001				
			[0.993]				
Union density				0.001			
				[0.926]			
EPL regular contracts					−0.012]		
					[0.056		
EPL temporary contracts						−0.002	
						[0.376]	
Barriers							−0.005
							[0.306]
Observations	284	252	284	270	203	203	284
Countries	13	13	13	13	13	13	13
R^2 within	0.635	0.623	0.635	0.596	0.74	0.739	0.638
R^2 between	0.589	0.614	0.589	0.566	0.63	0.562	0.595
R^2 global	0.571	0.571	0.571	0.536	0.607	0.54	0.578

Note: *p*-values in parentheses.

falling relative productivity in the aggregate service sector in Europe relative to the United States in recent years should have also contributed in closing gap between US and European service sector employment shares and is particularly apparent for the community, social and personal services sub-sector. Results on the female participation variable suggest that the stronger increase in the labour market participation of women in Europe relative to the United States over the period considered has also helped to reduce the

Table 11. The Determinants of the United States–Europe Employment Share Gap, ISIC 50-55 and 60-64, Panel Regression.

	Wholesale and Retail Trade; Restaurants and Hotels (ISIC 50-55)						Transport and Storage and Communications (ISIC 60-64)					
	Core	I	II	III	IV	V	Core	I	II	III	IV	V
Constant	0.26	0.256	0.221	0.321	0.322	0.263	−0.1	−0.092	−0.067	−0.219	−0.175	−0.098
	[0.000]	[0.000]	[0.000]	[0.000]	[0.000]	[0.000]	[0.075]	[0.093]	[0.258]	[0.000]	[0.004]	[0.082]
GDP per capita	0.172	0.168	0.155	−0.002	0.017	0.149	−0.265	−0.215	−0.23	−0.042	−0.108	−0.257
	[0.038]	[0.044]	[0.064]	[0.984]	[0.833]	[0.069]	[0.016]	[0.046]	[0.038]	[0.714]	[0.337]	[0.019]
Cycle	0.001	0.002	0.004	0.015	0.015	0.002	0.006	0.003	0.004	−0.011	−0.009	0.005
	[0.767]	[0.697]	[0.422]	[0.004]	[0.005]	[0.581]	[0.323]	[0.659]	[0.489]	[0.075]	[0.155]	[0.372]
Productivity gap	−0.04	−0.039	−0.043	−0.101	−0.09	−0.04	0.042	0.04	0.052	0.12	0.11	0.043
	[0.135]	[0.136]	[0.108]	[0.004]	[0.010]	[0.129]	[0.194]	[0.221]	[0.108]	[0.002]	[0.005]	[0.191]
Government consumption	0.126	0.127	0.153	0.2	0.194	0.123	−0.091	−0.091	−0.13	−0.205	−0.197	−0.09
	[0.000]	[0.000]	[0.000]	[0.000]	[0.000]	[0.000]	[0.020]	[0.020]	[0.001]	[0.000]	[0.000]	[0.020]
Education		0.002						−0.007				
		[0.582]						[0.048]				
Union density			−0.062						0.066			
			[0.000]						[0.004]			
EPL regular contracts				−0.011						0.002		
				[0.331						[0.863]		
EPL contracts temporary					−0.006						0.009	
					[0.087]						[0.026]	
Barriers						−0.014						0.013
						[0.122]						[0.216]
Observations	284	284	270	203	203	284	284	284	270	203	203	284
Countries	13	13	13	13	13	13	13	13	13	13	13	13
R^2 within	0.467	0.474	0.419	0.611	0.611	0.468	0.261	0.277	0.251	0.522	0.567	0.276
R^2 between	0.238	0.234	0.062	0.363	0.369	0.206	0.24	0.318	0.098	0.179	0.181	0.244
R^2 global	0.077	0.077	0.002	0.108	0.104	0.055	0.329	0.386	0.107	0.1	0.143	0.328

Note: *p*-values in parentheses.

Table 12. The Determinants of the United States–Europe Employment Share Gap, ISIC 65-74 and 75-99, Panel Regression.

	Finance, Insurance, Real Estate and Business Services (ISIC 65-74)						Community Social and Personal Services (ISIC 75-99)						
	Core	I	II	III	IV	V	Core	Core + Female Participation	I	II	III	IV	V
Constant	0.3	0.254	0.243	0.21	0.31	0.297	0.151	0.174	0.162	0.179	0.052	0.058	0.151
	[0.001]	[0.004]	[0.004]	[0.034]	[0.001]	[0.001]	[0.002]	[0.000]	[0.001]	[0.001]	[0.279]	[0.201]	[0.002]
GDP per capita	0.283	0.238	0.324	0.178	0.281	0.261	0.251	0.3	0.262	0.276	0.276	0.287	0.251
	[0.106]	[0.170]	[0.059]	[0.352]	[0.143]	[0.136]	[0.015]	[0.005]	[0.012]	[0.008]	[0.002]	[0.001]	[0.015]
Cycle	0.008	0.013	0.009	0.031	0.029	0.009	−0.019	−0.018	−0.02	−0.024	−0.024	−0.025	−0.019
	[0.370]	[0.162]	[0.329]	[0.004]	[0.008]	[0.295]	[0.001]	[0.001]	[0.000]	[0.000]	[0.000]	[0.000]	[0.001]
Productivity gap	−0.05	−0.045	−0.056	−0.079	−0.058	−0.05	−0.089	−0.099	−0.09	−0.095	0.0001	0.002	−0.089
	[0.347]	[0.385]	[0.309]	[0.249]	[0.407]	[0.337]	[0.006]	[0.007]	[0.005]	[0.003]	[0.999]	[0.950]	[0.006]
Government consumption	0.236	0.245	0.263	0.289	0.329	0.237	0.366	0.419	0.363	0.313	0.235	0.238	0.366
	[0.000]	[0.000]	[0.000]	[0.000]	[0.000]	[0.000]	[0.000]	[0.000]	[0.000]	[0.000]	[0.000]	[0.000]	[0.000]
Female participation								−0.212					
								[0.000]					
Education		0.017							−0.004				
		[0.002]							[0.223]				
Union density			−0.059							0.061			
			[0.110]							[0.006]			
EPL regular contracts				−0.061							−0.004		
				[0.010]							[0.668]		
EPL contracts temporary					−0.006							−0.001	
					[0.437]							[0.851]	
Barriers						−0.028							0.0001
						[0.104]							[0.994]
Observations	284	284	270	203	203	284	284	252	284	270	203	203	284
Countries	13	13	13	13	13	13	13	13	13	13	13	13	13
R^2 within	0.36	0.395	0.374	0.46	0.483	0.376	0.511	0.535	0.519	0.481	0.555	0.55	0.511
R^2 between	0.425	0.406	0.581	0.495	0.401	0.43	0.657	0.57	0.655	0.53	0.604	0.601	0.657
R^2 global	0.367	0.367	0.502	0.464	0.352	0.377	0.6	0.508	0.598	0.472	0.555	0.551	0.6

Note: *p*-values in parentheses.

service sector employment share gap between the United States and Europe, being again particularly driven by the community social and personal services sub-sector.

There is also some evidence that the institutional framework in Europe has an important role to play in the expansion of service sector employment in Europe relative to the United States. Tables 11 and 12 show that US–European skill differentials significantly affect the employment share gap in two sub-sectors transport, storage and communications (a negative effect on the negative gap) and finance, real estate and business activities (a positive effect on the positive gap). This latter results is especially interesting in finance, real estate and business activities which – as shown in section earlier – is a major employer of high-skilled labour and one of the sub-sectors where the employment share in Europe is significantly lower than in the United States; in particular, it would suggest the importance of upgrading the skill composition of labour supply in Europe in order to reduce the gap. A wider differential between the United States and Europe in the degree of union density significantly influences the US–European employment gap in three service sector sub-sectors, higher average union density in Europe increasing the US employment share advantage in wholesale and retail trade and decreasing the European employment share advantage in transport, storage and communications. The positive effect of the differential in the degree of union density on the US–European employment share in the community, social and personal services may be being driven by a higher rate of union density in the United States than in Europe in this sector. There is also some significant evidence of strict EPL on either regular or temporary contracts reinforcing the positive US–European employment share gap, both within the aggregate service sector and across three out of four of the sub-sectors. Finally, the lower level of barriers to business start-up is found to increase the positive US–European employment share gap in most sectors, although this effect is never significant.

CONCLUSIONS

Our investigation into the determinants of the service sector employment share in Europe confirms the results of previous studies which show that as European economies have grown richer, the demand for services, and thus the employment share in this sector has increased. In particular, we find that richer countries tend to have a greater proportion of employment in the finance, insurance, real estate and business services sub-sector, as well as in community, social and personal services. Our results also confirm that, on aggregate, a decrease in productivity in services relative to manufacturing is associated with a higher employment service share; however, this effect is found to be smaller in magnitude than that of final demand.

Moving to a finer disaggregation, results suggest that the productivity differential between services and manufacturing has a far smaller effect on the employment share in those branches facing stronger competition and/or principally involved in the production of intermediate goods. This applies in particular to the branches of transport and storage, financial intermediation and real estate activities. In contrast, service sub-sectors more domestically or locally oriented, such as service provision in community, social and personal services, face less competition, are aimed at final consumption and the effect of the productivity differential has a larger effect on the employment share, in-line with Baumol's cost disease. Furthermore, results support the hypothesis that countries with larger governments have a greater proportion of the workforce in services – the level of public sector expenditure is found to have had a positive and significant impact on service sector employment share in Europe over the period under analysis. However, the increased labour market participation of women seems to have played a less important role in the rising employment share in Europe. Differences in female labour market participation between Europe and the United States seems instead to play a significant role in explaining the *gap* between European and US employment shares, as it is the case for the remaining macro-variables belonging to the core specification.

Moving to the investigation of the possible impact of the regulatory environment, we also find evidence that some institutions have affected the pattern and thus development of sectoral employment in Europe. Countries with more union prevalence seem to devote more of their economy's employment to manufacturing and less to services. Furthermore, employment in services is found to be highest in fully centralised or decentralised systems. On the contrary, the degree of strictness of employment protection legislation does not seem to be particularly relevant in explaining the European services sector employment share; this is also the case for the OECD indicator of product market regulation. Finally, the finding of a significant negative impact of the vacancies to unemployment ratio on the aggregate employment share supports the hypothesis that a lack of flexibility in European labour markets, in particular its inability to match the skills of the workforce with the skill requirements of the service sector (e.g. in response to a sectoral shift) has inhibited the growth of the service sector employment share. The US–European differences in the human capital content of the workforce-measured by the level of educational attainment – as well as in the union density and employment protection legislation seem to matter in driving the US–European differences in the employment share.

Summing up, these results suggest that structural policies to boost human capital accumulation and to address rigidities in the labour market are supportive of job creation and increased employment in the services sector. Policies implemented in these areas over the last decade in the context of the European Employment Strategy seem to have contributed to the catch up of the European employment share with the United States. However, the dramatically lower levels of employment protection legislation and unionisation in the United States relative to Europe, together with the low levels of educational attainment in some European countries, seem to be among the main factors behind the persistence of this gap. Work by, for instance, the OECD (2004a) highlights the dramatically lower levels of employment protection legislation and unionisation in the United States relative to Europe. Studies such as OECD (2004b) show that whilst some European countries such as the United Kingdom and Sweden hold among the highest first university-level degree completion rate of OECD countries, and many countries have seen a rise in the average education levels of their citizens over the past decade, low educational attainment levels remain a particular concern in Greece, Italy, Portugal and Spain, which are also among the countries where the gap in the relatively high-skilled sectors is largest. Our analysis confirms the importance of addressing these remaining institutional and skill differentials to close the US–European service sector employment share gap, and more generally, to increase overall employment levels in Europe.

NOTES

1. Austria, Belgium, Denmark, Finland, France, Germany, Greece, Italy, the Netherlands, Portugal, Spain, Sweden and the United Kingdom – i.e. the EU-15 minus Ireland and Luxembourg.
2. This increase in the share of the workforce employed in services may in part be due to the practice of manufacturing industries to increasingly outsource their service activities. In this case, since National Accounts define firms according to their main product, the higher share of the employment in services would emerge merely as the result of the reallocation of activities. On the importance of taking into account changes in firms' organisation, particularly the practice of contracting out, see for instance Elfring (1989). According to Greenhalgh and Gregory (2002), Russo and

Schettkat (1999, 2001) and Petit (1986) outsourcing from manufacturing has in fact increased; however, they find that this effect is not sufficient to explain the trend towards service sector employment, as well as the difference in the share of service sector employment between the United States and Europe. That also seems to be confirmed by the upward trend in the share of "white collar" jobs (OECD, 2000).

3. Data on service employment rate in Europe show an even higher negative gap relative to the United States, due to the strong increase in the United States employment to working age population ratio.

4. Although not exactly overlapping, the ISIC classification broadly corresponds to the grouping in four service activities – namely personal, distributive, producer and social services – proposed in Singelmann (1978) and Elfring (1988).

5. Supporters of the income effect have compared the output of richer and poorer countries, finding a positive relationship between wealth and the share of services in GDP. However, it has been argued that this effect disappears if one allows for the higher relative prices of services in richer economies – and that 'real' service sector shares may not bear relation to a country's level of prosperity. Along this line, a number of studies find that the share of services in real output remained constant as per capital income rises. See, for instance Summers (1985), Baumol, Blackman and Wolff (1989) for the US 1947–1976, Ramaswamy and Rowthorn (1997) for the United States, Japan and Europe as a whole 1960–1994.

6. The nature of several service activities, which cannot be automated and have to go through set standardised processes (e.g. a doctor's diagnosis, a live orchestral performance), is behind the relatively stagnant productivity growth in the service sector. According to Baumol (2001), while some services (e.g. postal delivery times, rubbish collection) may have benefited from technological advances and many in particular from computerisation (particularly in the financial industries), he argues that so far, these productivity gains had been modest, whereas in other services no significant sources of productivity gains can be identified (e.g. care of the elderly).

7. Baumol (1967) argues that as technical progress in the industrial sector increases, wages will rise; if wage increases at the same or similar rates across sectors, labour cost per unit will remain constant (or even decrease) for manufacturing goods, but will exponentially rise in the lower productivity service sector, thereby leading to strong increases in service sector prices (the only possibility to halt this mechanism is to isolate the labour markets of each sector and freeze wage increases in services – arguably unrealistic). The paradox lies in the fact that despite the increasing relative cost/prices of services, the demand for services persists. Baumol (2001) links this to the fact that some services simply cannot be produced more cheaply; that some are provided by the government so that price increases are not observed first hand by the consumer; and that people consider some services critical for their well-being.

8. Baumol (2001) identifies the strong existence of the cost disease for a number of service areas (e.g. health care, education, legal services, police protection, restaurant services and car repairs) over the period 1960 to 1993 in the United States, Japan, Canada, France, Germany and the United Kingdom, although to varying degrees.

9. Russo and Schettkat (2001) find evidence of a significant increase in final demand, an increase in the demand for services from the manufacturing industry and an increase in the demand of intermediate services in the production of services as explanations for employment growth in the United States and Europe.

10. These institutions have been found to truncate the lower end of the low wage job distribution in countries with high labour productivity and wage dispersion (e.g. Spain, Italy and Germany), and particularly to reduce female labour participation. Furthermore, Bertola (2001) argues that contractual arrangements tend to prevent wages adjusting to local labour market conditions – resulting in low incentives for regional mobility.

11. However, the causal relationship between the dependent variable and independent variables is not entirely unambiguous. This is mentioned where relevant in the interpretation of results below.

12. The employment share (for aggregate services, services' sub-sectors and branches) is measured as a ratio to employment in the overall economy. One might consider whether the relevant dependent variable in our analysis should be the employment in sector/working age population ratio (employment rate) or the employment share (employment in sector/total employment). The former measure gives an absolute measure for comparative purposes whereas the latter measure is affected by developments in other sectors. We consider shares, rather than rates, since we are specifically interested in the ease of (re)allocation of employment across sectors rather than the ease of entering the labour market and employment per se.

13. A drawback of the random effect model is that it assumes no correlation between the country-specific effect α_i and the explanatory variables x_{it}. To overcome the problem, Mundlak (1978) proposed another estimation method within the random effect model framework. To assess how strict the orthogonality condition is, we also estimate the random effect model in the Mundlak version; the results do not change significantly.

14. Some of the variables used in the analysis have a clear trend over time; we do investigate on its nature, i.e. stochastic or deterministic. Usual tests do not reject the hypothesis of stationary residuals, hence the consistency of our estimates.

15. Institutions are added separately in the various specifications because they are often highly correlated. Adding them jointly leads to multi-collinearity problems in interpreting the impact of institutions. As an alternative approach, once could use factor analysis to tease out the independent factors from the institutional variables and include them as regressors. The problem with this approach is that it is difficult to label and fully understand what such factors are capturing. Here, we have chose to simply include the institutional variables separately.

16. A better measure would be union coverage, which would take into account both union membership and non-members covered by union bargaining arrangements. Unfortunately comparable time series measures of union coverage for all of the countries in our panel dataset are not available. For countries with a low membership rate, but high coverage rate (e.g. France) our measure may therefore underestimate the effect of the union bargaining presence on the service sector employment share.

17. For an overview of alternative indicators of labour market mismatch and what they measure, see ECB (2002).

18. In order to account for possible decreasing returns to public spending, we estimated the model including a squared term. The hypothesis of a significant inverse U-shaped impact of government consumption is rejected.

19. In-line with the empirical literature exploring the macro-economic impact of product market regulations we use the OECD aggregate indicators produced by

Nicoletti, Haffner, Nickell, Scarpetta, and Zoega (2000). Although extensive and, in practice, a unique source of information about the regulatory framework, the OECD indicators present some strong limitations – in terms of sector and time coverage – making the results of the econometric analysis questionable.

20. That is in fact the case in OECD (2000).

21. It also reduces the magnitude of the coefficient on the variable cycle, consistent with this variable picking up some effect of the cycle, although the both variables remain significant.

22. Given concerns regarding the possible endogeneity of female participation, we test its significance in a separate regression.

23. The Checchi and Visser (2002) index of union centralisation is not available for the United States. The most comprehensive information available on vacancies for the United States is the 'Index of help wanted advertising in newspapers' constructed by the conference board. However, this is an index based on the total vacancies, rather than unfilled vacancies, and is therefore not sufficiently comparable to the vacancy information available for Europe.

ACKNOWLEDGMENT

We would like to thank participants in an internal seminar at the ECB, in the EEFS 2005 Conference, the AIEL 2005 Conference and at the EEA 2006 Conference for their very helpful suggestions on an earlier draft of this chapter. The chapter also greatly benefited from comments by two anonymous referees. The views expressed are those of the authors and do not necessarily reflect those of the European Central Bank (ECB) or of the Central Bank of Ireland.

REFERENCES

Appelbaum, E., & Schettkat, R. (2001). Are prices important? The changing structure of the industrialized economies. In: T. Ten Raa & R. Schettkat (Eds.), *The growth of Service Industries – The paradox of exploding costs and persistent demand.* Cheltenham: Edward Elgar Publishing Limited (Chap. 7).

Blanchard, O., & Wolfers, J. (2000). The role of Shocks and Institutions in the rise of European Unemployment: The aggregate evidence. *Economic Journal, 110*, C1–C33.

Baltagi, B. H., & Wu, P. X. (1999). Unequally spaced panel data regressions with AR(1) disturbances. *Econometric Theory, 15*, 814–823.

Barro, R. J., & Lee, J. (2001). International data on educational attainment: Updates and implications. *Oxford Economic Papers, 53*, 541–563.

Barro, R.J., & Lee, J.-W. (2000). *International data on educational attainment updates and implications.* NBER Working Papers 7911, National Bureau of Economic Research.

Baumol, W. J. (1967). Macroeconomics of unbalanced growth: the anatomy of urban crisis. *American Economic Review, 57*(3), 415–426.

Baumol, W. J. (2001). Paradox of the services: Exploding costs, persistent demand. In: T. Ten Raa, & R. Schettkat (Eds.), Edward Elgar Publishing Limited, Chap. 1.

Baumol, W. J., Blackman, S. A., & Wolff, E. (1989). *Productivity and American leadership: The long view*. Cambridge: MIT Press.

Belot, M., & J. van Ours, C. (2007). Unemployment and labour market institutions: An empirical analysis. *Journal of Japanese and International Economics*, *15*, 1–16.

Belot, M., & van Ours, J. C. (2001). Unemployment and labor market institutions: An empirical analysis. *Journal of the Japanese and International Economies*, *15*(4), 403–418.

Bertola, G. (2001). Aggregate and disaggregate aspects of employment and unemployment. Paper prepared for a central bank policy conference on "Employment and Economics", March, Bogota, Colombia.

Calmfors, L., & Driffil, J. (1988). Bargaining structure, corporatism, and macroeconomic performance. *Economic Policy*, 14–61.

Checchi, D., & Visser, J. (2002). *Pattern persistence in European trade union density*. Departemental Working Papers 2002-01, Department of Economics, Business and Statistics at Università degli Studi di Milano.

Clark, C. (1957). *The Conditions of Economic Progress*. London: MacMillan.

Conway, P., Janod, V., & Nicoletti, G. (2005). *Product market regulation in OECD countries, 1998 to 2003*. OECD Economics Department Working Paper, No 419.

ECB. (2002). Labour market mismatches in Euro Area Countries. Structural Issues Report, March 2002.

Elfring, T. (1988). *Service sector employment in advanced economies. A comparative analysis of its implications for economic growth*. Gower Publishing Company Limited: Aldershot, UK.

Elfring, T. (1989). New evidence on the expansion of service employment in advanced economies. *Review of Income and Wealth*, *35*, 409–440.

Elmeskov, J., Martin, J. P., & Scarpetta, S. (1998). Key lessons for labour market reforms: Evidence from OECD countries' experiences. *Swedish Economic Policy Review*, *5*(2), Autumn.

Erdem, E., & Glyn, A. (2001). Employment growth, structural change and capital accumulation. In: T. Ten Raa & R. Schettkat (Eds.), *The growth of service industries – The paradox of exploding costs and persistent demand*. Cheltenham: Edward Elgar Publishing Limited (Chap. 3).

Fisher, A. G. B. (1935). *The clash of progress and security*. London: MacMillan and Co. Ltd.

Fuchs, V. R. (1980). Economic growth and the rise of service employment. NBER Working Paper No. 486.

Gordon, R. (1997). Is there a trade off between unemployment and productivity growth in unemployment policy? In: G. de la Dehese & D. Snower (Eds.), *Unemployment policy*. Cambridge: Cambridge University Press.

Greenhalgh, M., & Gregory, C. (2002). Structural change and the emergence of the new service economy. *Oxford Bulletin of Economics and Statistics*, *63*, 629–646.

Hausman, J. A. (1978). Specification tests in econometrics. *Econometrica*, *46*(6), 1251–1271.

Hodrick, R., & Prescott, E. C. (1997). Postwar U.S. business cycles: An empirical investigation. *Journal of Money, Credit, and Banking*, *29*(1), 1–16

Lopez-Garcia, P. (2003). Labour market performance and start-up costs: OECD evidence. CESifo Working Paper no. 849.

Messina, J. (2005). Institutions and service employment: A panel study for OECD countries. *Labour*, *19*, 343–372. doi: 10.1111/j.1467-9914.2005.00298.x.

Mundlak, Y. (1978). On the pooling of time series and cross section data. *Econometrica*, *46*, 69–86.

Nickell, S. (1997). Unemployment and labor market rigidities: Europe versus North America. *Journal of Economic Perspectives*, *11*(2), 55–74.

Nickell, S., & Nunziata, L. (2000). Employment patterns in OECD countries. Centre for Economic Performance Discussion Paper no.488.

Nickell, S., & Nunziata, L. (2001). Labour Market Institutions Database. Available at www.econ.upf.edu/~reiter/webbcui/combineddata/LMIDB.pdf

Nicoletti, G., Scarpetta, S., & Boylaud, O. (1999). *Summary indicators of product market regulation with an extension to the employment protection legislation*. OECD Economic Department Working Papers, no. 226.

Nicoletti, G., Haffner, R., Nickell, S., Scarpetta, S., & Zoega, G. (2000). European intergration, liberalization and labor market performance. In: G. Bertola, T. Boeri & G. Nicoletti (Eds.), *Welfare and employment in a United Europe*. Harvard: MIT Press.

Nunziata, L. (2002). Unemployment, labour market institutions and shocks. *Nuffield College Working Papers in Economics, W16*.

OECD. (2000). Employment in the service economy: A reassessment. Employment outlook 2000, Chap. 3.

OECD. (2004a). Employment Outlook, Paris.

OECD (2004b). Education at a glance, Paris.

Oulton, N. (2003). Must the growth rate decline? Baumol's unbalanced growth revisited. *Oxford Economic Papers*, *53*, 605–627.

Petit, P. (1986). *Slow growth and the service economy*. London: Frances Pinter.

Ramaswamy, R., & Rowthorn, R. (1997). Deindustrialisation: Causes and implications. *Staff Studies for the World Economic Outlook, IMF*.

Rogerson, R. (2003). Structural transformation and the deterioration of European labour market outcomes. NBER Working paper no. 12889.

Russo, G., & Schettkat, R. (1999). Are structural economic dynamics a Myth? Changing industrial structure in the final product concept. *Economia and Lavoro*, *3–4*, 173–188.

Russo, G., & Schettkat, R. (2001). Structural economic dynamics and the final product concept. In: T. Ten Raa & R. Schettkat (Eds.), *The growth of service industries – The paradox of exploding costs and persistent demand*. Cheltenham: Edward Elgar Publishing Limited (Chap. 8).

Schettkat, R., & Yocarini, L. (2003). The shift to services: A review of the literature. IZA Discussion Paper no. 964.

Singelmann, J. (1978). *From agriculture to services. The transformation of industrial employment*. Beverly Hills: Sage Publications.

Summers, R. (1985). Services in the international economy. In: R. O. Inman (Ed.), *Managing the service economy* (pp. 27–48). Cambridge: Cambridge University Press.

Wölfl, E. (2005). *The service economy in OECD countries*. In: OECD (2005). Enhancing the Performance of the Services Sector, (Chap. 2).

Wölfl, E. (2006). The growth of information workers in the US economy, 1950–1990: The role of technological change, computerisation and structural change. *Economic Systems Research*, *18*, 221–255.

World Development Indicators. (2001). World Bank, Washington, DC.

APPENDIX A: ISIC CLASSIFICATION

Total Services (ISIC 50–99)

(ISIC 50–55) Sub-sector 1: Wholesale and retail trade, restaurants and hotels
50–52 Wholesale and retail trade; repair of motor vehicles, motorcycles and personal and household goods

Sale, maintenance and repair of motor vehicles and motorcycles; retail sale of automotive fuel: Sale of motor vehicles, Maintenance and repair of motor vehicles, Sale of motor vehicle parts and accessories, Sale, maintenance and repair of motorcycles and related parts and accessories, Retail sale of automotive fuel
Wholesale trade and commission trade, except of motor vehicles and motorcycles: Wholesale on a fee or contract basis, Wholesale of agricultural raw materials, live animals, food, beverages and tobacco, Wholesale of household goods, Wholesale of non-agricultural intermediate products, waste and scrap, Wholesale of machinery, equipment and supplies, Other wholesale
Retail trade, except of motor vehicles and motorcycles; repair of personal and household goods: Non-specialized retail trade in stores, Retail sale of food, beverages and tobacco in specialized stores, Other retail trade of new goods in specialized stores, Retail sale of second-hand goods in stores, Retail trade not in stores, Repair of personal and household goods

55 Hotels and restaurants

Hotels; camping sites and other provision of short-stay accommodation, Restaurants, bars and canteens

(ISIC 60–64) Sub-sector 2: Transport, storage and communication
60–63 Transport and storage

Land transport; transport via pipelines: Transport via railways, Other land transport, Transport via pipelines
Water transport: Sea and coastal water transport, Inland water transport
Air transport: Scheduled air transport, Non-scheduled air transport
Supporting and auxiliary transport activities; activities of travel agencies: Supporting and auxiliary transport activities; activities of travel agencies

64 Post and telecommunications

Post and courier activities, Telecommunications

(ISIC 65–74) Sub-sector 3: Finance, insurance, real estate and business services

65–67 Financial intermediation

Financial intermediation, except insurance and pension funding: Monetary intermediation, Other financial Intermediation
Insurance and pension funding, except compulsory social security: Insurance and pension funding, except compulsory social security
Activities auxiliary to financial intermediation: Activities auxiliary to financial intermediation (e.g. Administration of financial markets, Security dealing activities, Activities auxiliary to financial intermediation n.e.c), except insurance and pension funding, Activities auxiliary to insurance and pension funding

70 Real estate activities

Real estate activities: Real estate activities with own or leased property, Real estate activities on a fee or contract basis

71–74 Renting of machinery and equipment and other business activities

Renting of machinery and equipment without operator and of personal and household goods: Renting of transport equipment, Renting of other machinery and equipment, Renting of personal and household goods n.e.c.
Computer and related activities: Hardware consultancy, Software publishing, consultancy and supply, Data processing, Database activities and online distribution of electronic content, Maintenance and repair of office, accounting and computing machinery, Other computer-related activities
Research and development: Research and experimental development on natural sciences and engineering (NSE), Research and experimental development on social sciences and humanities (SSH)
Other business activities: Legal, accounting, bookkeeping and auditing activities; tax consultancy; market research and public opinion polling; business and management consultancy, Architectural, engineering and other technical activities, Advertising, Business activities n.e.c.

(ISIC 75–99) Sub-sector 4: Community social and personal services

75 Public administration and defence, compulsory social service: Administration of the State and the economic and social policy of the community (e.g. General public service activities, Regulation of the activities of agencies that provide health care, education, cultural services and other social services excluding social security, Regulation of and contribution to more

efficient operation of business, Ancillary service activities for the government as a whole), Provision of services to the community as a whole (Foreign affairs, Defence activities, Public order and safety activities), Compulsory social security activities
80 Education: Primary education, Secondary education, Higher education, Adult and other education
85 Health and social work: Human health activities, Veterinary activities, Social work activities
90–93 Other community, social and personal services

Sewage and refuse disposal, sanitation and similar activities
Activities of membership organisations n.e.c: Activities of business, employers and professional organisations, Activities of trade unions, Activities of other membership organisations
Recreational, cultural and sporting activities: Motion picture, radio, television and other entertainment activities, News agency activities, Library, archives, museums and other cultural activities, Sporting and other recreational activities
Other service activities

95 Activities of private households as employers and undifferentiated production activities of private households

Activities of private households as employers of domestic staff, Undifferentiated goods-producing activities of private households for own use, Undifferentiated service-producing activities of private households for own use

APPENDIX B: DEFINITIONS AND DATA SOURCES

1. *Service employment share*: ratio between total employment (number engaged in domestic production) in services and total employment (multiplied by 100, logarithm). Source: OECD, Structural Analysis (STAN) database.
2. *GDP per capita*: gross domestic product per head at constant prices and current PPPs (divided by 1000, logarithm). Source: OECD, National Account (NA).
3. *Cycle*: detrended GDP per capita (divided by 1000). Cyclical fluctuations are extracted by applying the Hodrick and Prescott (1997) filter. Source: authors' computation on OECD, NA database.
4. *Productivity gap*: Productivity in services/productivity in manufacturing (multiplied by 100, logarithm). Productivities are computed as real value

at constant prices over number of employees in the respective sector. Source: authors' computation on OECD, STAN database.

5. *Government consumption*: real public consumption expenditure, percentage of real GDP (multiplied by 100, logarithm). Source: authors' computation on OECD, NA database.
6. *Vacancies*: unfilled vacancies to unemployment ratio (multiplied by 100, logarithm). Source: OECD, Main Economic Indicators; AMECO.
7. *Education*: logarithm of average years of schooling (multiplied by 100). Source: Barro and Lee (2000). Data available at the web address: http://www.cid.harvard.edu/ciddata/ciddata.html
8. *Union density*: logarithm of union density (percentage). Union density is computed as the ratio of number of members to number of employees. Source: OECD.
9. *Centralisation*: logarithm of the index of centralization/co-ordination of wage negotiations (multiplied by 100). Source: Checchi and Visser (2002).
10. *EPL (regular)*: employment protection legislation on regular contracts index. Two values available for the years 1989 and 1998. We assume constant the first value from 1970 to 1989 and the second value from 1990 to 2001. Source: OECD.
11. *EPL (temporary)*: employment protection legislation on temporary contracts index. Two values available for the years 1989 and 1998. We assume constant the first value from 1970 to 1989 and the second value from 1990 to 2001. Source: OECD.
12. *Barriers*: barriers to entrepreneurship. It includes: administrative burdens on startups; regulatory and administrative opacity; barriers to competition. Only year 1998 and 2003 available. Source: Conway, Janod, and Nicoletti (2005).